A SUITCASE FULL O. ᴅ.ᴇᴀᴍ

(An Aeronautical Journey)

David Taylor

Delta Tango Publications

York, North Yorkshire

For the Williams in my life: father & son.

First published in 1998

by **Delta Tango Publications**

York, England, YO23 1AR

Copyright © David Taylor (1998)

The right of the David Taylor to be identified as the author of this work has been asserted by him in accordance with the Copyright, Designs and Patents Act 1988.

British Library Cataloguing in Publication Data.
A catalogue record of this book is available from the British Library, Wetherby, Yorkshire.

ISBN 0 9534082 0 5

Printed by Quacks of York.

A SUITCASE FULL OF DREAMS

by

David Taylor

Pen and ink drawings by
Arthur Whitlock of Robertsbridge, East Suffolk.

Paintings by
Rex G. Josey of York

Photograph on page 10 reproduced with the kind permission of
Anglia Television.

FOREWORD

David Taylor served with me when I was flying helicopters in Malaya during the early days of RAF rotary wing support operations. Exciting times, especially so in that the flying took place on the front line of a long-forgotten campaign - the Malayan Emergency, 1948-60. By today's standards the tactics, the flying techniques and the machines themselves were all rather primitive, so life was always interesting, frequently difficult and occasionally alarming.

Nevertheless, the campaign was very successful, and in his book, Dave has allowed the reader a nostalgic insight to those times, with tales that are usually confined to the annual reunion or the bar at the local branch of the RAFA or ACA.

Air Commodore Tom Bennett CBE RAF (Retd.)

INDEX OF CHAPTERS

TRAVEL LOG

From Cosford, in the midlands, to Dishforth, north of York,
And the countryside of Wiltshire, of these places we will talk.
All was peace and comfort, though something was amiss,
Those foreign lands I'd need to see, 'fore settling down to this.
My appetite was whetted at Her Majesty's expense,
Three years in Malaya; for my service, fitting recompense.
Next a clapped-out troopship; to England I'd go back,
From Alor Star and Ipoh, to Bradenstoke-cum-clack.

But life was just beginning, there being so much more to see,
And with a job that paid my way, the world was mine, for free.
So now began adventures in countries brought to me,
By boats and planes and cars and trains; by air, by land, by sea.
In ships, not tall, in fact quite small, and miles of walking most of all.
Fertile lands and desert sands, sunshine all the while,
Caribbean islands, ruins on the Nile.
Not just beaches, swaying palms, and placid waters, blue,
Bugs and nasty beasties; those, and fever too!

Lush green fields and wastelands. Mountains capped with snow,
Painted deserts; strangely named. Valleys, and plateaux.
From Yucatan to Cuzco, along the Gringo Trail,
On down south to Chile, and back again by rail.
Walk the Via Dolorosa, relive the past thereby,
Climb up to Massada, to learn the when, and why.
Memories too - though precious few - of a country called Iran.
The dust and heat, the sweat and sleet; Mullahs, mosques, and Isfahan.

Sunsets and silhouettes, how the memories flash by:
Of Springbok and Impala and tables in the sky.
In Aotearoa; Land of the Long White Cloud
Men and women, dressed for sport, roll balls along the ground.
What are they doing - what deeds pursuing,
All the way from Auckland, south to Milford Sound?

I have been and I have seen the wonders of this world,
As a veritable cocktail of sights and sounds unfurled.
Here, a Siamese temple, the chateau of Loire
By the Harbour Bridge in Sydney, I knew I'd travelled far.
So stranger, follow me, discreetly tread my path...
My! that sounds good, true as well; Let that be my epitaph.

INTRODUCTION

We all seem to harbour, to some extent, a latent, nostalgic desire to, one day, return to our beginnings. The old home town and the family abode. The older we get, the stronger the urge. This is not the way it should be though. One should look ahead, imagine how things will be in years to come. In fact, that's essential to future planning. But as this generates so many question marks and frustrations, I prefer the nostalgia of looking back over what has already gone. This also tends to greatly reduce the number of conditional conjunctions with which looking ahead presents us. There are, after all, enough of those already.

*

1991. It wasn't that I was afraid of death, just didn't fancy being around when it happened. This thought sprang to mind when an ominous shadow engulfed me as I stood there, out on the deck. Not immediately, of course, but it instigated the actions which follow such a thought, for the shadow halted, sinister, threatening. I looked up, seeking the owner, for even a shadow has to belong to someone, or something. This particular shadow was cast by the boom of a crane that reached up, high above. But it wasn't that which suddenly caused me to think about the dangers we sometimes face in life, it was the jib attached to the end of that boom which prompted such a thought. Well, to be truthful, that which hung from the jib, for directly over my head was a thirty-ton anchor - Admiralty Stockless type, if it's of any academic interest. Should that decide to fall, thought I - immediately engaging every instinct in the rush to relocate myself - it's not going to do a lot for me, cosmetically. Nor physically, come to that. Not that I was any great shakes in the tall, dark, and handsome department to begin with. No way. It wouldn't improve things is what I'm saying, for despite strict adherence to present day safety standards - coveralls, hard-hat, safety boots - I'd likely end up flatter than a jaywalking hedgehog. Nor was it merely the thought of my being squished into the deck-plates that hastened my rapid departure to a position of relative safety, but also - for at times I consider myself thoughtful - the mass of paperwork someone would be required to complete should the worst happen. That in itself didn't bear thinking about, but perhaps other things did.

When your very existence is threatened is the time you tend to think of all the things you were going to do, but hadn't, rather than the things you never intended doing, but had. Over the years I'd made few notes about thoughts such as this. My intention: to work on them, maybe with a view to eventual publication. So maybe now was the time to call them up, put them to some use. I could write about the everyday dangers with which we are often faced, for there are apparently many. In fact, when thought about, we don't really stand much of a chance at all. Most of what we eat, so we are told, is bad for us. If not bad, certainly not good. The same goes for smoking, drinking, sex, the "chemically polluted" water we drink instead of the wine we're advised not to, even watching TV. Anything, it seems, that gives pleasure. Not only that, the essentials and the unavoidable too. The rain, so they say, is probably acid; thought-to-be-lead-laden is the air we breathe; we shouldn't expose ourselves to the sun's rays for fear of contracting cancer, and like that. But these subjects have already been well covered. So why not go the whole hog, make it an autobiography, of sorts. Not of someone rich or famous, (impossible to be more anonymous than myself) but an autobiography of an everyday life. Certain names would probably need to be changed, thus dissuading people from issuing writs, or possibly seeking me out with the intention of doing even worse things to me than anything I had ever inflicted upon an insect. Situations and occurrences would, at times, need to be watered down slightly, so as to render them more believable. In fact, it would probably have been more prudent, or - depending on viewpoint - spineless, of me to moderate my views on certain people and places. But, being a forthright, honest Yorkshireman, there was little chance of that happening. Call a spade a spade, I say. Or should that be a shovel?

* *

NOTEBOOK ONE
SCARBOROUGH REMEMBERED

The sun was still low in the clear sky, would remain so. Attempting to be bold, it failed miserably, weakened by the time of year and its position in the heavens, for winter was almost upon us. There was a chill in the air, too, frost on the ground, which in itself could account for the lack of people. I seemed to be almost alone as I sought memories of my past. At the moment, all I had was a name in my head: Whin Bank. A name for which I sought substance. Possibly the family home at the time of my birth, or the home of a relative. Possibly a street, or area.

Scarborough, Yorkshire's premier seaside resort lay before me. I closed my eyes and created summer. Now the memories began to form, the start of it all. Sea, sand, gulls, entertainment, and a Knickerbocker Glory at the Harbour Bar; so good you know it's doing you bad. There were also fish and chip shops, kiss-me-quick hats, mussels, shrimps, winkles, and rock; followed by a trip on the Coronia. There again... maybe not.

Originally Skardborg, the town had been founded by a Viking chieftain named Thorgils Skardi. Way back in the fourteenth century he established a base here from which he hoped to attack Scotland. Whether or not he was successful in his venture remains in doubt. Regardless, Skardborg was now on the map; so the reference library told me. Naturally, with this all taking place well before I was thought of - before even my grandparents' grandparents' grandparents' time - I have no personal recollection of it.

*

I reopened my eyes to the present. This I did remember, of course I did: that curve of sandy beach on the South Side. It began just past the rocks below the Spa ballroom, stretched away from where I stood, along to the fish docks; lighthouse standing sentinel on the seaward arm.

The sea was to the east. Landward, the road replicated that curve of sand, as did the buildings bordering the road: theatres, amusement arcades, restaurants, interspersed among the shops - almost all closed at present. And there in the centre, looking very much miscast, stood what had once been St Thomas' hospital - originally the Royal Northern Sea Bathing Infirmary, and if that doesn't allow the imagination to run riot I can't think what will.

Behind me - and even were it still there I wouldn't have seen it - was where Galaland had once been. Built as an aquarium in the late eighteen

4

hundreds it reopened as a subterranean promenade and amusement centre in nineteen twenty-five, was thus well established by the time I came along. I recall rainy days spent down there wandering among the stalls and cafes, along with all the other people seeking shelter from the weather. Indeed, Galaland became known as *The Umbrella* for that very reason. Down there, among the Indian architectural pillars, were Palmists and fortune-tellers, waxworks, peepshows - what the butler saw, kind of thing. (By today's standards, not a lot, believe me!) There were slot machines (one penny - old type), and a slide down which you rode on a coconut mat. And of course, down there you kept dry.

Overlooking the bay, on the hill of the headland, stood the remains of the castle. Completed by the Normans in eleven fifty-eight, it was shelled by the Germans during the first World War. Who knows, maybe they had something against the Normans.

All this then, plus Jaconelli. A good Yorkshire name, eh? Fact is, the Jaconelli family seem to have been part of Scarborough society since time immemorial. Probably hitched a lift over with the Skardi's.

Then I had a sudden memory surge: myself, with my brother and sister, and our mother, at the seaside. Couldn't say when it had been, just one of those mental pictures which are now and again filed away. But it was clear, and it was at this very beach, although then it was crowded. There were deck chairs galore, rolled up trousers and handkerchief hats, and donkey rides. Seagulls wheeled about above the harbour, screeching noisily. One presumed they wanted fish, but they seemed prepared to accept chips.

A far distant life. An entirely different season. But that was exactly the kind of thing I was seeking.

In my mind I followed Marine Drive and Royal Albert Drive, ending up on the North Side. Peasholm Park. The miniature railway on which we used to ride out to Scalby Mills. And there was the swimming pool, along with the Open Air Theatre, where I recall watching a performance of Hiawatha. What I couldn't see I knew to be there. The Mere, Odeon cinema, Oliver's Mount - highest point in the town - and the cricket ground. But these were images formed during later visits, not those early days.

Leaving the seafront I now set off up the hill, southwest, navigation in the hands of my subconscious. Huntriss Row I had never forgotten. And as I continued on my way other vague recollections stirred the memory, but nothing too familiar. St Mary's cemetery passed by on my right. Anne Bronte was buried there, I remembered.

Eventually, I found myself out by the hospital, an area in which the tourists and day trippers would hopefully have little interest. I didn't actually recall making a decision to head this way, it was as if my legs, in collusion with my motor functions, had decided this was where I should be. So I wandered around, feet still seemingly taking me where they would. Stepney Drive, Stepney Rise, Stepney Road. The names meant something, triggered a faint spark of remembrance, but not the houses. These were archetypal upper-class homes: perfectly trimmed lawns, neat and colourful gardens. The kind of house I'd love to have been brought up in, but knew I hadn't.

Then I came upon Whin Bank. A road, then. Yes, this was more like it; solid, semi-detached suburbia. Now the memories surged forth.

'Can I help you?' a voice asked. 'Are you looking for someone?'

I turned, surprised to find my eyes moist. She was middle-aged. Obviously a friendly type, as had been the small-town way.

'Looking for lots of people, love' I replied. 'But they aren't here any longer.'

* *

Chapter One
MY DADDY SHOOTS GERMANS

'*Aviation?*' It was the way she said it that stopped me momentarily, but not for long, as by this time we were well into the drink and the getting-to-know-you conversation. The matter of what to drink had also created its own problem.

'Fancy some wine?' I asked of the girl with whom I was dining. Elizabeth was her name, a true Yorkshire lass.

'Yes, please, David. That would be nice.'

'What kind?' I thought it a natural question to ask.

'Well...?' She shrugged and smiled. 'You're not one of those connoisseurs are you?'

'Not a connoisseur, no.'

'Does it matter then?'

'Of course it matters.'

'Sweet or dry, you mean?'

'Or red, white, French, German, still, sparkling? Plenty of choice. What's your mood?'

'I hadn't really thought about...... What would be right for now?'

I ordered a bottle of Anjou Rose, which we drank whilst we talked. Not a girl of the world then, I surmised. It was a thought that seemed to gain strength during a later stage of our discourse.

'Aviation?' She repeated the word, furrowing her brow and wrinkling her nose, giving the impression that the word was incomprehensible to her. I, not wishing to lose her apparent attraction to me, decided on a lighthearted explanation.

She'd been probing as to my interests. In life, that is. As far as my immediate interest in her went I felt sure she'd be able to hazard a wild guess. Throughout life I had held similar conversations with lots of interesting girls, but this was one that had stuck in the memory, for she'd been different, this girl (very different, for she was eventually to become my wife). Along with the usual hobbies and pastimes - travel, photography, motor racing - I'd listed aviation, probably because it was one of my interests, a major one. And it was this she had queried.

'Yeah, you know,' I'd replied. 'Fuselage, wings, some form of propulsion.' I'd flapped my arms and craned my neck, imitating a swan on take-off. She'd laughed. A pleasant, tinkling kind of sound, which told me I was doing all right.

'And what first kindled your interest in that?' she'd asked, which is where we got bogged down, for that was something I wasn't sure about.

7

Never had been. All I can say is that I don't recall ever giving serious consideration to the idea of settling down comfortably in suburbia, with a conventional job. Not once. Nor do I remember staring into the sky when I was young, watching the birds swoop and glide around, wishing I could do the same. Though I do recall occasionally wondering what kind of a view those birds had.

*

THE THIRTIES & FORTIES: Poverty, unrest, war. It was a period of rationing and hard times. It was also a period of national unity.

There were not, as far as can be ascertained, any connections through the generations. Pubs and publicans, yes. Aviators? Not a one. The publicans were there by the barrel-load, and they were all in Scarborough, the place in which I'd popped into this world, sometime during the twenty-four-hour period that had become April 2nd, 1936; a vintage year for kings.

There was an advantage to being Scarborough born, so I was told. Grandad Sale, who had connections within the cricketing fraternity, made sure I was well aware of the fact almost as soon as it was possible for me to comprehend: 'Thar's lucky, tha knows, lad. Being Yorkshire born an' all.'

'Why's that, Grandad?'

'Makes thee eligible to play cricket for t'County is why, David. Should thee prove to possess t'talent and inclination, o'course. Long odds, like, even if tha does, but at least tha's eligible.'

Alas, as was to become apparent early on, balls and I - at least in a sporting sense - were incompatible. A school report relating to physical training states: "Tries hard but has no actual ball sense." Ah well, by the time I was old enough to understand what had been implied, Yorkshire didn't need help from the likes of me. They were way down the Championship table already, which didn't please the locals overmuch. As obvious as a neon sign at the North Pole, that, for another thing to be learnt early on was that Yorkshire folk are a proud lot. I was advised to remember that our county was the largest of them all. At least, I believe that was the implication.

"Rest o' t'country's just tacked onti Yorksher, lad," was how it was put to me by an uncle.

*

So, aunts, uncles, grandads and grandmas there were, publicans all, which would account for my father, in 1939, taking out a licence to run his own pub, in Norton, halfway down the road to York.

Along with Norton came Malton, the two towns effectively divided by a murky-looking waterway of unknown and terrifying depth: the river Derwent. Though when it came to declaring assets, Malton claimed not only the railway station, but also the racing stables, for which the area was justly famous. This, despite the fact that the majority, if not all, were sited in Norton, which made that boundary seem rather discretionary, particularly since we weren't even served by the same council. Malton was in the North Riding, Norton in the East. Or could these injustices be related to age, with Malton dating back to well before the Roman era? Possibly Malton's fame is related to the fact of its having two breweries, and around thirty pubs, for a population of just over four thousand. Doubt over the pub count has to be blamed on the function of the pubs themselves; I always seem to lose track after the first half dozen.

The Griffin Hotel was the place Dad took on, although Mum was actually the named licensee (seems they knew something I didn't), which is how I came to spend a goodly part of my early life in a pub. Not a propping-up-the-bar kind of life, not at four years of age, or fourteen, come to that. No, the drinking came later. So much later, I apparently felt I'd been left with quite a bit of catching up to do. At least, I imagine that's how it must have appeared to others.

So, publicans aplenty, but none that appeared to have been in any way connected with aviation. Strange, this, for one of my heirlooms is a silver-topped, Royal Flying Corps cane. Such a link would have been well before my time, of course, for the RFC became the RAF way back in April 1918.

When I knew them, Grandad and Grandma Taylor ran the Nelson Inn, on Scarborough's Victoria Road. Here they remained until retirement, which at the time made Grandad the oldest licence-holder in town. There was also an Aunt Peggy and an Uncle Jim Clancy, who between them managed the Rosette, out Newby way. Then there was Grandad Sale. Yet in all the time spent in their company, no mention was ever made of the RFC, or RAF. But despite this, it was likely that one or other of them must have served in the armed forces at some point, for their lives encompassed the "Great War." In fact, I believe it was Grandad Sale who told me he could never understand what people meant by the term Great War. 'Great for whom?' he'd questioned. He'd said he assumed it to have been so named by people who were never actually at the front! So maybe he had been?

I do know my father met my mother at the Cayley Arms, Brompton, at a time when Grandad Sale was landlord of that establishment, before moving to the Cliff Hotel, on Scarborough's Huntriss Row. Maybe this was the connection to aviation then, tenuous though it might be? For the Cayley Arms was named after Sir George Cayley (1773-1857): inventor of the first *real* aeroplane, which flew close by here.

Wilbur and Orville Wright? Wrong! Kitty Hawk, North Carolina? December 1903? Nay, lad, forget all that.

The above claim, although true, rarely fails to raise the odd eyebrow, principally because the bulk of Sir George's notes was not rediscovered until 1927, by which time Wilbur and Orville had grabbed all the glory. But even they had been aware of George Cayley, for in 1909 Wilbur did in fact acknowledge his pioneering work. To quote: "About a hundred years ago an Englishman carried the science of flying to a point which it had never reached before and which it scarcely reached again during the last century."

Perhaps this gives Sir George a little more credit than he was due, for it was actually 1849 when he built and flew the first glider capable of carrying a person - a small boy making two flights down the slope of Brompton Dale.

Replica of a Cayley glider airborne at Brompton Dale. It was flown twice by Derek Piggott, first during a re-enactment of the famous "Coachman" flight for an Anglia TV production, then, ten years later, for the IMAX film "On the Wing".

Four years later, came what Sir George described as "a governable parachute", in effect, another glider. And this time it was to be the turn of a full-grown man, albeit not himself. Sir George, an astute and far-thinking eighty year old, decided to forgo the possible fame, volunteering his coachman for the task instead. But by day's end there was a vacancy for the role of coachman in the Cayley household, the incumbent having handed in his notice upon landing, if such an inglorious return to earth could be so described. A few bumps and bruises, we hear, but can you imagine the scene?

"Ey up, Sire. Sitha. Yon shilling a month gets thee a coachman, an' that's all. Nay mention was made about't role o'test pilot. Me terms of reference don't include t'likes o' yon." (Not ejection seat trained, d'yuh see.)

"Now come on, John, old chap, you're only a passenger after all. Besides which, surely a few bumps and bruises are to be expected in the advancement of science?"

"Be that as it may, me lord, get someone else. I'm off."

And that - so we are told - was it, off he went. No sense of adventure, it seems.

So, there you have it, Scarborough - or at least Brompton Hall, seven miles distant - Yorkshire, the eighteen hundreds, the very heart of aviation's early days. And if not the actual inventor of the aeroplane, Sir George can certainly lay claim to being "The Father of Aviation", and of the science of aerodynamics. His ideas were far in advance of those of the Wright Brothers, for what he envisaged was an aeroplane with true tri-axis control. Wing warping? Forget it, that was for the future! Indeed, it seems the only impediment to your actual powered flight back in the 1800's was lack of a suitable engine, internal combustion not yet an option. Had it been so, Wilbur and Orville - not yet born - would likely have missed out. Big time. Not many people know that, as Michael Caine might say. And, if it's of any academic interest, Sir George was also the inventor of both the linked-plank-belt - from which were eventually derived tank and caterpillar tracks - and the tension wheel: the spoked wheel used on the modern day cycle. I don't suppose many people know that, either.

I later discovered a photograph of Grandad Sale, at a dinner, seated alongside Sir Kenelm Cayley, the 10th Baronet - Sir George being the 6th. So, was there a tenuous link here? Maybe that cane originally belonged to a Cayley? Now there's a thought.

*

Despite the above, it's more likely the seed was subconsciously planted during those wartime years of my early life.

No evacuation for us, indeed ours was an area upon which the evacuees descended, a lot of them experiencing the countryside for the first time. But this was a time when the Yorkshire countryside also became saturated with the airfields of Bomber Command. Norton *was* the countryside; we were therefore literally surrounded. Like mushrooms, these airfields seemed to spring up overnight, twenty-five in all. Amongst their number could be found the emergency landing ground at Carnaby; Driffield - the very airfield from which, years later, I'd make my first flight. There were also the Halifax repair facility at Clifton, York, and the training base of Marston Moor - site of a decisive battle from another era: July 1644, perhaps the biggest battle ever fought on English soil, when, during the Civil War, close on fifty thousand combatants faced each other across this piece of then barren ground.

*

Although most of these airfields are now defunct - abandoned to some unrelated activity, or returned to the plough - during the Second World War they were hives of activity. Whitley and Wellington, Halifax and Lancaster, would depart from those airfields' extensive runways, filling the night sky with a synchronised, cyclic throbbing as they formed up prior to departing *en-masse*, heading for the continent.

In my freezing cold bedroom I'd climb into bed, pull the covers up to my chin and lie there, snug and warm, thinking and listening. I didn't really consider the idea of there being brave young men up there in those aircraft. But of course there were, and, dressed in sheepskin-lined leather they were going to war on my behalf, just like Dad, who was away doing his bit on the Indian subcontinent. By now a warrant officer, he was serving in the Royal Electrical and Mechanical Engineers, sorting out the war, or my future. But that's not quite how I saw it then, according to an entry in what could possibly have been my very first schoolbook, dated 1941. Amongst childish script not of the joined-up kind: "Mother likes my kitty"; "Rover can catch the ball"; "My daddy rides in a car"; is the declaration:

My Daddy shoots Germans

Ah well, don't suppose there was a notable difference between Germans and Japanese - at five years of age they were all classed as baddies. And never mind that Dad was unlikely to find himself in a situation that required him to shoot at anyone, he was a soldier, wasn't he? Anyway, that book also made reference to a Ruth and John - whoever they might have been - and in it I also declared myself to have two more brothers, "one called George, the other, Maureen"! (Morreen, actually. Not too good on the spelling back then. Not too good on genealogy, either, as there were only three of us children.) But that book does bear the subtitle, *A free expression book*. It also has some recognisable aircraft drawn inside the front cover, so at five years of age there must have been at least an inkling of something deep down in the subconscious.

I don't recall the details of Dad's departure. There'd been no tearful goodbyes, no signs of a uniform that I remember. He suddenly seemed not to be around any more. And it was to be four years before he returned, invalided out, suffering from climate-induced bronchitis and emphysema even before it was all over. Pensioned off by the War Office, he was to suffer breathing difficulties for the rest of his life. Then again, he *had* returned. A lot didn't, so at least I had that to be thankful for. Some of those airmen overhead would likely not return on the morrow, either. Some would never return, for this was a period when "Goodnight" could very well turn out to be "Goodbye". Not stupid, the Germans, you see. Soon figured out that if bombs were being dropped, there had to be someone up there dropping them, so they retaliated. Didn't bear too much thought that, which is probably why I mainly listened. A reassuring sound to lull a young lad to sleep, those engines. Almost an aeronautical symphony, Merlin's Twelfth, by Rolls Royce.

Come dawn they'd be back. Not all. Rarely in formation. And now the sound would be of an inferior quality: ragged. Engines would be running rough, out-of-sync, some not running at all, their propellers feathered. From what I'd heard I knew some of those airframes would be in bad shape, too, punctured by flack and cannon shells. But if they got that far they just about had it made. Just about. Though in war, it had been pointed out to me, there were no guarantees of anything.

In the beginning, I'd abandon my bed to peek out of the window, which called for considerable fortitude. A lack of heating allowed Jack Frost the opportunity of carving his intricate designs all over the glass. On the inside! That was the residue of my frozen breath there, which I now unfroze with a few early morning exhalations. It didn't take too long to clear a patch large enough to peer through, but by then there were no aircraft to be seen. Ah well, a minor discomfort for me, another lesson learned.

Other odd images of the period occasionally come to mind, rare though they were up our way: the muted stutter of machine-guns, the thump-thump of cannon-fire from somewhere distant. Scratchy white contrails would be etched across the sky, and dark specks could sometimes be seen, writhing and twisting in some deadly game, often in silence, sun glinting off a canopy. A smoky trail or flicker of flame would signal the death of an aircraft, severed wing or tail fluttering down, slowly, gracefully. Perhaps a parachute, perhaps not.

On the ground, life went on as normally as was possible. Up there was another world, almost passing unnoticed by those not involved, especially us kids. For us, war was a word almost without meaning.

There were crashes during training as well. More aircraft than the Luftwaffe would account for, in fact, for men barely out of school were being taught to fly. Not boys, you'll note, men. Deprivation and war causes people to grow up fast.

Sometimes, if the wreckage was close by, friends and I would visit the site. We'd search for pieces of plexiglass, fashion rings out of them, and model aircraft.

All around was open countryside. Elysian fields could become Agincourt or the OK Corral. Woods and copses, hills and valleys, became Sherwood Forest or Darkest Africa. We could be anywhere our imagination chose to place us, though it was hardly pirate territory. Pirates would have to await the end of the war and a trip to Scarborough, for there, on a lake known as The Mere, was a replica of the *Hispaniola*. On this we would sail out to an island nearby (the lake was very small). Here we could really search for buried treasure, digging for the imitation doubloons with which the sand had been liberally seeded. Meanwhile, to get in the mood, I read the popular stories of the time: Peter Pan, Treasure Island, Lady Chat ... oops! (It was actually Hank Janson.) There was also Captain W.E. Johns with his Biggles adventures, which I found enthralling.

Despite frequent air-raid warnings - from the rise and fall wailing of the siren's "Alert", to the steady, calming tone of its "All Clear" - I don't recall ever hearing the sounds of bombing, just hearing *about* it, that on the RAF station at Driffield resulted in the first WAAF casualty of the war, along with a dozen or so airmen. Then came the attack on York: April 29th, 1942, one of the Baedeker raids. So called, I later learned, for targets selected by the Germans from the Baedeker Handbook for Travellers. Cities which featured buildings of historic and architectural interest were to be given priority. A response, we are told, to the allied fire-bomb attacks on Lubeck and Rostock. Over thirty percent of York suffered; the Guildhall destroyed, station and marshalling yards severely damaged. Let's face it, the German bombers had been allowed ninety unchallenged minutes over the city!

During these years the only contact with Dad was via the odd, mimeographed, censor-approved letter, and an occasional parcel of, among other things, sugared almonds, which I didn't particularly like. But in war-torn Britain they were the first sweets I remember seeing, or tasting.

There are images of the walk to school, a tousle-haired child in mismatched clothes: short trousers, shirt and jacket. Not out of place though, for everyone was the same, dressed in whatever was available. And we all clutched an identical brown cardboard cube by a string handle. Not lunch, these contained a rubber and metal monstrosity, black, and ugly. The then ubiquitous gas mask. And of course, drills were frequently held during which we were compelled to wear the things, giving us the imagined look of wide-eyed beings from a distant planet. Still, as an effective means of reducing excited childhood chatter to a muted background of wheezing, hissing and grunting, the exercise could be deemed a success. Even if, inevitably, someone would end up clamping a sticky hand over the air intake of someone else's mask, face positively aglow with the discovery that the unfortunate lad's eyes appeared to be almost sucked out of their sockets. And, in the way of all boys, others would eventually follow suit, the less intelligent sometimes ending with their hand over their own air filter!

Later images are of the Italian prisoners who were billeted in a large building across the river in Malton. They must have been officers, for the main camp was out on the road to Pickering. I recall one of the cooks stationed here, at the house in town, a jovial Welshman: Taffy, of course. He used to give us various bits and pieces to take home. Things I later learned none of our prisoners were afforded by the enemy: butter, sugar, maybe tea.

There was no barbed wire to be seen, just soldiers who patrolled the area. Though why, I have no idea, for the prisoners seemed to be allowed almost a free rein. We'd see them in town, and they worked quite happily on the surrounding farms. Seems they had no wish to escape. Shrewd thinkers, those Italians - soon had it figured: WW2 wasn't going to be as spectacularly successful as had been the Lions v Christians in those Coliseum fund-raisers two thousand years back.

We also came across swarms of Yanks, and I can tell you now, the old saying is true, they really did give us gum, chum. That was one of the complexities of the time, to us kids, there seemed to be lots of American soldiers, few British. It was only later that I learned those American soldiers had actually been airmen.

Although money was never plentiful, we didn't go hungry. We got our ration, possibly a little extra, living in a farming district. The odd rabbit, for instance. The war didn't seem to have affected their prodigious rate of reproduction, and they too, like Bomber Command, were out there, all around us. We didn't starve, but there was certainly no abundance. We each had our own jam-jar - Maureen, George, and I - which, once a week was filled with sugar. Our very own ration, to do with as we pleased. When it was gone, that was it until the following week. Good schooling in self-discipline and moderation, that.

*

My most lasting memory of the war years is that of Maureen, shaking me awake one day. It was May 8th 1945. 'It's all over,' she told me. I was nine years old.

Regardless of the celebrations - the bunting and the street parties -

peace didn't seem to make a lot of difference for a while, the country taking time to recover. But eventually, Father returned from wherever it was they'd been treating him, food, sweets, and clothing came off ration, and there were comics, too: Beano, Dandy, Rover. Then came the Eagle: Dan Dare, spaceships, and technical cutaways. Wow! Goodbye, fairies.

But there were no fairies at the bottom of our garden; my bedroom window afforded me an uninterrupted view of both the gasworks and the railway. Back then, pre-Beeching, it was the London North Eastern Railway, trains every half-hour or so.

Over the years, passengers on the York to Scarborough run, would have seen - had they cared to look - various changes at the back of the Griffin (even to label it "garden" was taking flattery to the extreme). The tumbledown, brick garage was as permanent a fixture as vibration from the trains allowed. The outside loos and the boundary fence were of a more stable nature, the fence fabricated from old railway sleepers. Which reminds me, I was in the wars from day one of our move to Norton, losing half a finger to that fence in a macho, climbing incident. But fences and loos apart, things at the back of our house were apt to alter. Sheds, cars, pigeon lofts - the siting of which was also prone to change - chicken runs, rabbit hutches, washing flapping in the breeze. There had even been a boat at one time. A sort of offshore cabin cruiser affair, propped up on poles. Handy, eh? Twenty miles inland.

But the boat, sadly, was not there back in 1947, the only time it could really have felt at home; the Derwent, little more than an ambitious stream, took ambition beyond the limit, overflowed into the pub.

That was a great winter for us kids, '47: lots of snow, and unscheduled school holidays when the heating failed to cope, and the milk froze. But nature really is neutral, swings and roundabouts kind of thing. When the snow went, the river came. Weather forecast? Forget it. What we needed was a shipping report! For a period we were obliged to live upstairs.

During normal winters the pub lounge was a place that attracted me, for it was the only warm room in the house. It was where our first TV was located, and there was always a good fire for the customers - who always came first. Sound thinking, when reappraised in later years. After all, was it not they who put bread on the table, milk in the fridge? I always thought that fridge to be a waste of money, for, lounge apart, the whole house was a bloody fridge! The upstairs loo in particular, which is why I used those outside, which were just as cold, but closer. I favoured the Ladies, it being closest of all, and less draughty, although favoured may not be quite correct. Suffered, I suppose. But one has to look back at these things philosophically. It was part of growing up, and a few difficulties early on in life never hurt anyone. At the time though, I begrudged those customers their comfort, primarily because I was not allowed to share it, at least, not during opening hours; conflict between my age and the law, it seemed. Little things that mattered back then.

There had been pets, both before and after the war, but not during. Rabbits, for instance. A pair to begin with, but, rabbits being what they are, in due course a bunch of small ones magically appeared. Lovely little things, all ears and fluff, cuddly and furry. Then a dog got in. A Rottweiler, and.... Ah, well, no need to draw a picture. So much for the bunnies.

Dogs we'd always had. Small, friendly types, terriers, mainly. They were replaced every few years, naturally, but the funny thing is I don't recall ever being around when the end came. To my mind they suddenly seemed to change. One went away somewhere, another took its place. Nothing to do with a diet of leftovers, by the way, despite the fact that, after the briefest twitch of a canine nostril, those dogs would vacuum up almost anything within sight.

I recall a Patch - white socks on his pitter-patter front paws - and a Spot. Then there was Mickey, he who had a confrontation with an adder up on the moors. No harm done, apart from a swollen nose and possible loss of face. Or was it Tessie who sniffed out the adder?

There'd been budgies as well, at odd times. Not what one could term a successful line in pets, the budgies. They somehow never seemed happy with their lot, even though they were frequently given the opportunity to fly around the room, despite their tendency to crap all over the furnishings. A carelessly left-open window, and they were off like a prisoner from Wormwood Scrubs, two at least. I suppose this must point to a certain degree of unhappiness, as it's a known fact budgies would rather perch than fly. One even contrived to hang itself from the cord supporting its mirror. Mum tried to hide the fact from us, replacing it with an imposter before we returned from school. Alas, the difference was soon spotted, so she was reduced to admitting to the truth. The replacement was the second of those that winged away, out the window like. Scratch the budgies.

There was an escapee among the rabbits as well, almost forgot about that. A female. Only this time we avoided the mistake of getting her a mate, something which she perhaps took as an affront. We made sure she was always fenced in, which didn't bother her in the least, for, being a very efficient tunneller, our garden soon had the look of a training ground for Stalagluft 3. She was forever digging her way out, only to be returned by an irate neighbour.

'Bloody rabbit's taken a fancy to my lettuce and carrots, again. It's into the pot next time.'

She'd apparently taken a fancy to something else, too, for a few days after her return came a period during which she showed a distinct lack of interest in escape. And it had nothing whatever to do with the neighbour's threat. Obviously the magic wand had been waved, for the cage suddenly became home to considerably more than a single rabbit!

Then there was that other episode. Not pets exactly, but close.

'Ah could see t' point, Bill if tha'd done it durin't war; could have been tha contribution to t' "Dig for Victory" campaign. But what's this, "A Chuck for Luck?"' I recall a customer, saying at the time.

I hadn't understood what he'd meant, until I discovered my play area - aka the back yard - was to be shared. Dad, ever the optimist, acquired some hens and a cockerel.

'We're about to go into t' egg production business, Olaf, ' Dad had replied. 'Not commercial like, t' help things along.'

'Cost summat will that.' He was a regular, Olaf Wilson, and I'd heard tell he knew about such things. 'Need to feed em corn, tha knows. They aren't like cats and dogs,' he advised Dad. By which I was beginning to understand. Cats and dogs *were* different, weren't they. No specialist foods to buy for them. They ate what we did. Or, to be truthful, what we didn't; the leftovers. And believe me, there wasn't a lot back then. Not a lot to start with, so there was little waste; but the cats and dogs seemed healthy enough for all that. (And why not? If you think about it, they probably eat now what we ate then!)

As far as eggs went, I was all in favour. Anything would be better than the powdered variety. Spam I could take, actually liked it, but dried eggs? No thanks. Even the dogs and cats turned their noses up at those. So I welcomed the hens, and we got along fine. They just scratched about, pecked at this and that, kept out of my way; no problem. But that cockerel was another matter entirely. An evil bastard, if you'll excuse my French. (Yes, from the French, batard: child of the pack-saddle.) Anyway, that cockerel had mean-looking eyes and a vicious streak. Malevolent and hostile. He definitely ruled the roost, so to speak. A real bully, this, chasing small, frightened children. I mean, I had to be very young, didn't I? Otherwise I wouldn't have been afraid.

He'd lurk close to the back door, ready to pounce. I knew, because I'd sneak a look from behind the curtains first. He knew I knew, for there the old sod was, cocking his head and peering at me. He'd fix me with a baleful look. First one beady, red eye, then the other, jerking his head round officiously, comb flapping, almost daring me to venture out.

What did I do? It was back to the upstairs loo, I'm afraid. I had to use it at after dark anyway, for I knew the bogeyman would get me if I went outside then. Similar thoughts made me thankful to be sharing a big, old-fashioned double bed with brother George; despite the constant bickering about who had all the blankets, or more than their fair share of mattress. The way I figured it, two in a bed meant the bogeyman wouldn't get me. Or him, come to that. Therefore an advantage to both of us. But at that age I tended to worry only about me.

Anyway, that cockerel was to get his, for one day he aspired to downright bravado, foolishly challenging a customer going about his natural business. Naturally, when drinking, you occasionally have business to attend which requires your presence outside; if that's where the loos happen to be.

'Hey, Bill, yer bloody cockbod's deed,' "Chick" Hopper - as this particular customer was known - revealed upon his return. An apt name in the circumstances. The cockbird had - it so transpired - caught a convincingly aimed workboot about the audio sensory canal, cocking its toes as a result, so to speak. Well, it would wouldn't it, the boot was size ten.

I wasn't at all sad. After all, that's life. One minute, king of the castle, next, lunch for five. Don't suppose I thought that at the time, but no doubt would have had I been capable. Even so, I think I secretly declared Chick to be, "my best friend. Ever." One more thing, it was now so much quieter at daybreak. No, didn't miss that cockerel at all. Maybe the hens did, for there suddenly seemed to be few eggs; a temporary glut of roast chicken.

Now I could get back outside, Dad's heavy, leather-covered brass binoculars to hand. He was a racing man, was Dad, only natural in Norton - jacket and tie, trilby on his head, enclosure ticket in his lapel, those binoculars slung casually over a shoulder - but between times those glasses were mine, for exciting things were to be seen up there in the skies.

*

It was a time when springs seemed to drift easily into long, hot summers, and living in the countryside became a decided advantage. I remember them as lemonade and ice-cream summers (both home-made). They were also swimming-in-the-pool, or river, type summers. The pool, or swimming baths, were a bare hundred yards up the road from the Griffin, on Church Street. But there was no church, although there must have been at one time, for entry was by way of an ancient graveyard, its moss-encrusted headstones tilted this way and that, the church site now occupied by the pool, I suspect.

At the height of summer, that pool would echo to our excited yelps and chatter, the high-pitched voices of pre-pubertal youth. But whereas most dove in without so much as a ripple, I held my nose and jumped. For although I was an accomplished swimmer, I hadn't yet plucked up the courage to launch myself headfirst. From the edge of the pool, that is. Those other clever dicks, not satisfied with the height of the board, were, like lemmings on steroids, hurling themselves off the balcony, which ran across the top of the changing rooms. They would also use the boundary wall, separating the pool from the railway, with its steel-upon-gravel tracks.

Fields, which previously had been predominantly green, were suddenly interwoven with red and yellow, and they seemed to stretch away forever. Days were peacefully quiet, despite the sounds of aircraft, which were music to my ears. There seemed to be little but the laughter of children, and the sounds of nature: the cooing of a dove, the perpetually buzzing bees. Such days seem hard to find now. Possibly they were not common then, either, just those rose-tinted, retrospective images? But this was the tranquillity which followed the years of war. Heady days, when summers appeared to be just that, with sunshine in abundance.

But that day in September 1950 had not been such a day.

'Mum has gone away,' Dad told us one morning.

'For a long time?' I asked. It hadn't really sunk in what he was telling us.

'Forever, David. She's gone to Heaven.'

'Like Patch, you mean?'

'A bit like Patch, yes, although different as well. Dogs can be replaced, you see, Mums can't.'

Later that day I discovered there was another difference: dogs didn't get wreaths, Mums did. "Always gentle, always kind, a wonderful memory left behind." I cried a little that night, for that had been the first major event of my short life; the experience of losing someone close.

I later learned that Mum had been admitted to the hospital with some fairly minor ailment, developed pneumonia and failed to recover. It was only after she'd gone that I realized I had never really known her. But isn't that always the case? Sister Maureen, being female, had been closest, which is also normal. I suppose I'd have been closer to Dad, had he been around to get close to.

Now he was. Goodbye, Mum. Hello, Dad. My introduction to the realities of life. And death.

As if in compensation for my loss I now found girls starting to take me seriously. Well, as serious as it got at that age, in those times. I'm not suggesting they stepped out of their knickers and threw them in my direction. Wouldn't have known what to do about it if they had, apart from suspecting it would probably be fun finding out. Sex? As far as I was concerned it could well have not yet been invented. That's not to say the attraction didn't exist, it was there all right, from my side; it just wasn't being reciprocated. But the girls did now speak to me, laughed at my jokes rather than my disasters, which unfortunately still occurred, albeit rather less frequently. It was a start, even if I was clumsy and ill-at-ease in their presence.

Maybe Mums could not be replaced, but I discovered they could be substituted. Our substitute was a lady named Mabel. She was to be live-in nanny, barmaid, cook, cleaner, and a shoulder to cry on. She was good at it too, had a wealth of experience. During the war, Mabel had served in the WAAF, on the balloon sites. Previous to that she had been "In Service", and the tales she had to tell would make yet another novel for Barbara Taylor-Bradford.

Along with Mabel came her daughter, Pamela. Another female for me to tease. And whenever we had chips for dinner, Pamela, being female always got served first, so I would "borrow" one or two of hers until such time as mine appeared. Laughs and tears all round.

Mabel was eventually to be welcomed as our stepmother; remains so to this day.

*

In the true manner of boys I participated in all the youthful activities of the time: Cubs, Sunday-school, church choir at St Peter's (Honest! Cross my heart and hope to die). Well, they paid didn't they.

'As a choirboy, David you'll be working for Jesus. You'll also earn threepence every Sunday,' the choirmaster explained, during his attempt to recruit me.

'He doesn't pay a lot, sir, does He? I mean, they pay a shilling for delivering the papers.'

'Ah, yes, the newspapers. Well, it's not actually Jesus who will be paying you, that's the church's job. And we too pay a shilling, for weddings.'

'Oh, that's OK then, I'll just do weddings.'

'No, David, it doesn't work like that. To be considered for a wedding one is required to be a regular Sunday performer.'

Talk about bribery and corruption, and this from the church. I didn't say that, I thought it. But I joined anyway, for a while.

As things went I didn't seem to get a lot of weddings, probably a result of too many Sundays spent on the riverbank, where I'd taken to fishing, in all weathers. A bout of bronchitis was the result of one episode of such foolhardiness. Ah, but on a summer's evening it could be glorious, fish or no fish, often the latter. Not too successful then, the fishing, except maybe from a fishy point of view. Luckily there was a chippy close by - Jackie Taylor's - where I could get my maggot-tainted hands on threepennyworth in the evening's dying light. I was usually able to scrape together enough coppers for that; pennies and halfpennies saved from when people gave them to me. They meant a lot, those coppers, both to me and to those who gave them. But they gave them anyway, that was the way people were.

Then there were mishaps. Like the time I was distracted by a girl whilst riding my bike along Commercial Street. Full exposure, too, for this was Norton's major thoroughfare.

'Hi, Jennifer.'

A beautiful name, Jennifer. Nice ring to it. It certainly suited this girl. Matched her face, matched her budding young curves. Definitely a looker, I told myself. Like, *kaboom!*

So, in the act of trying to impress one of the graceful beauties who were constantly to reject my feeble advances, I took my eyes off the road, one hand off the handlebars, gave her a smile and a wave. It was an opportunity not to be missed, for, once you'd conquered the basics, a bicycle was a means of showing off. It seems I attempted it far too soon, for at this point I became vaguely conscious of something being not quite right. Nor was it. Bang! Slap into the back of a parked car. I don't remember the make, but that wasn't important. What was important was that it had a sloping back, nay, a launching ramp. For a moment there I seemed well placed to beat Gagarin into orbit, possibly could have had not gravity finally claimed me.

No wonder I was forever being rejected. She could set my heart aflutter from fifty feet, that Jennifer. I seemed to have no effect on her from as close as arm's length. Was never allowed closer!

I'd always assumed Jennifer's lack of interest to be related to my pre teen physique: skinny arms and legs, spotty face, unworried innocence. I once miscast myself for a local fancy dress parade, felt afterwards I must have looked pretty ridiculous dressed only in swimming togs, tan, courtesy of Rowntrees. Probably the skinniest, meekest Tarzan the world had ever seen. Had it rained I'd no doubt have been the weirdest, too. I hadn't felt foolish, there again, at ten I didn't exactly have a greatly developed sense of honour. I could have starred in those Charles Atlas adverts of the time, as the guy *not* kicking sand. Girls tended to agree, I hadn't been slow to notice.

So I suppose it was only to be expected Jennifer wouldn't even crack a smile as I picked myself up and dusted myself down. In fact I swear she turned her back on me, stuck her pretty little nose up in the air. Ah, well, not the first or last time disaster had struck in the process of my trying to impress a girl. God can be so cruel at times.

There were to be many similar incidents, a lot, admittedly, nothing to do with girls. The extreme macho, late-late braking technique, for instance. This involved building up a fair lick of speed as you approached the gang, straddling their stationary bikes and lost in some group discussion - probably by now relating to aviation. Anyway, the idea was to leave your braking to the last second, jam all on, skidding to an impressive halt only inches away. This, naturally, required precise judgement and timing, possibly also that missing ingredient, the consummate "ball sense". Not exactly my forte, I was to discover. And, to complicate matters further, if the road happened to be damp, or one brake block had fallen out, unobserved..... Those bikes were bloody heavy; no fancy alloys then. As for seats, they appeared to have been designed with no particular part of the anatomy in mind, least of all that which relates to sitting. But planting both feet firmly on the road slowed you hardly at all, and served only to wear out the soles of your shoes that much quicker. And even if it did warn the gang that something untoward was about to befall them, it was far too late for them to take evasive action. Scree... 'Look out! Ahhh....'

No, never did quite master that one. What the hell. Some people have it, some don't.

Then there was the time we were returning from a day of spud picking, an activity for which we were given two weeks' holiday from school. We weren't required to pick potatoes, of course, but as we were paid something like ten bob (shillings) a day to do so - in days when a single shilling was a fortune - we did. Let's face it, money only becomes unimportant to those that have it by the sackful. Our sacks were filled only with spuds, which was to lead to an incident on the ride home.

It was another case of "Hi ho Silver!" as I once more parted company from my bike, taking a header over the handlebars.

"Thick Mike" was deemed to be the cause this time, though the likely proximity of his own death could well have been a contributory factor. He was blue in the face, due to his carrying his knapsack - full of freebie potatoes - with the strap across his Adam's Apple, rather than over one shoulder.

'What are you doing, Mike? Move ov...er, ahhh...' Too late. The lamp-bracket protruding from the hub of his wayward front wheel, penetrated the spokes of my front wheel. That incident was to cost me half a front tooth. My fault again, should have remembered: Mike was one of the kids who used to stick his hand in front of his own gas mask. And to think, he was probably the first person to be declared, "my best friend. Ever." A status that had just been automatically cancelled.

*

The late forties, early fifties, were times when every schoolboy showed some interest in what was happening, aeronautically. More than a few no doubt harboured ideas way beyond their potential. Me? Apart from wanting to wear my underpants outside my trousers, and possess x-ray vision, I had absolutely no aspirations towards becoming a pilot. In fact, with a parcel of fish and chips in my hand I was already in a world of my own, a Yorkshireman through and through. But yes, the aircraft did attract me.

As well as finding a use in the fish shop, newspapers also covered all the aviation stories. They were probably the most spectacular news available back in those more tranquil days, for apart from travelling at unbelievable speeds, those early jets appeared to fall out of the sky at a phenomenal rate. At times, it seemed as if even the immutable laws of flight had suffered a temporary setback.

I read about trial flights of the prototype aircraft of that period. Such classics as the Hawker P1067 - eventually to become the Hunter - Vickers Supermarine Swift and the butterfly-tailed 535, plus all the prototypes which led up to them. Strange new shapes were to be seen, too. Aircraft which carried nomenclature such as DH108, Avro 698, and AW52. There were Javelin, Valiant, and Victor. A.V.Roe had a model 707, a delta, long before William Boeing brought out his airliner. Peter Twiss captured the world airspeed record for Great Britain in another delta-winged model, at well over a thousand miles per hour, if headlines were to be believed. And in those days they usually could be. (Anyway, he told me so himself, in

1998.)

Given the preponderance of bases still active in the area, Yorkshire skies were never quiet, our particular area a designated low-flying zone. But most of the interesting stuff flew way up yonder, with the result that Dad's binoculars worked overtime, tracking twinkling silver specks at thirty thousand feet. Those planes trailed vapour across the stratosphere, thin white scars defacing the canvas of ice-blue. But the sky is self-cleansing; we may tarnish it, blemish it, stain it, but not for long. That first breeze, the falling rain, the passing storm, all play their part.

One aircraft that didn't require the use of optical aids was the giant B36D; Strategic Air Command's "Peacemaker". Recognisable by sound alone - the distinctive harmony of six piston engines and four jets - they sounded like they were powered by high-revving, multi-cylinder two-strokes. Then there was the mighty Brabazon, which put in an appearance on its finale, an around-the-island flight.

Nostalgia? Of course. As Grandad Sale once said, 'Nay, lad, there's nowt wrong wi' nostalgia.' So here's more. *My* boyhood heroes bore names such as Lithgow (who was to lose his life to that T-tail deep stall phenomena, when testing the BAC1-11), Duke, Falk (who rolled the mighty Vulcan, thus earning himself the nickname, Roly). And there was Derry (tragically killed in the DH110 at Farnborough), and "Cat's Eyes" Cunningham, (the night-fighter ace, and of Comet fame). Others, too: Dave Morgan, Jock Bryce, Geoffrey Tyson, Weldon, and Zurakowski, test pilots, all, and superstars of the day, for their names featured regularly in the pages of the press.

*

Meantime, from across "The Pond", tales filtered through of strange happenings at Muroc Army Air Base, on America's West Coast. This was the place that would eventually become known as Edwards Air Force Base, after Captain Glen Edwards - a pilot who lost his life testing the Northrop YB49 flying wing from there. That aircraft - competing for a bomber contract at the time - was thought to have exceeded its structural limits whilst in a dive. Whatever the cause, that crash was to result in Muroc becoming Edwards - indeed, most of Edwards' streets are named in honour of deceased test pilots - and the bomber contract going to Convair. I, via Dad's binoculars now spotted B36's rather than B49's.

There were no computer predictions then to give a clue as to how an aircraft was expected to handle or perform, no supersonic wind tunnels to aid design. So, as if in a bizarre effort to prove Murphy correct, the designers occasionally got it wrong, as did the odd pilot. (It is said that Captain Edward Murphy, an engineer at Edwards, gave cause for the age old, previously unnamed law, "If anything can go wrong, it will" to become eponymous, because of his frequent use of the phrase.)

Edwards was "way out yonder" in the shimmering heat of California's Mojave Desert, and, from runways built upon its dusty, dry lake-beds, flew the X-planes. These were piloted by such as Crossfield, Bridgeman, Walker, and White. But most famous of all was Charles "Chuck" Yeager, my real boyhood hero, the man who finally destroyed the myth of a barrier by exceeding the speed of sound - and him with a broken collarbone at that! Which only went to prove it was a job that called for courage, skill, and, by all accounts, copious amounts of alcohol, a handy little watering hole known as Pancho's dispensing the latter. Named after the young aviatrix - Florence Lowe (Pancho) Barnes - who founded and ran it, Pancho's was part of the Rancho Oro Verde Fly-Inn Dude Ranch, nicknamed by the WW2 pilots who trained nearby, "The Happy Bottom Riding Club Ranch."

*

If not a direct result of the war, then perhaps this was when the avian bug was contracted, for it was certainly a stimulating period. The Great Adventure, dawn of the jet age. The sound barrier, fast jets and record breaking, a new era entirely.

But no matter how or when the seed was sown, this was the time propagation occurred. I became mad keen on aircraft. That I was hooked became clear the very first time I walked into a lamppost, my attention being directed towards the sky rather than on where I was going. Much the same as had happened that time with Jennifer. The main difference between my riding into a parked car, and walking into a lamppost, was that the distraction now went under another name: aviation. My next love affair had well and truly begun: I'd become a dedicated aerophile, thus beginning a long affinity with aircraft, and aviation in general.

But there was a problem: the aircraft were too distant. They were minute, inaccessible; optically-enlarged specks in the sky, pictures in a book. I had to find a way to get closer, actually to touch them.

The answer came in a flash of inspiration. I'd already gone the Cubs route, was not yet into girls, as it were. My sole preoccupation became aviation, rather than procreation. So, immediately exchanging neckerchief and woggle for blue serge and beret, I joined my local branch of the Air Training Corps, 1323 Middleton Squadron, and from that day on, the obsession really took off, it could be said. Aviation was to become the major attraction in life, to which even girls took a back seat, although not literally. There was room for a passenger on a bike, as some of the lads proved, but as I appeared not yet to have fully mastered the art of remaining on board alone, thoughts of carrying girls were to be dismissed. At least until the old biological urge asserted itself more fully. After all, I was only thirteen, going on fourteen, the Sixties yet a distant decade ahead.

*

It was the ATC that eventually led to that first cryptic entry in my logbook: 4-5-50, Oxford X7279, air experience, Driffield. A mind-boggling flight, that, and one of some significance, the entry, naturally, featuring at the top of page one. It was the high point of my life so far, a real charge to the system. I had touched the sky before. Of course I had, as has everyone, for the air we breathe is also the sky, it begins at ground level. What I hadn't experienced was the kind of levitation that spells flight.

It is sometimes difficult to recapture certain memories and feelings from a distance of forty-eight years, but ones that do stick in my mind are those of that first flight. Even today I only need experience that sudden surge of power and adrenalin which signals the start of a takeoff, and there I am, at Driffield, up into the clouds and down memory lane. Been that way forever, it seems.

It was a glorious day, skies a clear blue, not the deep blue of summer, but a sort of cornflower colour. The sun was high, the clouds small, white and puffy, the air still. Birds and bees twittered and hummed above the green grass of the airfield.

'God couldn't have arranged things better,' my friend, Pete suggested. 'A perfect setting to put us at our ease.'

'Yeah,' I agreed. Yet, despite the glow of excitement which coursed through my body, it was with trepidation that I stepped from the mundane into the first machine that would lift me off the face of this earth. It carried the yellow bands of Flying Training Command, I noted, and as we climbed aboard I looked across at Pete, gave him what I assumed to be a macho smile. 'Hope the pilot is an instructor, and not a recently-converted pupil,' I whispered. I also secretly prayed.

The aircraft had been built by Airspeed, a company born nearby, in the city of York, Neville Shute its founder. Not that it's of any significance, for all aircraft seem to possess that same, familiar, difficult-to-describe smell. Particularly military aircraft; a world apart, those. There is a mishmash of hydraulic fluid, rubber, leather, high-octane fuel, and sweat. Possibly a touch of wood, glue, fabric, and dope, back then, too. The combined odours of machinery and man. That was the first lesson to be learned when, on that sunny spring day, I traded fresh country air for that which now assailed the senses.

The interior had a used look about it; a thousand scuffs and scratches, chipped paint, crazed perspex, leather seats shiny with wear. I, along with Pete and the others, lowered my bum into one, and secured myself with a canvas lapstrap. Not a lot of help in the matter of gaining my confidence, that. Especially once the door was slammed closed, sealing us in. Still, I had my faithful parachute to hand - the harness I wore, clip-on chest pack by my side. (As had everyone, despite the fact that one lad - totally disregarding the canvas handle - elected to pick his up by that nice, shiny, D-ring. This of course released the silken contents to fall about his feet like an impatient bride discarding her wedding gown. Not the first time that had happened - the parachute, I mean - but being a cadet rather than a fully-fledged airman he was excused the normal repacking fine of two shillings and sixpence.)

The pilot looked back, checking that everyone was as ready as he was. He then reached forward and began the process of start-up.

A propeller turned jerkily a couple of times, cylinders coughed and died intermittently, belching blue-grey smoke rings, until the engine finally caught, sending a shudder through the airframe. To begin with, that engine ran as raggedly as my heart, but as it warmed so it roared into healthy life, exhaust gasses now a rich blue. The act was repeated, engine number two, which is when the previously inert machine suddenly became alive with noise and vibration. We then began to taxi across the grass, hollow-sounding thuds echoing throughout the cabin. Tailwheel, bumping over uneven ground? Or my still-ragged heartbeat?

At the end of the active runway, with the tarmac stretching ahead in diminishing perspective, each engine was systematically checked:

magnetos, temperatures, pressures. All must have shown the right kind of readings, for the throttles were pushed fully open, machine active, eager, straining against brakes which were suddenly released....

Up to this point it had been little different from riding a farm tractor, but now my heart was really pounding. Excitement, or fear? I attempted a little self-assurance. Nothing to be fearful of. People fly all the time. Nothing magical about it. Nothing new.

To me there was.

We moved. Disappointingly slowly at first, with some reluctance, it seemed. Then we were pounding along, gathering pace rapidly. On and on. An apparently ineffectual attempt. We were bumping, bouncing, the tailwheel lifting, but we weren't flying, until, parting company with our shadow - as Peter Pan had once feared - we were. On the way to Never-Never-Land? It felt that way, to me, for we were floating, the only vibration an out-of-sync rumble, which ceased as the pilot juggled the throttles.

Airborne at last, the machine seemed really to come alive. It hadn't, of course, it couldn't, it just felt that way, climbing, banking, turning this way and that. The fields and villages of my native county slid past below, filling my mind with cascading thoughts... The earth was down there, I was up here, up where the clouds formed, where the birds flew. At last I was seeing what they saw, and it was wonderful. Not only was the aircraft in its element, so, I was soon to realize, was I. The familiar Yorkshire landscape dropped away, below and behind, along with any misgivings I may have harboured. It was velvet smooth, almost dreamily peaceful, reassuring to discover that the theory of flight was in fact reality. A fact, in fact! The Air Training Corps had taught me about such laws: basic aerodynamics - lift versus drag, and so forth. I imagined air flowing above the wings speeding up relative to that which passed beneath, creating low pressure and suction on the upper surfaces, a prerequisite to the defiance of gravity.

The country that now passed below seemed foreign to me, for I couldn't recognise a thing from up there. What I had always imagined to be fields of enormous dimension were now being revealed as small green patches divided by hedges of a darker green. Cows and sheep had become unrecognisable brown and white dots. Woods and copses were transposed into mysterious dark patches, rivers and streams became threads of silver. But, significantly, birds flew by *below* me!

But it wasn't to last, for all too soon we were descending. We banked into a final turn, horizon tilting in the windscreen, that distant crescent of hangars drifting past, nose coming round until we were lined up with the runway ahead. The pilot, leather helmet on his head, held the oxygen mask to his mouth and spoke briefly into it. Oxygen had not been required at the altitudes at which we had flown, therefore the mask was left hanging until such time as the pilot needed to talk on the radio. Now he reached over to fiddle with something else, the aircraft slowing as flaps and gear sighed into place ready for the landing. We were on finals, engines throttled back, nose high, floating, floating, until, with a barely perceptible bump, we were down. That was it. Flight over. We were taxying in, earthbound once more. I was back on that farm tractor, and the hollow-sounding thuds echoed as before, but everything else was different. The sounds and the smells were now familiar rather than new, and apprehension had given way to wonder. But, most significant of all, I realized bonds had been severed.

Often, it seems, we don't recognize the good times in life until they are well past, but for me there were to be two exceptions, of which this was the first. It was absolutely fantastic (as would be the second). I experienced a sensation I was unlikely ever to forget; I'd become intoxicated by the science of flight, had broken the bonds which shackled lesser mortals to earth. My growing love of aeroplanes became even deeper.

*

Within the month our squadron travelled north for the annual summer camp, all the way to Leuchars, Scotland, another land, at last. It had to be, for they spoke kind of funny up there: och, aye, dinna ken, and stuff like that. They also played something called golf, drank a lot of something called whisky and, on occasion, some of the men took to wearing skirts.

On the RAF base at Leuchars a venerable old Anson was to provide the means of defying gravity, but also in the offing was a flight in something rather special, even back when there was more than one around. This flight, we were informed, was to be awarded to the cadet who had already logged the highest number of hours. Unfortunately, that information proved to be false. I say unfortunately, and such was to be the case for that high flying cadet, for, with but a piddling thirty minutes in *my* log, and some quirk of fate, I found myself en-route to RAF Waddington, down among the Lincolnshire potato fields. I'd apparently traded a flight in an Anson for one in a Lancaster. Was this to be some kind of omen?

To my everlasting shame, I have to admit the only moments I am able to recall of what should have been a memorable flight, were clambering over the main spar on my way forward. Then, at the end of it all, of standing by the aircraft on the ground.

Surely, at that age, whilst avoiding flak, I would have kept a wary eye peeled for an imagined attack from "the Hun in the sun"? Or did I crouch in the nose, watching Holland slide past below as we headed for the dams of the Ruhr? And what about the sound of those famous Merlins, that aeronautical symphony of the war years? Not a bit of it.

I do remember the touchdown - difficult not to - although I won't dwell on it, apart from saying we thumped down in a landing the pilot certainly shouldn't have been proud of. In fact, had he been honest he'd have logged at least two.

Whatever the reason, for 1950, that was it. A particularly barren year of but two flights, not counting the gliding at nearby Rufforth. These flights were in the Slingsby Sedburgh, also built locally, in Kirkbymoorside. But those two powered flights did account for five and a quarter hours, an annual total not bettered for the next five years, although, to me hours were less important than types. There was the Wellington, in 1951 - another coup, that. ATC summer camp again, Finningley this time, with day and night flying on the agenda. Next was the Anson, at Dishforth - another place that, two years hence, was to play a significant role in my aeronautical life. The Anson, too, was to perform a significant function, for apart from fifteen minutes aerobatics in a Tiger Moth, the Anson was to be the only type on offer for the next two years.

*

And so to that Tiger Moth (N5130). Although fifteen minutes may seem rather short in the matter of flight time, these were to be action-packed minutes for a lad, for during this flight it seemed the intention was that the wheels should point anywhere but at the ground.

I waddled out to the aircraft, parachute already strapped to my behind, a difficult and ungainly performance, even for a grown man. I recalled seeing a lad at school, walk like this, after he'd been caught short and suffered an embarrassing accident. I felt it to be entirely possible I might duplicate his act at any moment. As for climbing aboard, that was doubly difficult. But in this I was helped by the pilot, who then strapped me into the biplane's open cockpit, fitted my helmet and goggles.

'You all right?' he asked.

'Of course,' I told him. What did he expect me to say? Even if my mouth was as dry as a Muslim's wine cellar.

I could see little ahead but the instruments, and there are not too many of those in a Tiger Moth. Then came the start-up, and take off from the grass strip, exhilarating stuff. Biggles, the wind in my face. I imagined the only things to be missing were a silk scarf and a moustache. Or perhaps a touch of panache?

Too late now to change your mind, I told myself. Anyway, I was all right, wasn't I?

In perfect conditions we climbed to fifteen hundred, apprehensive, heart-thumping feet, high above Doncaster, my degree of anticipation climbing to match the altitude. Then we levelled out, and I noticed the pilot's grinning image in the rear-view mirror. He raised a thumb, I responded likewise. But I was too enthusiastic, raised my arm too high. The slipstream caught my hand and shook it around so much I felt I must look like a hitchhiker with diarrhoea. Well, the next few seconds will reveal all, I thought, dragging my arm back in to safety. And so they did, for this is when it happened.

The nose dropped and we were going down, absolutely vertical,

speed increasing as green fields filled the windscreen. Back came the stick, forces pushing me down in the seat as we recovered, and we were on the way up again, into a loop. Green fields to brown earth to blue sky to brown earth to green fields. Wow, what had I been worried about? Bloody fantastic.

It was when we went over the second time, to remain inverted, that I said my prayers, and my goodbyes. With the engine popping and banging away, my goggles, not fitting too well anyway, disappeared off my head. So what? Didn't really need them, seated as low as I was, thought I. Which is when *was* suddenly became the operative word.

My being relatively small meant there was a lot of slack in the Sutton Harness, I therefore found myself to be sliding up in my seat, which of course meant *down,* towards Donny racecourse. Oh, no!

For a heart-stopping second or two I thought I was a goner, about to be involuntarily ejected. One hand, the one that didn't have a white-knuckled grip on whatever piece of airframe happened to be convenient, shot towards the ripcord release. It would have been embarrassing if I'd popped the 'chute, but I didn't. I couldn't. Don't know what it was I had hold of, but it certainly wasn't the D-ring. No matter, my departure was firmly halted when the shoulder harness finally did its job, preventing me from emulating Icarus, albeit with myself starting at a much lower altitude.

Then we were right side up again, the sky in its rightful place, wings level, engine running sweetly, my heartbeat decreasing. A further bonus was that, apart from the pilot retaining his seat, my bum was back where it belonged, firmly on that parachute pack. The stands of Donny racecourse seemed destined to remain deserted after all.

After that nothing mattered, which was as well, for we went through the repertoire: loops, rolls, stalls, even a spin. OK, the spin had me worried, but only a little, and not for long, for recovery from it saw us on a sideslipping approach to that grassy runway. The only remaining worry was whether or not I would be charged for what had amounted to a rather tatty old pair of goggles. But even that turned out to be a negative problem; I discovered them hanging off the back of my leather helmet once we'd landed and I was taking a stomach-settling walk back to join the rest of the group. Naturally, they were there, well secured, just as I had been.

'How was it?' my mates asked.

'Fantastic,' I replied. Well, what else could I say?

*

1951. The Festival of Britain, war in Korea, unrest in Iran and Egypt, the first hydrogen bomb test, the Goon Show, that kind of year. It was also the year I decided to quit school. I left when I was fifteen, not realizing at that age just how important education was. It was goodbye to the exams, those sighs of relief, or groans of despair as we opened papers and scanned the contents. Goodbye also to the smell of chalk dust, to school meals, and free milk. An undistinguished schooling from an undistinguished state school, then, though I don't suppose I fared too badly, according to a report dated 1950. Third in class? Not too shabby, I suppose, out of a class of around twenty, though I must have had some pretty dumb schoolmates, given my results in certain subjects. Take art, for instance: "Has done better". And art was one of my favourites, even if I wasn't much good at it. The trouble was, I could visualize things perfectly. It was when those images were transferred to paper that discrepancies were to be found. Like giving a Rubik Cube to a chimpanzee, I'd occasionally produce something recognizable - aeroplanes dropping bombs; square cars; rectangular buses - but even those were more by luck than talent. (Although over the years I did improve, especially on the aeronautical side. Lockheed's beautifully curvaceous Constellation and the Handley Page Victor, with its smooth flowing lines, both were to become positive favourites. But by then I suppose I was at last becoming aware of just how beautiful curves could be, when applied to the right body.)

Perhaps I'd been elevated up the order because my failures were in relatively minor subjects. Things like gardening, religious instruction, and woodwork. But science? Can't understand that. Possibly my very favourite subject. Must have been an off day when I sat the science exam. As for biology, well... a little practical during the birds and bees phase could have proved useful in later years. For me, at least. Some of the lads seemed to have done all right, getting a little private tuition on the side, as it were. I recall one lad who became known as "Shaggy" McDonald. No need for details on how one acquired such a nickname; suffice it to say, it had less to do with his appearance than it did with the fact that he reputedly "got plenty". "Can't keep away from it", they said. And there was I - no doubt along with scores of others - the enigmatic "they" - couldn't get near it. Whatever "It" was supposed to be!

'It's not just for peeing through, thar knows.' That's all Shaggy was prepared to say, when broached on the subject.

OK, so the biology would come naturally, but upon leaving school I didn't exactly feel truly conversant with the mechanics of the three Rs. In fact they were so far removed from my frame of reference I wasn't even sure if three was the number of R's there were supposed to be.

There was to be no further education, but the lack of a piece of paper didn't seem to hinder me, apart from the fact that I couldn't decide what it was I wanted to do. I therefore took a job as a low-paid, trainee motor mechanic, and between bouts of stripping and cleaning engines, remetalling bearings, making tea, sweeping up, and liberally coating myself with oil and grime, I continued to pursue my new-found love.

*

Along with twenty thousand others I directed my eyes heavenwards. We awaited a sign of some kind which had nothing to do with the Almighty, although we were a kind of cult. Why else would ten thousand presumably sane people gather at an almost deserted airfield?

'See anything?' I asked my friend, Ivan, who lay nearby on the grass.

'A seagull just flew over, but apart from that, nothing but sky and clouds,' he replied, but he kept looking. 'How about you?'

'I'm looking.'

What we sought was the aircraft the commentator advised was now beginning its dive, aiming itself directly towards us. But as Ivan had said, there was nothing to be seen, apart from a few puffy white clouds set against a familiar background of blue. I'd even missed the seagull.

My day had already been fulfilling, for earlier I had been close enough to Neville Duke to be able to take his photograph, along with that of the Hawker Tomtit he was later to fly, but the real excitement was here and now, building all the time.

It was yet another of those almost-perfect sunny days, peaceful and comforting. The air felt so dry it hummed with stillness, yet there must have been a modicum of humidity present. Not exactly conditions that were likely to generate excitement, but it was there all right, I felt it, as did everyone, you could sense that.

Neither of us knew quite what to expect, but my adrenalin was certainly flowing, and I was carried away by it. Up on that plateau I felt less exposed, less vulnerable, lying on the ground, on my back. Watching. Waiting.

Still nothing, and now the place was almost silent. Apart from a few muted words it was as if the rest of the crowd, too, was holding its collective breath.

Suddenly, a voice broke the silence. 'There!' A finger pointed. Another voice, another finger, this to be followed by a plethora of fingers.

I sat up, turned my eyes in the direction indicated, caught a minute, brief flash of silver, then it was gone; if it had even been there. Was my imagination running wild?

'You see it, Ivan? I did.'

'You sure?'

'I think I did.'

No. It was there all right. The excited babbling of the crowd told me so. The tension rose. 'How loud d' you think it'll be?' I asked.

'Dunno,' Ivan replied. 'D' you think it'll harm our ears?'

'Dunno,' I said. 'Ask that fella next to you. Surely someone's heard it before?'

Then, before Ivan could ask anyone, so had I. Not once, but twice. Boom-boom! In rapid succession. The characteristic double report of an aircraft breaking the sound barrier. Not ear-shattering at all. Nor was it faint. A sound you could actually feel; the supersonic shockwave. A truly magical moment.

It was to be many long seconds before the aircraft put in an appearance, a low whine announcing the arrival of an F86 Sabre. It continued its dive, headed our way, wings swept back rakishly. As yet distant and small, it looked incapable of generating any great degree of sound.

That was Yeadon, on a warm spring day in 1952, the first of my many visits to air shows.

In those far-off, gung-ho days of public entertainment, the rules for display pilots were apparently few and far between. No health and safety executive then, so they flew fast and low, almost skimming the ground. Towards the crowd if that was deemed most effective. And it often was, for there is little to match the effect of a fast jet travelling directly towards you, as had that Sabre.

Even the faint whine diminished to almost zero as the aircraft grew larger and larger, wide-open mouth gulping air.

'Looks like one of those desk-top models, floating in the sky,' Ivan observed.'

'Yeah. But why no noise?' No matter what else I had learned, I was obviously as yet unaware of the difference in speed between sound and light. But Ivan was. There again, he'd always been smarter than me. Not that I'd have told him so.

'Science, remember? Sound and light? Only a difference of one hundred and eighty-five thousand, nine hundred and ninety-eight miles per second,' he quoted.

'Huh! Must have been asleep when that came up. Had to be. Let's face it, a difference of that magnitude I wouldn't have missed.'

'Tell you what, he's shifting all right,' Ivan said. 'Full chat, I reckon.' (It was the phrase we used; these days it would probably be "mega".)

He was, too. Unburnt Avtur was being chucked out the back at a ferocious rate, vortices shimmering above and below the wings as he finally levelled out. And, even if it did still the crowd, that silence was deceptive, nor was it destined to last. A fraction of a second after the machine flashed past it became a silence torn asunder, a thunderous blast leaving the air crackling in its wake.

'Bloody hell!' my friend exclaimed. But by then the aircraft was gone, a rapidly decreasing speck travelling in the vertical plane, the visual thrill heightened by the aural effect. Truly spectacular, for those were pre afterburner days.

It still wasn't enough for me. I had actually touched an aircraft, yes. I'd even flown in one or two, and almost fallen out of one, I often kidded myself. But my opportunities for flight were too few.

I decided I'd become a collector of types rather than a mere spotter - a collector of registrations. And for a type to qualify I had to fly in it. So far I'd bagged the Oxford, that Lancaster, Wellington, Anson, and Tiger Moth. Not bad, but I needed more. Lots more. And I thought I knew just where to get them.

*

1953. Frankie Lane, Guy Mitchell, David Whitfield. But for me the year was a turning point. Unable to accept my station in life as an eight-to-five nonentity, I decided to make a break for freedom, to seek excitement, stretch my wings. Perhaps I'd been born with the spirit of wanderlust.

For eighteen months I had been a trainee mechanic. What I learnt at that was to serve me well in future years, but right now, I decided it wasn't what I wanted. Nor, it seemed, was I what the girls wanted, for regardless of the fact that incident-filled outings on *terra firma* were becoming more of a rarity, I was still having little luck in the biology department. This despite the fact I regularly attended the local dances; the drapes, the blue suede shoes, quiff in my hair, condom tucked away in my wallet. (But beware the telltale outline, could be embarrassing when pulling out your wallet to buy a girl a drink?) I'd obtained a pack from the barber, the least humiliating place from which to buy them, as, when paying for my haircut, the standard question had been asked: "Would there be anything for the weekend, sir?" A mumbled reply had them palmed across, along with my change.

Three of us split them among us, for there was little hope of getting to use even one. Still, if I learned nothing else in the scouts, I knew what it meant to "Be prepared".

Come to think of it, I believe I may still have mine!

*

About the time the posher and tub were replaced by a rudimentary washing machine, and the telephone lines began to resemble sheet music, swifts and swallows - crochets and quavers - travellers about to seek the winter sun, I was to leave home for the first period exceeding two weeks.

I'd been presented with a travel warrant, the first of many. I suppose it was really a one-way ticket to the future, for it was no mere journey I was about to take. It had to be an adventure, in that I wasn't sure where it would end, what I would be doing, or what I was about to become. It could turn out to be a road to nowhere, but I had to find out. One thing was for sure, I had but two choices: slide further down the social scale, or climb up it. I figured I'd try for the latter. In this I was helped by a quote from Dad: "It's not the start you have in life that matters, Son, it's how you conduct yourself from that point on, and the finish. That's how you'll be judged."

I would return to Norton, of course. Eventually. But by then things would have changed. Childhood was behind me, already part of the past. Life would never be the same again.

* *

THE WAY WE WERE.
1998

Where have all the years gone? It seemed like only yesterday when horse-drawn ploughs tilled these fields, rich, dark earth curling over like heavy surf, gulls following close behind looking for all the world like they were being towed along. And what of those rainy Sundays when I would sit with friends in Malton's only fifties-style coffee bar - up Saville Street - they too seemed eons in the past; both coffee bar and friends. They are, of course, for it *had* been the fifties. Even so, the recollections were clear: Gaggia - a glass and chrome monster with a vast array of knobs, levers, gauges, pipes and tubes; like something out of science fiction. It sat on the counter, hissing and gurgling in accompaniment to the juke box, but it did produce a good cup of cappuccino; Expresso, to us.

Gentler, more tranquil times that, now, viewed over the decades, seem to have passed far too swiftly. But isn't that always the way; some hours pass quickly - especially if you are pressed, and there is a girl involved - others can seem like a lifetime. Years are obviously subject to a similar analogy. Did the sun really shine more in the days of our youth, I wondered? Did we really enjoy the picture card qualities of snow and frost at Christmas? Or were these just memories, viewed through the rose-tinted glasses of retrospect?

But things were different back then, just as *we* were different. Not only in the obvious ways of having less money, no television, and no luxuries; life in general. It seems there are few luxuries today, either. But for a far different reason: luxuries are now taken for granted; demanded, almost.

These thoughts came to me as I took a nostalgic walk along the banks of the Derwent, each thought providing the inspiration for another.

When we were young this river had appeared to be grand. A wide, silvery waterway of unknown and terrifying depth, which effectively divided one town into two. Today I saw it for what it was: an unimpressive brown smear, a river of laughable minuteness, across which, in places, I imagined I could probably wade. I also saw it as a political ruse. After all, two towns require two sets of bureaucrats as opposed to one!

Or could it be these injustices were related to age? Malton dating back to well before the Roman era - when it was thought to have been called Derventio. Doubt creeping in because the Romans recorded Eboracum (York) as being only seven miles distant, rather than eighteen we know today; Malton the first of the two settlements. It was certainly well established by the eighteen forties, when Charles Dickens would occasionally visit. In fact, it is said the area provided inspiration for both Martin Chuzzelwit and Scrooge.

Possibly Malton's fame is related to the fact that it had two breweries, and around thirty pubs; for a population of just over four thousand. Got to know some of those pubs quite well eventually: Gate, Green Man, Ginger Dyson's, a couple more in the market, maybe the Blue Ball. But I'd invariably end up at Paddy's; the Cross Keys, on Wheelgate. Still, no matter, a lot of them are now history, as are the breweries.

Whatever, Norton was where I grew up, so it is that Norton affords memories aplenty, for they are now only memories. There is the glow of the forge at that blackie's shop which I passed on my way to and from infants school, up Wood Street. Embers were fanned to a white heat by means of a long wooden pole which operated the bellows. I hear the "ring, ring" of the hammer as the smithy bounced it off the anvil between blows, the dull thud as it struck white-hot metal, smoke rising as a glowing shoe seared a hoof, myself flinching as it did so, expecting the animal to lash out with its foot. It didn't, even as the nails went in.

I went through the usual gamut of boyish things. Collections of this and that: bird's eggs, cigarette cards, the odd Dinky toy. (Today the bird's eggs would be illegal, cards and Dinky toys probably worth a fortune.) There'd also been the Meccano phase.

Ingrained memories of Norton, then. This, after all, was where I spent my boyhood, in a pub; the Griffin Hotel.

Almost directly opposite the Griffin had been the local cinema, the Majestic, handy for freebie viewing, that. And it had been rather majestic, certainly the most imposing building in town. Impressive steps led to small-paned glass doors which, bracketing the "stills" display, gave access to the foyer. Another pair of doors bracketed the box office, but were set back, out of its line of sight. Ease one of these open a crack, lo and behold, there was the screen. It was a vantage point from which I viewed the clips of many a movie; occasionally warranting the odd clip round the ear from an unusually alert commissionaire. But the Majestic is no more, for the record reads: Built 1923, closed 1953, demolished 1966. In fact the whole block had gone: Elliot's, the corner shop where I'd once squandered my pennies on the few sweets that were available, the chemist next door - Timothy White's - and Nestfield's forge. All demolished long before the days when people began to appreciate old buildings. Not even given over to bingo; a garage and filling station now occupied the site.

*

The old home town I found to be somewhat depressing. It wasn't that the memories of childhood had been swept away. Not at all. Most of it was still there; but not as I remembered. Nor had it changed for the better like a lot of places had, for it wasn't a tourist town; more degeneration than modernization.

The atmosphere was shabbily authentic, but it was no longer complete. Gone was the family grocer up Castlegate, now a hardware store. I recall the way that store used to look once rationing had been lifted. The window, the legend it bore; raised gold lettering on a dark green background: Thos. Taylor & Son, Purveyors Of Fine Foods. Walk inside and a blend of sights and aromas would assail the senses. Coffee beans, the large silver and red contraption which ground them taking pride of place on the long, wide, oak counter. From the ceiling hung cured York hams, ready for slicing, or to be sold whole. On the floor were sacks of this and that: tea, sugar, flour, rice. There were tubs of butter. Little was pre-packed, apart from the crisps. Service was a pleasure; and personal.

Gone too was the little house up Wold Street from which, over the top half of a stable door, we used to buy that home-made ice-cream. More like iced custard really, delicious for all that; in the memory.

Even had the house remained I knew the ice-cream would now be banned by modern hygiene laws. Ostensibly introduced to protect us from ourselves, but which more and more appear to be a ban on anything that offers satisfaction. It's as if Brussels, finding something that gave pleasure or enjoyment, immediately felt need to dream up masses of legislation, effectively to ban it. Same thing applies to the few "chippies" that remain. So as to compete with the Chinese and Indian take-aways, pizza parlours and the like, the "chippies" had been driven to offering battered sausages and hamburgers. Fish and chips *are* available, though it's doubtful they'll be cooked in anything other than some refined, homogenized, low-cholesterol, vegetable concoction; with a full complement of those mysterious E number additives, of course. Mustn't forget those. And what are they doing to our bodies over the years? Only God, and time, has the answer to that. Then there are the chips themselves: frozen, and crinkle-cut. Signs of the times; maximum profit for minimum effort.

I turned into a road I'd once known so well yet now hardly recognised. I was a stranger to this street.

But no. Some of the older buildings looked vaguely familiar when studied up close. For instance: replace the double-glazing in number ten with a small-paned bay, imagine that fancy PVC door to be paint-flaked wood, remove the pseudo-concrete finish from the brickwork, and presto! That was where Mike had lived.

Not a stranger after all, then; the street was a stranger to me. I'd expected it, though. They said it happened; people returning to a childhood haunt. But even if some of the originality did remain, the magic had gone.

Gone too was the corner shop where I'd once squandered my pennies on the few sweets that were available. Gone was that forge next door. There used to be two forges, I remembered. Absolutely necessary, what with two breweries, whose drays were horse-powered, and a farming community in which tractors were a rarity. Not now. No breweries, no blacksmiths. A sad loss all round.

That town held the history of my childhood, the Griffin, particularly so, and now it was no more. The building was intact, only its days as a pub were history, my father seeing it through to the end. But I realized I couldn't expect the place not to have changed, for it to remain my own private museum of nostalgia; on the off-chance he may one day return.

Mabel still lives across the road at number 10 (the Griffin had been number 7), but Dad was gone, even if his spirit remains.

But it was outside town where the memories really came flooding back. Yes, you need to travel further these days to find yourself out of town, but once there, you could almost be back in the past; if it wasn't for the school.

Norton Boys Secondary was the last school I'd attended. What today would be termed Comprehensive, were it still in existence, right there on Commercial Street, next to the cop shop. That it is not, accounted for this more modern, less aesthetic structure out here in the country. At least, what *had* been country; now the outer fringes of town.

Gone too were the bike sheds. Pity that. Handy, those bike sheds. Chiefly for what purportedly went on behind them. The thought produced a smile. Rumours and stories; some of which I dismissed as untrue. After all, it had never happened to me. Difficult really, in a boys-only school.

Of such are boyhood memories made. Or shattered!

* *

Chapter Two
TAKEOFF

Railway stations are generally cold and depressing places at any time of day, particularly so at seven o'clock on a February morning, yet here was I, at this unearthly hour, already on my second station of the day. The first had been Malton, from where my parents had seen me safely on my way for the first short leg of a very long journey. Here, in the gloomy cavern of concrete, steel, and glass that was York station, things seemed different. This was the real beginning, for I was now alone, mentally at least. And even though a number of people did await trains, they were silent and moody-looking, despite the fact it was already Tuesday. No fractious children charged around, no dogs barked, there were no loud goodbyes, no station announcements. There was, in fact, nothing but a distinct chill in the air, and a lonely silence. This was to be disturbed only by the arrival of a train. Mine.

It was the 17th of the month. The year was 1953. My only luggage consisted of a small, cheap, compressed-cardboard suitcase. My first suitcase. The first of many, though I wasn't yet to know that. This one held little apart from my hopes and dreams. Where I was going I wouldn't need much more.

My boarding was to be followed by a slamming of doors, the last minute rush of late-comers, the search for seats, the stowing of luggage, the shedding of gloves, of hats, and coats. Then, with a blast on his whistle and the wave of a flag - answered in turn by the engine, shrill and echoing - the guard boarded the train just as it gave a jerk and prepared to move off. The wheels of adventure had begun to turn, though we weren't yet underway. Steel wheels on steel tracks momentarily slipping and spinning. Then they found traction, and we did move, forward, on into the unknown. But there was sure to be more than adventure ahead, for wasn't this a new life I sought? And me without qualifications of any kind, apart from my secondary education, and the will to learn. Though my face remained stoically calm, internally I was in turmoil. Being a shy lad that was something I'd already learned: to put a brave face on things, no matter what. (When challenged by Norton's dreaded "Beverley Road Gang" it was either that or the shame of bursting into tears, for you were likely to get beaten-up, anyway.)

The engine hissed steam and chuff-chuffed clouds of sulphurous grey coal-smoke which broiled upwards, collecting beneath the already soot-encrusted roof arching high over the platform. The drive wheels again spun briefly, the smoke followed the curvature of the blackened, rivet-studded girders, and the glass, dissipating as it rolled down the sides depositing grime upon grime. Pigeons cooed and fluttered about as they were engulfed, not seeming too perturbed at all. "Should have been here when the bombs came down," you could almost imagine them saying.

I was travelling on my own for the first time in my life. Leaving home. And - although I didn't realize it then - apart from short visits, I had left for good. It was the start of a journey which, I fervently hoped, would surely bring me fame and fortune. At the very least it might satisfy a craving.

I settled myself in the Third Class compartment. Bit degrading, that, to my mind, but the railways only offered a choice of First or Third, my warrant assigning me to the latter.

Out of the eight seats on offer, four faced the future, the rest looked back to where I'd been, an arrangement that left me the choice of either staring my fellow passengers in the eye, looking beyond them, out of the window, or inspecting their luggage - located in the mesh racks overhead. Pictures, mounted mid-way between face and luggage, did offer an alterative to the embarrassment of staring, but even the most avid art critic would be hard pushed to find more than a few minutes interest in those. Gaze at them for any length of time and they started to affect your mind. Colours mutated, lines became blurred. Let's face it, how long could a print of Filey Beach or Scarborough Castle command the attention? I chose to look towards the future.

The carriage smelled of smoke and soot. It seemed to be ingrained in everything connected with the railways. They had their own special smell too then? Just like my aircraft.

Slowly gathering speed we passed the backs of houses, not noted as being their best profile: sorry little gardens filled with ramshackle sheds and greenhouses, just as ours had been. But once we got up speed the city soon fell behind, taking with it my past. Norton/Malton left behind, York left behind, the world I had known, had seemed condemned to forever, all left behind. Urban gave way to suburban then once more to rural, and though the lines were now national, the scenery still belonged to Yorkshire. Ploughed, deckle-edged fields, trees and meadows, rivers and streams, hills and valleys - the playgrounds of youth. Despite a lust for change, I'd miss all that. I'd miss home, too, and the rolling moors. I already did. The hollow cry of the curlews, the bleating of the moorjocks, the wind in the heather. It could be a lonely place at any time, deadly in winter. But my images were formed during the summer months.

Forget it. All behind you now.

I switched focus to the telephone lines beside the track. They, it seemed, wish to droop towards the ground, but were not allowed to. It was like watching a piece of elastic being jerked this way and that: down, down, down, up, down, up, up, down, then zooming skywards as the train approached a tunnel. Quite fascinating... for a while. I turned my attention instead to those steel wheels; listened. They were talking to me. A familiar chant. Leaving home, leaving home, leaving home, they said. Then, as we crossed a junction: "never ever to return." But I didn't believe that. Truth be told, they say whatever you wish them to say. So I let my mind wander instead, piecing together events that had led me this far. I looked upon this journey as turning a corner on the past, what little past there was at the ripe old age of sixteen and a half.

To me, it seemed endless.

I took the other alternative to Filey Beach and Scarborough Castle, lay my head back and closed my eyes. The idea was to concentrate on what may greet me upon arrival at my destination, but as I relaxed I again found the images to be those floating back from over the years.

*

It was a sunny September, and the school was on holiday. I was in a field which, to young eyes, seemed to stretch away to eternity. Row upon row of potatoes. Armed with a bucket, I, and a dozen others, trudged along behind a tractor, picking the spuds by hand, the earthy smell of freshly turned soil heavy on the air. It was back-breaking work for ten to twelve hours a day, but we were well-paid. And the lunch breaks were something else: fresh, home-made apple pies, and buckets of strong, milky tea. And to think they actually gave us time off school to partake of this, which made it a double bonus: no school dinners, and lots of aeroplanes zooming around. I could stare to my heart's content without the threat of being thrown out of the classroom window. Oh yes, they didn't mess about, our teachers, there again neither did some of the pupils. I recall a rather meek English master whose mild manner was exploited by the tough kids. They knew of course, the tough kids always know, in school or in life. Clem could never throw anyone out of the window, would likely have gone himself had he tried. I remember one lad being pulled out for punishment, but it ended up with Clem in a headlock, being punched in the face. His glasses fell to the floor, were immediately stamped on by someone else.

At least back then a teacher could retaliate. Or, if necessary, have the headmaster retaliate for him. He didn't mess about either, it was six of the best. Only choice we had was hands or backside.

*

I awoke to the clamour of movement, people standing, preparing to disembark. We had arrived. Wolverhampton, almost the end of the beginning of my new life, to paraphrase Winston Churchill. Just the branch line to negotiate now. Albrighton, Shifnal, and that would be it.

As I wasn't in farming, or any other "reserved occupation", nor poised to enter university (what, me, a lad from the sticks?), Her Majesty would shortly have made demands upon my person. This would have been in letter form, but rather than an invite to a Royal Garden Party it would have requested my presence for two years in the service of my country. National Service, it was called. Nor would there have been any chance of escape on medical grounds, for I had already been passed A1: fit to serve. So I decided not to let conscription claim me for the Army, to pre-empt the call-up, volunteering instead to serve ten years in the Air Force - on completion of Boy Entrant training. Surely a much better option than two years in the Army? Had to be, didn't it? After all, I'd be around my beloved aircraft.

That was the way my thinking went, though my arrival at RAF Cosford left me to conclude that perhaps I had slightly misjudged the situation - not an unusual position for me to find myself in, given my age, and lack of worldly experience.

Upon reporting in I had requested the use of a toilet, somehow became detached from the rest of my group. On enquiry I'd been told to remove myself to some other location, an Induction Centre, or some such. 'You'll find it over there,' said a bored looking airman, waving a hand vaguely in the general direction of the rest of the world.

OK. Nothing for it but to show some initiative. I headed off towards the area indicated, in a general sort of way. Well, let's face it, it had been a general sort of indication.

I set off along what I hoped was the right road; no doubt would have been had I chosen to travel in the opposite direction. A couple more roads - backtracking as it were - brought me to an open area. Which is when I saw them, away in the distance, a group of civilians. Could only be the rest of my intake, I decided, setting off in their direction like a bowling ball towards the pins. Which was about the time I discovered that open area to be "the hated parade ground": that large expanse of tarmac which forms the central point of any military barracks, and to be regarded as sacred. To walk across the hallowed surface, using it as a shortcut, is a definite no-no. (I later remembered someone telling me we'd been taught that in the ATC, and surely we must have been. Anyway, by the time whoever it was told me, his data was irrelevant.) It seemed I'd barely set off when I was suddenly overcome by the feeling that there was somewhere else I would rather be. Anywhere but where I was, halfway to my destination, via the shortest route.

Too late. Didn't require a master's degree in sociology to spot that, my secondary education served well enough.

'You, lad! Come here!' About six thousand decibels!

That was something I did remember hearing about parade grounds, they were reputed to be places where loud voices shouted orders and hurled abuse about. No abuse as yet, but the voice - if not six thousand, definitely on up there on the top end of the decibel scale - *was* issuing an order. And although I knew the command to be directed at myself, I imagined at least fifty other lads within hearing range automatically looking round, wondering what in hell it was they'd done wrong this time.

Considering this could be the end of the world as I knew it, I thought I coped quite well. I ran smartly to where he stood, coming to attention before him.

'Yes, sir?' Oops! That was something else I remembered, albeit again too late: never address a senior NCO as sir. That, to them, is as good as an insult. Seems they felt it degraded them, for many considered themselves to be better than officers, especially the drill instructors. This was one of the unwritten rules of service life, of which there appeared to be many. The written rules - of which few but the Service Police and lawyers seemed to have an interest - were contained in a rather unnerving tome known as Queen's Regulations, abbreviated to QR's. Which at present was of academic interest only. The sole exception to this rule was the Warrant Officer, who was definitely a "sir."

'Not sir! Sergeant! You'll address me as such. What am I?'

I could have told him. 'A sergeant, Sergeant.' So am I, I felt like adding. Would have, had not the thought occurred that there are times when it pays to be frank and times when it doesn't, even if I was a sergeant in the ATC. In fact, just as well I hadn't turned up in uniform, for, as a yet to be initiated civilian I was let off with a stern warning. Maybe the fact we were both named Taylor had a bearing, though I seriously doubted it. A tolerant and understanding admin sergeant, then, if there was such a thing?

Turned out there was, a positive pussy-cat, relatively speaking. He was also later revealed to be our flight commander. Our drill instructor, yet another Taylor - corporal this time - nowhere near as forgiving a creature, I was to find. I took to him much as would an arachnophobic to a tarantula in the bed. There were others, too. Some who appeared to have been recruited on decibel count alone. Certainly nothing that in any way related to IQ, so we told ourselves.

So, I was off to a grand start. Within a couple of minutes I had succeeded in transgressing two of the sacred rules of military life, rules of the unwritten variety. The good news was I'd done it before taking the oath of allegiance. I was still a civilian therefore, and, in theory, could walk out. Others would not be so fortunate, for once we had been inducted and kitted out, that would change with a vengeance. Walking out at that point would constitute being AWOL - absent without leave - a rather serious offence, to say the least.

It took no longer than a couple of days for us to be accommodated, documented, indoctrinated, and medically inspected, en-masse; the works. Even at school all they ever did was check my head for nits, this guy poked and peered everywhere, even going so far as to put his hands where previously only I put them, to relieve myself, in one way or another.

They were gruelling days, the evenings of which were spent relaxing on our beds, which made them seem not so bad (the days, that is). This, I suspect, was a deliberate ploy, for as soon as we'd signed on the dotted line laying on a bed became a thing of the past, along with any freedom we might have had. The drill instructors would see to that, making frequent, unexpected and decidedly unwelcome visits, suddenly flinging open the door.

"On your feet you 'orrible lot. What do you think this is, Billy-bloody-Butlins?" They never actually said "bloody", you understand, something a little livelier. Type of word you may use to express displeasure when hitting your thumb with a hammer! (And us just innocent young lads!) Then, after a few beds had been routinely overturned, kit scattered, they'd deliver their verdict. "This place is a pigsty. Get it cleaned up." An extremely rude awakening, that.

What we had thought of as gruelling days were now seen to have been nothing like. We could well have been at Butlins, as the drill corporal suggested. Not any longer. "Lights out" was sounded at twenty-two hundred, "Reveille" at zero six hundred, a bugle player from our recently-formed marching-band allotted the honours. Served him right for volunteering. Seemed I was to be the only one who could manage such foolishness with impunity, and even that was for the future.

Nor did lights out mean only that, it also meant "get to sleep", we soon found. Not advisory either, it was as good as an order.

'Did you hear the one about the old guy who was being questioned with regard to his sex life?' The words drifted across in the darkness.

'Go on, I'll buy it,' another voice replied.

'He was asked how often he "did it"?'

'And?'

'"Infrequently", was his reply.

"That one word, or two?" the questioner asked.'

It raised a chuckle from some, a comment from one lad who had obviously already enjoyed the experience.

'God, don't mention sex. I could use some of that right now.'

'You've done it then have you, Jonesy?' I asked.

'Definitely be two words in my case,' Jonesy replied.

'What the hell am I doing here?' someone else asked of the room in general. 'I want to go home, wish I hadn't signed on.' Seemed like he was missing something, too. Was I the only inexperienced lad here? I wondered.

All his remark did was to evoke some unsympathetic advice.

'Too late now to change your mind, boyo.' This from our tame Welshman, named Farmer, but for some reason we called him Taff! Which is when the lights flashed on again.

'Quiet in here,' bellowed a voice from the end of the room. Big Brother, in the form of the Leading Boy in charge. He lived in a one-man alcove, a separate room incorporated in the end of ours.

A loud fart rent the air. I knew who that would be; he of the blue-flame trick. No matter, next time the lights went out, so did we, for even Boy NCO's had the full weight of the service behind them. In fact the room became so quiet it would have been possible to hear a goldfish fart, never mind old Tillson.

Next morning came the production-line haircut, the old short back and sides trick. I saw lads almost burst into tears as well tended locks dropped around their feet like underwear at a medical inspection. Out went the DA and the Tony Curtis, not enough left to warrant the use of Brylcream. Me? I didn't care. My hair was nothing to begin with; styled by Multimix, kind of thing. What I now sported could only be termed an improvement.

Clothing fit where it touched, and although our dress uniforms were "tailored", this appeared to be the work of tailors who had probably been butchers in civvy street, nor did they bother asking on which side you dressed. There again they did have quite a task on their hands, almost every derivative of the humanoid form being on display before them.

'Are we actually supposed to wear these?' one lad asked, referring to underwear and socks that were almost certainly a hangover from the recently concluded days of the clothing coupon. I knew just what he meant. They did feel uncomfortably rough and itchy.

'These shirts don't have collars,' complained someone else.

'They do now,' replied the storeman, passing over collars of the detachable type, along with studs to hold them in place. 'They'll need starching,' he advised. 'No problem, though, the laundry will attend to such matters. With a vengeance,' he added.

Too true, I later found. Almost required the use of a metal press to bend them into shape.

One other small matter: little was of any use in the form in which it was issued. The pimply surface of our boots needed to be smoothed and shined to the mirror-like finish of patent leather, as did dimpled brass badges and buttons. There were various tricks to this of course, passed down from more experienced boys of the senior entries. (One of my ex-school, ex-ATC friends was in the Seventeenth Entry, that was Ivan, another was to follow on behind me, in the Nineteenth; Jimmy.) For the brasses, fine emery-paper - although our blankets would probably have made a good substitute. The emery was followed by cardboard, liberally doused in Brasso. Last of all came the lifesaving, Duraglit. Boot-leather was painstakingly smoothed by a mind-boggling combination of Cherry Blossom and a heated spoon. I often wondered who first thought that one up, for it worked a treat - as long as you were careful with the heated spoon. The final polish was down to old-fashioned elbow grease.

Most important, at least as far as we were concerned, were the knife, fork, spoon, and mug. 'Essential items, those,' the storeman advised. 'Guard them with your life. No eating irons, no food. No mug, no tea. Naturally, there *were* losses, which meant keeping your own in sight, or under lock and key, when not in use.

I suppose in these days of high ideals, with hardly anything remaining in the luxury category, the food we received would be classed as rubbish, but to us ration-book kids it was wonderful stuff. Well, for a month or so it was.

Although medical facilities were first-class, the procedure for attending sick parade, then facing the MO (for Medical Officer), were complex and labourious.

'Six o'clock, sarge!' one lad exclaimed, when we were advised of the time needed to report. 'That would mean getting up before Reveille!'

'If you're ill enough, lad, you'll make the effort.'

'If I'm that ill, sarge, I'll be dead.'

'Just don't die while I'm in charge, or you'll be bloody sorry you were even born.' We had a laugh at that, but only after the sergeant had left.

I suppose this did tend to weed out the malingerers, as it was no doubt designed to do. May as well get on the parade ground with the rest of the lads, unless you *were* seriously ill. Same thing went for church parades: pointless declaring yourself to be an atheist, that only ensured you'd be peeling spuds until long after the church service was over.

All this the price of becoming an airman, should I be so lucky as to survive eighteen months of it. Even then it was no guarantee I would get to fly any more often than I had in the ATC. But that wasn't all. We were shouted at and subjected to base humiliation, expected to take it. No choice. Discipline was tight, blank obedience expected, though not always forthcoming. With lads of our age the natural temptation was to flaunt the regulations, even though lapses rarely went unforgiven. A minor infringement - brasses or boots not shining to a standard deemed acceptable to the drill corporal, hair a touch too long for his liking, or maybe just because your face didn't fit today - could see your name featuring on a form 252. Not exactly one of life's more pleasing experiences, for sure.

The Air Force, I discovered, was run on forms, some of which you needed, others you certainly didn't. 1250 was your identity card - important, that - one you definitely needed. 700 was the aircraft log book, in which every detail of a machine's life was recorded. This would become important, once you arrived on a squadron. (Another point to remember about the form 700, extremely important, this: it must never take to the air in the aircraft to which it relates.)

There was the 1443: railway warrant, the 1771: travel claim - extreme care required here, no cheating allowed. Then there was the 295: leave pass, a much-prized and highly sought after item, that.

Form 252 was the exact opposite, this was a charge sheet. Definitely one to steer clear of. Your name on one of those would earn you seven days jankers in a jiffy, requiring your presence on the twice a day defaulters parade, in full kit. And if you believed discipline to be already tight, here it was extreme. A wayward piece of fluff, a unavoidably rain-spotted button or badge; such carelessness could earn you another seven days in an instant. Nor did it do any good to sulk, or refuse to answer a leading question. Such was construed as dumb insolence, a catch-all offence, that. You could find yourself reporting for weeks.

There were numbers for us, too. Most important, for that is what we were reduced to; a number. There could, after all, be any number of Taylors - as I had already discovered. Possibly more than a few David Taylors. But I was the only one with that unique seven-digit sequence which identified me: 400, my last three. The whole sequence needed to be committed to memory, for it needed to be registered on every form you signed, and every officer or NCO who addressed you seemed to want to know your "last three". Who knows, maybe they collect them, like train spotters, compared results in the mess, over a beer: "Got a four hundred today, and a two nine seven."

So important was your number deemed to be, you'd probably have had need to cite it before being allowed to die, should such a misfortune befall you while still in the service.

*

Slowly, we were gelling as a group. Friendships began to form from day one, total strangers in a strange environment ensured that would happen. Even so, as is normal with such a cross-section of society, there would be the occasional serious disagreement among our ranks (minor, really, but not seen as such to macho youth). And although we were not yet men we were grown up boys, therefore disagreements needed to be settled. Away from the eyes of authority. In one of the storage or laundry rooms. Toe to toe, a group of blood-thirsty onlookers seated on the shelves, for blood was sure to be evident.

It was like a scene from a Western: "I'll meet you in the laundry room at nineteen hundred. Be there." (Yet another discovery, that, as the sharp eyed reader may already have noticed: the military worked on the twenty-four hour clock. Nineteen hundred relating to seven pm. Although for some reason there was no midnight. It was either twenty-three fifty-nine, or zero zero zero one. Twenty-three fifty-nine was also our private designation for, how shall we put it? Anyone of less-than-white pigmentation? Yeah, should sneak that past the race relations board.)

Fighting, of course, was a chargeable offence, but walking into a door, or falling downstairs, was just plain carelessness. It was all a far cry from the childish performances I recalled taking place in the school playground.

"Fight! Fight!" The cry echoed across the schoolyard of Norton Boys County Secondary, an indication that yet another minor dispute had failed on the diplomatic front, degenerated to the fisticuffs stage. Well, sort of.

Two lads grappled with each other, and after swinging a few inept blows one now had the other in a secure grip. Both were head down, face to bum, one with his arms pinned, the other apparently wondering what to do next. They staggered this way and that inside the circle of onlookers. The kind of movement one would expect of an elephant turning around: done without regard as to who, or what, may be nearby, the onus being on those within range to remove themselves, or face the consequences. We duly did, giving them the room in which to do absolutely nothing.

Then, disaster struck the lad doing the holding. His nose started to run, and not a spare sleeve within reach, not without releasing his grip. Ah, but - and here you could almost see his mind at work, cogs rapidly resolving the situation - there, right in front of him, a cotton-coated back. Without a moments hesitation, nor a thought as to the consequences, nose dragged its way across shirt, a snail-like trail marking its passage. Everyone saw it, of course, and we all broke up. Nobody let on what the laughter was about, but within seconds the fight was over, unresolved, anger dissipated. Who knows, his mother probably thought it had been a snail.

That had been my friend, Brian - although I don't believe he'd been awarded that highest of accolades, "My best friend. Ever." I'd meet up with him again, thirty years hence, in New Zealand.

*

52

So, what of those aeroplanes that had been the catalyst to my joining up in the first place? Well, here at Cosford, two weeks passed during which I hadn't so much as been within sight of one, although I had learned the rudiments of close order drill. Naturally, us ex-ATC cadets were a jump ahead of the rest, we'd done it all before: shoulders back, chin in, arms straight, thumbs uppermost, wrist cocked towards the ground. Only here it was slightly more serious, in that if you didn't like being shouted at, or verbally abused, you could hardly pack up and bugger off to the chip shop.

'Squad, att..en..tion,' barked the drill instructor, in answer to which a hundred polished boots recorded ten point five on the Richter scale as they simultaneously stamped out a tattoo on the tarmac. In open order we were commanded "From the right... dress." "Close order... march," came next, after which it was, "Right... turn. By the left... quick...march." We'd then be wheeled right and left, about-turned, marched some more, then halted. We'd be commanded to "Slope arms, Present arms, Order arms," then, after an hour or so, we'd then be marched off to wherever it was we were due next. And so it went, day in, day out. Physical fitness featured prominently in our training, too, with many an hour being spent in the gymnasium.

Come Sunday we'd be marched to church, in Number One Blues; our best uniform. I hadn't been in a church since I left the choir and took to delivering newspapers; more money the incentive there. The Air Force also paid me, even more than I'd received for a wedding: two shillings and sixpence. But that wasn't so much for going to church, it was my weekly stipend. And I had to salute for it, a measly half-crown. Which got one lad to wondering: 'Once I'm in the Air Force proper, receiving paper money, what will be the requirement then? A full bloody march past?'

I soon had gleaming buttons and brasses, had learned to spoon, spit and polish my boots to that mirror-like shine, wash and iron my clothes, press my uniform - pleats and creases razor sharp. (A little soap helped keep them so.) I'd also learned to make my own bed. No, not really. Make it in the Air Force approved manner is what I mean. This called for it to be unmade: one blanket was stretched across the mattress, drum-skin tight, the rest of the sheets and blankets folded in a precise shape and form - rather like a large rectangular Swiss roll, pillows on top (from here on, to be known as a bedpack) - the whole kit and caboodle was then placed at the head of the mattress. How you arranged the sheets and blankets at night was left to your own creativity. Or - as in the case of the apple pie bed - occasionally someone else's. An apple-pie bed was probably bottom of the pile when it came to misdeeds, for, being young and wild, some incidents were absolutely unbelievable. How about a little friendly arson, for starters. We weren't all blue-eyed boys, you see.

After the first month we were reassessed, which was when - personal reservations notwithstanding - I found I had done rather well. Almost too well, it seemed. I was recommended for transfer to the Apprentices, at RAF Halton, but as this was also to entail a change of trade, to Air Wireless/Radar, the decision was left to me. So it was I escaped that fate. I didn't fancy the trade at all, turned it down, this despite the fact that Halton was No 1 School of Technical Training, Cosford being No 2. But that wasn't all. The Apprentice course was a full three years, as opposed to our eighteen months. Forget it. I'd stick with what I'd got. Besides, I was by then beginning to settle down at Cosford, had established friendships. Anyway, I hated sudden change.

* *

PHOTOGRAPHS-1 :

Page 56: Top: Leader of the pack; the author, aged four, with "my two other brothers" (George, five, & Maureen, seven).
Bottom: Much later, jungle bashing in Malaya.

Page 57: Top left: Aged about seven.
Top right: In ATC uniform, wearing a parachute, ready to take a chance in a Tiger moth.
Bottom: Civilians, RAF, RAF Auxiliary, & Boy Entrants - a group of ex-ATC friends.

Page 58: Father in floods. Not as bad as 1947 but the cellar was always first in line. Inset: The big one,1947; taken from upstairs, naturally.

Page 59: Top: Farnborough, 1961 - Javelin.
& Bottom: Hp115.

59

Chapter Three
THE CLIMB-OUT

Shotguns apart - and that fired from the hip (of which, more later) - I had used a rifle before, in the ATC, but that had only been a .22. Here we were taught to shoot the venerable Lee Enfield .303, a much more serious piece of kit, even from my position, at the friendly end. The target was a hundred yards distant.

'On my command. Squaa..ud, load.'

I quickly worked the action, loaded the five-round clip with what I felt was some expertise, snapped the bolt closed, loading a round into the breech. Easy this. The weapon was ready, so was I. Ready to take on the world at large. John Wayne at Guadalcanal.

'Squaa..ud... Five rounds grouping... In your own time... Fire!'

I did so. Albeit with some trepidation, squeezing the trigger slowly. That this was more through not knowing what to expect than teaching, I don't mind admitting to. It's the next bit I'm not too proud of. The effect wasn't quite as anticipated. Nothing happened. Not a bloody thing! World War Two was being re-enacted all around me, yet the weapon in my hands remained stubbornly silent. Not even the dull click of the firing pin descending on a dud round. I assumed the gun to be jammed. Which, in a way, it was.

'Let's try again, shall we, dumb-cluck?' the instructor said, reaching down to release the safety-catch. (At least I think that's what he said.) John Wayne's image retreated in disgust as I once more squeezed the trigger.

BANG! Bloody hell! Much louder than I imagined. Well it would be wouldn't it, this explosion was taking place an inch from my right ear, stock kicking me in the shoulder like a pissed-off mule. It left my head ringing, my arm numb. If I wasn't careful this thing would do me more damage than it would the enemy. As if to confirm its presence the gun exploded again. I wasn't at all happy, but carried on until the magazine was empty.

'How's that for grouping, sarge?'

He gave me a look of utter contempt. 'Possibly very good,' he replied. 'Who the hell knows? One thing's for sure, we aren't about to find out, are we. I don't know where you were aiming, lad, but that target is in pristine condition.'

OK, but I did have an excuse, I'd been distracted, hadn't I? I just couldn't believe what was happening on the next mat to me. Had to be on my right, for my left eye was closed in that squinting-down-the-barrel pose. One minute he was there, then he was gone. So small and light, I swear he had to wriggle forward a couple of feet to regain position every time he pulled the trigger. A lot of good he'd be in the field of action. Me too, come to that, and I had previous experience. I'd been quite good with that .22, at fifty feet. So much for my first visit to the range. Next time will be better, I promised myself.

They even taught us the rudiments of throwing a hand grenade. Dummies, of course, but they did toss the odd thunderflash around, just for effect. Big boy's fireworks, those.

'The reason we use dummies,' the sergeant explained, 'is that, although the grenade is somewhat more lethal than a bow and arrow, in your bloody hands it would probably be nowhere near as accurate. Anyway, it's what you do after the throwing that's important: get the hell out of it. Lie down behind something solid.'

Next came the Bren. 'More like it, this, sarge,' I said. 'Hardly any kick at all.'

'No, lad. That's because the recoil is used to stuff the next round up the spout. But it's no second division piece of tackle when it comes to dealing with the enemy,' he assured me. That was something else I'd discovered: these Regiment types could become almost human if you showed the slightest bit of enthusiasm. Still, I couldn't think why it might be possible I needed to become familiar with any of these weapons. I was in the Air Force wasn't I, not the bloody army. Wasn't that the main function of the RAF Regiment, to protect us? Anyway, I would have thought one of the first rules of combat should be to put your opponent on inferior terms. Not a lot for the enemy to worry about with us then. Not in those days there wasn't. Although it was always possible they would have died laughing. One could only hope.

*

Naturally, above all else we received training in our selected trade. Mine, given its full title: Instrument mechanic (Navigation), under training. I.mech(Nav) u/t, in Air Force parlance.

It was like the first day at school all over again, and in a way I suppose it was. Different only in that our classrooms were now located in cold hangar-like buildings, known as workshops. Wood and sackcloth dividers formed separate cubicles, each dedicated to a different subject. But there were blackboards and chalk dust, notebooks to scribble in, lessons on this and that, and, of course, more of those dreaded exams. No free milk.

They taught us state-of-the-art electronics, although back then in the dark ages this probably bore closer relevance to fish and chips than it did to microchips. As transistor technology had not yet fully asserted itself, fifties state-of-the-art came mainly in the form of vacuum tubes, heavy gauge wire, and seriously high voltages which, when wired to some unsuspecting lad's metal chair..... Well, no need to go into detail is there, save to say the results were usually effective enough to engender many a curt, crude, and often colourful, remark. We were slowly getting the hang of things.

We also wallowed in the principles of navigation, pondered over the intricacies of the equipment necessary to put those principles into effect. These were the data providers: compasses, sextants, altimeters, airspeed indicators, drift recorders and the like. There were mirrors, lenses, prisms, collimators, and other such devices used to reflect, refract, or focus, beams of light. These could, with a little ingenuity and guile - we weren't slow to discover - redirect and focus a ray of sunlight onto a specific target - say an unsuspecting earlobe - with spectacular results. They could also quite effectively to burn holes in sackcloth.

We had Pitot heads and static vents, upon which those altimeters and airspeed indicators relied for their readings (which could be made to reach spectacular levels by the simple expedient of placing ones mouth over the end of a Pitot tube and blowing into it. But be wary, that tube had a built-in de-icer - which got extremely hot extremely quickly when not subjected to a three hundred knot, high-altitude airflow - and there was always one joker who would just have to switch it on. Gave a whole new meaning to the phrase, Hot lips, that).

We then got the standard lecture on airspeed: why it is of critical importance to a pilot. Why - because it is measured in knots, and one knot equates to one nautical mile per hour - there is no such thing as knots per hour. The difference between airspeed and groundspeed was revealed to those of us who hadn't served in the ATC: 'Groundspeed matters only in so far as establishing an ETA (estimated time of arrival), and has no bearing on flight. It's quite feasible for an aircraft to have a negative groundspeed when faced with a strong headwind; it will remain airborne, but it could be travelling backwards over the ground. Speed of the air over the wings is the important element. That's what keeps us airborne.'

So much for the theory of flight then. Pretty ancient stuff really, for old George Cayley had that sussed back way in the eighteen hundreds, remember?

There was much hilarity and ribald comment when the instructor produced an instrument whose dial was graded in something listed as FART. This, he revealed, was the German measurement for airflow. I'd always assumed it meant the same in English.

Then there was George of another kind: the SEP2 autopilot -

developed by Smiths Industries (hence the nomenclature: Smiths Electric Pilot, version 2) - so advanced it smacked of science fiction. Yet compared against today's programable marvels of technology and miniaturization it did next to nothing, apart from fly the aeroplane, would now be considered positively Jurassic. Bombsights also came under our jurisdiction, whereas gunsights bore the classification, Instruments - General, a separate trade as far as training went. Oxygen systems, engine instrumentation, and the like, fell under the same category. In the Air Force proper we were to find there was no such demarkation.

On top of all this trade training came our further education. We were reacquainted with maths and geometry, introduced to algebra, calculus, and trig; mysteries and miseries I seemed to have escaped at secondary school. No chance of that at Cosford.

*

Although I slept on a mattress that bore closer resemblance to a cement waffle than to a feather bed, it didn't matter. I was usually too tired to care. There were times I even slept on the floor, after prematurely preparing my bed for next day's inspection, or when one or other of the senior entries had made the traditional, early-hours bed-tipping sweep through our room. Though these were not as frequent as they would have been were it not for our accommodation advantage.

Whereas other entries found themselves billeted in POW style wooden huts - through which a raiding party could enter at one end and depart by the other, wreaking havoc along the way - we at least had the luxury of a modern, centrally-heated, multi-storey fortress named Fulton Block. Single entry/exit rooms, stairs and corridors offering us a kind of minimal security.

I also learned new songs during my time at Cosford, the words of which they seemed to have forgotten to teach us at school. These were picked up during the occasional cultural evening, when a group of us would gather together in harmonious accord around the NAAFI piano, words and arrangement attributable to servicemen over the generations. Let's see: There Was A Monk Of Great Renown..., Ring The Bell, Verger..., The Ball At Kerrimuir, and, Little Angeline. A favourite, that last, though at a family gathering all would probably be about as welcome as a french kiss.

They were a mixed bag, the eighteenth entry, as are bound to be any group of individuals, male or female. There were a number of oddities among us, too. The guy on the parade ground who got it all wrong when marching, left arm with left leg, right to right. The harder he tried the worse it got. I bet he felt a right prat. Then there was an armourer who looked like a boxer, or maybe he'd just been released from prison. Well, why not.

Robert Mitchum made it from prison to the silver screen, and Jack Palance looked like he could have, even if he hadn't. Come to think of it, that's who he reminded me of, this armourer, Jack Palance. Though it wouldn't have been in my interests to voice that opinion. At least not in his presence. Or out of it, come to that; too many individuals around who might see dropping you in it as a way of gaining his friendship. And that was one thing I wouldn't have wanted: him as an enemy. Especially as he seemed to be a regular participant in the laundry room punch-ups. (I can still see that face today, can't put a name to it.)

Then we come to someone I can definitely put a name to: Titch Nelson. No, definitely not related to the Admiral so named. Titch was the dwarf-like creature who had experienced problems with that nasty Lee Enfield. Alternate nickname: short-arse. Oops! No, of course he wasn't dwarf-like, or short-arsed. Well... what I mean is, he was then, but in this crazy era of political correctness the term would probably be, vertically disadvantaged, or some such. Silly bloody description, really. I mean if you're down there where you can look up a girl's mini-skirt you're hardly disadvantaged, are you? Be that as it may, having never been an avid subscriber to the concept of PC, to me he would forever be a short-arse. But whatever he was, he shared our room. And in common with most small folk, especially one as meek as Titch, he was the one to be picked on.

Also sharing our room - along with about twenty others - was a lad who proclaimed himself to be an accomplished hypnotist. And if he wasn't, there were certainly some among us who should have been up there with Mitchum and Palance, or even Gielgud and Olivier, he was that good. Certainly had me convinced. This despite the fact he was never successful with me; apparently not an ideal subject. Titch, it seemed, was. It took about a minute to put him under, a couple of seconds to bring him back. No problem. Unbeknown to Titch, in between, his subconscious had been primed. He'd been told to collapse every time he looked in a mirror. And so it was. Even a brief glance as he walked past was enough. Nor was there any way for him to be faking it, not the way he hit the floor. It was instantaneous, as if his bones had suddenly become non-existent. And he didn't so much as move a muscle until brought round by a click of the fingers, for which he'd also been primed.

But there were some sad buggers among us, too. The Leading Boy in charge of the room, for instance (yes, he who lived in the one-man alcove). It happened to be Friday, bull night, when the room had to be prepared for that rigorous, Saturday morning inspection. This guy allotted Titch the job of polishing the mirror. Well, sad or not, it was so unbelievable I had to laugh. It was like watching a reverse jack-in-a-box, the subconscious in serious need of a de-prime were our mirror ever to pass inspection.

In time these weekly inspections became fairly routine. Not only the room and ablutions, our kit was also on display, a rigorously enforced arrangement, each item allotted its own place on that drum-tight blanket which covered the mattress. The perfect layout took quite a time to achieve, hence the need to occasionally sleep on the floor. It was clean anyway, that floor never lost its shine, everyone skidding about the room on felt pads, and woe betide those that forgot.

'Pads!' The call would echo down the room the moment anyone so much as thought about stepping in, minus the required protection. In this, we became our own strict masters, especially if it involved that sacred patch of floor known as your bed-space. My bed, and the floor surrounding it was my own private little island. This was where I lived, where my kit was kept - either in the tin locker beside the bed, or beneath the bed itself, along with my little cardboard suitcase full of dreams - and no one but no one set foot in that space without my express permission. Well, senior entries apart, that is. And NCO's and officers. And those tougher than myself. All right, probably everyone except Titch. But they shouldn't have, is what I'm saying.

The initial polishing of the floor was achieved by use of a device known as a bumper. Basically a felt pad attached to a cast iron base, hinged to a long handle. Swing the handle and the base did the lion's share of the work, for it was heavy. So heavy, that if released mid-swing it would charge off down the room like a herd of elephants run amok. It was another mindless game we occasionally played, though not too often for any irreparable damage was our responsibility, had to be paid for. Awful trouble too, should it slam into the door, the moment the duty sergeant happened to be entering the room! Not me, sarge. Honest.

Didn't matter who it was. Certain in the knowledge he would never find out, we all paid. Took ages to sort out our kit, set it out again.

The rest of the bull eventually became monotonous rote, even the monthly ritual of the Commanding Officer's parade. The only fly in the ointment was if we required a new pair of boots, or a new uniform. We then had to start again, from scratch. But the most likely item for replacement was the SD - for service dress - cap. As these looked rather silly in their official form, most were heavily doctored, turning them from duckbill, to something more akin to those worn by the Gestapo. Mild doctoring you could get away with, cut and slash to excess and you were ordered to replace the item. Most, therefore, had two caps; one for use on camp, a heavily doctored version for use when on leave.

The annual ritual known as AOC's inspection (Air Officer

Commanding) was something else again. Paint was applied anywhere paint would stick. You know the old service adage: If it moves, salute it, if it doesn't, paint it.

*

A total of eighteen months were spent at Cosford. Little flying, lots of learning. Had to make up for the loss of that advanced education somehow. Even this early I'd begun to realize adulthood was not something conferred upon one by time, by reaching some magical age. It had to be earned. And earn it I did. Life was one long learning curve, the end of which we seemed destined never to reach. But there were aircraft around for us to get our grubby hands on, training airframes, long since retired from flying. Better than nothing.

One thing I wasn't able to get my hands on were the girls, for as far as I was concerned, there weren't any. At least none that fancied the likes of me. Not much chance, really. We weren't allowed off camp for the first month, after that, only in uniform. (All civilian clothes were required to be posted home almost as soon as I signed on the dotted line.) The only time I did get to wear civilian clothes was on leave.

But uniform wasn't really the problem, for the girls seemed quite attracted to them. No, it was the other three to four hundred like-minded, lusty lads, that were the problem. Some, by their own account, no longer virgins. I was inclined to believe them, too, for I recalled "Shaggy" McDonald, at school. He'd apparently been into it before he was fifteen.

I, being inexperienced and shy could never have expected to compete with any degree of success against the likes of these guys, especially if the rumours were true.

'You know what?' Mike said one day. And it was obvious we didn't, because he hadn't yet told us, but we knew he was about to.

'Those sneaky bastards are resorting to the use of bromide in the food.

'Who, Mike?'

'The authorities, of course.'

'What the hell's bromide?'

'Don't you know anything, Taylor? Chemical that's supposed to curb our natural tendencies, ain't it.

'Ah, I see,' I said, though I didn't really.

'Just a rumour then,' replied Jim, who we knew to have a girlfriend in town. 'I seem to manage all right.'

And suddenly I did see. Well, good for Jim, but never having had a girlfriend to call my own, I didn't really miss them. Not yet. But the old biological clock was certainly ticking away. And I had to agree with Jim. At that tender age, the bromide, if used seemed to have little effect, if the state of the sheets was any indication. There again, maybe it was delayed action stuff? Is there a possibility it actually takes forty-five years to penetrate the system? Now there's a thought. I'll bet even "Shaggy" McDonald is facing hard times these days. No, poor choice of words. If you get my drift, he won't be, will he?

*

The only real disadvantage of having to wear uniform, then, was that it precluded any thoughts of a visit to the pub, everyone being only too aware that, as Boy Entrants, our age was well below the legal minimum. Which only made a drink all the more desirable.

Nothing to stop someone else procuring a bottle or two from the off-licence on our behalf, of course. Which is exactly what a group of us did. Once. Alas, I may have assumed myself adult enough to handle it, but my metabolism thought otherwise, leaving me nursing a brain-to-eyeballs headache next morning. Didn't enjoy my breakfast second time around either. Put me off Port for years, that.

Apart from the novelty of being able to wear civvies, there was another facet to going on leave. From the very first it felt strange, for despite the hard times, the inspections, the shouting, the bullying by NCO's, I found I missed the life at Cosford almost as soon as I stepped out through the gates. The camaraderie, and the friendships, that was what would be missing.

Another thing missing was my flying. Eighteen months, two flights. Both extremely welcome, for sure, though it was the first of them that affords the most detailed memories. It was taken during summer camp, at Millom, Cumbria. It was also the first time I had flown without the back-up security of a parachute. We were in the Air Force now, no longer pampered-to ATC cadets.

I have a vivid recollection of lying in a glassed-in nose, watching the ground float serenely past. I was in my element once more, the earthly shackles broken. But I had cause to worry. Nothing to do with the lack of a parachute, for in this situation a parachute would have been as useful as a chocolate fireguard. We appeared to be on course for a collision with the crest of a mountain. It lay dead ahead. With the accent on dead, of that I was sure.

The ground rose gently, seeming about to bisect our course about a hundred feet below the peak. And remember, by this time a had been afforded some little insight into basic trigonometry, and navigational procedures. The closer we got, so the impression of speed gathered pace. Grass and rocks blurred past at a fantastic rate - everything being relative, of course - until, flash, we cleared the summit by inches. Well, it seemed so. OK, so maybe my little insight fell short of the required experience, or maybe my eyesight was faulty. Would you believe two hundred feet? Whatever, I was immediately imbued with a tremendous feeling of elation. Only natural when finding you are still alive, after expecting to be dead. And not only did the peak disappear, so did the earth beyond. The reverse slope fell away, a thousand feet or so, almost sheer. Quite dramatic, that. As was no doubt the intent.

This was also the flight during which, still prone, in the nose, I found myself to be floating around, weightless, when some wag, commenting on the machine's inability to perform aerobatics, invoked the pilot to put it into a stall. About as aerobatic as an Anson got to be. Not that exciting an aircraft, you see, but at least I was flying again. For that I was thankful.

*

The gathering at Farnborough was an event anticipated with pleasure. In those days the display was staged annually, but due to service commitments, and lack of resources, I was lucky if I was able to attend every second or third year. But as a member of the Boy Entrants' Aircraft Recognition club, my 1953 visit was courtesy of the Air Force.

Recognition had always been my thing, even before my ATC days. Hazy shots of aircraft in cloud; small sections - a wing, nose, or tail - long distance shots; esoteric shadows or fuzzy silhouettes, it made no difference, I could name them all, type and mark. I didn't need to think, they registered themselves immediately, it was automatic.

After the John Derry disaster of the previous year, new rules were in force at Farnborough. These restricted height, speed, and direction of the demonstrations, though the show was nevertheless full of spectacle. We were still to be allowed our sonic booms - Hunter and Swift - and the Victor, plus Shorts' Seamew, both made their debuts.

Digging out my programmes I see that year it cost one shilling and sixpence (7.5p), a year later, one shilling (5p). Not a trend that was to continue.

So the months came and went, as did members of our group. We lost a couple at the three month crunch-time, more over the duration: those unable or unwilling to cope with the rigours of the discipline-for-disciplines-sake, or score well enough in exams. Most were given the opportunity of dropping back an entry, to start again with the Nineteenth, four months behind. Ernie Cornish was one who joined us, stepping back from the Seventeenth. Those deemed unsuitable for service life were said to be released, a phrase more suited to the end of a term in prison, I would have thought. There again...

I guess I was lucky, or foolish, made it all the way. We were the senior entry. Those blue and green checkered hatbands made us top dogs.

It was September, 1954. Summer was coming to an end. A good time for it. Not September, that always falls in September, as does the end of summer - officially - although summer itself appears to fall in July; usually around the twentieth. But forget all that, when I say a good time for it, what I mean is the one parade we'd all been eagerly awaiting: pass out. Not physically, mind - well, maybe one or two - but this was the parade which was also to signal the end for the Eighteenth Entry. Tomorrow, the Nineteenth would be top dogs, but this was to be the Eighteenth's very own, special day. And so it had been. Top brass gathered, parents and guardians were in attendance, the sun even shone, and the parade was in the hands of Boy Entrant NCO's. Cue in the music. Not orchestral, for we had our very own band, remember: bugles and drums. And while probably not quite up there with the likes of Cleckheaton and District, it was good enough to march behind. And our drum major was in a class of his own. (Often fancied the job myself, but too many accidents with a broom told me I wasn't to be the one. Should have practised outside, I suppose. Well clear of light fittings, mirrors, and windows.) The guy who did have the job could twirl that mace over the water pipes which crossed twenty feet above the road, no problem whatsoever, though I doubt he'd be so foolish as to attempt anything so pretentious on this day. Even if it was more spectacular than a mere twirl round the neck, it was sort of frowned upon by people in authority, of which there were a considerable number present. Nay, there were even people in authority of authority in attendance, way up there in the lofty realms of Air rank.

And so, with bugle and drum packed away for the last time, and the sound of marching feet gradually fading, so the shadows lengthened as the sun slid down the sky. Another hour and those shadows would have spread like a damp stain, the entire camp becoming wrapped in the cloak of dusk. Thirty minutes after that, it would be dark. Which didn't matter, for by then, we'd be gone.

School was out again. More like college this time, but I was the better for it. Transformation from apprentice motor mechanic to fully fledged, Senior Aircraftsman, Inst Mech (nav), was complete. I was fit, well, and full of a confidence I'd never felt before, even if I was still a virgin. Excitement was high. I was about to be let loose on an Air Force that had bases in all kinds of interesting places, for we then still had the remnants of an empire to protect.

I had, in fact, already completed six months full-time service, for, being a late starter I'd reached the qualifying age of seventeen and a half before completion of training. This meant I had been earning substantially more than the seven shillings and sixpence I was by then being paid, the balance deposited in an account on my behalf.

'Been that way from day one,' the accounts sergeant revealed. 'That half-crown was an allowance, not your full worth, lad. You now have a substantial sum in the Posbee (from the initials POSB, for Post Office Savings Bank, a government institution, therefore favoured by HM's Armed Forces). The residue of eighteen months pay, plus interest,' he told me. Welcome news indeed. And as I was now of an age where I could legally take a drink, I'd feel more at home back home, in the Griffin. I was legally entitled to those home comforts which the law had previously denied me. I was also of an age at which I could fight for my country, even if I wasn't yet entitled to the vote.

My departure from Cosford was unique as far as my future service career went in that I was not given chance to volunteer for my next assignment. I was told where I was to go.

No matter. Had I realized I was not yet qualified to serve overseas, it was probably one of the places I'd have chosen, given the chance.

So it was, blue kitbag now supplementing my cardboard suitcase - its complement of dreams as yet unfulfilled - I was off into the wide blue yonder of the outside world, to begin yet another adventure.

* *

Chapter Four
A PASSION FOR FLIGHT

𝕿 he dying hours of night brought with them an aura of stillness which settled itself over the surrounding countryside along with the morning dew. Through the remnants of a hazy mist could be seen strange, spectral shapes, these too were silent and still. Taken as a whole the scene looked as tranquil and undisturbed as a Constable landscape, yet those somewhat abstract qualities weren't destined to survive, were already being threatened by nature itself. To the slightly fuzzy mind, the early morning chorus seems overly enthusiastic. Is it possible the birds are already aware it is to be yet another fine day?

The air was as fresh as it was likely to get, which was a help in clearing my hangover. Chill and crisp. Early morning freshness. The combined aromas of moist grass and earth, even if they were tainted with overtones of Avgas and Avtur. Out here, even the sounds are of a different calibre. Gentle sounds on the brittle air: the swish of canvas as covers are removed; voices, muffled, indistinct. Early morning voices. There were also the harsh, metallic sounds of equipment on the move, of preparations being made. All in all, the sounds of a new day coming to life.

Given time the first gold rays of an early sun poked their way through, and the voices gained strength and vitality, became terse, authoritative.

'Switches off?'

'Switches off.' Confirmation from the cockpit, high above the oil-stained tarmac of the dispersal. (From close up the interior of that Hastings was large, in comparison to any other aircraft I'd been in. The cabin looked huge, and, being a tail-dragger, the walk up to the cockpit was therefore steep; more a climb than a walk.)

So, with no chance of an engine inadvertently bursting into life, the huge, four-bladed propellers were turned by hand, one man per blade, two complete rotations, a check against hydraulic lock; oil collecting in the lower cylinders of a radial engine could wreak havoc on start-up. Four engines, four props.

Different sounds now: electric motors, pumps for fuel and hydraulics. Hatches, doors and panels are secured, controls checked, equipment removed.

'All clear?' The voice from the cockpit: captain, his face framed by the clear vision panel, and the blue, cloth helmet he wore.

A final check of the surrounding area to ensure start-up procedures were being observed, chocks and fire extinguisher in place, superfluous ground equipment removed. 'Clear one,' I answered, raising the forefinger of my left hand. My free hand pointed to the engine in question - number one, port outer - right forefinger describing a circle in the air, a signal the area was free from obstruction, that the propeller wasn't about to transform an errant airman into Pedigree Chum.

'Starting one,' came the reply. It was to be the last verbal response between us.

A starter whined. The propeller turned, labouriously it seemed, as if reluctant to pick up speed, or unable. A half-hearted cough appeared to test the quiet as a single cylinder fired, then died. A blue smoke-ring spun through the still air, drifting gently away. One more cough - full-throated this time - then another, until the comparative silence was finally shattered into a million pieces, Bristol Hercules bursting into angry life. The torque, as it attempted to tear the engine from its mountings, pointed to the vast amount of power available, propeller eventually disappearing in a whirling black, yellow-tipped disc, the wash from it putting paid to that smoke-ring once and for all.

With the pilot also now reduced to using hand signals the three remaining engines were started in sequence: port inner, starboard inner, starboard outer, each initially belching out fearsome clouds of blue/grey smoke. This too was flung away by the swirling propwash, to disappear over and beneath the wing, over elevators which were held in the full up position - to prevent the tail lifting - then away behind to flatten the grass back there where it was untrimmed. Barely visible tongues of flame erupted from exhaust stacks which would soon glow a healthy red. Cowl gills are set, brake pressure checked, flying controls - full and free movement. With engines now warm, settled into a steady rhythm, the trolley-ack (a mobile battery-accumulator, used during start-up) is unplugged, then the chocks are waved away. I relay the signal to the airmen who stand waiting, bare inches behind those whirling, lethal steel discs. Then, in response to a throat-clearing burst of power, the machine was taxying off in response to my signals until, with a final salute, I hand over control to the pilot. The aircraft was now his responsibility. Up to that point it had been mine.

A quick dab on the brakes, to verify their operation, and the aircraft is out onto the perimeter track. They'd be running checks all the way to the end of the runway: temperatures, pressures, magnetos, fuel cocks, flaps. The list was endless. In God we trust, everything else we check and double-check. That could well have been the pilots' motto, and a good one, too. More than one aircraft has been lost by taking off with the flying controls still locked. Hard to imagine, yet it does happen. (Even today, in the older type of aircraft.)

As control surfaces - mainly elevators and rudder - could be damaged by being blown around in the wind, aircraft on dispersal have these controls locked. This sometimes took the form of an external lock, a red-flagged contraption attached to the control surface itself - as on the Hastings - or, like the Valetta, a control lock located in the cockpit, on the throttle quadrant. Sometimes the ground crew would release them, sometimes not. But no matter what aircraft, ultimate responsibility to ensure they were removed, or disengaged, before flight, rested with the pilot. Which, when it came to the Valetta, was often cause for an entry to appear in the F700: "Port oil-temp gauge inoperative". The reason? As it had been known for the Valetta's locks to engage during flight (rather embarrassing) the release spring on this type had been subjected to a manufacturer's modification; the spring was re-tensioned. One slight problem: it was now so strong that extreme care needed to be exercised when disengaging the locks. The lever needed to be eased off and held firmly, if not it shot forward with such force it would hit this gauge dead-centre. Many a time I've stepped into the cockpit only to find the shattered remnants hanging down behind the panel on the end of their cable.

'Yeah, well, it would be bloody inoperative, wouldn't it, sir. Stands to reason, what with its face stove in and all.' Still, better the loss of a gauge than an aircraft. No problem with the Hastings, though, and I knew all was well with the controls here, I'd checked them myself, kept an eye open as the pilots did the same as part of their pre start-up checks.

So began another day out on the flight-line. Which, by this time, was well and truly where my heart was.

*

My full-time service began with a posting to Transport Command, at RAF Dishforth, North Yorkshire. Probably one of those very airfields that had taken root during the war years, fashioned out of farmland. It's possible some of the bombers that used to lull me to sleep at night had departed from these very runways. Likely, in fact, for here had been based Whitley, Wellington, and Halifax. Not exactly one of the more exotically-interesting type places to which I'd hoped to be posted. Places that were talked about way back when, as they say. Names I'd heard bandied about when old timers got to waxing nostalgically, as old timers tend to do. Far away places, with strange sounding names, to quote the words of a one-time popular song. Only these were different. Far away, yes, but not places referred to in the song. These mysterious and strange sounding places were dotted along the routes to our colonies: El Adem, Mersa Matruh, Fayid, Wadi Halfa, Habbaniya, et al. (Not an airfield, that last, just a bit of

Latin I threw in. Evidence that my education was proceeding apace, for I certainly didn't learn that at Norton School for Boys.) Anyway, at the time I imagined I'd need some experience before I could expect a posting to somewhere along those lines, and Dishforth didn't seem like a bad place to get it. Dreams of travel would at present have to remain just that, but at last I had my aeroplanes. No more fixing imaginary problems on imaginary aircraft with imaginary tools, this was for real. A mistake now could lead to far more serious consequences than a poor result, or a failed exam.

I was literally a stone's throw from home, and most week-ends were free (as was any off-duty time. I could wander off camp whenever I liked, wear whatever I liked. My free time was my own, to do with as I pleased. Quite a change from having no free time at all). But, what with timing of the buses and the number of changes required, the quickest way to *get* home called for hitching a lift. Not too difficult back then, that post-war/national service period when a certain amount of goodwill was extended by the public towards members of the Armed Forces. To the wearers of uniform, hitch-hiking was a simple matter. Of course, there was also the fact that, back then, one didn't need to be so mindful of picking up a "wrong 'un," as they say. More likely to be the other way round, in fact. Plain-clothed service police, posing as civilians, would occasionally pick up a hitch-hiking airman. They'd readily proceed chat them up, posing leading questions on station layout, aircraft types, and strength, etc. Any information that might be deemed of use to an enemy power. This was particularly common practice around the fighter and V-bomber stations, but I did hear tell of cases in our area. It made us wary, as it was no doubt meant to.

Had I so chosen, I could have gone home quite often, but found I rarely did. By this time I had come to realize that home was wherever I wanted it to be, and the bonds of camaraderie were such that the preference was often with new found friends. The Air Force, you see, had already made me more discerning, independent, self-reliant, aware of my capabilities and limitations. I could now have aircraft and girls. Still in that order, but girls were certainly making headway up the list of priorities. Obviously so, for I seemed to devote a considerable amount of time to the act of trying to lose my virginity. I was also of age as far as drinking went, I read the New Musical Express, and Melody Maker. I smoked, too, as did almost everyone, the atmosphere in our crewroom often rivalling that of a misty autumn day. Senior Service and Players were the popular brands, but the multi-coloured Sobranie Cocktail or the strange, oval Passing Cloud were ones with which to impress the girls. Life was almost as good as it got to be.

Our stamping grounds were the surrounding villages: Dishforth itself, nearby Norton-le-Clay and Marton-le-Moor, or the more distant towns: Thirsk, York, Ripon, Knaresborough, and their wealth of pubs; Chicken-in-a-Basket, good ale (all Real, back then). Black velvet was as lo popular, a mixture of cider and stout. And there was the odd bird of the female type, along to feather my nest. In fact Dishforth was proving to be a revelation after the seemingly hostile environment of Cosford. Yes, we still had inspections and parades, a regular part of service life, those. Here, though, they were nowhere near as frequent, nor as demanding. And, given a little ingenuity, it was possible to avoid a lot of them. Well, ingenuity was something with which I was familiar, mine having been developed and tuned to a fine pitch over the past eighteen months. But at Cosford it had been almost impossible to implement, other than on the Wednesday sports afternoon. Cross country had been the standard option. A gentle trot along the road, out of sight, only to return via a hole in the fence round the back. There you go, a quiet afternoon on your pit. No falling asleep though. There were spot checks, so one needed to remain alert at all times.

Dishforth required nothing so devious. Now designated a recreation period, Wednesday afternoons no longer posed a problem. We could do as we pleased: York races, Thirsk races, Ripon races, Wetherby races. Sport, you see. After all, I had been raised among the stables of Norton (known as Malton, you may recall). As for parades, an air test, shift work, or some carefully arranged leave would take care of most. Even missed one during a visit to London on Air Force business. I'd been selected to represent Transport Command in the annual All England Aircraft Recognition competition. I was proud to be so honoured, but was soon to be put in my place. Show some of those guys a rivet and they would relate not only the aircraft type and mark, probably give you the serial number, too. Still, I didn't fare too badly; and perhaps they didn't miss a parade?

But if there was one parade it would have been foolish to miss it was the weekly pay parade. Not the full march-past that lad at Cosford had so foolishly envisaged. In this respect, Dishforth didn't differ from Cosford at all. Well, not often. But one week it did, for the paying officer happened to be a friend from my schooldays. Only he was now a Pilot Officer, and trainee transport jockey, which ruled out my calling him Trev, or even Trevor. Nor would it have been prudent to suggest he slip me an extra quid or two, for old-times' sake. (He had, after all, at one time also been proclaimed, my best friend. Ever.) All he got now was a snappy salute, and my last three. I got what I was due, along with the hint of a smile.

On the subject of pay, a rather outspoken National Service airman friend once related to me how upset he became when the amount he received seemed to vary week by week, with no explanation forthcoming.

Well, it wouldn't would it, on pay parade? You saluted, quoted your last three, signed, took what was offered then moved off. This went on over the weeks until eventually, deciding to take matters in hand, he phoned accounts, expecting a lowly clerk to answer. All he heard was a background of typewriters click-clacking their messages of bureaucracy.

'What's wrong with you lot?' he demanded. 'If you don't have anyone that can count I'll come and do it for you.'

'Just a minute. Do you know who you're talking to?' came the startled reply. 'This is Flight Lieutenant Wilson, accounting officer.'

'Oh, is it? Well do you know who you're talking to, Flt Lt Wilson?'

'No,' the officer replied, suddenly not sounding at all confident.

My friend wisely hung up.

*

Dishforth was the home of 242 OCU (Operational Conversion Unit), its job, to train fresh-faced young pilots - wings on their left breast still white and sparkling - the rudiments of handling multi-engined transport aircraft: Handley Page Hastings, and the stubby, cigar-shaped Valetta, by Vickers, the last piston-engined transport to be built by them. The Valetta was also operated by the resident, and fully operational, No.30 squadron.

At last I was among machines that actually took to the air rather than simple training airframes. The servicing was for real now, all our training coming to the fore. But I was soon to realize that training was only a small part of it, experience counted for a lot, too. Take for instance the F700 entry for a Valetta: "Autopilot will not engage." It wasn't long before I too was able to proclaim, "Not again", without even setting foot in the cockpit. The autopilot featured an emergency cut-out button on the control wheel, within range of the pilot's thumb. Trouble was, the wires for this switch were routed down inside the control column, and given time they would chafe, thus shorting out, disengaging old George just as effectively as it would if the pilot punched the button. A quick rewire saw the problem cured, aircraft again ready to take to the air, George back in control. Not only that, I found I was able take to the air with them, just to check things out. As a result many hours were logged on these two types during the next three years. There were also odd trips in the Anson and Chipmunk, assigned to the Station Flight.

Air tests apart - for which I usually volunteered - all my trips were scrounged. Flights were there for the begging anyway. I didn't care what kind of sortie they were on, nav-ex, night flying, even pounding round on circuits and landings. Monotonous, people said, but heavy-handed trainee pilots almost guaranteed life would never be monotonous, which is why such an exercise was known as circuits and bumps. These guys had been trained to fly Percival's Prentice and Provost, and the Avro Anson, toys to what they now had in their hands. Believe me, the Hastings, with its huge, ultra high profile doughnut-like tyres, really could be made to bounce if not handled correctly. I was to find they could also be - often were - bounced off the surface of the nearby road, too.

The main runway on any station is naturally aligned so as to take advantage of the prevailing wind. At Dishforth, ours ran north/south, parallel to, but at a slightly lower level than the A1, the Great North Road. But adverse winds would occasionally force a switch to the shorter east/west runway, the threshold of which was extremely close to the boundary fence, which almost guaranteed an undershoot would take in the aforementioned road. ATC controlled traffic lights, and the rubber streaked surface of the A1 served as confirmation of this.

Engines were shut down during take-off, and in the air. There were flapless landings, and overshoots galore. How could it ever be boring?

Then we came to the good part. I soon discovered that upon completion of their course each crew was required to make what was termed a route trip; an overseas flight down a specific route - Air Force supply lines to the Middle and Far East. To add authenticity, some freight and a few passengers were taken along, a list of volunteers' names kept for this very purpose. Add your name, and as soon as it reached the head of the list you were contacted. The only problem then lay in persuading your section commander he could afford to release you for the required period: two or three days, a week, whatever. Well, volunteering was my forte, so in went my name, quick as a flash. This, despite the fact that the first rule for survival in the forces appeared to be, never volunteer - for anything. Forget all that, I saw here the chance of fulfilling some of those dreams. My collection was about to begin.

Maybe I had an understanding section commander, maybe not, but my absence was to become a regular occurrence. As soon as I returned from one trip, my name was back on that list. And I don't recall ever having to turn one down. Or perhaps my section commander happened to be looking out of the window the day I almost trashed a Hastings. My fault, I'm afraid. Certainly would have been in the eyes of the Air Force, simply because I was in charge of moving the aircraft, although relying on other people to know what they were about.

We were set to tow the aircraft from in front of the hangars out to a dispersal, a job I'd done many times. None of your fancy towing gear in those days, mind. There was a simple arm which hooked onto the tail wheel, allowing a modicum of directional control (providing the guy manning the arm had scoffed the appropriate number of Weatabix for breakfast, that is!). David Brown was to provide the pulling power, via what appeared to be a modified farm tractor. This was attached to the aircraft's main wheels by a wire towing bridle. It could move the aircraft ahead, therefore, but - a steel cable being nothing if not flexible - contributed zero in the realms of retardation (unless aircraft caught up with tractor. It would stop then, for sure!).

So here we go. The guy on the tail wheel was ready, the tractor driver was ready, I was ready, as were the guys beneath each wingtip, ready to check clearances between other aircraft, and buildings; the sort of immovable objects it was felt undesirable to approach too closely.

'All ready?' I enquired of the guys in the cockpit. 'Brakes on?'

'All ready,' came the reply.

'Chocks away,' I called, signalling to the airmen beneath the wings. 'Brakes off,' this to the cockpit crew. 'Take it away.' I signalled to the tractor driver.

With a sharp, angry hiss, the brakes were released, and as the tractor took up slack on the bridle, so the aircraft began to move. Didn't take much, for it was on a slight downhill slope. In fact it gathered momentum rather quickly. Too bloody quickly, thought I.

'Brakes on,' I called as the bridle resumed its slack state, aircraft moving faster than the tractor was pulling, which was not a good moment to discover that the guy in the cockpit had either misread the gauge, or failed to check the pneumatic pressure before giving me the go-ahead. Naturally, according to sod's law (or was it Murphy, up to his old tricks?) the pressure was far too low, even if existent. This became apparent quicker than almost immediately, for not a lot happened. Not a lot in the way of retardation, that is! Emotionally, all hell let loose. And, as such circumstances do tend to make one sit up and take notice, it felt like my bowels were about to do likewise.

'Brakes on,' I called again, desperation beginning to show through when nothing happened. Not even the courtesy of a reply.

'Cockpit,' I called, loudly, was rewarded as a head briefly poked its way out, only to tell me to, 'Stand by.' The head then made a rapid withdrawal.

'What do you mean, standby?' I called, hoping someone was listening. 'We're rolling here, get those bloody brakes on.'

'We're working on it,' said a seemingly disembodied voice.

Working on it? Bloody hell. Ahead I could see nothing but gloom and doom; the squadron's crewroom looming large in our path; a very bleak outlook as far as myself and the Royal Air Force were concerned. With a future that looked about as stable as a ten-storey tower of playing cards, my brain was rapidly evaluating the options, attempting to arrive at a magic solution.

I looked across at the guys on the wingtips, perhaps for inspiration, but they seemed to have lost interest, or hope, not a sign of help forthcoming from that direction, forget it. Nor did there seem to be a glimmer of hope from the tractor driver, in fact he looked ready to abandon ship. Couldn't really blame him, what with that lot bearing down. But when I waved at him, rather frantically I suppose, he remained aboard, actually followed my instructions to the letter, attempting to turn the wayward beast, albeit without success. I could well imagine his thoughts: bail out and the blame could fall on me. Stay with it and... "I was just obeying orders, sir." Covering his arse, was what. Something I had obviously failed to do.

I looked aft for salvation: no way. The aircraftsman supposedly controlling the tail wheel struggled to do so, to turn it, failed miserably; one more hope shot to hell. Obviously *hadn't* had his bloody Weatabix.

I noticed the lads upstairs in the office had now applied full corrective rudder, seemed to me we were rapidly approaching the speed at which it would become effective. Yet despite all these efforts it still appeared the aircraft was about to make an interesting addition to the fixtures and fittings in the pilots' crewroom, a generally inadvisable practice, I would imagine. After all, it's usually the other way round, aircrew going out to join their aircraft. And how would that look on my CV? Experienced at towing aircraft into hangars, via the fire door! Forget the bloody crewroom, that was a mess anyway. Luckily, it didn't happen, for the Lord dealt bountifully with me that day, or with those guys in the cockpit; they, after all, were closer to Him than I was.

"Never before had I seen the hand-pump operated with such frenzy (so that's where all the Weatabix went), so many eyes willing the pointer of the pressure gauge to rise," I was later told by one of the observers from upstairs. But rise it did, along with my hopes and, one presumes, theirs also. Seems they'd started on the pumping bit the second they released the brakes, realizing their error immediately; mistaking brake pressure for system pressure.

Not sure if the tailwheel actually left the ground once pressure was restored, I doubt it. Seemed the guy at least had the sense to apply the brakes progressively, as soon as that once more became an option. In fact, it obviously didn't appear at all dramatic to anyone not in the know, for there were no repercussions, no startled personnel rushing out to lend a hand, or offer advice. Nor was there a scattering of tables, chairs, and newspapers, in the crewroom, white faces pressed against windows, bodies flying out the door. Not a bit of it. No, repercussions are probably for the future, when I pass away a year or two earlier than I might otherwise have done. Grey haired and withered, at forty-two. Tell you one thing, I checked the system pressure personally before moving another aircraft. Nor did I take any chances either; that pointer almost needed to be wrapped around the top end stop before I'd even have the brakes released!

But I wasn't the first or last person to overlook things.

'How are we doing, Dave?' the mechanic asked, poking his head through the over-wing escape hatch.

'Hardly seems to have moved,' I replied.

'Um, OK, keep an eye on it.'

He was out on the starboard wing, refuelling the Hastings on which I was working in the cockpit. It was night. To save himself walking back and forth into the aircraft he'd asked me to keep an eye on the relevant gauge.

'Still no change,' I informed him a little later. I'd finished my work, was ready to go and sign the F700. 'I checked the guage, that seems OK,' I told him.

'Strange.' Then, after a pause for thought, 'Hey! anyone there?' he called down to the ground.

'Yeah, mate, you finished?' the bowser operator replied.

'No, something appears to be wrong. We don't seem to be getting any fuel.'

'Getting fuel all right,' the operator replied. 'It's pissing out all over the tarmac. Has been for a while.'

'Well why the hell didn't you say so?' the mechanic shouted.

'Just, bloody did, didn't I.'

It turned out to be a fuel management problem, someone had left a crossfeed pump on, a result of which the fuel was being transferred into already full tanks on the port wing, thence out of the overflow! Knowing how keen the Air Force were on details, I often wondered how that fitter explained away all those extra gallons of Avgas.

*

The call came. I took the phone and listened, learned that my name had topped the magic list, and was I ever excited. I was going abroad. Abroad! The very word was exciting, those far away places at last. Dreams about to be fulfilled. Where would it be? Mersa Matruh, in Egypt? Wadi Halfa, Sudan? Maybe as far as Hyderabad, in India, or on east, to Singapore itself. The excitement soared as the seconds ticked away, dwindled rapidly, to be replaced by disappointment when I learned what was to be my destination.

RAF Valley is in Anglesey, North Wales. OK, a different country, but still part of the British Isles. Bleak and miserable, too. On top of which, the bloody aircraft, a Valetta, went unserviceable, big time. They had to send an engine fitter, along with the parts to fix it, and another aircraft to carry the passengers back home. I'd certainly been hoping for better. Ah well, one has to begin somewhere, and after that it did get interesting. UK, Europe, the Mediterranean, Middle East, I visited them all. Even dropped in at some of those exotic-sounding places to which I'd at one time hoped to be posted, was suddenly pleased I hadn't been. Fayid was one, in the Canal Zone (Suez, of course), and Castel Benito (later renamed Idris, after their last king), in Libya. I can still remember the smell of the place, sort of peculiar to the Middle East. Don't know what though: Dates? Camels? The desert? Who knows, probably a combination of things.

During this early, educational, phase of travel I was learning too, about not allowing myself to be ripped off; a painful process. I recall one instance in particular, probably the first. It involved, a country where spirits of the earthly kind were at a premium, a number of duty free bottles, and someone who knew someone with an interest in acquiring same. (Aka, himself, as it happened!)

Servicemen weren't paid a lot back then, and the price mentioned would probably have sounded good even to such as Rockefeller. Which should have alerted us to begin with. Anyway, a deal was struck. This man would introduce a buyer, would even drive us to his house, which he proceeded to do. There were numerous delays en-route, of course. He had to see this man and that, make arrangements. "Much lire, my friends. Have patience." But we eventually arrived, somewhere. Then it was time to walk, down a side street off a sidestreet in what must have been the least populated area in town, perhaps the world. A respectable-looking area though, reassuring, that. A maze of streets and alleys - well lit - an open door, long, marbled corridor, sparkling clean. Now the crunch. We must wait. He'd take the bottles, see which were acceptable. We demurred, vociferously. Not that bloody stupid, even if we may look it.

"Okay, no deal." Just like that, not willing to compromise.

We demurred less, needed to money, could pick up more duty free on the way home.

"Trust me. Haven't I gone out of my way for you?"

Smooth talking bastard. Capitulation. He slipped away.

Had we awaited his return, with piles of loot, we'd be at that door still. How could anyone be so gullible? But that's how one learns about life. So obvious. Isn't it always, after the event. Like they say, hindsight is twenty-twenty vision. We laughed about it among ourselves, what else was there to do? But inside I was fuming, determined it would never happen again. Ha!

So much for Europe and the Middle East. Yet for some reason the Far East seemed to evade me. Maybe someone knew something I didn't?

My next trip took me to Malta, via Istres, in southern France, the French equivalent to Boscombe Down. Many experimental aircraft were to be seen scattered around the base. Types such as the Leduc O.21 ramjet aircraft were observed, plus the Sud Ouest Trident, and the Hurel-Dubois HD31 high aspect ratio research aircraft. (I was to meet up with the HD31 again, more than twenty-five years later. Long since decommissioned from test flying, it had been put to work in Gabon. What a coup for the logbook that would have been. Unfortunately, it never happened.)

At present, life, as the saying went, was "swinging". This, the current euphemism that defined anything that was OK, good, or excellent, was the catch-phrase of Norman Vaughan, of "Sunday Night At The London Palladium" fame. The word became vogue during the fifties, as these things occasionally tend to do. Today's equivalent would probably be "Didn't they do well?" or "To see you, nice," as used by Bruce Forsythe. But then it was "Swinging". Which brings to mind a particular evening at the Astra, the camp cinema at Dishforth - and almost every other RAF base. It happened during a particularly dramatic sequence: no music, no dialogue, no sound effects, not even the cracking of a branch or a whisper of wind, on screen or in the theatre. The cowboy hero, prowling the woods in this stillborn silence is seeking someone or other, finds him; a pair of boots at face level, the attached body out of scene, above, obviously strung up. Suddenly, from out of the hushed auditorium and threatening gloom came a solitary voice; loud, clear, quick as a flash. 'Swinging,' it said, drawing the word out to its full extent. And did that ever wreck the suspense.

Back on the flying front I was to discover that relatively few people seemed to bother volunteering for the route trips, for which I was eternally grateful. But I never ceased to be amazed by the number of airmen who showed no interest in aviation whatsoever. How could anyone join the Air Force and not want to fly, or at least fail to be excited by the presence of aircraft? Was it possible to spend two years of your life surrounded by the elements of aviation, yet remain untouched by them? The answer seemed to be yes. I loved this environment, surrounded by all the things that went to create it. Not just the aircraft, but also the hangars in which they lived, the specialist equipment required to service and operate those aircraft, the taxiways, the runways from which they flew, even the grass which makes up the bulk of a military airfield. I could *accept* that others wouldn't find it so enthralling, found it hard to understand why. There again there's no accounting for taste. Let's face it, I've heard tell some people are actually turned on by columns of figures, a visit to the ballet, railway engines. "One man's meat...," as the saying goes.

Still, this was the age of National Service. And if one were being offered a choice: Army or Air Force? I suppose.... Well, not really much of a choice at all, is it? I'd come to that very same decision over two years ago. To me, being around aircraft, working on them, touching them, was my nirvana. First line servicing gave me even more scope than ever, for *all* arrivals were within my domain. In this there was another bonus to my being at Dishforth. This station was classed a Master Diversion, so I was also treated to a wide variety of visiting aircraft. I recall Hunters, Swifts - remember them? - Meteors, from Mk4 through to NF14, and Ansons. The Navy occasionally dropped by also, bringing with them such aircraft as the Avenger, Gannet, Skyraider, Seahawk and Attacker. There were Yorks - Dan Air calling in nightly for a time, delivering the newspapers during a national rail strike. Which was how we got to read the Daily Mirror at three in the morning. Yes, I know, but I was a Yorkshireman, and it was free. Sophistication would come with time.

There were Neptunes too, from nearby Topcliffe - at times a little too nearby, it seemed. Close enough for the heading of their main runway to be on a par with ours. We actually had a Hastings land there thinking he was at home base. His error only became apparent when Dishforth tower questioned his request for taxy instructions once he'd reported being on the ground; no aircraft to be seen by Dishforth Air Traffic Control. I believe I did mention these pilots were trainees, didn't I?

We had visits from F-86 Sabres - my introduction to the sonic boom, back there at Yeadon. Even the incredibly ungainly-looking Blackburn Beverley, just entering service, put in the odd appearance. In fact I well recall the first visit of this lumbering giant, it's departure in particular.

The aircraft began its take-off roll, pace unhurried, engines roaring, seemingly in frustration, for it rolled, and it rolled, and it rolled. It appeared to have as much enthusiasm for flight as would a block of flats, which is exactly what it reminded me of. But it was eventually successful, clawing its way into the sky just as quickly as multi-thousand horsepower and limited aerodynamics allowed. Well, the aerodynamics were fine as far as the coefficient of lift went, but I imagine form drag was a bit of a problem. Not exactly stealth technology, this! Such a performance, that once it was safely airborne I felt as if I should applaud. Others were less gracious.

'Well, even a chock would become airborne if you whirled it round on the end of its rope.'

This was one of the less disparaging remarks overheard at the time. And I did hear tell of one bemused American who - upon first setting eyes on Blackburn's biggie - was heard to comment, " Sure as Hell won't replace the airplane." (Nor did it, but over the years it did do an excellent job in the role for which it had been designed.)

Me? I was the proverbial dog in the sausage factory. My only regret is that I have no photographs of this era, security being so tight at the time. Cold War and all that. Photography on or near the base was not just frowned upon, it was a definite no-no. Although I do have a photograph of the Beverley, in its prototype form, then known as the Universal Freighter, or GAL60 (for General Aircraft Limited). It was taken at Brough, near Hull, back when, as ATC cadets, we'd been invited to act as program sellers during an open day at the airfield which was Blackburn's base.

Another frustration of this period was that I never did get to fly in the trainer version of a single-engined fighter, piston or jet. But although it was something I longed and hoped for, I didn't really need to, I'd sat in plenty. Given my imagination, it almost amounted to the same thing.

My first priority was to check the safety pins were fitted to the ejection seat. Although were I to have been splattered all over the hangar roof I certainly wouldn't have been the first. Then, after recharging the oxygen system, carrying out my cockpit checks, servicing the flight instruments, I'd remain awhile. Right hand on the stick, my eyes would traverse the multitudeof dials, switches and buttons, left hand fancifully flicking, tapping, and pushing. My salute, as I prepared to taxi, was returned by the imaginary groundcrew. I could smell the oil and exhaust in the imagined slipstream outside the open cockpit of a biplane, feel the sun streaming through the pressurized canopy of a modern jet. I'd speak into the dead radio, requesting clearances and landing instructions, performing a zero-zero high-speed pass before zooming round to join the circuit, managing a quick burst with the Aden cannon at the station commander's car on the way. The lighter side of life.

These harmless imaginings in no way satisfied the urge to fly in such types, but they perhaps helped ease acceptance of the fact that the chances had anyway been minute, especially on a transport base.

Dishforth was to introduce me to the darker side of aviation, too. The realities and dangers brought home one night as I wandered along the dispersal to work on an aircraft. Flying was in progress, a chubby Valetta - nicknamed "pig" because of its appearance - charging urgently down the runway on its take-off run. Even though it was dark, the red and green navigation lights defined the dim silhouette as it roared away from me, exhausts glowing red as they spouted blue flame. A take-off, or landing, being something I was never able to pass up, I watched until darkness enveloped the aircraft, then turned away.

Suddenly, a deathly silence replaced the healthy-sounding roar of its twin engines, as if my turning had switched them off. Then the silence was gone, to be replaced by a fearful noise which chilled me to the core; the heart-rending whumph of a fuel-heavy explosion. In a field over on the far side of the A1, the resultant holocaust lit the night sky. Overcome by a feeling of helplessness I gazed at it briefly before turning away once more. I couldn't watch the fiery demise of one of our aircraft and its crew. With heavy heart I trudged back to my work. Nothing I could do to help. Nothing anyone could do. No possible way for anyone to escape from such an inferno, I imagined. Wrong again. I subsequently learned that all on board escaped with only minor injuries. The aircraft was a total loss. Amazing.

We later had a Hastings go down over Ripon golf course, and that crew were not so fortunate. All perished in a crash which was to feature in the national press, front page. Must have been a slow news day, though I do recall there was something strange about the photographs. None of the propeller blades were bent back. The lower ones stuck straight in the ground, as though the aircraft had hit with no forward speed whatever. A flat spin maybe? The date: September 13th 1955 - but not a Friday.

I was airborne again that evening, the aircrew questioning my sanity. They were flying because they'd been detailed to, and it was what they were paid to do, they said, didn't want to. Why was I volunteering to accompany them? To me it was a question that didn't really need answering.

That crash had an even more profound effect on me, for I seem to recall being forcibly volunteered to join the funeral party - rest on arms reversed, the final salute, and such.

But these were unobserved crashes, events disguised by darkness, or hidden behind a newspaper headline. Next time was to be different, for it's a sickening sight to watch helpless as an aircraft falls out of the sky.

*

A DC3 of 1325 filight - on detachment before heading for Christmas Island and the British Nuclear Test Program - overflew the airfield, an ominous trail of smoke evident, belching from the starboard engine. Smoke became visible flame, fierce, obviously well established. He was up around three thousand feet, people down below willed him to bring it in. Surely he had the room, if only he had the time. The nose went down, a steep dive. An attempt to douse the flames by forcing the airflow to snuff them out. It seemed to work. But as the pilot recovered from the dive so the burning engine detached itself from the wing and fell away. Which is when reality struck home, the cold and terrible certainty of how things were going to end. Time, space to manoeuvre, options, had all run out at once. That aircraft was doomed.

Now clear of the station and nearby village, but totally out of control, KN129 seemed determined to follow the path of its missing engine. A wing dropped lazily and you could imagine the pilot fighting to regain control of a totally uncontrollable machine. He had no option, for, naturally, Transport Command crews rarely carry parachutes, bad for passenger morale. Those watching, probably three or four hundred by this time, seemed dumbstruck, and if willpower alone could have changed things there would have been no problem. But there was little chance that willpower could achieve that, nor did it. The aircraft spiralled down, seemingly in slow motion, looking as though it was about to begin a display routine. Then, in the final seconds of its avian life it rolled onto its back before vanishing behind distant buildings. A muffled explosion and the tell-tale column of oily-black smoke mushroomed up to signal the inevitable outcome. Other aircraft circled overhead like vultures over carrion.

We later learned the chances of landing had apparently been fifty-fifty, but the pilot had seen his priority as clearing the married quarters and nearby village, before making the attempt.

Three lives lost. How many saved?

*

Two years and I was on the move again. Melksham this time, in the rolling Wiltshire countryside. After the modern barracks of Dishforth it was back to the wooden hut regime. Ten beds a side, a pot-bellied stove in the centre. I recall many an hour seated by that, soaking up the heat. The beds closest to it were too warm, the rest of us freezing.

It reminded me of home, the Griffin:

Our fire was an old cast-iron grate affair with back boiler, oven built in to one side. Apart from being the sole source of heat it also provided us with toast, my bread - spiked on a brass fork - vying with sister, Maureen's bread for sight of the glowing coals. I spent many an hour standing in front of that fire, too, back to the coals, legs astride. It was the only warm place in the room, which is why damp washing hung above my head, suspended from one of those ceiling rack things. But, (as with this stove) there was heat only if you stood close.

So the huts were cold, but at least the were weatherproof. No leaking roof, no rebellious winds whistling in through badly fitting doors and windows, and the cold I was used to.

Melksham was yet another training establishment. Technical. Another six months of schooling, trade and academic. Albeit the square bashing and the bull were part and parcel of any training camp. But successful completion of this course did offer a step up through the ranks.

It was effectively two steps, I found, shortly after my return to Dishforth. I'd volunteered for overseas service, was promoted corporal in a vain effort to keep me where I was. Presumably as the overseas post called for a junior technician, my present rank. Too bad, Dishforth, seemed they required corporals as well.

This phase of my service career saw me through to late 1957. I'd enjoyed it, was in a way sad to be leaving.

Looking back there was the camaraderie, and places remembered. Knaresborough, particularly the bus station on a Saturday night, awaiting the last bus. We'd always finish up in the Board Inn, next door; wouldn't miss that. The memory of being legless, I mean. The old carrot and peas on the pavement trick! Then there was the Black-a-moor, a pub name that springs to mind, though for the life of me I can't recall the location. Must have had some good times there, one imagines.

As I tramped around the station collecting signatures on my clearance chit, I recalled how it had looked three years ago, when I went through the reverse procedure upon arrival here, my first operational posting. The contemporary accommodation, matching blocks (a vast improvement on Cosford), that crescent of hangars which overlooked the airfield proper, Hastings and Valettas, crouching there, almost looking as if they were awaiting my presence, possibly even wondering where I'd got to. Real aeroplanes at last. A Hastings stood there now, fresh from yet another sortie. I could visualize the atmosphere up in that recently vacated cockpit: the whine of gyros running down, instruments dead or dying, switches off. Outside it would be the clicking of metal as it cooled and contracted, everything awaiting the attentions of the fitters and riggers who would shortly arrive to put the machine to bed. I also recalled working out there in the depths of winter, in the ice and snow, how I'd discovered almost by accident that working at night in such conditions entitled us to a tot of rum. Only problem was, the rations were dispensed by the medical staff, in sick quarters, rather a long trek in the middle of the night. Too far, and I never had been keen on rum.

The memories seemed fresh, yet so much had happened since that first day. Anyway, time now to move on. New experiences to record. So I forgot about the past, filed the memories, packed my suitcase with my newly acquired tropical kit - issued during a trip to RAF Innsworth - along with my dreams, looked ahead to my new posting.

Apart from being kitted out for the tropics, my arms appeared to have been used as dartboards, each receiving several innocculations and vaccinations. Not taking too many chances, the Air Force. Still, I was going overseas. Aviation in imagined paradise, what more could one ask of life? Well, a little more cash, for starters. That wouldn't have brought with it too many objections. Be that as it may, I was ready. All I needed now was an aeroplane. The thought of a troopship never even entered my head, although maybe it should have.

* *

Chapter Five
EN ROUTE TO THE WORLD

𝕿he garden, with its hibiscus and travellers palms, was enclosed and well shaded. Not only that, for, attending to one's every wish, uniformed waiters flitted silently amongst rattan furnishings set out on the grass beneath tropical skies. It was in this tranquil setting - ensconced in luxury, surrounded by the gifts of nature - that Somerset Maugham and Noel Coward took tea and wrote, for although humidity in the Lion City is generally high, out here in the garden the climate almost always seemed bearable. Lion City? A direct translation from the Sanskrit: Singa, meaning lion, Pura, city; the island state of Singapore.

This oasis for novelists, the Palm Court - to be found within the encircling arms of the Raffles Hotel - is probably one of the few places in the area which remains basically unchanged since the heady days of Empire. But in 1957 the whole island sat there, redolent of another age. I know, for it was the place to which I was posted.

No quirk of fate, this, I'd volunteered again. In fact, opening my mouth was probably the most dangerous thing I did in my military career. I always seemed to be volunteering for one thing or other. Singapore, though, was acceptable. No, better than that, it was great. The exotic location I had long craved was finally mine, come what may. What else could I want for?

Well, an aircraft or two would go some way towards making things perfect. Aircraft on which to practise my trade, not the one I'd flown out in. I'd already been issued with my first passport (still the impressive blue and gold version back then of course), courtesy of the Home Office and Air Ministry. It accorded me the status of Government Official as my occupation. We wore civilian clothes during the flight, you see; a precaution. I assumed it had to do with the need to overfly unfriendly territories, that should an emergency occur in such airspace, which was to force us down... well, a civilian aircraft full of civilians, wasn't it?

*

The image of my arrival is still perfectly clear, for it had been a totally new experience to that which I had so recently left behind: green fields, English beer, Elvis getting "All Shook Up", fish and chips and the like. Out here there was a soft, tropical night to greet me as the doors opened on my new environment: a velvet sky, the sweet, scented air, the incessant clicking of the cicadas. A warm blustery breeze flicked at me like a feather duster. It was the kind of night most people back home could only dream about. It also served well to embellish the truth - a white lie that embroidered the ordinary with a colourful and imaginative border - for what didn't greet me out there at the airport was the fetid smell of open storm-drains, the rancid pools of stagnant water, the mosquitoes, and the cockroaches. Oh, there was also the durian, a popular, and apparently very tasty tropical fruit. But the durian had its downside, so grave it was banned from being consumed in most public places, for reasons which became obvious, once you got a whiff of it. A smell which equated with the winner of a vile nappy contest.

But none of these things was I to discover, or notice, until later; kind of things that seemed to have been kept secret from the writers of the guidebooks.

Then there were the people, Chinese-looking and all. I somehow hadn't expected that. Don't exactly know what I had expected, hadn't really thought about it to tell the truth, too wrapped up in excitement. (I have since. After Singapore every new location was researched thoroughly, well before I set foot in the place. Even the two weeks holiday was subjected to the same scrutiny. With so short a time on offer no point squandering a couple of days finding out about something you could already be doing. The only exception to this was to be Nigeria, for the market was not exactly awash with guide books on Nigeria. Well, it wouldn't be, would it?)

I immediately fell in love with Singapore. The atmosphere was magical. Though this was the first, there would, over the years, be innumerable such arrivals, such nights.

Off course it wasn't all sun and powder-puff clouds. The occasional storm would sweep through, fierce winds and heavy rain. Which is when those vast, open drains soon filled to the brim with swirling muddy water. But such storms rarely lasted, sun eventually breaking through, temperature climbing again, steam rising from concrete and bush alike. OK, not quite paradise, yet. But I could imagine paradise as being only a few short steps away.

I had been overseas before: Malta, France, Libya, Egypt, those training flights from Dishforth. But those visits had been fleeting. They served to stimulate the wanderlust in me, but that was about all. Besides, this was the first of the truly exotic locations. Here I wore khaki cotton rather than blue serge - shorts by day, longs at night - the standard issue fitting about as well as a three-fingered glove. Lily-white skin apart, I soon discovered it was my ill-fitting uniform with knee-length shorts which made me as conspicuous as a tarantula on an iced bun. Everyone else seemed smartly dressed, and I was quick to ascertain the reason why. So it was quickly down to a local tailor, whom I had outfit me from scratch. As this area was to my theatre of operations for the next two and a half years, I decided I may as well look the part, especially as it cost so little. Out went the shiny black shoes, to be replaced by the soon-to-be-scruffy, fawn, suede desert boots, whose wear seemed almost universal. (Shoes were for parades only.) Then there was the matter of arms and legs. Compared to those who had been here for some time I was ghostly white, a result of which was that I - along with all the other new arrivals - became known as a moonie. Just had to grin and bear being addressed as such by the well established inhabitants, along with the cries of: "Get yer knees brown," and "Get some in." Meaning, time out here.

I also had to suffer the embarrassment of being lectured by the medical officer on the dangers of sunburn and venereal disease, both apparently rife in the area, if one did not take adequate precautions. Both were chargeable offenses under the heading of, self-inflicted injury. On "active service" a charge like that could be serious enough to warrant a Court Martial. And let us not forget, this was an "active service" area. The threat of VD was serious enough for them to make us watch a film showing its possible damaging effects on certain parts of our anatomy. Which is where the embarrassment came in, for the audience also featured moonies from the Women's Royal Air Force; all lily-white and blushing pink.

The obvious answer would have been for us lads and lasses to get together, as it were, thus evading the possibility of picking up anything untoward. But life is never that simple.

Care needed to be taken all round, then, for as well as nut rot, foot rot and gut rot were also prevalent, not to mention the dreaded malaria-carrying mosquito. (Hence the insistence on our having to wear trousers and long-sleeved shirt after dark; anti-malarial precautions. It was an order we tolerated, most of the time.)

When volunteering for overseas service I'd actually opted for Hong Kong, but then so had everyone else. So I wasn't surprised or dismayed to find I didn't get it. Singapore had been my second choice, and I look back on my time there as a series of images; half-remembered dreams.

Fortune smiled upon me from the start for, with trooping by sea the norm, I was flown out. At a time when Singapore direct was still little more than a dream, G-ALDV, a Handley Page Hermes of Skyways carried me from Stanstead to Paya Lebar in all of three days. A total of thirty-seven flying hours, for a trip which today is but a comfortable twelve hours non-stop by Boeing 747-400.

No in-flight drinks, and no movies back then, either. Meals were in sandwich form, came in cardboard boxes; often tasted like they were made out of them, too. Nor could we always climb above the worst of the weather, despite the aircraft being fully pressurised. The choice lay between, through, or round. The aircraft also required refuelling down-route, which meant sectors of around four to six hours duration. A leisurely trip for us, then, but if dwelled upon one had to wonder about crew fatigue, for they didn't slip en-route as is now the norm. Of course, dwell on it was what I didn't do. Not back then, and by now it no longer matters, to me. But that aircraft did crash a couple of trips later, which gives one cause to wonder...

Brindisi was our first stop, down on the heel of Italy. From there it was Baghdad, Delhi, Calcutta, Bangkok, with a couple of hours in each, to stretch the legs, then that spectacular arrival in Singapore. One nightstop was made en-route, at Karachi. Ey up! as they say back int' West Riding. Not one of life's more exhilarating experiences, that. Karachi, I mean. The rest of the flight was great. I felt pity for those unfortunates who were down there bobbing about on the oceans. They had no doubt left long before us, would arrive long after, which would make them our "moonies", provided they didn't take steps to circumvent that minor embarrassment during the voyage out.

Upon arrival at Seletar I was to find that not only was the island recalling days past, the RAF was caught up in it too. To me, Seletar resembled a museum. A living museum, dedicated to aviation, in that its aircraft were also of a bygone era. There was the Sunderland, Beaufighter, Mosquito, Spitfire - aircraft which had long since been retired from front-line service in the UK Commands, as was the equipment with which they were fitted. From the electronic marvels of instrumentation on which I'd been so painstakingly trained I was now faced with the wonders of an ancient science; air and oil driven contraptions as fitted to the remnants of a World War Two air-force. My first thought was, Boy, talk about crude! But of course they weren't, were they, not back when they'd been designed. Interesting enough now, for sure, but even they, it seemed, were not to be honoured by my presence.

My luck, apparently, had at last run dry. No first-line servicing for me. No second-line, either. Worse. Much worse. Not even any aircraft.

Assigned to the maintenance unit, I soon became bored with the testing of instruments in a climate controlled environment. It was like working in a refrigerator, then walking into an oven. An insight as to what frozen fish might feel when transferred to the microwave, were it possible for fish to feel anything, that is. Especially in the frozen stage.

The staff were multi-lingual - meaning we either conversed in a recognizable version of the English language, or waved our arms and pointed. And believe me I can wave my arms and point with the best of them.

I didn't care for this place at all, nor did I possess the enthusiasm needed to repair instruments, rather than the aircraft they came from. Besides, it was like working to union rules, we had to clock on, and our daily routine was logged and recorded: time in and out, equipment checked, hours logged, which was to create something of a problem in itself. I discussed the situation with my compatriot, "Smudge" Smith, apart from the Warrant Officer in charge, the only other Englishman around. There were Scotsmen, too, but they didn't appear to speak our language any better than the Sikhs or Malays, the balance of the workforce.

'I see there's a set schedule for the testing of each item, Smudge, a time specified for each test, right?'

'Yes. Well, a theoretical time. One that could well have been set by a militant, union boss. Take this altimeter, for instance.' He held it up. 'That is allotted ninety minutes, which means you can manage five in an eight hour day.'

'So, what's the problem?'

'The problem is, these times are nowhere near realistic. Give me fifteen minutes and this altimeter will be finished. Five times fifteen?'

'Ah, yes, I see.' Even my secondary education could figure that out.'

'The problem therefore...' Smudge was intent on spelling it out, '...what to do for the next six hours?'

He was right, too, I was to find. Every day felt like it was Monday. So boring, NAAFI breaks became the big event of the day. But you can only stuff a limited amount of sticky buns and sarnies down your neck in a given time. As for NAAFI tea, well, there must be an absolute limit on how much of that one could safely sup in a day, leaving room for the odd pint of *Tiger*, naturally.

Even school bus detail became a boredom-breaking change. Did it ever. This entailed escorting the children of RAF families to school, utilizing RAF transport. And I use the term "children" in the loosest sense possible. Even the kids seemed to assume the rank of their service parent, but although I was only a corporal I could be seen to have the advantage, for I was armed. Which got me to thinking: was this ancient Lee Enfield meant to offer those kids some protection from the communists - who were at present waging war, over there in Malaya - or was it meant to protect me from the kids?

Then there was that other mindless pastime which I and Smudge - who also happened to be my room-mate - dreamed up.

We were into model aircraft - those highly detailed plastic-moulded things - were, in fact, rather enthusiastic builders, which eventually posed a problem: where to hang them all in the limited space allotted us in which to live? Answer: Impossible. So it was that the older models found themselves loaded with Chinese firecrackers - small, but loud and powerful - suspended from a fan blade, set in motion, fuse lit. Wow! Quite spectacular. But as we'd inevitably end up picking pieces of plastic out of our clothes for days on end, we eventually devised an alternative method of destruction. A length of cord was stretched from our second floor balcony, to the trunk of a distant palm tree. The aircraft would now slide gracefully into oblivion, wreckage scattered over a wide area of grass, leaving the clearing up to the native bearers.

This was another feature new to me, proving once again that RAF service overseas was on an entirely different plain to that in the UK; much more relaxed. Out here, as long as we did our job, we were basically left to enjoy life to the full. No bull, few parades, hardly any restrictions. The bearers were just another facet of this easy life. For a couple of dollars a month these guys - mainly from the Indian subcontinent - would clean the rooms, make our beds, change the sheets, and see to the laundry. And, being as they were earning much more than any of us, they were also quite happy loan us the odd dollar or two when we ran short; at a rate of interest that would make even a loan-shark blush!

Smithy and I also acquired a stuffed panda, whom we promptly named Fred. It was Fred therefore who volunteered to test our state-of-the-art parachutes from the second-floor balcony. A much better option than the childhood kitten which had "volunteered" to serve in a similar post. (Much like George Cayley's coachman, I suppose.) In fact, I rather suspect that was the point at which my subliminal interest in aviation first began to assert itself. Just an inkling, mind, but it was enough. Which was to be unfortunate for the kitten. For although I eventually reached the stage where the parachutes worked quite well, as with most experimental projects the early models left a lot to be desired, especially for that kitten. Came down rather rapid-like, at times. Yes, you get the idea; roughly the same velocity it would without a parachute, should it foolishly choose to jump from such a height. No problem though, they do always land on their feet. Well, almost always. If not, it would looked a bit bemused for a second or two, but as long as all four legs worked it would flick its tail and ears - as if also checking their operation - then off it would charge. Anyway, if all else failed there was always that old "nine lives" backup.

But that was ten years in the past, you can bet even the kitten would have used up its tally of nine in that time. No such problems with Fred then, which was just as well. Especially as the state of our particular art left a lot to be desired. Seemed I'd forgotten all the lessons learned during my earlier erudition.

'Fancy a trip down the village?' Smithy enquired of me one evening. And as I was doing nothing in particular, I readily agreed to join him.

'How about a curry?' he suggested, once we were settled in air-conditioned comfort, a glass of *Tiger* to hand.

'What! That foreign muck? Come on, Smudge, you know me, your typical Brit abroad, I'll eat anything, so long as it features sausage, egg, and chips.'

'Right, you get what you like, I'll order curry, you can have a taste of mine.'

'I won't like it, it can tell you now.'

'Can't say, until you've tried it.'

'I just did say it.'

But he ordered anyway, and he watched me as I tried it. He 'd known I would for I hadn't rejected his offer out of hand.

'There you are,' he said, 'told you you'd like it.'

'Who said I liked it? I replied, reaching across for another forkful. 'Need to try a bit more, that's all.'

'Good, eh?' he persisted, as I shovelled it down.

'Well, yeah. Not good, but maybe not so bad,' I admitted, somewhat reluctantly.

'Okay, I'll order another, and we'll share it,' he said, which he promptly did. And that was my introduction to the world of the curried egg, from where, I at first imagined, it was but a short hop, skip, and jump to unrefined napalm. Which it almost was, literally, for across the road was a pukka, Indian place, complete with dirt floor. And it was to here we went from then on. Although I did at first demur.

'No bloody air-con, Smudge!'

'What do you need air-con for, hardly any walls.'

'Yeah, and the place is full of cockroaches.'

'Ah, but wait 'till you try their curry. Get that beer down your neck and shut up.'

As usual, when it came to curries, Smithy was right. Should have been, he'd spent part of his youth in India. But that curry was to change my outlook on foreign foods forevermore. And given the circumstances, it was probably as well he did introduce me to the dish, being as we shared a room.

So, curried eggs, beer, barbecues at the Malcolm Club, exploding plastic models, and unsuccessful parachutes, what an interesting social life we led. There again, we did occasionally venture into town, when funds permitted. I even replaced my plastic Kodak box with a new type of camera: the revolutionary, Ashai Pentax. That was another fact of life of the personnel stationed in the Far East: they probably owned more quality cameras than the whole of the Royal Photographic Society back home. Cameras were cheap, so everyone went for the best: Twin-lens Rollei,

Leica, Contax. All made in Europe, you'll notice. The same went for watches, mainly Swiss: Rolex, Patek Phillipe, Omega. Seiko were but a thought in some Japanese head, though not for long. Just as the photographic world was about to be turned on *its* head with the introduction of that Pentax, the Japanese were about to stake a claim in the chronology market - big time, it could be said!

There was a thriving photo club on the base, of which I became a member. It all helped keep madness at bay, but I did pine for my aircraft. I could photograph them, get close, but that wasn't the same as giving them my loving attention.

As the days dragged inexorably by it seemed there was to be nothing. But, just when I was of the opinion that - so far as my welfare was concerned - God had taken early retirement, along He comes and hands me a bonus. I'd been keeping my eyes peeled, an ear to the ground, looking and listening, hoping something interesting would come up for which I could volunteer my services; aircraft-wise, that is. Anything had to be better than my present situation.

After barely a month with the MU - though probably the longest month of my life - the section commander, a rather personable and astute Warrant Officer, called me into his office one morning.

'Corporal Taylor', he began, 'How's it going?'

'Okay, sir, I suppose.'

'Not happy here, are you?'

'No, sir, not really. I'm a first line man at heart.'

'Just the man then. There's a requirement for an instrument fitter on the one of the station's other units, would you be interested in a one month secondment?'

The fact that I was being asked, not forcibly volunteered, made me suspicious right away. This, after all, was an active service posting, people were being shot in the jungles to the north. But my suspicions were soon to be dispelled. Anyway, what the hell, I was dying of boredom where I was, would prefer to go out with a bang.

*

Singapore is separated from those Malayan jungles by a body of water known as the Straits of Johore, across which lies the only physical link between the two countries: a one kilometre causeway which carries road and rail traffic, and the pipelines which do likewise for Singapore's water supply, bringing it over from Johore Bahru. But apart from forming the border, the Straits had another function: their waters served as runways for the joint No.205/209 squadron, a Sunderland equipped unit known as the Far East Flying Boat Wing. This was what I was being offered.

Last of the services' flying boats, the Sunderland first flew in 1937, had given sterling service during World War Two, the Berlin Airlift, the communist takeover of China - remember the Yangtze Incident? A Sunderland had been involved there, managing to transfer medical supplies and a doctor behind enemy lines to HMS Amethyst - and on through the Korean conflict.

These aircraft, last of the almost seven hundred and fifty produced, were now approaching the end of their time gracefully, serving in one final conflict.

More like it, this. A situation made for the likes of myself.

'I realize you aren't familiar with the aircraft, or their equipment, but instruments are more or less the same no matter which type of aircraft they are fitted to.' he said, 'So that won't pose a problem, will it?'

'No, sir. I've never yet trained on any specific aircraft on which I've worked. Pick it up as I go along: the quirks of each particular type.'

This was true, as he was no doubt well aware. On arrival at Dishforth I'd never before set eyes on either the Valetta or Hastings. And, needless to say, each of the visiting types was also new to me, so this was no different. What's more, the position was on offer, a few steps closer to paradise. I said yes ever so indecently quickly, never for a moment regretted doing so. In fact I enjoyed it so much I eventually contrived to turn what was to have been a detachment of a month, into a posting lasting a year. Just as well, for I'd dreaded the thought of ever returning to that MU.

*

As on any operational squadron there was considerable rapport between the aircrew and their mechanics on the ground. Team spirit, the essential bond that is plainly evident, for let's face it this was the front end of the Air Force, what it was all about, its very reason for being: getting those aircraft into the air and keeping them there. The unity and loyalty of squadron personnel lasts a lifetime - evidenced by the number of annual reunions, the majority relating to squadrons that no longer exist.

It was during my time with 205/209 that I finally made it to the Crown Colony of Hong Kong. One of our aircraft was kept there on air-sea rescue standby - airborne lifeboat tucked beneath the port wing, Lindholme gear (inflatables and emergency stores) carried on the internal, underwing bomb racks on the starboard side. It was based in the bay at Kai Tak, where I was lucky enough to be detached for a couple of months. With but a couple of training flights, and thankfully no emergencies, there was not a lot for us to do on base, but ah the memories. Honolulu Bar: "enchanting music for dancing, genuine drinks(?), delicious food", read their gaily-coloured business card. It was something all bars gave out, possibly so you could later remember where the hell it was you'd been. Lucky Star Bar

& Nightclub was another, in the Wanchai district - oh, oh, Suzie Wong territory, that; think maybe I met her sister. Said she wanted to improve her English, didn't she? And I thought she meant the language!

*

A myriad of aromas permeated the atmosphere, so many they intermingled into a deliciously confusing amalgam, the nose requiring help to separate them: petrol fumes, coffee, wood shavings and dried fish. Incense and sandalwood, too. Joss-sticks burned in a temple across the way, smoke rising vertically in the still air. The temple was small, but magnificent in red, gold, and green - significant colours here in the east. Carved and gilded dragons wound themselves everywhere, green-glazed terracotta examples forming the upturned corners of the green tiled roof.

I wandered on, fascinated, past open fronted shops and stores. From within one came the click clack of Mah-jong pieces being rapped on a marble-topped table, and the unintelligible, sing-song voices of the players. Another, doorway, and a happy, grinning face looked out to wish me "Goodbye", which I assumed was meant to be "Hello". On second thoughts, depending what went on in that dark and mysterious interior, it could well *have* been goodbye.

I came across a market in which bowls and tins were piled high; spices of every type and colour. There were mountains of chili powder, weird and wonderful mushrooms, root ginger and ginseng, and garlic by the ton. Then there was an "exotic" section; dried bugs, beetles, and centipedes, the latter fully six inches long, bundled and boxed, ready for .... whatever!

In the evening there was noise. The noise of the traffic and the sing-song voices of the locals, plus the music which seemed to blast out of every bar and club. Neon bottles poured neon champagne into neon glasses as neon can-can girls kicked their neon legs. "Kit Kat Klub" read a sign around which endless red neon arrows chased each other, before diving down towards an otherwise anonymous doorway. To one side a svelte Chinese girl with long, glossy hair, balanced on high heels. Her form-fitting cheongsam provided an ostentatious display of tight buttocks and slim thighs. The cheap scent she wore mingled with a hundred other assorted aromas; food, carbon-monoxide, garbage, and sweat. Those, and more, ebbed and flowed in the night air.

The girl made a pretence of looking in the window of a nearby shop, but her actions made it plainly obvious she was selling, not buying. And I had to admit, the goods appeared to be quite stunning. Or maybe she just wanted to improve her English?

High overhead, against the black roof of the night, a star streaked across in its death arc.

This whole area was a wonderful, colourful kaleidoscope of shops, bars, restaurants, clubs, hotels, and "girlie bars". All were dimly lit, airconditioned, and comfortable. Homely type places with cheap drinks and obliging hostesses. And this being well before the days of the long-haul package tour, or the American invasion, we had the field almost to ourselves.

Luckyman Hall, The Sportsman's Arms, they sound ominous, too. Must have been, for their cards are still lodged in the back of my photo album, as is the one they gave you to hang on your glass if you found a need to leave the bar for a while: "Do not touch, gone to wee wee," it stated. The Waltzing Matilda gave us a scroll.

Hate think how much I spent in these places, time, or money. But, unless my memory is playing tricks, it was well worth it. It beat Norton and Malton into a cocked hat, that was for sure; to say nothing of Cosford.

It took a Sunderland just five minutes short of twelve hours to haul itself up the coast from Singapore to Hong Kong, a time I was to see progressively reduced over the years: seven hours forty-five by Hastings, three hours fifty-five by Comet 2, three and a quarter hours by Boeing 707, as opposed to days by B-O-A-T.

*

Those Sunderlands may have been vintage but the facilities at Seletar were probably a hundred percent improvement on what had been available during World War Two, especially at the remote outstations. I'd heard tell of bush huts for the crews, and refuelling by handpump from makeshift jetties. We refuelled by barge, and our jetty was substantive. A long concrete affair with a control station at the seaward end. Next to this was a magnificent slipway, complete with winching system for bringing the aircraft ashore once the beaching trolleys had been fitted. Major servicing could thus be carried out in comfort, hulls kept reasonably clean. Though one prankster pilot would probably disagree with the latter, especially after the take-off run that took him down the Straights as far as the Sembawang naval base, aircraft still firmly attached to the water. What the hell, maybe he was seeking some assistance from the earth's curvature to get him airborne. No matter, the exercise was a failure in more ways than one. Apparently not too chuffed about having a Sunderland tearing about in what they saw as their territory, the Navy types. Neither was our Wing Commander too chuffed about receiving a call from the Admiral, or whatever. Shouldn't have joined if they couldn't take a joke. I thought it hilarious, can still see that plume of spray disappearing from view, well past the area cleared for take-off, aircraft inside it rocking back and forth as the pilot attempted to unstick it. Took him quite a while to taxy back, too.

As far as the routine servicing of flying boats went, it was anything but. There was a marine craft section for a start, the Air Force's own sailors, with their floating fuel bowsers, ammunition scows, lighters, pinnaces, fire tenders, and crew transport. I'd ride a launch out to the aircraft, bobbing at its mooring buoy in the Straits of Johore, climb aboard and complete my task. One thing to remember - when working outside the aircraft - tools needed to be secured to ones person via a length of string, were they not to be lost forever. Oops!.. Clink.. Plop.. Damn and blast! Look out, fish, here she comes: 5/16 x 3/8 Whitworth o/e.

With my servicing complete I'd reach for the Aldiss lamp and signal the piermaster, requesting the launch's return, which I knew could take some time. So, imagine if you will, the intrepid fitter, task complete, ninety plus in the shade, palm trees on the nearby beach barely stirring in a lazy breeze, sea as flat and smooth as unrolled silk, a wing that made a perfect diving platform (I had eventually mastered the art of entering the water head first). But, as usual, paradise did have the odd flaw. For instance, I lacked of a glass of something long, cool, and wicked, close to hand, and I knew my swimming hole was domicile to venomous snakes. (Come to think of it, they probably fit the "long, cool, wicked" description to a tee, albeit minus the glass.) Like most snakes, though, they offered no harm unless threatened, but try telling that to a naive airman. Still, I never heard tell of any personnel being attacked, either when swimming, or when beaching the aircraft. Though, over the water in Malaya they apparently lost more lives per year to snakes than they did on the roads, the majority of the victims being fishermen. What with snakes, and some kind of conflict going on, didn't sound like too healthy a place, this Malaya.

The hardest part of these impromptu swimming sessions, unless you had help, was the difficulty in getting back on board the aircraft. The base of the entry door was naturally well above water level, with a step down once inside. Oh-oh! Watch out for the family jewels.

*

So excited was I at the time that only brief fragments of my first waterborne take-off are lodged in memory. A launch had first made a sweep down the watery runway, checking for debris - any flotsam and jetsam that could wreck an aircraft travelling at speed - our engines were running, we'd cast-off from the mooring buoy and we were now lined up and ready.

With throttles pushed open and the roar of four engines at full power, the spray flew back, obscuring the view .There was a reluctant build-up of speed - degree of reluctance dependant upon hull cleanliness (barnacles the problem here) - as hull and wing-tip floats cut creamy furrows in turquoise water. Then we were "on the step" and the foam subsided as we we charged across the surface. A lunge, a couple of bounces, and we were airborne, water-streaked perspex clearing as we clawed our way into the tropical sky. A boat had become an aeroplane. Fleeting but emotional recollections.

My services were requested one morning to make adjustments to an autopilot, a task which was completed whilst airborne. It usually took less than an hour, but this time I found dusk to be settling with us as we floated back down to the Straits again, Pratt & Whitney Twin-Wasps roaring healthily, just as they had for the past twelve hours and twenty minutes.

As the bow wave shortened to a feather of creamy ripples, we slowed, wings creaking and groaning as weight was transferred from them to hull and floats. It was as though the machine itself was sighing with relief, secure in the knowledge it was all over for yet another day. The aeroplane had once again returned to the maritime environment, engineer in the forward hatch ready to hook the buoy, pilot controlling speed and direction. (No easy task, for there was no way of braking on water, can't throw an aircraft in reverse like you can a boat - at least not a Sunderland.) A miss and it was round again, plus a round of drinks on the luckless engineer. The pilot would find himself facing the same forfeit should he forget to dress the propellers upon shut-down: ie one blade up, two down. This allowed clearance for the crew launch on its approach. But care was still required, for the tips and leading edges of those propeller blades could be deadly on flesh and bones. The spray attacked them relentlessly, eventually creating very effective saw-like edges. An additional job for the riggers was to file the roughness out every so often. (Not too healthy in the interests of blade balance, I wouldn't have thought!)

It had taken me all of twenty minutes to check the autopilot fully operational. We had then proceeded on a routine sortie: Borneo and back. At Labuan we actually made an approach to the runway. Not exactly a touchdown, of course not, but extremely low. Some would have said cutting the margins too fine. Maybe, maybe not, depends on the pilot. But this was so low he must have been very good, or lucky. In fact, had the beaching gear been fitted I swear we'd have laid rubber down the centre of the runway.

Probably effective relief from any boredom that may have accumulated in the interim, but it didn't affect me that way. I wasn't bored to begin with. Here I was, aviation venerator par excellence, actually being paid to fly around all day.

I later heard tell of a Royal New Zealand Air Force Sunderland pilot who cut the margins even finer. Too fine, in fact, actually managing to scrape his keel along the hard stuff. Not recommended, that, as he was soon to discover, assuming he wasn't already aware of the fact. And all he had to fall back on was the excuse of a sudden downdraught or possible wind-shear, just the kind of thing margins are meant to cover.

The incident took place during a public flying display at the opening of Wellington's new airport, and apparently it somehow caused fire to break out in the aircraft's bilges. (Yes, they were flying *boats,* remember. They had bilges, bulkheads, and ports. Stuff like that.) Anyway, fire wasn't the real problem. That was successfully extinguished on the flight back to base at Hobsonville, north of Auckland, where the aircraft was safely set down. Unfortunately, despite the pilot's attempt to make the slipway, the RNZAF found itself with one less Sunderland on inventory, the aircraft foundering well before it reached shore.

They were comfortable old aircraft, those Sunderlands, had been designed with long flights in mind, hour upon lonely hour of sub-hunting, far out over the Atlantic. The "lounge" - on the lower deck - featured leather-upholstered banquettes. These were arranged fore and aft, either side of a folding table, ideal for dining, or a game of poker. Meals were prepared on board, over an open flame stove. And if memory serves correctly, this just happened to be located beneath the wing centre section, in which was carried the hundreds of gallons of fuel required for such lengthy flights! Can't be right, can it?

I was once more happy with my lot. After dark I would occasionally take a relaxing walk along the jetty, as though not wishing to release the aircraft from my sight. The sky would be clear after the rain, night air washed fresh, scented with the blossoms of frangipani, Jasmine, Magnolia. In the background nature's symphony would be tuning-up: frogs and cicadas providing the percussion, mosquitoes, the strings.

At my side, a pale, liquid moon would match my pace. In such conditions a witch on a broomstick would not have been misplaced.

That was all it took for me to become melancholy, despite that fact that out there on the water, aircraft bobbed at their moorings, each with an armed guard aboard, for let us not forget, this was an "active service" posting. It was one of the more pleasant guard duties, though. A good chance to get in some fishing.

*

It was during the hours of darkness that the interior of the barrack blocks echoed to a sound of a different kind: lizard-like geckoes clung to ceilings and walls by means of their suction-cup feet, tiny heart pulsating visibly behind their transparent epidermal layer, every now and again issuing forth with the call by which they were more commonly known: chit chat. They provided a service, too; lapping up mosquitoes and other small pests. But every so often one of these harmless little creatures would miscalculate with it's fancy footwork - rather like the younger version of me on my bike. Down it would plop, possibly onto a bed, charging off immediately, but not before startling the occupant more than it had itself. This was especially true if that occupant happened to be a moonie: one who'd been primed by the old hands to watch out for these "deadly poisonous creepy crawlies that are apt to launch themselves upon you". I've seen guys almost mesmerized, laying there staring at them, afraid to close their eyes, until some kind soul let them in on the ruse.

Aerial invaders of the larger kind were usually accounted for by the ceiling fans. I'd lay there in the dark, beneath my mosquito net but above the sheets, wearing not a stitch, louvred windows thrown wide open, for even with the fan at a fair lick it would be hot in our two-man room. Heat another disadvantage conferred upon us by the room being so small, apart from the lack of space to hang models.

Of course, an open window was an invitation to all and sundry, and I'd often hear the familiar whine of a dung beetle. They'd whistle and whang their way around the room, ricocheting about like a bat with faulty radar, as if involved in some clumsy suicide bid, until inevitably they'd meet up with a fan blade travelling in opposition to the direction of flight. Whack! Straight back over the bowler's head for six. Splat! against the wall, end of story. Very yucky. Quite something, that. Especially when a flip-flopped foot would merely pin the tough little sods to the ground. As soon as you lifted clear, they'd be up and away.

Given the chance, so would I. And here the opportunities for flight were endless, and encouraged. There were air-tests - after major maintenance - and it was seen as an act of faith by the aircrew if a number of tradesmen volunteered to join the flight. I was there in a flash, every time. As frequently demonstrated, I didn't need any encouragement when it came to volunteering. There again, I suspect my IQ may begin with a decimal point.

Air-tests apart, there were mail-drops to Royal Navy vessels - buoyant waterproof container being tossed out of the open (under-wing) bomb-doors, aimed to land as close as possible to the waiting launch, though I don't suppose a direct hit would have been at all appreciated. There were anti-piracy patrols, routine flights, and saturation bombing missions over Malaya. Hard work, the latter, for the lightweight metal - up to twenty pounds - was dispatched by hand, no precision required. The bomb racks were reserved for the heavy stuff.

*

All too soon my time with the squadron was up, my first year in the Far East drawing to a close, but by then the Sunderland's days were numbered, too. It was obvious the end was approaching the day the whole squadron was ordered to pose for a group photograph in front of one of the aircraft. Beached, of course. A bit difficult lining everyone up otherwise. Bags I the top row!

Then we became plain old 209 squadron, No.205 being reformed at Changi with the Shackleton Mk1, just entering service in the Far East Air Force. Not too much longer and 209 would follow suit. But they too would reform and re-equip, this time with the Scottish Aviation Pioneer, moving up country, closer to the front line.

Singapore was still officially in the war zone, even though it had long since been declared "white" (as opposed to "black" for the operational areas in Malaya). Testimony was in the dog tags with which we were issued, and required to wear: name, rank, serial number. Further evidence was provided by the exercises which were occasionally foisted upon us. I recall one such where an SAS troop were the attacking force, the idea being for them to enter the hangar and symbolically blow up our aircraft. We, of course, would prevent just such a thing happening, so we were told. A game, really, to check on security, but it was a game which kept us up all night.

I was patrolling an area alongside squadron headquarters when I caught a movement out of the corner of my eye, a shadowy figure was attempting to sneak past along the storm drain. Almost dry, of course, but none too pleasant for all that, enough slime and gunge to keep Noel Edmonds happy. Still, from what I'd heard I doubted that would worry the SAS a great deal.

Gotcha, you bugger, thinks I. 'Halt! Who goes there?' I challenged, as required. Yes, still the same old procedure. I made a production of cocking the weapon I held; an ominous sound that echoed in the night. It was almost guaranteed to stop anyone in their tracks, as it did this joker.

Back through the darkness came the authorized reply: some password or other, just like this fictional fellow, James Bond, who was becoming popular at the time.

'Advance and be recognized,' I called, sticking to the script, even though I wasn't too sure about the scenario. It might be a game to us, but from tales doing the rounds those SAS guys played rough. To them the game was always deadly serious. Fine, so far as my country's enemies were concerned, not too pleasant a thought for such as me, in this kind of situation. For although in reality we were on the same side, tonight we were technically not; we were enemies. So I wasn't going to him, that was for sure. If he was who I thought he was, nasty things could await me. He'd likely floor me and head for the hills, disappearing into the darkness. I could end up with anything from a sore head, to a bayonet up the arse! No thanks, he could come to me, out here in the light where I could see.

And where I had a mate to back me up.

Advance someone, or thing, did, emerging from out of the murk and gloom, heading in the general direction of the business end of my rifle. Gradually, almost as if by parthenogenesis, a figure took shape. A figure dressed as an RAF officer, Flight Lieutenant no less. Yes, well... Maybe, maybe not.

'Could I see some identity, sir, if you don't mind.' I didn't ask so much as ordered, enjoyed doing so. Felt I was quite within my rights in such a situation. Especially as I was at the advantageous end of a weapon, which I pointed threateningly. It was the usual, an ancient Lee Enfield. Unloaded, of course, they weren't taking too many chances. But would he know that?

When he handed me his ID, I realized he would. It was a card: photo, name, rank. Official observer. OK, due etiquette, he now got a salute, for he had his rights, too. Silly sod had been testing me, which made me feel quite chuffed, even though he had been easy to spot. Should have known the SAS wouldn't have been so careless, or compliant. Still, it was enough to keep me on my toes. No one else tried it on that night, I can almost guarantee. Almost? Well, yes. You see, when we entered the locked hangar next morning we found it to be a bit of a mess. A bit good these lads. (There again, don't suppose we were the fiercest opposition they had ever faced.) Paint was everywhere. "SAS were here", and other such messages, plastered across walls and floor. Take some cleaning off, that. But they were welcome to it, this "gweilo" (literally, white ghost, even if I was by now well bronzed) was off "up country", as they say. Goodbye SAS, goodbye Sunderlands. Goodbye the All Services, Britannia Club, downtown Singapore, directly opposite the luxurious splendour that was Raffles Hotel. The Brit Club, with its home-from-home food, good social atmosphere, and its swimming pool, was usually the first stop on any visit to town. After some time here our behaviour would usually degenerate to a level not acceptable in the area of the Raffles, so we'd be off to various local bars and clubs, often travelling by trishaw (bicycle powered rickshaw). If the requirement was for more than one machine - as was often the case - we would coax the drivers into a race.

" Come on Johnnie, you number one, you beat him. No winee, no payee."

That's all it took, and off they'd charge, like Ben Hur on steroids. They'd cut corners, rush willy-nilly down unlit streets, spindly legs going like pistons. It was a game they joined in, well knowing that not only would they be paid, but could expect a handsome tip. It wasn't in our interest not to pay. Too much hassle. For although, to us, they did all look alike, the reverse didn't necessarily apply. They had a good memory for faces, and the RAF Police tended to get slightly upset should we in any way distress the locals.

Occasionally, if we'd drunk enough (OK, somewhat more than occasionally) we'd sit them in the seat and have a go ourselves, for a couple of yards or so! Nowhere near as easy as it looked, which made me realize just how fit those scrawny-looking Chinese must be. Well, it was goodbye to all that. Goodbye too, that Indian curry shop, outside the camp gates, where my room mate had first converted me to the curry platter. Here the air was spiced with a combination of coriander, tumeric, cumin, chilies, garlic. Not an English smell. A different form of cooking from a different land.

A rickety, open-fronted affair, that shop, its hard-packed dirt floor patrolled by cockroaches the size of... well, bloody big cockroaches is what they were. But even those were not enough to deter Smithy and I from frequently partaking. Washed down with ice-cold *Tiger* it had to be one of the great egg curries of our time, a real sinus clearer. There again, maybe not. But ah, the memories. I now have only to pass within sniffing distance of an Indian restaurant for the images to flow. Palmed paradises of the Asian continent: Hong Kong, Malaya, Singapore, Thailand.

It was goodbye also to the joss-scented Chinese restaurants that formed the bulk of Albert Street. The real thing, these, forget your fancy high class places, with high class prices. Good as they might be, we couldn't afford them, so we took to the street.

The Albert Street kitchens were located on Tilly-lamp lighted barrows, positioned at the roadside. Marble-topped tables were sited in the mysterious-looking depths of the buildings behind, up rickety wooden stairs. Up there the floors were polished wood, a step or two up from packed dirt, solid, yet uneven. The lighting was dim, but the inescapable cockroaches didn't seem to mind. Forget the decor, the food was great, the aromas, out of this world. Real flip-flop food.

In matters of hygiene, of course, eating in this fashion did have its drawbacks. It could mean an extraordinary amount of time needed to be spent in the toilet, and third-world toilets are not exactly places where one would wish to spend an extraordinary amount of time.

One place we did seem to spend an extraordinary amount of time was in the bars of Bugis Street. (Pronounced boogie.) It was fun to sit at tables set out on the street, drinking beer and watching life pass by. Especially the girls who flaunted about, attempting to sell themselves to us. The best looking girls in town worked the bars of Bugis Street. Only they weren't! This was a street of transvestites. We were well aware of the fact, but many strangers were not. They were that convincing, and it was interesting to watch the wheeling and dealing going on. Were some of those strangers to be in for a shock and a load of disappointment if it eventually progressed as far as the sliding a hand up a shapely leg stage! Imagine the scene as he reaches what he imagined to be his objective. The "girl" turns on all her charm. 'You like?' she asks.

'I regret, sir,' replies the man. 'I am not cognisant of the body in question'. At least he'd probably use a group of words which more or less amounted to such a reply, though perhaps not so elegantly put. This would occasionally be followed by a fist in the face.

Close by was Thieves Market, alongside the Rochor Canal. You could buy almost anything there, real or fake. Buy your own watch if you weren't careful. Same thing went for Change Alley, in Raffles Place. I'd forever remember the times spent haggling down there: the cheongsams that no one at home would want, those garish velvet cushion covers, decorated with dragons, likewise.

Yes, I'd miss all that. What I wouldn't miss were the storm drains: a mere trickle of water four feet down. During the monsoon season, a raging torrent. Nor would I miss the colourful but hideous Haw Par Villa, otherwise known as Tiger Balm Gardens. Their graphically explicit sculptures depicting various acts of barbarism, enough to give anyone nightmares. If that's an example of Chinese mythology - to which they are supposedly related - you can keep it. No, I certainly wouldn't miss that.

What I would miss, probably most of all, was the Seletar Yacht Club, located on the seafront, next to our crewroom. In fact it as good as was our crewroom, during the day, especially towards that day's closing, for many an evening had been spent sitting out on the veranda of this simple, single story, wooden structure. I'd sit there, taking in the sultry night air, *Tiger* to hand, watching the effects of the sun's setting over the Straits of Johore, Malaya less than a mile distant. Out at anchorage, aircraft bobbed on the water, mooring lights aglow, for when afloat these leviathans of the air needed to comply with the laws of the sea, even so far as being required to carry an anchor. It was a piddling little thing that would have found difficulty holding a rowing boat in position, but it adhered to the letter of the regulations if not the spirit.

Yes, it was to be goodbye to all that, good and bad. This was how it was then, I could well imagine how it had been in the very early days of Sir Stamford Raffles. A time when tigers roamed the island. No lions though. Never had been. The place got its name after a Sumatran Prince encountered what he *thought* was a lion. He was probably leaving the pub after a heavy night. Lucky him, I saw much stranger things than lions when in that state. You see, the way I had it figured, the bedtime drink was absolutely essential in the tropics. Yes, I often started very early, I realize, but by the time I'd finished it would be bedtime, wouldn't it? Anyway, my point is, the drink helped me sleep.

So, goodbye Singapore, hello Malaya, a place I'd longed to visit ever since I'd been based in the area, looked across at it every day. I had travelled the length of the peninsular by train - on my way to Penang, on leave - but that was different. Apart from jungle, and the occasional kampong, all I managed a glimpse of were the domes and minarets of Kuala Lumpur, of which - being a predominantly Muslim city - there appeared to be an abundance. In fact the most spectacular were those of the city's Moorish-style railway station, at which we made a brief halt, en-route to the north.

Our train wasn't even ambushed, as they were occasionally subject to, the very reason we were obliged to travel fully armed, weapons actually loaded this time. It was the first time in my service career that I was issued a rifle where the intent was that I use it to shoot someone, should that become necessary. I don't even recall there being any restrictions as to rules of engagement. If the train was attacked we went into action (or out of it, whatever the case may be). The thing to remember was that not only would I be held responsible for the return of the weapon, but I must also account for every round, whether used or not (ie, if it came to a firefight, there'd be a need to scrabble around and recover the empty cases. Naturally, they didn't hold you to this were you not to survive. Not too clever an option, that). Trains were an easy target, for the only line ran all the way up the west coast, passing through the fringes of the jungle. Little did I suspect that one day soon I would be able to study that jungle in extremely close detail. As well it didn't happen on that journey (even if I did secretly wish for it to), I could well imagine the confusion and chaos that would have reigned if it had.

England it certainly wasn't. In fact, out here, England was best forgotten. I didn't like to think about it. Cold and snowy, rather than hot and humid; roast beef and Yorkshires', as opposed to those curried eggs and chapattis. No, it didn't pay to think of England. That was some place far away across the sea. A place from which you occasionally received a letter. Or, to which you sent one.

So, it was to be goodbye Singapore, hello Malaya.

Hey! Hang on a minute! Didn't I say people were being shot up there?

* *

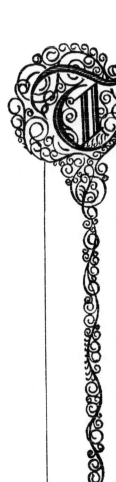

THE PRESERVATION OF MAN

THE horse and mule live thirty years,
And nothing know of wines and beers.
The goat and sheep at twenty die
With never a taste of scotch or rye.
The cow drinks water by the ton
And at 18 is mostly done.
The dog at 16 cashes in
Without the aid of rum or gin.
The cat in milk and water soaks
And then in 12 short years it croaks.
The modest, sober, bone dry hen
Lays eggs for nogs, then dies at 10.
All animals are strictly dry
They sinless live and swiftly die.
But sinful, ginful, rum-soaked men
Survive for three score years and ten
And some of us, the mighty few,
Stay pickled till we're 92.

With Compliments of

Chapter Six
UP COUNTRY WITH 155

𝕬 quick look at a map of the Far East showed me that mainland Malaya was that dragon's-head-like peninsula that appears about to devour the island State of Singapore. Not that I was unfamiliar with the geography of the area, just felt I should refresh my mind. Malaya is, in fact, that area referred to by service personnel in Singapore as "up country".

In my case, "up country" was a reference to the airfield associated with the capital city, Kuala Lumpur; commonly referred to as KL. KL is located on the western side of the peninsular, as were the majority of towns and cities in Malaya. There were one or two in the east, but these were accessible only from down south, or by air. There were few cross country roads back then, and, having ridden it, I was already aware that the railway traversed only the west coast. Almost the entire central region, from the Thai border down to the south of KL, was covered by a vast, mountainous green jungle, known colloquially as "The Ulu." To me, KL itself looked to me like the ideal vacation spot. I was soon to learn otherwise. 'Be advised, lad,' a grizzled Regiment sergeant told me, 'this is the front line. The terrorists infest that jungle, not to mention snakes and wild animals. On top of which you've got aborigines, armed with blowpipes from which they fire poison-tipped darts.'

As far as the terrorist threat went, the proof was all around me. Just eight miles due north of the city, in the hills, are located Batu Caves; a Hindu shrine that was especially relevant during the festival known as Thaipusam. But at the time even this area was still declared to be "Black"; evidence that Chin Peng and his boys were that close to the capital city.

As seemed often the case in Southeast Asia, come the end of the Second World War, the communist-inspired guerilla bands who had fought against the Japanese - with weapons supplied by their allies (in this case, the British) - did not always have the allies interests at heart. Their idea was that, with the cessation of hostilities, they would take over the country for themselves, even though few of the leaders were nationals. With this in mind, here in Malaya, Chin Peng had secreted away countless stores of weapons. He'd also had his followers indoctrinate the populace in the ways of communism. And they were now well familiar with that jungle.

Separating towns and jungle were the rubber plantations, vital to the country's economy in the days before synthetics. Just such a place was that in which the trouble began: Sungai Siput. Barely warranting a name on the map, this innocent isolated outpost was deemed ideal for a communist incursion, with three expatriate plantation managers being slaughtered. This all happened long before I arrived in the area, the conflict by then in it's eighth year.

I was flown up to KL courtesy of the Royal New Zealand Air Force, in one of 41 squadron's boxy-looking Bristol Freighters. Not exactly first class, but what military aircraft is? (The answer would become evident a couple of years hence. One of them was also built by Bristol; a sort of scaled down Brabazon.) That the Freighter was known to its crews as the Vibrator, or Frightener, says it all, but at least it got me safely to my destination.

The RAF base at KL was also the civil airport, or vice versa, the single runway shared with international traffic: BOAC - Comet 4, Malayan Airways - DC3 and Viscount, and Cathay Pacific - Douglas's varied piston-engined range, and the Electra, vying for space with Air Forces of the UK, New Zealand, Australia, and the fledgling air arm of the host country. It was also where I saw my first 707, by Boeing, Qantas making a low pass on a delivery flight. With such an amount activity taking place it would be embarrassing should the runway be rendered *hors de combat*, even for a short time: which is where Murphy once more came into play.

The noise carried clearly to the squadron crewroom. It sounded like someone had loaded the cutlery into the spin-dryer in mistake for the dish-washer. Rushing outside I saw an RAF DC3 voice aircraft sliding ignominiously along the runway on its belly, sparks flying, emergency crews arriving on scene even as it ground to a fiery halt - by which time you could colour the aircrew gone! It turned out to be another case of the taking-off-without-first-removing-the-control-locks syndrome. Remember that? Someone obviously hadn't, which resulted in that runway being closed for a time. What made things considerably worse, at least from the Air Force's point of view, was the fact of that aircraft being one of a kind. It was fitted with recording equipment and high-powered amplifiers, with equally high-powered speakers hanging from beneath the wings. At least, they had been! The job of this aircraft had been for it to fly over the jungle, broadcasting messages to the terrorists, and dropping leaflets advising them as to the benefits on offer should they surrender.

There had been an earlier incident involving this aircraft, when it was found the recording had inadvertently been erased. Rather embarrassing, that. Or had proved to be, for the Malay radio operator. Now the flights had been permanently erased, for there wasn't a replacement DC3 available.

So this was KL, the place at which I joined number 155 squadron.

Quite a change from the Spitfires the squadron had flown during World War Two, Westland's Whirlwind Mk4 was the aircraft which would provide me with a new and vastly different experience of flight; rotary, as opposed to fixed wing. A quantum leap, one might say. Vertical take off, hover, sideways and rearward flight. Almost a new language, too: Casevac - for casualty evacuation, and Fort Express, with which I was later to become familiar. And how about Lima Zulu - landing zone: a temporary clearing hacked out of the jungle at a convenient location, for as well as suiting the enemy, this place was ideally suited for helicopter operations, the type making an immeasurable contribution to the communists' eventual defeat.

Other talk related to pull-off checks (not what you might at first think!), the ground cushion, translational lift effect, and blade tracking. There were droop stops, a collective control (the up and down stick), and a cyclic control (the back, forwards, and sideways thingy), and the tail end was fitted with an anti-torque device: something that resembled whirly hair trimmer.

I'd expected it to be different, and was it ever. This was military helicopter flying in its infancy, at least as far as the British forces were concerned. The Whirlwind Mk4 was a far cry from the relatively safe, computer-assisted, turbine-powered, clutch-less machines of the eighties and nineties, and the potential for an incident was never too far distant. But we didn't allow such thoughts free rein at the time, couldn't afford to. Besides, comparisons between era are only possible with hindsight, the dangers only then becoming obvious. Anyway, we were full of ourselves, had very good pilots who practised incessantly. Sometimes, on the way back from a day's operations I would be asked to switch off the hydraulics to the flying controls, so my pilot could get used to the feel of it, in case of a failure. Looked like hard work to me, and it apparently was.

'Much like losing the power steering on a car,' Taff told me, 'but a necessity here, rather than an added luxury. Five minutes is about my limit,' he said.

There'd be practice autorotations, too: power off, collective to zero; the procedure to be followed in the event of an engine failure, or should the tail rotor drive shear. (That anti-torque device: no power, no torque to correct for.) Autorotation allowed the rotor to freewheel, which - much like the fruit of the Sycamore tree - provided for a reasonably gentle, fairly controllable descent. Just like riding a big, Big Dipper. I got used to those, quite enjoyed them in fact, which was to stand me in good stead in later life.

Maybe ours were a special breed of pilot, for they certainly instilled confidence, and I never once felt anything but at ease when flying with any of them.

But incidents there were, aplenty. In fact I recall Pete, an egotistic crewman if ever there was one, becoming rather disgruntled by the fact that he was one of the few who hadn't yet been involved in anything untoward! Well, neither had I. Nor did I want to be. I was sane and selfish enough to wish my share upon someone else, he was welcome to them. Still, takes all types, as they say. And, merry gathering that we were, we were certainly no different when it came to the matter of varying personalities.

Pete (or Lofty, as he was known. Not so much for his ego as his size), must have been away the day the recruitment branch came to take publicity photographs, for he, no doubt, would have leapt at this chance of fame and glory.

What was called for was a shot that could have been entitled "inspecting the tail-rotor gearbox", though for some reason there seemed to be a distinct shortage of volunteers to fill the role of inspector. Then Fred had a bright idea.

'What about whatisname?' he suggested. "Whatisname" being an airman - who shall remain nameless - who had taken to drink; this a result of the Dear John he'd recently received. Unfortunate, that, for he was one of the rare breed that were unable to take more than about half a pint before reaching the "absolutely legless" stage.

'Brilliant,' replied Cheify Henderson, an ex Dambusters flight engineer. 'Go get him. And make sure he's in a fit state to do the job,' he added, a twinkle in his eye.

Problem solved. "Whatisname" was so plastered they just draped him over the tailboom and took their pictures, confident in the knowledge he wouldn't be going anywhere in a hurry.

This guy's drunken escapades also bought him into constant conflict with the "Snowdrops" (the RAF arm of the Military Police, so-called because of their white cap covers, and the white webbing they wore). So, to prevent him going downtown and getting into trouble, his friends would buy him a pint in the NAAFI, then put him to bed. Even so, he escaped often enough to become well known amongst the local community. So well known, the local taxi drivers took to carrying him back to camp in the boot of the car, so as to keep him from being apprehended at the gate.

*

We were operating at the front line in the 'Emergency' - Malaya 1948-60 - and aircraft operating away from base required the services of a crewman - ordinarily the domain of fitter (engines), or rigger (airframes), at least as far as official policy was concerned. But I was determined not to be excluded. I learned quickly in those days, soon acquired sufficient knowledge to enable me to carry out the necessary duties: ie, I could refuel and inspect the aircraft, knew basically where to kick and tap when a problem occurred. (Throw away the manual, old chap, use your initiative. Especially out in the bush.) For instance, the starter motor developed a habit of not always engaging, the cure for which required the clamshell doors - which formed the aircraft's nose - to be opened, allowing access to a little toggle on the starter itself. A tweak on this usually cleared the problem, but in certain cases it could create another. As happened the time a Flying Officer, transit pilot, was ferrying an aircraft down to Singapore, with an officer of Air rank as his co-pilot passenger. They'd stopped off en-route, to refuel on the village green at some out of the way place. Oh-oh! An ideal time for our old enemy, Murphy, to strike. He always seemed to be hanging around backstage, awaiting just such an opportunity.

'Not again,' wailed to FO, as the starter failed to engage. 'A common occurrence, sir, unfortunately,' he explained.

'So what is the procedure now? asked the Air Commodore.

'Well, sir, being as we don't have a crewman on board, one of us needs to tweak the thing whilst the other initiates the start up. I wonder if you'd mind doing the tweaking, sir?'

'Point me in the right direction,' says the senior officer.

This was done, but with the result being a marked lack of success, they decided to trade places. The Air Com would climb back into the cockpit, the F.O. would do the tweaking.

Success at last, but success that was to swiftly translate into failure. The starter engaged all right, and the engine fired, but unfortunately, "Sir" had the throttle wide open. Engine revs rose in rapid response, the clutch made a snatch engagement, the rotor suddenly turned. In this situation, the weights in the sagging blade tips tend initially to droop even further, rather than lifting the blades, which can result in damage to the tail-boom, across the top of which runs the tail rotor driveshaft. Which, as dictated by Murphy, is exactly what did happen. Oops! Chop, chop, no drive to the tail rotor, a damaged boom. And guess who took the blame for that little lot? A clue: it wasn't anyone of Air rank.

But I could handle that. More importantly, I could safely climb into the cockpit once the rotor was turning; an essential attribute. Use your head, don't loose it, could get messy! Yet that too did happen.

It was November 1958, and somewhere west of Tanah Rata, in the Cameron Highlands, the jungle was about to be filled with drama of a different kind.

A Sycamore (XL822) of 194 squadron was on detachment at Ipoh, when a casevac flight was called for. The incident took place on the return trip. Flying the aircraft was Master Pilot "Nobby" Clarke - an aviator renowned for his nicotine intake. In fact Nobby's navigation was said to be related to the number of cigarettes it took for a particular trip (he'd use the Verey pistol outlet as an ashtray/extractor). Along with him were his crewman - fairly new to the job - with a mental patient in a straight-jacket cast in the role of casualty.

'I experienced sudden engine failure,' Nobby later told me, 'so I set it up to autorotate, selecting a nearby river as my target, the only clear area to be seen. But it turned out to be a white-water rapid, didn't it, filled with huge boulders. This called for a last minute change of plan. No option of overshooting and going round again, in autorotate you pick your spot and aim for it, and here was I, collective in the fully up "help me Jesus" position. Nothing for it but a quick jink on the cyclic, which had us ending up in a nearby bamboo thicket, scything down a hundred Sunday Times editions worth of unprocessed newsprint. The blades shattered, naturally, being made of wood, but before the remnants had ceased rotating, myself busy shutting down, the crewman was halfway out of the door, being struck on the head in the process. Despite wearing a helmet, that was him unconscious. There was mention of the helmet not being a good fit, or of it not being fastened correctly, though that was probably irrelevant. Let's face it, Dave, a bone-dome is scant protection against a blade hitting it at any kind of speed.

'I had managed to get off a distress call, but with darkness encroaching I found myself to be deep in the sh... er... bandit country, with only a nutter and an unresponsive crewman for company. Tell you what, though, that patient made an amazingly swift return to the realms of the sane, upon being offered his release.

'This conditional upon you helping me tend the crewman,' I told him.

'OK,' the guy replied. 'But first you must give me back my gun. It's packed away with the rest of my kit.'

'Well, I balked at that idea, didn't I, but then I thought about it. I definitely needed help, so went ahead anyway.'

(No wonder Nobby was a fully paid up member of cancer incorporated. This incident apart, he was also one of the few pilots to have survived the runaway-tailplane-actuator-syndrome; a problem endemic to the early mark of Canberra bomber.)

Unbeknown to Nobby the eighth cavalry were on the way (the seventh were wiped out at Little Bighorn, if I memory serves me), and another Sycamore was already airborne, in search of them. This second aircraft was eventually forced to depart the area before locating the wreck, due to the same darkness which was encroaching upon Nobby and Co. It diverted to Fort Brooke, spending the night there. The third and final

Sycamore of their detachment did manage to land a medical team - doctor plus one - in a nearby clearing (nearby as the crow - or helicopter - flies, that is). But as this coincided with the very moment darkness finally descended (yes, the very same), the arrangement was that the pilot would allow them fifteen minutes, after which, if no word was received, he also would retire to Fort Brooke, returning at first light.

Retire he did. Very daring too, it seemed.

'I was new to the Sycamore,' the pilot later said. 'In fact I had never flown any helicopter in the dark, so most of my time seemed to be spent hunting down the switches for the cockpit lighting. And when I found them, the lights were so dazzling I felt I'd be better off without. Only I realized I needed to keep an eye on the rotor rpm! But it did ensure my eyes were well tuned for the landing at Brooke. They'd positioned the bloody Land-Rover so that the headlights shone straight into my eyes, rather than away from the direction of approach!'

Meanwhile, back on centre stage, the doctor had managed to break an ankle - his own. A bit careless to say the least, but it was that kind of country. Still, he didn't have far to travel for medical advice, didn't need worry about bedside manner, and there were no prescriptions to scribble out.

They were all found the next day, brought out, including, after a time, the aircraft, which was eventually repaired and returned to squadron service.

'No such luck for the poor old crewman,' Nobby told me. 'He succumbed overnight.'

So, could I handle that kind of emergency, if necessary? Well, who knows for sure until it happens? But I was confident. On top of which, I could rough it with the best of them during night-stops in the field.

All it required now was a course in jungle survival at the school located part way up Fraser's Hill, on the peak of which was a leave centre. The fresh, cool air up there called for a log fire in the evening, but it was hot and sweaty enough during the day's activities. They possessed all the key ingredients to make it so: heat and humidity, secondary jungle, mud and slime, deadly snakes and such.

'A supply-drop parachute makes a fine bed, and forget about trying to swat the mosquitoes, next morning they're so bloated they're grounded.' That was the kind of advice we were given. I found it to be true enough.

Splat!

'Hey! Check the size of him. That red blotch on the wall used to be my blood.'

'Look, don't worry, Dave, we have ten to twelve pints of the stuff.

Enough to provide Dracula with a three course lunch, never mind the odd mossie.'

'What about Malaria?'

'Never heard tell of anyone being so afflicted. Cast it from mind. Enough to worry about already without piling on the agony.'

I must have performed well enough, for I was issued a set of jungle green: shirt, trousers, boots, and the vital floppy hat, the means by which those in ambush differentiated between the good guys and the bad. Along with the kit came a commando-type dagger, handy when refuelling in the field from five gallon cans (known as flimsies). A quick stab and a deft flick of the wrist had the seal removed, another stab in the opposing corner so as to allow a steady flow. Refuel through a chamois filter, fling the empty well clear, providing the rotor wasn't already turning. Notorious for sucking loose debris into the disc, a helicopter. The downwash would blow loose items out and up, where they'd be drawn in from above.

I was also awarded RAF form 1767 - Aircrew Flying Log-book. Bureaucratic English, that. I flew of course, the log-book remained safely back at base. The only thing I missed out on was the meagre flying pay awarded to official crewmen, but that didn't bother me at all. A minor sacrifice for the honour of occupying the left-hand seat: in fixed wing terms, the captain's position.

For some reason - the true facts about which appear to have disappeared in the mists of time - the captain of a helicopter sits on the right. Something to do with airfields having left-hand circuits, so one story goes. The apparent thinking behind this was that it would separate the helicopter circuit (slow) from the fixed wing circuit (fast) thus avoiding confusion between conflicting traffic. But there are other versions as to the reason, one of which is said to originate in the States. This has the very first rotary wing instructor (Les Morris, of Sikorsky) taking the left-hand seat, as on a fixed wing type, thus putting the pupil on the right, where, upon qualifying - having become used to the position and not now wishing to reverse his control orientation - he remained. Sounds feasible. Especially if you consider the cabin door - thus winch - were usually to starboard, therefore a pilot seated on the right would be better positioned to keep an eye on things. Then there's the idea it was purely to facilitate exit in the event of an emergency, it being easier to exit from the right due to the positioning of the collective control. Myself, I favour the American version, as vacating the cockpit with the collective raised - when it would impede exit - hints of abandoning ship with the rotor still turning! Ask any helicopter pilot the reason and you'll get any amount of conflicting ideas, though most never seem to have spared it a thought, have no idea whatsoever.

Anyway, the left was where I now sat, making me feel even more like someone out of a Biggles novel. An up to date version this time, what with my bone-dome and throat-mike, plus newly-cultivated moustache (which wasn't destined to survive for long; made me look old when I was still very young. Anyway, Biggles didn't have a moustache). One more thing, the cockpit - no matter on which side one was seated - was a far better option than the cabin, for believe me, nobody flew first class in an S55, either, Royals apart. The interior wasn't just spartan, it was bare. Anti-corrosion coated aluminium skin and stringers, ribbed and skeletal; none of your fancy airliner panelling here. Even the seats, when fitted, were basically... er... well, basic. Sound proofing? Forget it. Those quilted covers appeared to be more decorative rather than of any practical value. Though they did prevent *some* of the gearbox oil from dripping onto the passengers. The floor consisted of a plywood sheet, to help spread the load, and prevent wayward bayonets and suchlike from penetrating the aluminium skin, beneath which were located the fuel tanks.

Because of the hostile environment in which our helicopters operated, we carried a wealth of firepower: one pistol - pilot, for the use of - one M1 carbine, crewman, ditto. A little short of what would be required to start World War Three, but that was never the intention. All that was needed was for us to protect the aircraft, and ourselves. Not exactly the *creme de la creme* in the hardware stakes, neither were they the best weapons for the job. But all that was to change. After assessment of our ability on the firing range, the rifle was replaced by a lightweight machine-gun, with two magazines, taped together back to back, just like in the movies. The assumption, one supposes, that so armed we may stand a chance of hitting something. At least we could look and sound the part.

Although I was by now quite adept with a rifle, at a target - that ATC and Boy Entrant training finally paying off - it would probably be a far different matter when faced with the reality of another human. Someone who meant business, who was able, and willing, to return fire. Well, I now had a serious weapon in my hands. One that could possibly reassign the odds in my favour. Basically, just point and let fly. It was a thought that only needed a hook on which to hang it. A hook that was readily supplied by a subconscious which appeared to be of the reckless type. A subconscious which seemed continually to seek adventure, not caring a damn what happened to the body it served. An instant and imagination ran riot. In my mind's eye I could see it clearly, the way it *might* happen.

A couple of guys charging out of the jungle, myself engaged with the refuelling, George - the human pilot - still strapped in the cockpit, controlling things from on high, finding himself not to be in a position that enabled him to make a fast draw. Restrictions of harness and space resulting in his pistol being pointed at a vulnerable part of his anatomy, its removal dictating a need for much care, therefore time. Sid James rather than Jesse James.

No matter, help was at hand.

Now I don't go around advocating violence and such, but that wasn't the Salvation Army out there, not dressed the way they were: clothing that gave the appearance of having been designed in such centres of haute couture as Moscow, Peking, or Ulan Bator. No, it was fairly obvious these buggers weren't here to carry out a sociological study on the travelling public. With this in mind - plus the thought that, as crewman, protection of the aircraft was one of my functions - I'd immediately hurl the fuel can aside and, aided by the reflexes of youth - instinctive, faster than thought itself - I'd swiftly snatch up the Sten. In a twinkling, with all the dexterity of a yet to be discovered Schwarzenegger, I'd quickly cock the weapon, flick off the safety, and hose the area down. (I saw myself as having come a long way since those early days at Cosford.)

'It's OK, sir,' I imagined myself shouting above the racket. 'All under control.' And so it would be, at least in my head. Chackka... chackka... chackka - though faster than you could say the words - flora, fauna,

and terrorists, disintegrated in a hail of lead as the air was filled with the

120

sharp tang of cordite.

'Take that you commie bastards. Teach you to mess with One Five Five.' Blowing smoke from the barrel I'd then calmly switch to the fresh magazine, make the weapon safe, placing it within easy reach. After which I imagined myself carrying on with the task of refuelling, whistling away merrily, with not a care in the world. An extraordinary act of heroism against an insidious and determined foe. That, I imagined, would surely earn me a medal. At least a Mention in Dispatches. Well, are we not all allowed our one moment of glory?

It never happened, of course. Luckily, I suppose, for - recalling my schooldays, my bicycle, my pitiful efforts at the late-late braking technique, the ensuing pile-up - I suspect no one would have had much to fear, with the possible exception of the flora and fauna. Hell! Maybe even, George. Not good for pilot-crewman relations, that. And how would it look on my resume? Doubt it would qualify me for a lawful job. That apart, how then would I get home? Occupation of the left-hand seat did not magically engender one with the necessary skills required to fly the thing, though we were allowed plenty of practice. I harboured few doubts about my ability to keep the thing in the air, once it was up there chugging along merrily, not too difficult, that. *Getting* it up, then putting it down again was where problems were likely to occur. Well, maybe not so much the putting down bit, provided Her Majesty was prepared to strike thousands of pounds worth of aircraft off charge.

One MiD was "allocated" to the squadron during this period. Not that any of us had done anything say, "above and beyond the call of duty", as it were. There again, maybe we all had. Well, most of us. Anyway, the decision was made to put the names of all squadron personnel into a hat, but by some quirk of service life the "draw" was won by the admin clerk. Still, he was a good friend of mine, so maybe I qualified by association.

Pete, MiD, was also the person responsible for my future addiction to the sport of motor racing. His enthusiasm, augmented by the discovery that these machines also operated close to, and occasionally beyond, the limits, ensured my immediate interest. Besides, as he pointed out, those fellows, Moss and Hawthorn, did seem to be doing quite well. Apart from which, they were Brits, in there among the foreigners, showing them how it should be done. At least Moss was. Until recently, Hawthorn had been.

*

A trip to the Cameron Highlands showed me another face of this diverse country. Were it not for tea plantations and the sun I could have been back home in England. Cottage, and village green type place. This hill resort was located one hundred and forty miles to the north of KL, at an altitude of six thousand five hundred feet, where the air was cool. It was also an area of dense trees, and waterfalls, the hills - a profusion of wildflowers - were alive with beautiful butterflies. It was yet another resort area which didn't seem at all hostile - especially when, in the evening's dying light, you saw the plantation managers relaxing on their verandas, gins and tonic to hand - but the bandits were out there all right, not too far away. Waiting, no doubt with malice aforethought.

Mention of hostile environment brings to mind our odd forays into KL itself, for as far as I was concerned, this was where the real danger lay. The capital played host to diverse regiments of not only the British Forces, but those of other members of the Commonwealth as well, some of them apparently expert in the field of unarmed combat. And like all experts it seemed one needed to continually practise the art so as to remain on top of things. This they certainly did. All too often. Usually in the various bars and clubs dotted around the area - Juke boxes firmly secured and caged, so as to prevent improper use. The troops were just honing their skills, as it were, upon one another. Indeed, one was left with the impression their skills were in dire need of a honing, so enthusiastically did they become embroiled. Only natural really. These guys had been trained this way, aggression was now part of their make up, although the fact didn't seem to be taken into account by the authorities when arrests were made. I witnessed action aplenty on that front, but during my twenty-one month spell with the squadron the only terrorists to cross my path were either as dead as a Monty Python parrot, or prisoners. I did see a lot of jungle though.

We flew into small strips and clearings hacked out of the wilderness. Many of these were located in mountainous regions, accessible only to the Pioneer and its larger, twin-engined brother, or by helicopter, with a limited load, as I was to find.

I figured we were well short of our destination, one of the forts - way up in the mountains - yet here we were, descending. I looked across at George, the question clearly etched upon my face.

'Can't make it, Dave. Not with a full load. At this altitude the engine can't handle it. Going to have to dump you, make a couple trips.'

So, down we went, out I got, taking part of the freight with me. It looked a decidedly lonely spot. A small clearing, with only the jungle for company.

'Forty minutes,' George assured me, before departing. 'Then I'll be back.'

I waved him off, then watched as my helicopter climbed away, to disappear in the distance, a dot that became gradually smaller and quieter, until it finally vanished altogether. Then the silence closed in. It seemed like a total silence, almost eerily quiet now that helicopter was gone. I was on my tod (from the rhyming slang, on one's Tod Sloane - own), twiddling my thumbs, out in the middle of hostile territory. At least I hoped I was alone. And if not? Well I did have the trusty Sten at my side, cocked and ready. I also had death on my mind. The only question to be answered: whose? Still, nowhere is it written that if you play safe and hide you will live to be a hundred and die happy.

George had his ETA figured pretty close, I knew because I'd been checking my watch, rather frequently as it happens. Thirty-five minutes and forty-two seconds had ticked away before I picked up the familiar sound of a Pratt and Whitney Wasp, of blades slapping the air, the signal that my whirlybird was on the way back. Then there it was, a fairy godmother, curving in over the trees, preparing to land. Relief, for I knew then I would soon be on my way. And so I was. Good experience, for it was at times like that I realized just how much we meant to the Army in the field.

There was one time I got rather worried though, the day my machine curved in over the trees trailing smoke. Had me worried for a while there, until it landed, and the rotor brake was found to be not fully released! Didn't really need to look, the air reeked of overheated brake lining. Not a big problem, all had cooled down by the time I'd finished refuelling. Then we were ready to depart once more, my thoughts now on beer, bath, bed.

* *

Chapter Seven
A RABBLE OF BUTTERFLIES

Some of the strips we flew to were attached to forward bases of the Malayan Police Field Force. Known as forts, these bases - a dozen in all - were in reality little more than an armed enclosure set in an isolated jungle clearing. Reminiscent of something out in the Wild West, with but a simple barbed wire fence replacing the log walls. Ineffective at stopping bullets, but it would give flesh and blood pause for thought. From here patrols would head off into the jungle for weeks at a time, carrying with them most of what they needed to survive, being resupplied from the air.

The forts, too, relied on the Air Force for their supplies. Brooke, Betis, Keemar, Shean, and Legap, for starters. Evocative names to those who were there. These names, and others, were to feature regularly on our operations board, especially those without the luxury of a grass strip attached. Often we would visit two or three on an operation spread over two days, spending the night at one or another of them; as in the aforementioned Fort Express. I've often thought it would be nice to know how those forts came to be so-named, what stories lay behind their choice. Where in fact did the names originate? Who were, or had been, these people, or places after which they had been named, what had they done, or been? Never did find out, just assumed them to have been Generals, or State Representatives.

They were interesting places to visit, too, for, upon invitation, a short walk from most forts would take you to a clearing in which would be situated one of the native longhouses.

'A prime reason for the existence of these forts,' I'd been told upon joining our squadron, 'is to protect the aborigines who live nearby. Actually to prevent the communists from subverting them, and from stealing their crops and livestock.' To which one of the squadron pilots had later added a chilling postscript. 'Not for philanthropic reasons is the odd sack of cooked rice left laying around for the terrorists to find. Those bags are rumoured to have been liberally seeded with bamboo slivers, a particularly nasty way to die, so I've heard,' he'd said.

'A bit dirty, isn't it?'

'As they say, fight fire with fire. The terrorists are said to play far dirtier tricks on the Security Forces.' (The name given to the Combined Services operation.)

The longhouse visit was a trip I made often, Pentax in hand.

Built on stilts, one of these bamboo, rattan, and thatch dwellings would be home to a multitude of families, often with no form of interior division. Not that it mattered, bamboo floors are extremely springy; one couple humping and everyone would be bouncing up and down in unison. The floor space would also be shared with the dogs. Pigs and chickens rooted and scratched around in the dirt, ten feet below where I stood. Dust motes and smoke drifted in the air, accented by the shafts of light which poured through gaps in the barely adequate exterior walls.

Such a visit, encompassing as it does a different culture, was like stepping back in time, to visit an ancient world. A blend of remote primate and exotic environment. It was a world of wood fires, and of cooking beneath the sun, and stars. Women would sit around weaving, making things from whatever grew, roamed, or lived close-by. Men fashioned darts for their elaborately-decorated blowpipes, coated them with poison. With these they'd hunt monkey, and deer, which the women would cook in their cast iron pots. They also concocted a fearsome grog, for which, after one sip, I dreamed up all kinds of excuses as to why I had to refuse more. Yeah, that bad! But they seemed to enjoy it. Truth be told, had I been living here rather than just visiting I'd no doubt have become rather partial to it myself.

Basic living, basic comfort, basic dress, it was all they wished for.

Then there was Fort Chabai - located in a remote valley deep in the jungle - where I once elected to spend a week's leave. (Could have gone to Singapore, Hong Kong, Bangkok, almost anywhere in the Far East really, but I chose Chabai. Today it would be no contest. There again, today I'm no longer in jungle-bashing shape, back then I was. And had I not taken advantage of the opportunity I could well imagine the result: a nagging thought, forever wondering what I'd missed. No problems now; been there, done that, as they say. All the other places as well.)

But that Chabai break really was novel. It seemed like a different country out there, away from the cities and towns: KL, Ipoh, Penang. It was different of course, this was the "Ulu". Nature in the raw. Mountainous, primary and secondary jungle. Absolute peace on earth, so long as you omit the occasional mindless foray during which we discharged a multitude of weaponry on the make-shift range.

'Got something here for you to try, Dave,' the Malay commander said one morning. 'Anti-personnel, semi-automatic shotgun. A fearsome tool, this.'

True enough I found. It really could devastate the greenery - and, one imagines, anyone or thing lurking within - with impunity. All it required was to be pointed in the general direction of a threat and fired. Not that different from my first encounter with a really serious weapon, in point of fact. A sparrow decimation exercise, if I recall the facts correctly.

It was one day after school, long before I joined the ATC. I went home with a friend who lived on a farm. Not the first time I'd been, for he too had also once been declared, my best friend. Ever.

'Ever fired a shotgun?' Mark asked me. I told him, no.

'Never fired a gun of any kind,' I said.

'Fancy a go?'

'If it's OK. I mean, is it allowed?'

'Dad won't mind,' he said, which didn't answer the question but, let's face it, at that age you tend not to question morality too closely, never mind the safety aspect of such a move. So, as there was no one around, borrow it we did.

'Better take a few of these,' Mark suggested, grabbing a handful of cartridges. 'Not exactly borrowing those, they're not going to be returned.' He laughed at that. We then set off across the fields.

Keep your eyes open, Dave. What we need is something upon which to inflict untold damage, preferably something that moves.'

'Loads of cows and sheep,' I said.

'Come on, you silly sod. The demise of one of them is unlikely to pass unnoticed.'

'Guess not,' I giggled. 'Especially if it happens to have a bloody great hole in its flanks.'

'Yeah, right. What we need is vermin of some kind. Something too stupid or trusting to realize the nature of the threat, thus less prone to dash off.'

'Like a hedge filled with twittering sparrows, you mean?' I indicated to just such a target, right there in front of us.

'Get em,' he said. And as it just so happened to be my turn to carry the weapon, I aimed in the general direction and let fly, if you'll forgive the pun.

'Bloody hell! I didn't expect anything like that,' I told him.

'What, the noise and recoil? Yeah, I suppose I should have warned you. Anyway, your aim was good.'

'Not aim exactly,' I told him. 'It just happened to be pointing in the right direction when I pulled a trigger.'

'No matter, you actually hit the hedge.'

And so I had, but whether or not I hit anything else was open to question. Certainly, feathers and leaves flew in abundance, as did a wisp of sparrows, heading for pastures anew, as sparrows will, given the slightest encouragement. Never did find anything they'd left behind. Not so much as a scrap of wing, or any other limb or organ. Not even a trace of blood and gore.

'Yeah, but look, a twelve gauge from five feet? Well, I mean, what else could you expect?' That was Mark's reasoning. And after much discussion it was agreed I could chalk up at least five probables. It was a phrase I recalled being used by the RAF.

Similar then, though this shotgun at Chabai was intended to deal with somewhat larger prey, therefore the size of the shot was somewhat larger, maybe a dozen balls as opposed to a few hundred! Ideal, should a wandering patrol inadvertently stumble upon an ambush situation - though stumbling upon an ambush in the first place would hardly constitute an ideal situation. Could spoil your day, that kind of thing.

*

Outside the area cleared for the camp and its barbed wire perimeter was the oh-so-short airstrip - carved out of a nearby hillside - its length effectively further reduced by lack of a straight-in approach, or exit. One way in and out; no choice being the choice. But at least he'd be going out lighter than when he came in. This was where the Pioneer came into its own, with its low-speed manoeuvrability and STOL characteristics - short-take-off-and-landing, that is - employing as it did such high-lift devices as leading edge slats and Fowler flaps. Quite something to stand and watch, that steep, twisty, terrain avoidance approach, flaps and slats at full stretch, Alvis Leonides snarling defiance. Even more thrilling was the view from inside the cabin, directly behind the pilot, whose eyes were the only form of ground proximity radar fitted to this machine. I'd be perched atop sacks of rice and suchlike, attempting to wedge myself in place, hands grasping whatever there was to grasp. Always bearing in mind the pilot required full and free use of his arms, and the controls. It was another very basic aeroplane that did exactly what it had been designed for, and did it well.

Beyond the strip lay an all-encircling wilderness of untamed jungle. A verdant barrier of flora, limestone cliffs and mountains, along with their associated silence. I say silence, because that's the way it sometimes appears; sounds so natural, serene and comforting, they could often be disregarded. A background of echoey, tropical-rainforest-type music. Nature's nonstop symphony: a cawing, croaking, creaking, buzzing, and whining, with possibly the occasional thought-provoking roar thrown in for good measure.

Meandering around two sides of the camp - and twenty feet below our level - ran nature's contribution to our comfort and well-being: a small river, or large stream. Fast-flowing, self-cleansing, ice-cold. And there is a pureness to be found in the waters of a mountain stream which is apparent nowhere else. This was ideal for washing, drinking, and, when the sun was at its height, a cooling dip.

'An important point,' I'd been told, upon arrival. 'Make sure you wash, drink, and swim upstream of the camp. Downstream is the place to take a crap.'

Days began early out here. Not with the crowing of your common-place cockerel, but to the chattering chorus of gibbons and monkeys, high in the treetops. Dawn itself was six-thirtyish and, being up in the hills, surrounded by mountains, as we were, it was sure to be cold. So, whilst the morning shave may not have been one of mankind's more enjoyable experiences, washing in those waters was certainly guaranteed to either kick-start your heart into life, or to end it prematurely. But the first sight of that river in the early morning was something else again, for the surface would be mirror-like. So calm it appeared to be still rather than flowing, thus enhancing the tranquillity of the place.

I say the days began early, not sunrise, you'll note. It would be three or four hours past dawn before the sun was high enough to smile down and chase the shadows out of our valley. I'd realized it would be something like this, for I'd seen it many times on the way to early morning operations, a helicopter being a much better option from which to view this event.

A sea of wispy cloud-like mist would slide down the tree-covered slopes, to collect in the enclosed valleys below. Lakes of cloud which obscured everything but the mauve, tree-layered peaks which poked their way well clear. Nothing else to be seen from up there, apart from the occasional, yellow-beaked toucan, gliding from one area of high ground to the next.

Here at Chabai the air was so fresh it was almost pure oxygen. Tasted like it too; sweet, untainted, regenerative. And there was something else I'd noticed about the place that made it rather unusual, a total absence of that uniquely-shaped soft drink bottle with which America appeared to have swamped the face of the earth.

Just as the days began early, they ended early too, for in the tropics darkness descends rapidly - around seven thirty in the evening - which is when the jungle bursts into life. Patrols apart, that is. They need to be settled well before then.

With darkness came the incandescent, pulsing glow of the fireflies.

It was a vacation you couldn't possibly buy, although maybe most wouldn't wish to. After all, paradise is a personal thing. In fact, it has been said that paradise is often close by where you live, that we don't recognise it as such until we are no longer there. If for me that meant Yorkshire, with its Dales and Wolds, then I'd possibly agree, but right now I was happy where I was. If not paradise, this was close to perfect tranquillity. Until I once more lost my mind, that is, jumping in with both feet this time. Not the river, you understand.

Infallibility not being within man's scope, I actually volunteered to go on a three day jungle patrol, a situation that could well have been positively unhealthy. Talk about crazy, I mean there were people, and things, out there, intent on doing us harm. I just felt it would be something different, something new. There again, let's face it, so is death; new to everyone, that. A first time, once in a lifetime thing.

It hadn't yet filtered through to my subconscious: the fact I wouldn't have been cleared to take leave in Chabai were it not considered to be reasonably safe. Had I picked a fort that had recently been subjected to an attack, as some of them occasionally were, it wouldn't have been allowed. The thing was, all intended destinations in this theatre had to be officially approved before leave was granted. Getting killed on duty, in the service of your country was one thing, getting killed on leave, apparently a different matter altogether. To start with, given such an eventuality I'd immediately become AWOL, on top of which the amount of paperwork would be horrendous. Not that any of this would be my worry, but it would have been my squadron commander's. There again he hadn't appeared too worried when I'd approached him about it. He'd merely waved a finger around his temple and grinned at me. I'd wondered what he'd meant by that?

But volunteer to go on patrol I had, and now we were on the way, I wished I hadn't. Okay, we were armed, but so were the terrorists. And this was their kind of terrain. They'd had years of experience, knew how to make best use of it. There was something else to consider, too: Death wasn't the be all and end all, there were degrees of discomfort to be endured in the interim. That verdant barrier for starters. It now turned out to be more than just that, it was a barrier in all three dimensions, each apparently filled with malighn intent. We soon found ourselves surrounded by a dense wall of foliage, through which we had to hack our way. By we, I mean the Malay police and their Iban trackers who plunged ahead, machetes flashing and slashing. I tagged along behind. It was OK for the first hour or so, as we followed a well defined track, but then we veered off, into the unknown, it seemed.

'Naturally, we choose the path of least resistance,' Mustafa, the leader, and my self-appointed guide, told me. 'This is a kind of track,'

'Could have fooled me,' I said. 'Well disguised and protected, eh?'

'No, Dave, it's just not used much. Well-used tracks are the very places ambushes are likely to be set.'

Track or not, that jungle was a green hell that fought back. It whipped, slashed, and tore, seemingly totally intent on preventing any forward progress whatsoever. Branches and barbed vines plucked at my clothes like malevolent hands, flicked dangerously near my eyes. My feet churned up the spongy carpet of the forest floor, releasing its musty fungal smell. Rivulets of sweat trickled down my back; or were they the feet of insects on the prowl? Difficult to tell, really. But for the circumstances they could well have been a lover's fingers working their magic, the feeling was similar, the reaction entirely the opposite. Nor was there any chance of disregarding the sounds when you were in there among them. Sounds which now took on a more eerie quality rather than serene and comforting. Not just the cicadas and bullfrogs, or the whine of a mosquito, for they were always around, even back in the city. Out here there were new sounds to consider: the screech of a monkey, the shrill cry of a bird - echoing - even the roar of a tiger - distant and receding. Mustafa identified them all for me as we moved on. Occasionally he'd suddenly stop, hold up a hand, motioning me to freeze. Pointing to a bush, he'd whisper a name, "Lesser-spotted gol-gol", or whatever. I'd look, see nothing but still leaves, the bird splendidly camouflaged by splotches of shadow. Then, movement would catch my eye and it was gone. I was lucky if I managed to snatch a brief glimpse. Ah, well, so much for the gol-gol. By now I was almost ready to give up, too tired to talk.

'Nothing to fear here,' Mustafa said, 'normal sounds. Those we welcome. It's a silent jungle that spells danger. Nature quietened by a human presence,' he continued. 'Then is the time to stop and exercise care, create a matching silence, listen for that tell-tale crack of a branch being stepped on by a carelessly placed foot, the muffled curse, or a negligent cough. They're the kind of sounds that indicate the presence of unwelcome attention.'

He seemed to have surplus energy, Mustafa, I could have used some. Real jungle-bashing, this, to me. Cue in the haunting refrain and subtitles if you like, but beware of airborne teeth. The fauna had come out to play.

*

The sun's light didn't penetrate too well down here - trees over a hundred feet tall (that third dimension), and the almost impenetrable canopy they formed, saw to that - but its effects did, as did the frequently heavy rain.

'Probably the reason it is known as rain forest, eh?' Mustafa quipped, in reply to my muttered curse as I almost went down.

The ground was wet and slippery, the air as still as a dead man's breath. It was hot and humid. Rather like being fully dressed, trapped in a sauna; a thought that had me longing for a dip in that ice-cold stream back at the fort. Wouldn't even bother to undress first. Wouldn't have mattered anyway, I was already wet through, would remain so until it was time for bed.

'Always keep a dry set of clothing to sleep in,' I'd been told at the pre departure briefing. 'Next morning it's back into the damp set.'

'Be a bit chilly, won't it?'

'At first, but they'll soon warm up. Keep the dry set on if you like, but they won't remain that way for long, then you'll have nothing to sleep in.'

Dark thoughts flooded my mind as I tramped along mechanically beneath the shrouding green canopy. Things occasionally squished and crunched beneath my feet. I didn't look, didn't wish to know. We'd only been underway three or four hours, even if it did feel more like a month. Out here, time, days of the week, they were irrelevant.

I was sweat-stained and weary already, facing the stigma of looking defeat in the eye. A situation that was unlikely to improve in the near future. Possibly the distant future, as well, for we appeared to be advancing with all the speed of a badly crippled snail. The men at point, machetes flashing, were by now having to hack a path through almost virgin bush. Sweat trickled down my cheeks, or were they tears?

But I couldn't quit now, be worse off if I did: no one to take me back, sure to get lost on my own. I thought briefly about how that would sound back at the camp. 'Took this Air Force type on patrol with us but he couldn't hack it, decided to return to base on his own. Never saw him again.' And wouldn't that merit a barrelful of laughs down at the Pig and Whistle? Not from me, mind. Given that scenario coming to pass, by then I'd probably be dead.

Oh that one of our helicopters would make an unexpected appearance; a quick, passing thought. But even had that happened I knew it would depart without me, for there was also ego at stake here. Some of these guys were smaller than me, much older, yet they were carrying twice the gear I was - mine as well as their own - making out quite nicely, thank you. Or so they made it seem. No, best to face facts: the aching tiredness, the sweat, the pain, all had to be endured, they would last but days. Failure to carry this through would haunt me for the rest of my life.

So I pushed the dark thoughts to the back of my mind, silently cursed to myself - along with the rest of them, I was sure - and carried on. It did seem to get easier with time, though time itself was definitely dragging. And despite the fact my pack only weighed probably a meagre twenty pounds, compared to the fifty or sixty the rest carried, it definitely contained enough momentum to bring me crashing down more than once.

By the use of hand signals, a halt was called every hour or so. A welcome break, I'd at first though. Not so.

'Leeches,' Mustafa explained, peering down the inside of my collar. He had me pull my trouser legs out of my socks, and there they were, sucking away. He used the glowing end of his cigarette to burn them off, the rest of the patrol assisting each other.

'There'll be more,' he told me. 'Buggers get everywhere. Well... almost. We'll have a full clean-up tonight.'

I didn't like the sound of that, but there was no time to think about it, for in came the next assault: mosquitoes in combat formation, peeling off like fighters diving to the attack.

'Big buggers, eh?' Mustafa was grinning. Not a lot seemed to worry him.

'Big? Could have been designed by De Havilland, at Salisbury Hall,' I said. But the humour was lost on him, for I had to explain it.

'What about nets?' I asked, for I knew I didn't have one. And now it was Mustafa's turn with the humour.

'Nets!' he exclaimed, somewhat dramatically. 'Forget em. These guys work in pairs, one lifting a corner, the other dragging you clear.'

I could almost believe it. Come out to play? Wouldn't have surprised me to find this lot had been lined up in columns of three, smacking their lips and presenting arms at the first sound of our approach. (But why did they all seem to target me?) And let us not forget the snakes and tigers that lived hereabouts, they too could do you a lot of no good, too.

*

My heart skipped a beat. I felt fear steal through me. Icy coldness raised the hairs on the back of my neck. There was something up ahead, I just knew it. An ambush? Or maybe it was a tiger on the prowl? Watching? Crouching? Awaiting the moment?

Whatever, I prepared myself for the expected rattle and crash of automatic fire, or of teeth and claws launching into an attack, rancid hot breath on my neck.... No. It couldn't be either. Too much noise from the area's full time residents. Not the aborigines, these were nature's tenants. The odd monkey which gave advance warning of our approach, the brightly-coloured birds which chattered and screeched, complaining of our intrusion into their territory. But by the same token I realized they were sounding the all clear, for it is a lack of noise that normally presages danger, as Mustafa had explained. Even so, I sensed there was something. The feeling was too strong to disregard.

I wasn't wrong. But it turned out to be a threat of another kind.

I don't know what made me look up, other than intuition, but it was as well I did. A black and yellow banded krait was coiled round an overhanging branch. In my mind, poised to drop, wrap itself around me, sink its lethal yellow fangs into throat.

Discretion at such a moment seemed definitely the better part of valour, so, moving quickly enough to secure myself a place in the Olympic squad for whatever, I stepped aside, foiling the assault. I now felt a new sense of awareness, exhilaration almost. Life would go on, of course, I realized that. It's just that, fifteen seconds ago I was certain it would be going on without me. Even so I imagined the agony as the poison attacked my nervous system: spasm, paralysis, death. That's the sequence, so I'm told. Hell, what next?

Breakfast was what. Dawn found me jerking awake in my makeshift bed, beneath a makeshift shelter, both thrown together for me by someone more experienced in these matters. The idea was to get your arse clear of the ground, and to keep as dry as possible. The bed was constructed from two poles and a canvas sheet, the shelter - or basha - fabricated from more poles, ponchos, a plastic sheet and palm frond roof. But it had served well, I'd had a good six hours beneath my mossie-net (Mustafa had been having me on). Despite that, after yesterday's slog I felt like I could use another six. Not that I wasn't fit. There were no undue aches or pains, just a lingering tiredness, a bootful of blisters, and the marks where those leeches had latched on.

So, the imagined ambush, the snake, had only been figments of a departing dream. My foolhardy subconscious up to its usual tricks. But the threats were real enough, as was the pounding in my chest, dreams proving to be as powerful as reality so far as my heart was concerned.

Fortunately, we were due for a supply drop that day as not all the patrol would be returning to the fort with us. The majority would move even deeper into the jungle, where, close to a trail known to be used by the guerillas, they would lay in ambush. Whatever the outcome, it was unlikely they would return to Chabai within the week.

So, as preparations were made I relaxed as best I could, used the time to overcome my nightmare, cast aside the images. Plenty of time as it turned out, for we first had to await clearance of the usual early morning mist. It hung from the trees in wispy threads, had about it the look of rotting lace. At least the associated moisture served to curb the activities of tiresome flying pests.

The rising sun completed its task on schedule, almost as if programmed to do so, for even as it cleared we picked up the distant sound of an aircraft approaching; talked to the crew on the patrol's transceiver. They had spotted the smoke from our signal fire, had the general area located. Easy to see when flying over the jungle, smoke; a certain give-away. It was what we kept an eye open for when flying towards an operational area. Forewarned is forearmed.

Now, homing in on the carbide-gas-filled balloon which had been raised above the surrounding treetops to mark our exact position, a Valetta of 52 squadron dropped fresh supplies and other incidentals. An operation which allowed even more time for me to effect a recovery, although I suspected I wouldn't find it so difficult from now on. It was also an operation which left these guys with even more baggage to lug around for, groceries apart, those parachutes had to be recovered back to base. Well, a token number. Most would be reported as being "inadvertently damaged", or "deemed beyond salvage". Soldiers, it seemed, became quite attached to the material from which they were fashioned. The canopy made decent bedding, or was useful for keeping things dry, but the soft nylon cord was especially appreciated. Handy for lashing things together, that. Such things as the bed I'd used last night. And it was highly unlikely a team of accountants would be sent into the Ulu, to investigate the loss of a couple of 'chutes.

At times like this, what with excess baggage and all, I was thankful I'd joined the air force, that these guys held us in some regard. They occasionally had reason to rely on us. A five minute flight could save them a day's walk, less than an hour in the air was equivalent to a week on the ground. So a chopper was appreciated at any time, in an emergency it could mean difference between living and dying.

Then there was the patrol itself. No bloody stroll in the woods, that, bluebells and butterflies kind of thing. Butterflies, yes. Rabbles of them - which, I believe, is the collective noun for butterflies. They were exotic, both large and small. So colourful that, if there was such a thing as a deadly butterfly, these - given nature's propensity to use bright colours as a warning - were clearly prime contenders. As for the blood, of that there was an abundance. An abundant loss, that is. What with mossies and leeches I was surprised to find I didn't need a transfusion upon my return to the outside world. Who needed terrorists on top of that lot?

Anyway, at the time I suppose I was still young enough to think myself invincible. And even if the patrol did turn out to be uneventful on the action front, it certainly wasn't boring. Hard graft is what it had been. Absolutely unbelievable, my volunteering for something like that. OK, to a member of the SAS it would probably have been deemed a stroll, but I wasn't in that class, I was an instrument fitter in the Air Force.

But later, back in the relative safety of civilization, I regarded it as a satisfying, character-building achievement, during which I discovered the limits of my fortitude to be much higher than I'd dared hope. Still, as the saying goes, when the going gets tough, the tough get going. From here on I resolved I would; in the opposite direction. Not tough, me.

Seemed that vacation had been about as close as you could get to serious combat without an actual exchange of fire. Combat conditions in which the action never materialized, apart from in my head. So, there you have it. I never, knowingly, had a shot fired at me, nor did I kill anyone. On top of which, I hadn't *been* killed. Which is not a bad way to end the day, for getting yourself killed happens only once.

The above also holds true with regard to fully developed tigers, I never did see one in the wild. Which is not to say one didn't see me.

I did see a cub, though. It was a guest at Chabai for a time, awaiting transport out. Seems the mother had been shot by an army patrol when they inadvertently stumbled across one another. Both parties possibly a little careless, though the army better equipped for that kind of confrontation. And if they used that anti-ambush shotgun? Well... don't imagine the remains would have made for a decent rug. Regardless, from that point on there'd been no choice. Naturally, with a cub in tow she'd been overly protective. Anyway, it all went to prove the threat was ever present; as was the threat of terrorist attack.

* *

PHOTOGRAPHS-2

Page 137: Top: 50's Singapore: Raffles Hotel.
Bottom: Entrance to the Great World; one of three major recreational areas of this type.

Page 138: Upper left: Sunderland flypast - Labuan. Note clearance between wingtip float & ground, then compare with photo below of aircraft onshore - that is what I call low! (Twin pioneers in background are Borneo Airways.)
Upper right: In-flight meal; Sunderland style cuisine.
Centre left: Sunderland undergoes engine runs after servicing.
Bottom centre: Crew launch alongside.

Page 139: Top left: Seletar: MU, multi-lingual advice.
Top right: Fred, preparing to meet his doom.
Centre right: Sunderlands undergoing second-line servicing.

Page 140: Top: "On the Step" - a Sunderland on the take-off run, front turret now in the flight position.
Bottom: The all-analogue Sunderland cockpit.

Page 141: !8th Entry, Cosford; inst mechs group photo, 1953.

Page 142: 205/209 squadron photo alongside RN270, 1958. The open panel beneath the wing is the port bomb-door. Bombs/depth charges were carried internally, fitted to racks which then ran out on tracks beneath the wing.

Page 143: Top: The steamship *Nevassa*, which was to transport me home at the end of my tour.
Centre: GAL60. The prototype at Brough, 1950.
Bottom: The fully developed, service version of the Beverley, visiting KL.

Page 144: A short break before the trooplift of an Australian regiment at Lasah strip. From left to right, the pilots: Flt Lt's Tom Browning & George Puddy, Sdn Ldr Frank Barnes (the CO), and Flt Lt Deke Bradley. The crewmen: Sam Saunders, Merv Scopes, the author, Fred Macdonald.

WARNING!

DO NOT TOUCH THIS EQUIPMENT
UNLESS YOU KNOW HOW TO USE IT.
THERE ARE HIGH VOLTAGES PRESENT
WHICH ARE DANGEROUS!

請勿亂動!
此處的設備,乃是用高电壓的.

எச்சரிக்கை
அதிக மின்சார சகதி உள்ள கருவி இதின
உபோகிக்க தெரிந்தால......யதொடக்கூடாது அபாயம்!

WARNIN'!

LAY AFF THIS STUFF IF YE DINNA
KEN WHIT YER DAEIN. THUR'S AWFY
HIGH VOL'AGES AROOND WHIT UR
NAE GUID TAE YE!

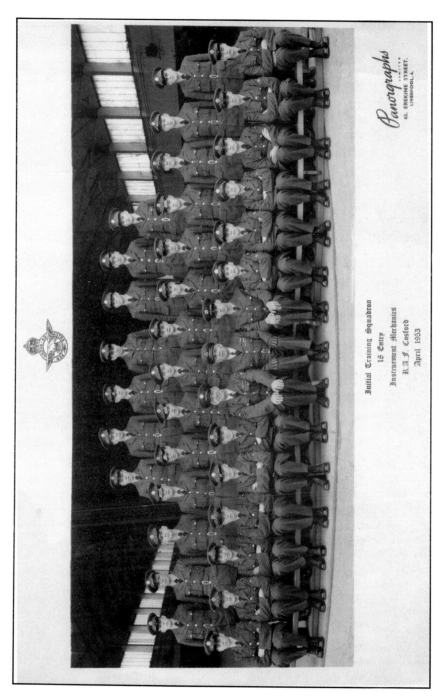

Initial Training Squadron
18 Entry
Instrument Mechanics
R.A.F. Cosford
April 1953

Panographs LIMITED
63, ERSKINE STREET,
LIVERPOOL, 4.

141

BRITISH INDIA S.N.Co's s.s. 'NEVASA' 20,527 tons.

Chapter Eight
ROTARY WINGS, SHIPS, & OTHER THINGS

𝕿 hey did give me a medal, after all. The General Service Medal on its mauve and green ribbon, with clasp: Malaya. It was engraved around the edge; name, rank, serial number. That unique sequence of digits confirmation that this medal was meant for me. Pretty insignificant compared to those passing by the Cenotaph during the Armistice Day parade, admitted, but we all had to start somewhere. Nor am I suggesting it was exclusive, or that I got called to the Palace. It would have been a bit hard on the Queen, that, being as everybody got one, right down to the cooks and admin wallahs safely back in Singapore. No fancy parade even, you more or less drew it from stores, much as you would a new beret or a pair of boots. It just took a little longer, was all. Fill in a form, wait a couple of months, and there it was.

To be doubly sure, I did check with the stores sergeant when I went to pick it up.

'Is there any kind of presentation ceremony, sarge?'

'Sure there is,' he replied, sliding a little white cardboard box across the counter towards me. 'Sign here.' The box was followed by the inevitable form. 'No need to trouble Her Majesty,' he said. And that was it.

As stated, even those back on the island got one. There was no basic requirement actually to set foot in the combat zone, it was enough to survive twenty-four hours in the general theatre of operations. OK, so Singapore had its dangers, too: Happy World, Old World, New World - dance hall, amusement park, sports stadium type places, the accent being on bedroom-type sport, naturally. At least, so I'd been led to believe, would you believe? Hazardous enough in itself, that kind of thing, I allowed, recalling the medical briefing we'd been given upon arrival in area. That aside, even though I saw my part in this limited war as being no more than a grand adventure, for which I was being paid, I always felt I was more deserving of mine. Medal, that is.

Pity the rudimentary stores procedure regarding replacement of boots and beret - or the issuing of medals, come to that - didn't also apply to the issue of aircraft spares. There again, beret and boots had to be paid for, personally, even if they did give us an allowance for such purchases.

With regard to procedure for the issuing of aircraft spares, there was one incident which caused me to question the commitment of personnel stationed in Singapore. It concerned one of our Whirlwinds, at the end of a visit to my old base at Seletar. The aircraft was urgently needed back at KL, but the pre-flight inspection revealed a blade to have been damaged, requiring replacement. Well, that shouldn't pose a problem, the MU was at Seletar, West camp, so they were contacted.

'Yes,' the NCO in charge of aircraft stores confirmed. 'We do have a blade in stock.' And 'Yes,' he would dispatch it to Seletar, East camp - where the aircraft was located. 'Just a moment, though. Isn't 155 squadron based at KL?' he questioned.

'Well, they are, but this aircraft is on detachment, here at Seletar.'

'Ah, but any replacement parts must go via the squadron, otherwise it will take forever to sort out the paperwork. I'll have it dispatched immediately, shouldn't take more than three days.'

'Three days! But this is an AOG situation' (aircraft on ground - the highest priority).

'Which is why I'm dispatching it forthwith.'

The next call stores received, less than ten minutes later, was from the 155 Squadron Commanding Officer, in KL, via the station CO of Seletar. He was said to have issued a curt reminder that this was actually a combat environment (attested to by the award of that medal), and that as, presumably, we were all working for the same Queen, they had better get that aircraft back up to the front line, immediately.

Within thirty minutes the blade had been transported from one side of the camp to the other, direct. A ten minute drive. The aircraft was back in squadron service the next day.

*

During a typical day's operations we'd depart base early in the morning, one, two, sometimes even three aircraft; a positioning flight whilst the sun was still low, the air reasonably cool. But by the time we were ready to begin operations, cool air would be a thing of the past, the sun now well into its arc, and we soon worked up a sweat. We would prepare the aircraft - refuel, yet another check - whilst the pilots briefed the Army commanders in the field. Troops would lay around in the heat of the day in full combat dress, trying to snatch a little rest while the chance was available. If it was some place not too remote the Salvation Army would be on hand with tea and wads. It never ceased to amaze me, the places at which the Sally Ann showed up, and I would forever be thankful to them for that. Even so, the forts were the best places from which to operate. The hospitality of the Malay commanders was legendary in our circles.

Then came time to begin the ferrying. Start up, troops and gear aboard, aircraft away. Depending on altitude and conditions - fuel load, etc - we were capable of carrying between two and six men a trip, though if six, they would need to be lightly loaded Gurkhas. (The goats and hens

146

could follow later.) Oh, and about those SAS guys I thought I'd said goodbye to in Singapore. Wrong. They were here, too. Seemed they were anywhere there was a hint of trouble. Those guys - plus all the gear they somehow managed to lug around - we could only manage two at a time.

The aircraft would return every ten to twenty minutes, ready for another load. (Couldn't drop them too close to their intended destination - especially if it was to be an ambush situation - helicopters were noisy, could be heard a long way off.) No shutting down on the return, either. Troops aboard, refuelling, all done with the rotors whirling. Even though the blades were well clear, the troops would duck their heads, as they had been taught. It's always advisable. Some helicopters are a lot closer to the ground, apart from the fact that it only takes a freak gust of wind to bring a blade down to decapitation levels. No point bucking the odds when the end result could be far worse than a Court Martial.

On and on it went, all day long, with only the odd break to give the aircraft a quick once over. A quick gulp of water, then it started again. Hard work beneath a pitiless sun. And the sun's rays not only beat down from above, they also rebounded off the parched earth, augmenting the effect.

Swirling clouds of dust blown up during lift-off and landing would cake our sweat-damped bodies, for we often worked naked to the waist. And no matter that we turned to face away and protected ourselves, it would still penetrate our eyes, fill our noses and mouths. Not only was it difficult for us, so it was for the pilots. With such short sector times there was not much chance for them to relax, either. Take-off, a short hop, descent into a jungle clearing - hopefully secure - away for another quick turn-around. And so it went, always with the chance of a mechanical problem, or of being shot at, to keep them on their toes.

It was a relief for us all when the aircraft settled for the last time at the day's end. One more service check, refuel, tidy up, then climb up into the cockpit, eight feet off the ground. It would still be hot, sun glaring in through the perspex above and to the sides., and I'd be sweating profusely. But I was always aware of that giant fan above my head. Once that began to turn I knew relief could not be far away. Nor was it. Ten minutes and we were a thousand feet up, and cool. Down below was spread that verdant carpet of jungle, looking peaceful and calm from our viewpoint.

And the troops we had spent all day flying into the interior, into that seemingly peaceful calm, what of them? Ah, yes. What indeed? They'd be tired, dirty, and hungry, as was I. I would be so again, tomorrow, and probably the next day, too. But in between I could look forward to a shower, clean clothes, a decent meal, a beer or two - possibly more - and a soft bed. I also had the advantage of having had a brief insight as to what those soldiers could expect; not a lot in the way of creature comforts, that was for sure. But the majority of them were National Servicemen, had no choice. Should have signed on for ten, lads, joined the RAF.

*

Many hours were logged on the Whirlwind during my time on the squadron, plus - continuing my resolve to fly in whatever to wherever, whenever - odd hours in numerous other types, including Cathay Pacific's, Lockheed Electra. Yes indeed, that one! I was on my way up to Japan, on leave. An interesting trip all round. Malayan Airways DC3 from the island of Penang, to Kuala Lumpur, via Ipoh. The Electra to Saigon and Hong Kong, where I switched to a DC6B for the Taipei, Osaka, Tokyo, legs. On the return trip the Electra transported me between Bangkok and KL. In fact the aircraft in which I flew, carried, among the in-flight reading material, the current edition of *Life* magazine, one article of which concerned itself with the way this very type had, until recently, been divesting itself of its wings, thereafter, proving Newton correct.

Renowned for the quality of its photography, the magazine featured shots of some very spectacular holes which had been bored into the US landscape when gravity triumphed over aeronautics.

Considering one actually had to purchase airline drinks in those days, I imagine profits on that flight were what could be termed "adequate". Especially as the problem was still to be resolved, the type being operated under a speed restriction.

But to me it was just another diverse entry in the logbook. If they hadn't already known the cause the aircraft would have been grounded. It's a bit like flying on Friday the 13th. Best day to fly, really, you can usually take your choice of seat. Not that I'm superstitious, but I am from Yorkshire, where superstitions and old wives tales abound.

*

Recalling times past: 205/209, the nightlife on offer sixteen hundred miles to the north, the good times we'd had up there, I decided my next leave should be taken in Hong Kong. It was an easy decision to make, once I discovered I could fly there, courtesy of the Royal Air Force rather than commercially. It was to be my first flight in an aircraft whose airspeed was measured in mach numbers rather than knots, and the only service flight for which I was ever required to pay: Two dollars fifty for a trip in a Comet 2 (around twenty-five pence, in 1959 Straits Dollars). I was termed an indulgence passenger: a phrase used by the Air Force to define service personnel travelling on one of Her Majesty's aircraft by courtesy rather than by right. Space available, as it was more correctly defined by the Americans. On RAF aircraft seats were allocated in reverse order of rank, at least that was the official line, though I couldn't imagine any movements officer being brave enough to bump, say a Group Captain, in favour of a mere Corporal. Whatever the case, I was offered a seat. This was the good news, the return trip was another matter altogether.

There being no flight available to get me back before my leave pass expired, I was required to make allowances, to return early. No mach numbers this time, and I doubt the rate of knots achieved would serve to get even a bee airborne. Which, incidently - according to one aerodynamicist - is an impossibility. Seems he'd figured the power, plus the lift to drag/weight ratio of a bumblebee not to be conducive to flight. Be that as it may, they *do* fly (so much for experts), so back to my mode of transport, which didn't.

Although this was my first view of a large passenger liner, its size didn't overawe me. Not at all. At least, not at first sight. But the troopship *Oxfordshire*, grew and grew with my every approaching step until, at the dockside, it literally towered above me, held there by ropes thicker than my arms. I cast a glance at the steel sides, followed them up to the superstructure, way above, was still unimpressed. Until I was up there on deck, looking down, that is. I was in aviation, a total land-lubber, so understanding none of the complexities of displacement, draught, and ballast, and choosing to disregard the fact that it *had* sailed in here, I felt sure that as soon as it cast off those heavy lines, and parted from the safety of the pier, the whole thing would turn turtle. But of course, it didn't. Twenty thousand tons moved away gracefully, an ever widening chasm developing between concrete and steel. People on concrete waved up at the people on steel, who waved back at them, and I, caught up in the euphoria of saying goodbye, joined in. I didn't actually know anyone down there, of course, and no one down there knew me. But they weren't to know I knew they didn't know, so they wouldn't care. Come to think of it, half of those people down there probably didn't know anyone up here, either. It reminded me of one of those film epics which feature the departure of a Transatlantic liner; albeit without the bunting and streamers. Then we were too far away for it to matter. Tugs fussed around like terriers, clearing us from the pier before casting us loose in the shipping lanes of busy Victoria harbour. Soon we were out there among the junks and sampans, the freighters and liners, warships of the American Sixth Fleet, the Royal Navy, the wallah-wallah boats, and the non-stop too-ing and fro-ing of the efficient old (circa 1898) Star Ferry; still the best means of viewing the city from seaward.

Then Hong Kong was but another memory, and we were cutting a path through the green waters of the South China Sea, its surface inviolate until our arrival. Flying fish skimmed the waves and sped down the valleys, porpoises played "chicken" across our bows, and during the night the phosphorescence in the wake enthralled us.

It wasn't a long trip. Four or five days after the ship sounded its own farewell to the Crown Colony, I was back with my unit, in the action zone.

*

As the front line moved north so did our area of operations, over the border into Thailand, although we still made the odd trip down the peninsula. One such was an operation around Kuantan, located over on the east coast. And it was here that I scrounged a flight in an Auster AOP9 of 656 squadron, Army Air Corps.

The mission called for the dropping of delayed action grenade simulators over a known guerilla area, just to keep them on their toes, so to speak. Hopefully to drive them into the waiting arms of the troops which were patrolling the area. The grenades were on a static line, attached to the airframe, and once thrown out this pulled the pin, thus activating the delayed action mechanism. My duty, as sole passenger, was to toss them out as directed by the pilot. Must have been two or three dozen in all, and once dispersion was complete, the pilot called for recovery of the trailing static lines. Which became a mission impossible, as they were caught round the tailwheel. Still, that was preferable to them flapping around in the breeze. Could have done a lot of damage to the fabric covered fuselage and control surfaces had that been the case. As it was they didn't seem to affect our landing back at base.

Ah, well. Perhaps not the spectacular success the Army would have wished for, but at least the grenades were on target. As for the representative from the Royal Air Force, well... much like Greece voting for Turkey in the Eurovision Song Contest, or vice versa, no points were to be awarded. Full points though for the eagle which mistook one of 209 squadron's Pioneers to be a tasty morsel: it attacked the aircraft at around two thousand feet, scoring a direct hit on the cockpit area, ending up half in, half out of the side screen. Max points for aim, though they couldn't be awarded, the bird perishing in the process.

*

So it was, in August 1959, the squadron now redesignated No.110 - ex Vultee Vengeance and Mosquito unit - we found ourselves regrouping at RAAF Butterworth, north Malaya, a base of the Royal Australian Air Force and their F86 Sabres. We moved up from KL lock, stock, and barrel, following the front as it progressed to the north. No period of consolidation though, operations continuing throughout.

Butterworth was purely a military base, with no civilian traffic vying for use of its single runway. But the implications of having a single runway, on a fighter base, were not lost on the Aussies, for shortly after our arrival,

150

a monstrous, runway clearance vehicle was also to appear on the scene. This was a specialist affair whose doughnut-tyred wheels were fully twelve feet in diameter. So large in fact that steering was by way of an electric motor mounted on each wheel. The whole thing could be operated by remote control, the driver punching buttons at the end of a long armoured cable, well clear of any wreckage, or fire.

For a couple of days, this very expensive toy, brand new, resplendent in its bright yellow paintwork, could be seen tracking up and down the seaward end of the concrete pan, the opposite end to where our aircraft were dispersed. It was obvious the Aussies were familiarizing themselves with the controls, checking out the capabilities of the machine. But it seems the smooth concrete was not enough of a challenge for them, for they next took it onto the beach, and into the sea!

As with my teen-age condom, I believe it may still be there.

*

There may not have been any civil traffic around to distract me, but across the dispersal from where our helicopters were based was where most visiting aircraft were parked. V-bombers would stage through here - Valiant and Vulcan - plus the odd fighter type. Then there were the Gannets, on delivery flights to the Indonesian Navy. It all helped break the between-operations monotony.

Butterworth was on the mainland, directly across from the holiday island of Penang. Duty free, and but a short ferry trip away. This was a place with which squadron personnel were to become quite familiar, if they weren't already, many of us having previously visited the island, stayed at the leave centre there, travelling up from KL, or in earlier days, Singapore.

With Penang bearing obvious similarities to Singapore, our visits to the city were rather like something out of Leslie Thomas' *Virgin Soldiers.* Well, they would be, wouldn't they? We were role models in a different uniform. Needless to say, I won't go into details. Suffice to suggest: them that's been will know, them that hasn't, wouldn't wish to. The undecided should perhaps read the book.

There were other places on the island worth a visit, too, on the cultural side that is. Up on the hill known as Ayer Itam was a magnificent seven tiered pagoda, reputed to contain a thousand Buddha. (Buddhas, maybe? Or how about Buddhi?) And what of that one thousand? Figure of speech, or fact? Never did count them, personally, but I must have taken a thousand photographs of the place. (OK, twenty.) And guess what, not one of them was smiling. There again, they generally don't, do they, Buddha? A short distance away was a Snake Temple - once only for me, I hate the buggers, even if they were drugged - and there was a

Waterfall Temple, too, all red and gold; lucky colours as far as the Chinese are concerned. Should one wish to soak up the sun, fine and dandy, the island was ringed with glorious, palm-fringed, sandy beaches. If not the beaches then how about a trip up Penang Hill on the funicular: magnificent views, cool air, so the guide book told me. There was a tea shop up there as well, a pleasant interlude until the pub opened, though in reality they were open all day.

Now don't get me wrong. Nothing wrong with culture, in limited doses, and during the hours of daylight. But of more interest to us at the time were the bars, clubs, and restaurants, which is where we would spend our nights on the island.

I recall some of the aircrew spending a night or two on the island, too. Literally. They'd been detailed for a survival course, set in the surrounding hills. Or maybe it was an initiative test. Survival, initiative, what does it matter, they were dropped off, without food, needed to fend for themselves for a couple of days. Which they successfully did; apparently well before the exercise had even begun!

Naturally, so as to avoid any chance of the whole process becoming overly burdensome, you understand, they had taken precautions, made previous arrangements. By a strange coincidence, a Whirlwind just happened to fly over a certain area at a certain time, and as it did so, certain items "accidentally" fell out of it. Strange how the toilet rolls - which formed part of the cargo - happened to partially unroll themselves on the way down. This, of course, should have made recovery relatively easy, had it not been primary jungle, the clearing into which the items fell much too small even for a helicopter in which to land. Ah well, someone would no doubt find a use for them.

So, survival? Initiative? To pre-empt is to prevent; is that not how the saying goes?

*

Making an escape from both the rigours and pleasures of Penang, another place with which we were to become quite familiar, was a forward operations base pronounced Gree; although spelt Grik. This was where that Chabai tiger cub ended up, eventually becoming quite tame. It was looked after by an officer of the Manchester Regiment, under whose bed it slept. Probably did other nasty things under there as well. Apparently this officer used to walk it around on a lead, until - so the story goes - it one day went missing. This caused a bit of a panic amongst the army brass, as it had been promised to Belle Vue Zoo, in Manchester. Iban trackers were engaged in the search for it, to no avail, so it was assumed to have returned to the wild, or possibly to have been cubnapped.

But no. Two weeks later, tired, filthy, and hungry, it returned to it's place beneath the officer's bed, apparently looking for all the world like it had had enough of life in the wild.

Hard to believe, maybe, true nevertheless. And it did eventually end up in Manchester. (Had it been aware of that it probably wouldn't have returned. Just imagine, having to look forward to the rest of your life in Manchester. I mean it's not even in Yorkshire, is it?)

Grik was also the place from which we performed troop-lifts into the interior, and carried medevacs out, especially if the Kiwis had a rugby fixture that weekend!

Taff Walker, a Master Pilot colleague from the time tells of one such operation in which he was involved. The op order apparently called for the evacuation of two "casualties", but when he arrived at the LZ there turned out to be eight, not one appearing to be in desperate need of medical attention, or assistance. And as they were all strapping lads, carrying loads of kit, it required four sorties to bring them out.

At least they did win their game, eventually going on to lift the end of season trophy. Win, that is, not steal.

*

It was about this time the roads round squadron headquarters began to echo to a rather different sound than the clattering roar of Pratt & Whitney's Wasp. This was the Honda 50, a rather neat little moped with automatic gears. Not loud in the singular, but a bit wearing when all the aircrew seemed suddenly to get the urge to own one, notable exceptions apart. One expatriate patriot pilot named Paul (Gray, that is) opted instead for the BSA Bantam.

'Absolute crap,' was the opinion of Tom Browning, one of the Honda owners.

Paul, who loved it, replied to the effect that at least it was, "British crap".

Nobby Clarke's selection was a very posh Vespa, which he almost immediately fell off (probably trying to light yet another fag), rendering himself *hors de combat* for quite some time. Then there was Tom Bennett. Tall, young, ginger hair, with matching moustache, good-looking (Ah, but weren't we all? OK, maybe not Nobby). Tom, being the proud owner of a "stinkwheel" (a bicycle contraption with a French built motor driving the rear wheel), was different again. He had a large wooden box made, which was then fitted to the rear. This was, he explained, "for putting things in". Of course it was. So one day some of the other pilots did. They filled it with the lizards which were a common feature around the area. That other Tom, the debonair Tom Browning (whom I suspect to be the instigator, for this was his kind of thing), says he was quite surprised when, during the round-up, capture, and box-filling operation, one of the little sods had the audacity to bite him when he grabbed it from behind.

Three rebels then, which left at least half a dozen Hondas; apparently available in any combination of colours, so long as they were cream and blue. And of course the noise became a little more than wearing when they took to riding in formation, round and round the block. Who knows, maybe they were working off the frustration of never having enough choppers serviceable at one time, or at base, for them to be able to achieve a decent formation in the air (and if moped form was anything to go by the airborne version would have been a sight to behold). Or maybe the idea originated with the monsoon fly, with which we were occasionally inundated. Like large flying ants they would magically appear in their thousands, nay, millions, shortly after a heavy downpour. On arrival they would immediately shed their wings, join up in long trains and wander around like strings of circus elephants playing follow my leader. (Imagine that. Unless you *are* in the lead the view ahead never changes!) They'd then disappear, just as suddenly and mysteriously as they had at first arrived, leaving us almost ankle-deep in obviously no-longer-needed wings. Where they came from, or went too, who knows, or cares? OK, maybe David Attenborough would.

As with all new toys, though, there was a slight problem with the scooters. Easy to handle, yet unlike a car, with a moped one needed to place ones feet on the road when stopping at traffic lights. It was something to remember. Not too difficult a thing, I would have thought, especially for a pilot. And it probably wasn't, at least when sober. You out there, Deke Bradley?

His antics, I heard tell, mirrored those of the German motorcyclist in Rowan and Martin's Laugh In. (In fact Deke, being Canadian, reminded me of someone about whom I had once read: a member of Alexander Graham Bell's "Aerial Experiment Association" of 1907. Apart from Bell, Glen Curtiss, "Casey" Baldwin, and Tom Selfridge - the first man to die in an aircraft accident - the group had included a Canadian engineer who, although reportedly could not be trusted to sit astride a motorcycle without falling off, was acknowledged to be one of the finest flyers of his time.)

That was the way in the Far East Air Force, every squadron I'd been on, people got up to some outrageous things at times - stunts that would never be contemplated back home (at least outside of the Officer's Mess) - but when it came to the aircraft, flying them, or servicing them, everyone reverted to being very professional, very serious, very quickly. We wouldn't have had it any other way.

Until early 1959, No.194 squadron - Bristol Sycamore equipped - also operated out of KL, but a couple of disastrous accidents - the cause of which was determined to be break-up of their wooden rotor blades (possibly due to the harsh operational environment) - led to their being grounded.

The intention was that the Sycamore would eventually replace the Whirlwind Mk4, which was rather underpowered. That changeover was then put on hold. RAE, (the Royal Aircraft Establishment), at Farnborough, later came up with a solution, so by mid-1960 we were being re-equipped with a modified version of the type, these working alongside - for a time - the ubiquitous Whirlwind Mk4.

Another slight hiccup in phasing out of the Whirlwind was experienced when two RAAF Sabres managed to collide in mid-air, over dense jungle. The last Whirlwind was retained for a couple of days as it was equipped to receive signals from SARAH - for Search And Rescue And Homing - whereas the Sycamores were not. (The almost appropriately acronymic, SARBE - Search And Rescue BEacon - would have been more fitting to this story, but these were as yet in the future.)

With this operation successfully concluded it was goodbye Whirly 4. And it was to be not too long before the Sycamore was also replaced by the more modern, much safer, turbine-powered, Whirlwind Mk10. Although by the time that event took place I'd become nothing more than a mere statistic in the squadron's past history. A very minor player at that, even if I had done my bit.

But before we leave it, a couple more Taff Walker stories, if only because Taff has a sackful of them. The first concerns another operation in which he was involved, over the Thai border at a place called Betong, yet another location with which we were becoming quite familiar as the front moved ever northward.

Taff was scheduled to fly some Thai police into a place known by them, somewhat tongue-in-cheek, as Fort Ha Ha, an area of really deep jungle. These guys were apparently carrying kit-bags, and as they placed them aboard the aircraft so the crewman, ensuring they were positioned with regard to the centre of gravity - rather important in a helicopter - thought he saw one of them move. Being a conscientious type, or maybe just plain nosey, he opened it up, and out popped a young Thai girl. Talk about home comforts out on patrol! We were used to the Gurkhas carrying edible livestock in with them - chickens and things - but this was ridiculous. Curried girl? I hardly think that was what they had in mind!

Then we come to a character known as "Whacker" Cox; presumably due to his tendency of addressing all and sundry as "Whack". An old Malaya hand, Master Pilot "Whacker" was awarded a DFC whilst flying the Westland Dragonfly on ops there, but this incident took place after his return to Blighty, where he had since been commissioned. Thorney Island was the venue.

Whacker had apparently been detailed for a late afternoon wet winching exercise in a Mk4 Whirlwind, and, regardless of the limited power of the engine, and prevailing conditions, he asked a pilot friend, Fred, if he'd like to go along for the ride. Fred, having never flown in a chopper before, but about to convert onto the type, said he would be happy to, duly hopped into the left-hand seat.

Fred now takes up the story.

"It was a hot, windless day, the sea like glass as we arrived over Chichester harbour and came to the hover - not exactly ideal conditions, I thought, given our all-up weight and lack of power. The heat and humidity only made matters worse, and still air meant an almost total absence of that rotary-craft phenomenon known as translational lift effect. This became self-evident when I looked out, surprised to see the port wheel in the water. As it was still attached to the aircraft, I pointed the fact out to Whacker, who said it was OK, he was working on it.

"I looked out again, just checking on progress, but by this time the wheel had disappeared completely, water now lapping at the underside of the fuselage. Not good, eh?

"Although I hadn't flown *in* a helicopter before, I *was* aware of the pertinent facts: we were overpitching, ie rotor rpm too low; as was, therefore, airspeed over the blades. Now the only way to recover from such a situation is to decrease blade pitch, or gain translational effect by picking up forward speed, both of which called for the sacrifice of a little height; somewhat difficult when part of the aircraft is already below sea level. To put it mildly, lacking any kind of floatation gear, it was obvious we were in deep trouble. Or should that be deep water?

"Don't you think it's time to get out, Whacker?' I asked.

"'You're right, Fred,' Whacker replied, calmly shutting down the engine, as if at the end of a day's flying. Which, in a way, I suppose it was.

"Don't recall the details but I was in the water in record time, heading for the beach at a fair rate of knots. No problem at all exiting from the left-hand seat, though I was a bit concerned about Whacker. Well, maybe not Whacker so much as the NCO winchman who was down in the cabin. Wasn't it, after all - as captain - Whacker's duty to remain to the bitter end? Nevertheless, I was about to turn back when I saw this guy waving at me from the shore. He was shouting, too, obviously keen to attract my attention, so I continued swimming towards him. I presumed he would have news of the others. Didn't cross my mind, the thought that if they were already ashore they'd have to have been really motoring.

"I eventually reached the beach and dragged myself out, knackered. 'What is it, mate?' I asked, somewhat breathless.

"'Oh, nothing, really. I was just trying to point out, you could have walked from where you were,' came the answer.

"He was right, too, the sea was barely three feet deep.

"We all survived of course, and the aircraft was eventually recovered, albeit, not exactly in pristine condition. In fact it was later struck off charge. Apparently, due to the advanced state of corrosion, odd pieces kept falling off. Not really fundamental to the safe operation of an aircraft, that.

"Whacker eventually left the chopper world, ending up on Beverleys. Bit of a change, for sure. I was going to say bit of a come down, but, given the circumstances, that would be cruel."

*

So it was that the carefree fifties drifted into the Swinging Sixties. I became aware of this when one fixed wing pilot with whom I was acquainted, insisted on replacing the formal, "Gear down, please" with the more trendy, "Dangle the Dunlops, daddio."

It should have been time to go home, for by then I was tour ex (for expired). But I wasn't yet ready. I was enjoying myself so much I actually volunteered for, and was granted, an extension of six months, making a total of three years in the Far East. In fact - as the astute reader may already have gathered - I found myself volunteering a lot during my service career. Normally acknowledged to be a foolhardy practice, in my case it generally seemed to bring about the desired result. Complete fluke, of course. It wasn't a matter of what suited me, it was what suited whoever was in charge. If our wishes happened to coincide - as it seemed they often did - then so be it.

In September, 1960, finding myself allocated a berth on the troopship, *Nevasa,* for the trip home - at a time when trooping by air was now *de rigueur* - it seemed my luck had finally run its course.

Not exactly cruise liner conditions. There again, as we were being paid, not paying for the pleasure, maybe it was not so bad after all. More experiences to add to the growing catalogue of experiences. Our first ports of call were Colombo, and Suez. Then we were off again, via the Bitter Lakes and Ismailia, through the Canal to Port Said. Next it was across the Mediterranean, to Gibraltar. Stepping stones along the route back to Blighty, all negotiated successfully.

Okay, discount Colombo, but that was my fault entirely.

What happened? Oh, a silly thing really. Hardly worth mentioning, but... Well, all right.

The hassling and bartering started even before we'd dropped anchor, bumboats drawing alongside, trading taking place over the rails. Voices called down, mainly unintelligible replies drifted back up. Baskets filled with dubious offerings were then raised to the deck. Some of the offerings were then removed, to be replaced with cash, baskets then lowered back down.

I watched with interest, but wanted for nothing, couldn't wait to get ashore, which I eventually did.

The visit went quite well, actually. Another day in another land, both new to me. New friends, too. A wander round - the sights, a meal (rather a good curry), a few drinks - and it was over. We then gathered on the quayside, awaiting the launch that would return us to our vessel, riding at anchor out there in the bay. And from that viewpoint I thought it looked rather glamorous.

As usual, everyone was bragging and showing off their purchases, each boasting about how little they had paid.

'Got this carpet for the equivalent of a fiver. Not bad, eh?

'Yuh was ripped off, I only paid three quid.'

'Obviously not as good quality, yours, is it?' So on and so forth.

Again I'd bought nothing, seen nothing that attracted my attention, despite the fact I had been almost dragged away at one point. It was some fellow who apparently had the most fantastic deal to offer me. He didn't speak English too well - in fact, hardly at all - but if I understood the terms correctly, it seemed to involve me giving him a rather large amount of money, for which he, in return, would give me some entirely worthless item.

'No thanks. Been that route before.' That was my Yorkshire upbringing coming into play. We can be rather frugal when the mood takes us, I'll admit to that. Instead, I joined the rest of the lads for a drink. Even then we weren't left alone. Local traders kept hassling us, trying to sell us gifts to take home. Their wares were pressed upon us, quickly passed around for close inspection: necklaces, watches, old coins, carvings "precious stones". Almost as quickly they were passed back, usually to the accompaniment of detailed instructions on what they should do with them, and themselves. The first almost a physical impossibility, the second more like wishful thinking.

It was here on the quay where I was to temporarily upstage everyone, producing a sparkling necklace which I swung around on a finger.

'Hey, look at that. Cost me nowt,' I declared. With which, the necklace flew off the erect digit, described a glittering arc against the dying sun, and plopped into the bay. Judging by the speed with which it plunged beneath the waves, certainly not plastic.

'Ah well,' I said, resignation on my voice. 'So much for my souvenir of Colombo. Could have been worth a fortune, that.'

*

So ended another phase of service life, the most interesting of all up to that time. More goodbyes, more memories to be filed away like snapshots in an album - more experiences, more friendships developed, before being left behind. Hopefully, more to be made in the future.

Were there though? For a fleeting moment I was suffused with the feeling that, during the last three years I'd seen it all and done it all. Left nothing for that future. Then, somewhat relieved, I realized that couldn't be possible. There still remained lots of exotic places I felt would be worthy of a visit. I had yet to set foot in the USA, Central and South America, Canada. And the whole of the continent of Africa had yet to feel my presence, and vice versa.

But they *were* for the future. All too soon, bright blue skies and high digit temperatures would be replaced by the predominantly grey overcast and the cold, the exotic by the mundane. Sun, sea, and flying fish, would be replaced by gulls, white cliffs, and the changing seasons. No bad thing, this last, for the mysteries and splendour of seasonal change - the colours and moods that change inspires, along with fluidities of light and landscape - are denied to people in the tropics. Three years I'd been away. Three springs, three summers, three autumns, three winters, yet I hadn't really noticed. The missing seasons had been just that; apparent only by their absence. Our years had been split basically by two seasons, a dry one and a wet one. Everything else remained basically the same: colours, temperature, the mood of the landscape. Even sun and sand can become boring after a time. Yes, I'd look forward to the seasons. Just as long as the change wasn't too drastic.

I also considered the certainties left behind, the uncertainties that lay ahead. Not sure if I was ready for all that. I missed the Far East already, but my only link with it now was this stretch of ocean upon which we cruised, and the sky above.

Then there were the memories. Of course there were.

I vowed to return, one day.

* *

The Ballad of One Five Five

Come one, come all, where'er you may be
Sit down a while and listen to me
The truth I will tell of the world's greatest skive
On a Whirlybird squadron that was named One Five Five

There was Clayton and Geddes, and a boss they called Ron,
And Browning and Puddy, but now Puddy has gone.
Best bunch of guys you ever could meet
We sweated together in tropical heat.

Old Wal' you know was in charge of the store.
Finding spares for our choppers, his biggest chore
For the kites they were ragged, all tattered and torn
And we worked like the devil to keep them airborne.

The aircraft themselves once totalled fourteen
The pilots and crewmen wore jungle green.
As they flew overhead, our hats we would doff
Thinking, there goes another, to be written off.

The first we lost went into a stream
Some parts of that one have yet to be seen.
From then on we lost them, 'bout every two weeks
On beaches, in clearings, even the creeks.

The end of the story is sad to relate,
They gave us Sycamore's "'fore it's too late."
And once these aircraft began to arrive
It was the end of our squadron, the bold One Five Five.

*   *

Thanks are due to the unknown squadron member who penned the
original words, of which I have taken the liberty of amending slightly.

NOTEBOOK THREE
SINGAPORE REVISITED
1997

𝕴 had once again left Yorkshire far behind, to depart on a journey which would carry me halfway round the globe. To be truthful, I suppose I could claim "all the way round," for I would cover the remainder on the return trip.

As the landscape of early morning fell away below we sliced our way through the grey opacity, up into the blueness of an empty sky, a scene of transcendent beauty. Our shadow - an almost perfect outline of the aircraft - chased across the cloud-bank below, the silhouette encircled by a mini rainbow.

Yeadon - now Leeds Bradford or, in airline parlance, LBA - was two hundred miles behind us. Heathrow was barely ten, though it was a thousand feet below. The machine, although heavy with fuel, freight, and around three hundred passengers, climbed steeply, such was the performance of the four Rolls-Royce turbofans slung beneath the wings. Engines like this are capable of converting aviation fuel into lots of noise, heat and, especially, power, which is exactly what they were doing. Air was being devoured by the ton, then compressed and superheated, to be blasted out at a hundred times the speed it entered. From there it was a simple matter of physics: equal and opposite reactions, thrust versus drag, lift, and suchlike; the immutable laws of science and aerodynamics. No problem. Twelve hours and I was back from whence I came.

*

It wasn't quite as I remembered, this place. None of the familiar smells greeted me as the aircraft opened its doors once again on Singapore. It was now the aroma of jet fuel which pervaded the senses, rather than those of mimosa and frangipani. And I'd arrived in the harsh light of day, rather than the softness of a tropical night. But these, I was soon to discover, weren't the only changes.

Was this really the place where it all began, thirty-five, forty years back? My overseas tour, that is. It certainly wasn't the same any more. OK, few places were untouched by the passing of time, but this island seemed to have changed more than most. For a start, it was now a republic.

The airport at Paya Lebar was a thing of the past. Changi had switched from military status to become one of the most modern airports in the world. It was now a huge complex, much larger than when it had been an RAF base, as was the island itself. Land reclamation had imposed vast changes to the south coast, completely redefining the waterfront area. The coast road we had so often followed out to Bedok Corner was now well inland. The city had changed, too. As well as growing out, it had grown up. Cloud-piercing up. Raffles Hotel now lay in the shadow of the world's tallest hotel: the seventy-three storey Westin Stamford and Plaza. Orchard Road, once on the outer fringes of almost everything, was now the hub; a shopping mecca for tourists. The Cathay Cinema was still there, at the bottom end. This, previously the most prominent building in the city, was also dwarfed into insignificance.

There was now an underground system, known as the MRT - for Mass Rapid Transit. It covered most of the island, though, strangely, not the airport. The trip to and from Changi is via either the Pan Island Expressway (PIE), or the East Coast Parkway (ECP), magnificent, tree-shaded, flower and bush-lined multi-lane super-highways, which become choked with traffic as you approach the city. Tampines still exists, for the moment. But it is scheduled to become the third expressway in the very near future.

Water is still imported across the causeway from Malaya, only now, after being purified, the majority is re-exported, back from whence it came, at a considerable mark up in price!

Bedok is alive and well. A picnic area now, with ten-pin bowling, Macdonalds, good restaurants, and play areas. And they do still play cricket on the Padang, against the backdrop of City Hall and St Andrew's cathedral - it too almost lost amongst the mega-storied architecture.

Occasionally, amid all the modern buildings, I'd stumble across one of the old, traditional merchant's homes. Concrete and wood structures, raised above the ground on cement piles so as to allow cooling air to pass beneath, and with an encircling veranda. Due to high humidity, the burnt-orange tiled roof would be darkened in places by patches of moss and fungus, and walls would be blackened with mould. It would be set amid a cool greenness of coarse grass and Traveller's Palms, with Flame-of-the-forest, Hibiscus, Bougainvillea and Magnolia adding colour to the oasis, the most famous of which is still to be found within the grounds of the Raffles. But even Raffles hasn't escaped the changes. Expensively refurbished, I was saddened to find their oasis, the Palm Court - where I had once sat and sipped on a Singapore Sling - was now out of bounds to all but registered guests; though none sat out there, for even the tables and chairs had been removed. Oh, and no photography inside the lobby, if you please; photographs are available from the many retail outlets which now form the exterior surrounds. But by the time I'd been informed of this my video was in the can. The laid-back era of Coward and Maughan, it seemed, was no more.

What the hell, now I could afford it I entered the Tiffin Room: light and airy rather than the staid, dark-panelled, clubby-type atmosphere I recalled from a previous visit. All I'd managed then was a drink. Could barely run to that. But what I'd really been paying for was the privilege of looking round. I'd even had a pee in one of their loos. Not that I needed to, but I'd heard how luxurious and lavish their loos were, wanted to see for myself. Not outstanding had been my verdict. Thinking back, I know which version of the Tiffin Room I preferred.

Now, amid the glitter and gloss, the damask and silverware, and the sunlit tables, I partook of their curry. Hygienic, tasty, impeccable service. But it was a white-man's curry. No sweat, no runny nose, which immediately had me pining for the old Seletar curry shop.

The Singapore river has probably seen the biggest changes of all. One-time hive of activity, with the coming and going of the lighters, carrying cargo to and from the ships lying at anchor offshore - known as the roads - its waters were now deserted. Back then those lighters would discharge their freight into the heaving clutter of godowns (warehouses) which lined the banks. Interspersed amongst the godowns were dozens of rickety, open-fronted shops, packed with everything from spices to incense, clothing, raw cotton, and silks, electrical and electronic goods, along with the latest offerings from the world of photography. There were fruits galore, and dried fish - very important, that, especially the sharks' fins.

An aromatic clutter of herbs and pungent spices would be piled all around, open sacks and tins, in bowls, and on trays. A dazzling kaleidoscope of colour. Greens and browns, saffron, white and orange. The red of the hot chili peppers, the green of the capsicums.

It was all gone now, replaced by touristy restaurants and bars. One compensation: the river was cleaner. Much cleaner, sweeter smelling by far. Of the lighters - still with eye painted on the bow, so they could see where they were going - the few that remained had been modified to run tourists up and down the river. For what? So they could see what was no longer there?

Change Alley? Would you believe Paris chic? High class art, Havana cigars, designer clothing; the real thing these days. There is a touch of the old place, if only in name: Change Alley Aerial Arcade. It spans the highway, but bears only a passing resemblance to the original.

The only thing to remind me of earlier times were the barrows which served fresh drinks, a hand-turned mill squeezing the juice from sugar-cane, or tropical fruits.

Not bad then, the changes, though not all good. For although it is probably one of the safest, cleanest, and greenest, cities to be found anywhere, it seemed to me that a lot of the character had been swept away. As in Tanjong Pagar Conservation area. The original buildings remain, yet the spirit seems to have departed.

After being shut down for a time - ostensibly to clean up its image - Bugis street is again open, now renamed New Bugis Street. Correctly so, for it too retains little of the original character; just another tourist street. The boy-girls who used to entertain us with their antics have moved to another area. Out of sight, out of mind.

Albert Street is another to have suffered. Its roadside kitchens, its rickety stairs, its balconied parlours, all gone. Replaced by something called the Albert Street Mall. And there are very few trishaws remaining. Just as well, really. Wouldn't catch me in one now, not in today's traffic, Ben Hur or not.

Lost my sense of adventure, you think? Not really. But I do now tend to think more about survival. These days the traffic is so horrendous that entry into the town centre, by car, is strictly controlled during the day. At night, it seems anything goes. Wouldn't exactly appreciate a three pointed star between the eyes!

Gone too are the open storm drains, the stench of rotting vegetation, and most of the cockroaches. Not really gone, I doubt. More like, rarely seen. The majority of mosquitoes also seem to have packed their bags, headed for pastures new. Probably "up country."

*

The entrance struck a chord. A familiar place in a once familiar area: Stamford Road. I peered through the window. Yes, of course. The basic layout appeared to have changed hardly at all, though forty years ago it hadn't been known as Harry Keely's Pub and Lounge, just a plain old bar. I even recalled one of the girls that worked there, answered to the name of Dumb-Dumb. Not because she didn't know what was what, because she was. Couldn't speak a word. Didn't need to; not exactly a barmaid, you see. One other change: the place was now airconditioned. It reminded me of how the MU had been, at Seletar; bloody freezing if you were dressed in anything less than a suit. Main problem with that: to wear a suit out on the street was to be slightly overdressed. Now, as then, I wore short-sleeved shirt and shorts. We used to sit in the heat to drink cold beer, an electric ceiling-fan stirring up the air enough to keep us comfortable, and to deter the mossies.

So, better, or not? I wasn't really sure. Cleaner, yes, but perhaps a little too clinical. And at a price, for it certainly isn't cheap these days, not with beer averaging six quid a pint.

Funny, that. How with such as myself beer always seems to be the yardstick. All right then: cameras, computers, and such? Forget it. You can buy them far cheaper in the UK. Happy now? All I bought was an illegal piece of ivory, which I picked up along Bras Basar Road. It depicts the four wise monkeys. Yes, I know there were; so I leave it to your imagination to figure out as to what it was the fourth monkey felt his hands should protect! Which reminds me: what of the Worlds; Happy, Old, and New? Yes, you've guessed. They also failed survive the cleansing. Wouldn't be surprised if my ivory turned out to be plastic.

But for all that, Singapore remains one of my favourite cities. I'll go back, anytime.

*

And what of Malaya, just over the water? Big changes there, too. Offshore oil to begin with, which automatically brings changes in the wake of the wealth it creates. These days the helicopter is associated with the oil industry rather than the military. You no longer require one to fly into the "Ulu", for you can drive there. Drive across country as well. In fact there is an East-West highway that cuts straight through our old, isolated, base of Grik, now known as Gerik. That is the northern East-West highway. There is another to the south, across from KL. You can even drive close by where some of those forts used to be located.

Only fly in the ointment: as with most Third World nations that find themselves to be suddenly rich, they've overspent on such prestigious and useful items as the worlds tallest building - but for how long? Now it all seems to be collapsing around them; the economy, not the building.

Time will tell. In the meantime, I'm off back to my favourite place of all time: New Zealand.

* *

Chapter Nine
TOP OF DESCENT

THE SIXTIES: The Beatles, sex and drugs. The Mini: car and clothes. Woodstock and Vietnam. There were maiden flights for both the 747 and Concorde. And in 1969, a year when the minimum wage for farm workers was set at a mere thirteen guineas, Prince Philip declared the Royal Allowance of £475,000 to be not enough. "We may have to move out of Buckingham Palace. We've already sold off a small yacht, and I may have to give up polo," he was alleged to have stated on American TV.

Then there was the event of the decade.

*

I first learned of the Kennedy assassination when I walked into the junior NCO's club at Lyneham on that fateful Friday in November 1963.

'What's going on?' I asked of the room in general. I was curious as to the story behind the scenes of mass confusion which were playing on the television.

'They've shot their President,' a stunned mate informed me.

No need to ask who had shot whose president, that was immediately obvious. And despite all the good things that had happened since my return from the Far East, three years previous, I remember that moment clearly. It was to be one of those time and place things that forever stick in the mind. I remember it far better than I was to recollect my demob, far better even than the final stages of my homeward voyage.

*

'Bloody weather,' Phil complained. 'Looks like summer's long gone.' Phil was one of the guys I'd hung around with during the journey home. A shipboard friend, nothing more.

'Yeah,' I agreed, for it was cold, considering the time of year. It was wet as well.

'Typical Europe, ain't it. Here we are, in the Bay of Gibraltar, and already the bloody weather is declaring its hand.'

'But the forecast did say it was expected to clear,' I reminded him.

'Never happen, mate, we aren't in Singapore now.'

'Seems those years in the tropics have reprogrammed your brain, Phil, effectively erasing all memories of a European sun,' I said. Mine too, I thought, for I realized the conditions hadn't exactly depressed me. It was what I'd expected September to be all about.

There had been a bit of a blow during our crossing of the Indian Ocean, which didn't seem to effect me at all. I recall the thrill of leaping up just as the vessel topped the crest of a wave; time it right and you could clear the deck by six to ten feet as it dropped into the next trough. Get it wrong and I suppose it would have been easy to break a leg! One more thing: no queues for the mess, even the thought of food having apparently lost its appeal to the majority. They seemed to have consigned themselves to a slow death below decks, heading above only so as to puke over the side. But most recovered quickly once we entered the Canal, at Suez. From that point on, the decks had resembled those of a cruise liner as almost naked bodies stretched out wherever it was possible for a body to stretch out. We all soaked up the last of the sun as the vessel slipped into the Mediterranean for the run to the Rock. After Gib the only remaining obstacle on my epic three-year journey was the Bay of Biscay, which, thankfully, we caught in a rare, benign mood.

Then came Southampton: more of the same grey overcast, tugs pulling and nudging, gulls screeching, salt air, docks and cranes, warehouses. Not much of a welcome then. There again, the major difference between my arrival here, and the departure from Singapore, was a weather-induced mood. I'd boarded under the sweltering heat of a tropical sun, full of joyful anticipation at what lay ahead. Even as I disembarked, anticipation remained intact, only now it was tinged with apprehension. My arrival back home in Yorkshire served only to reinforce this feeling, at least initially, for after the greetings, one of the first questions asked was, 'When do you go back?' Confirmation perhaps, if it was needed, that I was now "grown up". A man of the world.

Following disembarkation leave - where Dad's binoculars had once more been pressed into action (Canberra, Vulcan, Jet Provost, etc) - I found myself in the depths of the West Country. Wiltshire. Perched atop Dauntsey bank, to be precise, with Bradenstoke-cum-clack close by; who could ever forget a name like that? But there were many such names in this area. Upper and Lower Slaughter, for instance - so named, as when William the Conqueror granted the Saxon landholding to one of his knights, a Phillipe de Sloitre, the name proved such a tongue-twister the locals corrupted it to Slaughter. Just thought you should know that.

Although I wasn't to know then, RAF Lyneham was where I would be based for the final three years of my service career. I say based, and that was the reality of it, for I probably spent more time *away* from the camp than I did *at* it, which made them the most prolific years of my life to date. As far as travel and experiences went they were certainly that.

If people thought we spoke strange up in Yorkshire, down here was different, for sure. This became obvious as soon as I attempted to engage someone in conversation; my first visit to a local pub, I believe. A man stood next to me at the bar, and I asked him a question. He looked quite bewildered at first, and the time he took to reply made me feel that this was the most awesomely complex question he had ever been called upon to answer. Or maybe he was just winding himself up, for once he started, there was no stopping him. It sounded like he could have been relating Cook's first voyage, so long did he take. And, to confuse things yet further, his hands flew this way and that, like he was warming up for a bout of martial arts. Then he suddenly stopped. I think he may actually have just paused for breath, but I got in quick and thanked him. Hadn't the heart to tell him I barely understood a word - lots of arr's and ee's, but little else it seemed, not that it mattered, for by then I'd forgotten what it was I'd asked him. But I did manage to translate most of what it was he said as I downed my pint and prepared to leave.

'Tell ee what, young fella. Ee don't say a lot, but ee's awfy hard to understand.'

I was back, in my element, with Transport Command, though by choice this time, for I was a man with a mission. I had a cunning plan in mind, and although it was already in operation I realized I was as good as aiming for the moon, and even the Americans had not yet landed there. Live and learn, as they say. Well, after three years in the Far East I was still alive, and during that time I'd certainly learned something, quite what I wasn't sure, for it certainly didn't dissuade me from volunteering. Maybe three years in the tropics *had* effected my brain.

The Lyneham posting was phase one of my plan, the easy part, preference of choice being one of the perks offered on completion of an overseas tour. Not that your preference was automatically granted, for, naturally, service requirements took priority. But, without Lyneham, phase two was doomed to failure. In fact there would have been no phase two, for this base was my launch pad; the launch therefore, a success.

I was assigned to first-line servicing - out among the operational aircraft, second-line being AES (Aircraft Engineering Squadron), where major maintenance and servicing took place, not my thing at all. I'd always found first-line to be much more interesting, and this was, to be sure. Exactly what I would have wished for, had I not had something else in mind. Something I suspected to be an even better option; provided it was an option!

I allowed a couple of months to pass, giving myself time to size up the situation, gain experience, slot myself into the system as it were.

Although three squadrons were based at Lyneham, 99, 511, and 216, groundcrew were pooled rather than being allocated to a particular unit. Same thing applied to the Britannia. Whilst 216 Squadron had exclusive use of the Comet, neither 99 or 511 had any specific aircraft assigned to them. Both flew the Britannia, each drawing their aircraft from the pool, as and when required.

With the two months up, I played my hand. I was volunteering again, this time for an internal posting: to join Transport Command Mobile Servicing Flight, a select group that had come to my notice as far away as Malaya.

We'd had a flight of Vulcan's stage through Butterworth, en-route to New Zealand. They'd been accompanied by a Britannia, and, as was my wont, I'd wandered over to have a look round, both types being new to me, and of far greater interest than the by now familiar Whirlwind.

' Hello? Dave Taylor, isn't it?'

I looked up, recognised a face I hadn't seen for six years, at Cosford. Same entry, same trade, yet I couldn't recall his name. But he I think he realized that.

'Rex Chapman?,' he said, offering his hand. 'Instruments, general,' he stated, as if offering an excuse for my forgetfulness.

'Yes, of course. What are you doing out here, Rex?' Which is all it took. He showed me round and explained about what it was he did, which is when I became aware of the opportunities available with Mobile Servicing Flight. That was for me, I decided, and determined there and then that it should happen. And so it was that chance meeting had sown the seeds, the inkling of yet another plan.

Now, here I was, nine months on, at Lyneham, successful once again. And it had seemed so easy. Luck, fate, destiny? Who cared. It was what I'd set out to achieve, so I wasn't about to instigate a sociological study into the hows, whys, and wherefores. They'd accepted me, I accepted them. Common courtesy, isn't it?

So it was I joined the chosen few. A couple of dozen at most, Rex no longer among them. We, also, were pooled, flew with any squadron, any type of aircraft.

'Not just the Brit and Comet,' Willie Wilson - another instrument fitter with MSF - told me. 'Any of 38 Group aircraft, when they're operating away from base, in places where there's no RAF presence. Which, of course, means travelling with them to... Well... wherever.'

'Such as? I asked.

'Wait for the monthly planning requirement,' he suggested. 'It's due tomorrow, then you'll see.'

I found it to be an event that generated quite an air of excitement and anticipation in our crewroom, for those who happened to be there at the time, that is. Those who were away in some foreign land were likely to miss out, but it was a swings and roundabouts thing.

It was just as smoky as any other crewroom I'd been in, our fifteen by ten base at Lyneham. Enough seats for half a dozen, then came the toolbox; pretty bum-numbing after a while.

'Help yourself to tea or coffee,' Willie said, pointing to a Burco boiler which bubbled away, steaming up the windows.'

'An advance on the communal bucket we used to brew up in back at Dishforth,' I remarked.

'Bucket?' Willie questioned, wrinkling his nose.

'Yeah. Strong, sweet, and milky, stirred up with a broom handle. This is civilized, even fresh milk. We used condensed cow.'

In the Far East, the Coke machine had replaced the tea-urn.

*

Even our MSF training was different. As there were no RAF courses covering the civilian equipment fitted to the Britannia 312 and Comet C4 - which had, after all, been designed with the world's airlines in mind - I was to find myself dispatched afar, even deeper into the West Country. This time to Smiths Industries, in the heart of the beautiful Cotswold countryside. A timeless area in a region of rural calm. Thatched roofs and cottage gardens; butterflies and bumblebees kind of places. There were ancient churches, and the country pub; the very essence of all that is best in the English countryside. After that it was off to Hertfordshire, and the De Havilland factory, at Hatfield.

After the Comet 1 disasters of 1954 it was almost inevitable De Havilland would find themselves up against it. From being five years ahead of the field, with airlines knocking at their door, they paid a heavy price for stepping into the unknown. (A chance that had to be taken were we to compete in the field of air transport. A wartime agreement that had Britain concentrating solely on the design and production of fighters and bombers put the Americans way ahead, as had no doubt been their long-term plan.) And no matter how good later versions of the Comet might be, orders would be hard to come by, for tough competition was on the horizon - the 707. Boeing, after all, had the advantage of a military test program, and all that that entailed; the 707 being originally designed for the Department of Defence. In contrast, De Havilland had been left to fund their own research, a lot of which was presented to the Americans on a silver platter. Especially the results of the Comet 1 investigations: damning evidence of the dreaded, yet largely unfamiliar, metal fatigue.

Still, orders were forthcoming. The remaining Mk1's were rebuilt as C2's, originally to fulfil an order by BOAC, but all were eventually modified and sold to the RAF. The airline opted instead for the longer range Mk4, various models of which also went to such as British European Airways, and to a certain Middle Eastern airline. 'Which appeared to flight-test every safety device built-in to the seven they acquired,' one of the instructors told us. 'Almost every "test" attributable to "finger trouble."' (I was to remember that in later years, making a mental note to steer clear of that particular airline.) The Mk4C - last of the line - apart from attracting airline orders, was also supplied to Transport Command, becoming the C4.

Training complete, I was now about to begin a life living out of a suitcase. Not as bad as it sounds, for after the Sunderland, Valetta, Hastings, and other diverse types, the Britannia and Comet were magnificent aeroplanes. These were the service aircraft in which we did travel first class, relatively speaking. I hadn't been expecting anything as perfect as a Rolls-Royce, but these were probably the nearest avion equivalent, as far as Service aircraft were concerned, at that time. They were certainly technically far in advance of the Sunderland and Whirlwind. For instance, on the Britannia, there was no direct connection between stick and control surfaces. Ailerons, elevators, and rudder were free-floating, controlled by trim tabs, and it was these that were connected to the control column. As for engine controls, the throttles were all electric. Yet when it came to the navigation department, we were a generation behind the V-Bombers and high-tech fighters; albeit light years ahead of the Sunderland's "wind and piss" machinery.

This apart, living out of a suitcase was to prepare me well for future years. My suitcase was now of better quality, and much bigger, room for many more dreams; the formidable-seeming layer with which I'd returned from the Far East would barely line the bottom of this case. Just as well, really, I was to need the space.

The advantages of joining MSF were twofold - the varied nature of our work, and the amount of travel involved. The travel came in various guises: rapid response alerts to the world's trouble spots; liason exercises with the army; introductory trials with new aircraft types. We also participated in Royal flights and VIP tours, for which the aircraft were especially fitted out. For these, the Comet 4's exterior highly polished; a labourious and thankless task for those whose job it was - spit and polish, all arms and elbows. I knew that as I'd sometimes take a peek when they were in action, for if there is anything more satisfying than looking at a nice shiny aeroplane in which you are about to depart for warmer climes, it has to be watching someone else making it shiny. There was an exclusive interior fit, too, especially for the Royals.

Next in order of preference were much-prized flights with NATO Defence College personnel. A choice here, were you lucky enough to be selected: Southern Capitals, or Northern Capitals, (Europe, that is) where NATO staff officers familiarized themselves with their area of influence, and we familiarized ourselves with the women and bars, with lots of sightseeing thrown in. We alternated in these duties with the United

States Air Force, year and year about. (The tours, that is, not the women and bars. The Americans proved themselves quite capable on that front.)

NATO apart, there were trooplifts - both on exercise and for real - and, during England's cold winter-months, when the snow lay heavy across the Wiltshire countryside and the wind howled mournfully, there was the welcome advent of continuation training for the crews, in the much more agreeable climatic conditions which prevailed in Cyprus. Also to Cyprus were the so-called "Hot Load" flights. 'Don't ask!' I'd been advised. So I didn't. I never knew, didn't want to. Anyway, much better that than a snow clearance party back at Lyneham. In fact, so frequent were our visits to places such as El Adem, Nicosia, Aden, Singapore, and Gan, that they were to become almost second homes to us. And, due to our year-round tan and apparently easy life, we became known as "The Sunshine Boys" to certain elements of the Lyneham community. I suppose they saw us as the Air Force equivalent of the Jet Set, something I'd have found it difficult to disagree with, I'm happy to say. An altogether most enjoyable lifestyle.

*

Gan - then a staging post in the Indian Ocean, now popular with holiday-makers, who pay a fortune to go there - is one of the Maldive group of Islands, and it was during a departure from there that I was to face my only emergency in a Britannia. Not a lot to worry about, in retrospect. But isn't that the case with any emergency that is brought to a successful conclusion?

Take off, along with the landing, are the moments of greatest danger on any flight, combat missions excepted, of course, which I imagine to be dangerous in the extreme!

We were pounding down the runway of this palm-fringed semi-paradise, outbound to Australia. Full fuel load, maximum all up weight, ambient temperature on the high side. This was partially compensated for by a runway that was at sea level. (The lower the altitude, the higher the density of the air; the higher the density the greater the lift.)

In keeping with Murphy's law, V1 came and went before we lost power on an engine, we were therefore committed to take off. Even though it was an outer, it posed no real problem. VR, and the aircraft lifted off as the engine was shut down, propeller feathered, corrections applied. Even on three engines V2 came up fairly quickly, aircraft climbing away. At least, back where we were seated, that was the way things seemed to be. Procedures had been adhered to, the moment of risk vanquished. The only danger now lay in ejecting tons of fuel into the atmosphere before we could make a safe return to the runway, the aircraft at present well over the weight limit for a landing. There was no question of continuing, for to set off across more than three thousand miles of ocean on three engines was a definite no-go situation. Almost an invitation to disaster, that. Let's face it, is not gravity is far stronger over water? Either that, or golf balls have a fatal fascination for ponds and the like.

The next hour was spent circling, dumping fuel, fingers crossed. Out there were two sides of the fire triangle: fuel and air, conceivably in an explosive mix. Thankfully it wasn't put to the test, for the third component - sufficient heat to cause ignition - remained absent throughout, even if, to my mind, the possibility did maintain a slight presence: a wayward spark, a perverse burst of flame from an engine, a bolt of lightning. Yes, I know the chances are minute in the extreme (I believe the air force used JP1 in preference to the more volatile JP4), but it only needs lady luck to turn her back one time...

There *were* two other incidents. Not exactly emergencies, but could easily have become so.

Northern Canada. Goose Bay - previously coded Bluey West One - was well astern, our Britannia now lined up for a landing at the Canadian AF base of Churchill, Manitoba, when a situation occurred.

It was foggy and cold outside. Very foggy, very cold. Minus twenty-two degrees centigrade, to be precise; cold enough to spread major concern amongst the male brass monkey population, believe me. Difficult conditions, then. Instrument Flight Rules prevailed, naturally. And although approach aids had now advanced to the basic Instrument Landing System stage, radar and a talk-down (GCA approach) still played a part. In other words, it could be hazardous. Though in this respect service flights were generally much safer than their civilian counterparts. Service pilots took less chances, for the cost of diverting a service aircraft was borne by the taxpayer, didn't detract from the profits, as it were.

In this instance our first approach was a miss. Overshoot procedure: full power, flaps one third, gear up.

Oh, oh, small problem: three greens. The landing gear stubbornly refused to retract. Much better than the reverse, of course, but still a problem. Now what? Divert, with the gear down, or go round again? Much better to try again, it seemed, for round we went. A wide circuit, long, straight approach, concentration intense, one imagines. With nothing to be seen outside, attention would be focused on the instruments and, in the headset; the disembodied voice of a distant controller.

But not for us, back in the cabin. That our rearward facing seats gave us a view of where we had been rather than where we were going mattered not one iota at present, fog looks the same when viewed from any direction. We had only what our imagination allowed us, and faith in the crew. Just as the crew needed to have faith in that controller, and in what the instruments were telling them.

Down and down we went, as if gingerly feeling the way, which, in effect, we were. It was always reassuring to catch a glimpse of any odd light that came into view, more so if they happened to be the approach lights, as on this occasion.

We floated above the glistening surface, then, a slight bump, the rumble of rotating wheels, and we were down, worry replaced by relief. Suddenly the air smelt sweeter, the cabin felt warmer, more familiar. And once we were out on the tarmac, nostril hairs frozen solid, we discovered the answer to the problem: particles of freezing fog formed a solid sheet of ice on the forward surfaces of the undercarriage struts. It was inches thick, smooth and translucent, effectively welding the gear in place. Strong stuff, this ice.

A difficult place to work then, Churchill, due to the cold. In fact once the wind speed reached a certain level, all external doors on the camp were automatically locked. Taking into account the wind chill factor, it was deemed too dangerous for anyone to venture out, and as all buildings were interconnected via heated walkways there was really no need.

The next incident involved a Comet C4.

En-route from Gan to Aden with the Secretary of State for Air and his entourage, we were approaching the island of Socotra, in the Arabian Sea. With Aden due to be closed come the kind of independence that faced them once they kicked us out, interest had been shown towards the possibility of establishing a base on this island. So, as Socotra just happened to be reasonably close to the descent path into Aden, we were going down for a fly-by look-see.

The sky was devoid of cloud, the air clear, the island well visible. To me it looked like a sandy-brown-coloured Table Mountain, rising from the sea. Calm and tranquil as we approached from the north, but once we crossed that ridge the aircraft suddenly dropped. In no more than a second or two we lost around five hundred feet. The cause? I suppose something similar to what today is known as wind shear. Luckily it didn't extend to sea level, but it was bad enough. Scared the crap out of me, I'll tell thee that for nowt. Don't know what it did to the S of S's secretary, for he was seated in the cabin at the time, typing some report or other. We were strapped in, he, apparently, too busy to do so. And of course, when an aircraft goes down, anything not secured goes up, in effect: secretary, papers, typewriter, the lot. I can still see that guy floating around in the cabin. He looked like an astronaut in training. Luckily, his typewriter landed clear of everyone, though not so lucky for the typewriter. That, you may say, was a write-up write-off. More tax-payers' money down the drain, though that civil servant appeared to have more pressing things on his mind. He was in a seat as soon as equilibrium was restored, tightening his seatbelt fit to cut himself in half. Once on the ground at RAF Khormaksar, on the Aden peninsular, a check of the gravity-meter revealed readings which were way over the limits. A major airframe check would be on the cards back at Lyneham, and care would be the watchword on the way there.

I believe the Russians eventually established a base at Socotra, the British, either not interested, or not allowed to be.

*

Only slightly less familiar than the pseudo second homes mentioned previously were points of call such as Thule, in Greenland - a stopover on the Polar route to the Far East - Christmas Island (Pacific, not Indian Ocean), Ascension Island, and various bases in Australia, New Zealand, and the United States.

Not only did I travel worldwide, I began to cover a lot more of the UK, too. With money saved during my three years overseas I was now able to purchase my first car, a maroon Ford Anglia 105E. And why not? Willie had recently got himself a Mini, was having great fun with it.

What I'd have really liked was one of the recently-introduced Jaguar revelations, the E-type, but that was way outside my budget. Just about double, in fact; neither was it exactly a learner's car. (Although Flight Sergeant Henderson had taught me the basics, allowing me to drive 110 squadron's standard issue Standard Vanguard pick-up, up and down Butterworth's uncrowded roads, I had yet to attempt the DoT test.) My pride and joy cost six hundred and forty pounds, brand new. A good price I thought, though probably not too well received down at the Woolwich, where my account reached a temporary zero. But this acquisition gave me the independence to follow my growing passion in motor racing. And it wasn't long before the Anglia's engine had been lightly breathed upon at Rob Walker's Wiltshire premises: uprated valve springs, twin choke Weber's, etc. The suspension was beefed up, brake efficiency increased, and the car now boasted a wood-rimmed steering wheel, along with full harness seat belts - long before even basic restraint became a legislative requirement. With these mods, my Westover driving boots, the Jim Clark gloves, and the shades, I was ready. Oh, one other thing: the copper pipe on the end of the exhaust; to make it sound like the racer it almost was. After all, the 105E was one of the engines that really started Cosworth on the road to success.

The boots, gloves etc weren't just for show either, for I was a technical driver, understood about understeer, oversteer, and weight transfer. I drove for pleasure rather than a means of getting around.

I recall having a dice with a bog standard version one day. Out braked him by a mile going into a corner, pulling away easily - you could safely do that on the relatively uncrowded roads back then, so long as you knew what you were about, and were familiar with that particular stretch of highway. Not really a dice therefore, but when I stopped further up the road to check on the radiator water level or some such, this guy pulls up alongside.

'Jeez, what have you done to that thing?' he asks.

'Oh, it felt a bit sluggish, so I've just stopped to put the other plug lead back on,' I ad-libbed. He left in rather a hurry. Muttered something about heading for his local "go faster" shop.

Often was the time a group of us left camp at three in the morning, arriving at Silverstone well before the gates opened for practice. Breakfast would be taken at a local transport caff; what today would be called a greasy spoon. Not a bit of it; good, cheap food was what. So maybe the decor was a little sad: greasy walls, Formica tables, their tops marked by brown snail-trails - kind of thing unattended cigarettes are prone to leave - but what could you expect at those prices. After a feed we'd often nap in the car, waiting for the circuit to open. Then, at day's end, we'd call in for a drink at the Green Man, on the road to Brackley. This is were we discovered the Team Lotus drivers to be staying: Jim Clark and Trevor Taylor, along with C.A.B. Chapman himself. They were all sitting there in the very room in which we were drinking. One time as we arrived, Innes Ireland was just about to depart, in a white E-type. Made me envious, that. I thought about going over and asking him the age old question: 'What'll it do mister?' Trouble was, I thought about it too long. He leapt into it and was gone, blasting off down the road in a screech of rubber.

We'd drink the night away and be back outside the circuit entrance by two o'clock on race day. There would be probably a dozen cars queuing at that time, but when we awoke the line would extend a mile or more down the road.

Once admitted, we'd go charging off across the grass, all heading for that particular place at which each seeks to be first to arrive. Then out would come the scaffolding, the wooden planks, and the plastic seats; the impedimenta of a personal grandstand.

This was pre-chicane, super-fast Silverstone, when, in the wet, cars would howl down the straights, the treads of their fat tyres throwing great roostertails of water into the air. Then they'd be snaking and twitching under braking, to go slithering round the corners in heartstopping, opposite lock slides, barely under control.

I look back on them now as being the golden days of racing, at least as far as I was concerned. You could actually get close to your heros, take photographs, talk to them, have them sign autographs. We'd travel far and wide to the various international meetings, of which there were many: Thruxton, Snetterton, Aintree, Brands; all corners of the Kingdom held Formula One meetings back then.

I was glad I'd had seat belts fitted, too, came in handy, those. Especially the time I contrived to turn the thing over.

'Bit of a misjudgment there, Dave', Ginger, my mate suggested.

'Come on, the other guy was mainly to blame, him being on my side of the road and all,' I replied.

'Should have made allowance for just such a possibility. One of the basic rules of the high-speed driving,' he advised. Ginger was another speed enthusiast, older than me, possibly a better driver, though I wasn't about to admit it, naturally. Especially now, whilst we were both hanging upside down! I was, after all, an egotistic male.

'Hey, I don't care who the hell was to blame, let me out of here,' another voice cried.

Ah, yes. The three passengers in the rear of the two door car. They'd ended up in a heap on the roof, which was now the floor. My thoughts about safety belts hadn't extended as far as the rear seats.

We all clambered out and heaved the car back onto its wheels. No damage to personnel - ego apart - little to the car, really. Although one headlight was now focused on the treetops, as if searching out roosting birds, and if I used the wipers they tended to slap me about the face, the windscreen having scattered itself across the tarmac.

It was down to my friendly local garage early next day. This time, so as to reduce the chance of any get-out clause, I removed the Webers, etc, before the insurance assessor arrived to look the thing over. Not too bad, fifty quid and it was back on the road in a day or two. Taught me a lesson, that. There were to be no more such incidents. Well, apart from... No, it's not worth mentioning, really. But I must say, the lady was rather understanding about her poodle.

I got her a replacement, though, of course I did. Second-hand, like!

*

Meantime, back at Lyneham, my first overseas trip was a trooplift out to the Middle East, where Iraq was threatening Kuwait. That was in 1961, so it would seem things don't change a lot over the years. Another trip during my first year with MSF saw us dispatched from Benson to Wildenrath, West Germany, to take part in the Argosy proving trials. The flight out was by Argosy, that four-engined turboprop designed by Armstrong Whitworth (later to become part of the Hawker Siddeley group, eventually British Aerospace - God, seems like another lifetime). A Hastings brought us home for the Easter break.

*

We were to return to Germany courtesy of the lumbering giant; a Beverley of 47 squadron allotted the honours. Different again, especially when compared to the sleek grace of the Comet. A real workhorse, this. Descend into the empty cabin and it was like flying in a barn. All in all an interesting trip during which personnel stationed at Wildenwrath introduced us to some very agreeable pubs round about. Over the Dutch border, for instance, a place named Sittard. Remember the name of the town, you see, not too much about the pub, *that* agreeable.

What I do remember was the particular night we were invited to a house for supper, after the pub closed, which in fact made it early morning. There was a girl involved - of course there was - the fiancee of a friend of a friend; honest. She had invited us all back home along with her fiancee, to her parents house, where we were made welcome. Very much so, for the table was soon awash with plate after plate of cold cuts and salads. An early breakfast, or late supper. There was bread and beer too, enough to feed an army, and there were only six of us, plus the girl and her parents. But nine became ten when the girl's brother returned from his soirée to his pub, slightly the worse for wear. Not that we were entirely of sober mind ourselves, but we were all still capable, he proved not to be.

We were merrily tucking in to the food and drink, the brother by this stage well into a physical re-enactment of his escapades whilst serving with the Dutch paratroops in Indonesia. 'Ambush,' he suddenly yelled, grabbing a convenient umbrella, which magically transformed itself into an imaginary Sten, chattering away in his hands. Then, in an excess of enthusiasm, he flung himself to the floor, rolling for the nearest cover, which happened to be the table. Unfortunate, that, for his judgement was as poor as his reactions, his momentum such that he took the lot with him. Meat, salad, bread, butter, beer flew every which way, scattering themselves over the furnishings, and everything in the vicinity thereof, which meant us. This made things rather difficult when attempting to put together anything like a decent sandwich.

'Hey, Pete. Toss me some beetroot, will you? It's over there on the wall, just below the Rembrandt.'

'Chackka-chackka-chackka.' The brother, unperturbed by the chaos he'd created, was busily mowing down the communist hordes he imagined to be secreted away around the room.

'Yeah, right, Dave. Meantime, would you mind scraping some butter off the curtains for me?'

'Look out! Grenade!' A shell-less boiled egg flashed past my left ear, on its way to oblivion. That kind of thing. So much for the room, not to say the Dutch obsession with cleanliness and order; take some cleaning up that lot. As well he was family rather than one of us, we had enough of a reputation to live down as it was. We also had the Amstel trees to contend with. These were actually very solid poplars which lined the road on either side. They had been so named because, after a night on the Amstel, it wasn't unknown for one of them to apparently leap out in front of the car on the drive back to camp. There were so many they almost always got you. Couldn't miss really. Dodge the trees and you'd likely end up in the canal.

*

When travelling with the Brits and Comets, as MSF personnel we were usually regarded as part of the crew, which gave us access to the cockpit. I took full advantage, for I liked to keep an eye on things up front. Got some good movie footage from up there: the snowy crater of Kilimanjaro; the approach to Gan, though that certainly wasn't taken on one particular approach to the island. I remember that well.

During monsoon season the weather could be quite nasty over the Indian Ocean (on it, too, recalling that troopship). So when I noticed the navigator strapping himself in, full harness, I knew it was a signal for me to return to my seat in the passenger compartment, to do likewise, for, take-off and landing apart, the crew, with the exception of the pilot in control, rarely used seat restraints. A quick glance at the weather radar before departing told the story: solid cloud on display, bright in the centre; a sure sign of heavy precipitation and turbulence. Not nice at all. Kind of weather that makes the heart beat faster.

From the safety of earth, clouds appear as those fluffy, rose-edged or silver-lined picturesque additions to nature's canvas. But only when viewed as the backdrop to the speck of an aircraft, even one the size of a 747 - so large that some of the passengers are actually seated ahead of the crew - can their true enormity can be gauged, the forces within possibly imagined: high velocity air currents, rain, ice crystals, lightning. A boiling, seething, mass that, in the extreme case, could pluck an aircraft out of the sky and tear it apart as effectively as did those Chinese crackers to our plastic models, back there in Singapore. It is a big sky, and no matter how large an aircraft looks on the ground, up there it is very tiny indeed. Which is the very situation in which we found ourselves.

The pilots would now be relying solely on instruments and electronic aids, blind to anything outside the cockpit. Dexterously, by use of their weather radar, they would guide us around the most vicious of the storm cells. Even so, we seemed to hit every pothole in the sky, wings flapping and flexing, as they are designed to do, for they are an aircraft's shock absorbers; if they didn't flap they'd break. It's at times like that you really value your basic lapstrap.

I was certainly happy to touch down on a rain-soaked Gan that night. Happier still next morning to find we had a free day in this place where the sun once again blazed down, nature's tantrum of the previous night long forgotten, and forgiven.

Gan is one of a group of coral islands which form a rough circle around the still, blue waters of a deep lagoon. Addu Atoll is the name given to this particular group. It is surrounded by the vast expanse of the Indian Ocean, the tranquil-looking blue-green waters containing most of what is dangerous around here. Sea snakes, lion fish, stone fish, and sharks. Lots of sharks, so they say.

'Don't worry, Dave, they know and abide by the rules. You won't find them inside the reef,' Jim - my snorkelling companion and fellow MSF crew-member (radio and radar) - advised.

'Good enough,' I replied, for having recently been based here I assumed he'd be one to know.

Between the beach and the drop off, which forms the inner wall of the lagoon, is the stretch of coral-strewn shallow water in which I now lay, motionless. Through the faceplate of my mask I looked out upon the technicolour world which existed there. A magical world, in water barely two feet deep. Fish darted about at the least movement, wary, until eventually curiosity overcame caution and they moved closer. One or two braver individuals at first, but then, as if fearful they were about to miss out on something, they all edged in. Many shapes and sizes were observed, in colours only a rock star would dream of putting together. Reds, blues, greens, yellows, in any and all combinations. There were stripes and spots, wispy fins, transparent bodies, flat, round, long and slim, short and fat, the whole collection, though none appeared to be more than an inch or two in length. I was spellbound, but Jim, indicated I should follow him out to the edge of the drop off, where we could expect much bigger fish, so follow him I did.

As the coral sloped gently upwards we had to rely on the swell to lift us over the lip, a matter of precise timing. But once over, the wall was sheer. The coral was abundant, and multi-coloured, wispy tropical plants waved at us, goggle-eyed fish investigated, the vertical wall disappeared into the darkness below. Down there the world looked as mysterious and threatening as a gangster's sunglasses. Exhilarating? Would have been, but for the bloody great shark that cruised the depths. It appeared to be waiting just for us, or someone of matching stupidity. Munchies, I imagined it thinking; Fooled you. Tell you what, don't know how I made it back over the lip, but I was on the beach in no time flat. Sod the swell, colour me gone. Getting old, I suppose. Or maybe it was self-preservation coming into play; hoping to live long enough to reach old age.

As postings went, Gan was good with respect to environment, but in terms of just about everything else, it was poor. The expression "piss poor" didn't exactly fit the bill, for competitive drinking appeared to be a fact of life on the island. But no aircraft were based there permanently, it was merely a staging post and refuelling stop on the route to points east and west. Fine for a day or so, but a posting lasted a whole year (singles only). No thanks, deal me out. Given that situation, it was no wonder such inane diversions as the jetty cycle race were devised.

The jetty walls were three feet wide, fifty yards long, so, with a rider on each they would race to the end. Stopping - apart from being impossible - was apparently much less important than it had been to me during my youthful pile-ups. Winning was the prime aim here, which meant committing oneself, totally. Though, "the sensation of becoming airborne, to splash down in the warm waters of the Indian Ocean, is not too bad at all," so I was informed. Ah, well, whatever turns you on. We'd had our day, now had other places to go. Singapore, Hong Kong, Australia, New Zealand, and like that. The schedule was hectic, but we'd be sure to call in on the way back.

* *

PHOTOGRAPHS-3

Page 183: Oops! 1. **Top left::** Dropped! A Sunderland falls off the tail trolley. A case of mishandling the handle, perhaps?
Top right: S55 down in the Ulu after an engine failure - Not a lot of choice, you pick your spot and go for it. The aircraft was later stripped of its major components , then left to rot.
Centre right: S55 tail chop. A heavy landing after failure of the hydraulics to the powered controls.
Bottom: USAF C54 - last aircraft to attempt a landing on the old runway at Kai Tak. Still, as the saying goes; If you walk away, it's a good landing. (Don't suppose Uncle Sam would agree!)

Page 184: Oops! 2. **Top & centre:** This eagle apparently objected to sharing its airspace with a 267 squadron pioneer; the attack appearing to be deliberate. Ah well, can't win them all.
Bottom: S55 down in a rice paddy (another engine failure). Crewman, Gary Keen, appears to be awaiting the fellow with the lawn mower.

Page 185: Malayan forts. **Top left:.** Chabai, general view.
Top right: Chabai Officer's Mess
Centre: Chabai, aerial view. A small clearing in the dense jungle, with its oh so short airstrip carve out of the hillside.
Bottom: Fort Shean & its unique signboard.

Page 186: Whirlwind (now dressed in rescue yellow) offshore Penang Island. Another photograph from this series taken by a squadron pilot was used for the 110 squadron Christmas card 1959.

Page 187: Top: Fort Legap, I believe?
Bottom: XE515, a 267 squadron Pioneer at Chabai.

Page 188: Top: Tiger cub at Chabai (destined for Bell Vue Zoo - Manchester).
Bottom: Master Pilot Taff Walker (left) gets down to some last minute route planning in the field.

Page 189: Top: Lightly-loaded Gurkhas, disembarking for an op. Sam Saunders, crewman.
Bottom: Gurkhas, lending a hand with the refuelling, whilst I take photographs!

Page 190: Both: S55 clutch adjustment on the strip at KL. Pete "Lofty" Dace (shirtless, back to camera). The rest of the names I don't remember.

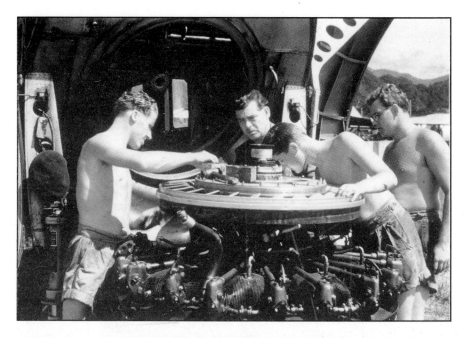

Chapter Ten
FINALS

On VIP flights, and specials, we were often afforded a temporary promotion to acting sergeant; unpaid, of course. It helped bridge the social gap between aircrew and groundcrew, did absolutely nothing for a bank balance that seemed continually to be in a state of shock. But there were occasions when even rank appeared to have been consigned to the scrapheap. One such was at RAF Changi, where we were due to make a nightstop at the start of an Australian tour. The aircraft captain was a Wing Commander, the squadron's commanding officer, in fact; a true "officer and gentleman" type.

'Everything is arranged, sir,' the young transit officer told the Wingco. 'Flightcrew to the Officer's Mess, ancillary personnel, the Sergeant's Mess.'

'Pilot Officer er.. Smith, is it?' the Wingco asked.

'Yes, sir.'

'Well, Mr Smith. As we are scheduled for an early morning departure, it would be rather helpful if we could remain together as a crew, be accommodated in the Transit Hotel.' Very pleasant, no hint of intimidation, though naturally, being at least a quartet of ranks down the ladder, the transit officer complied, magically finding rooms in a facility he'd recently declared to be full.

Things like that were what bound the crews together. We relied on them, they relied on us. It worked well, just as long as protocol was observed when necessary. Of course, all crews were different, and I heard tell of the occasional captain being considerably less accommodating. But they were either in the minority, or I struck lucky more often than not.

Apart from sharing the same hotels - these more often than not quite luxurious - we'd also socialize together. At Gan we'd load case after case of duty free beer into the aircraft hold, by the time we reached wherever, they'd be well chilled. We'd then all gather in one room or another, and start on the pre-dinner drinking.

Crew chief apart, as we only carried one rigger and one fitter - both of whose turnarounds were much more involved than ours - once we ancillary tradesmen had completed our servicing we helped out with refuelling and cleaning the aircraft. In fact cabin cleaning became quite popular. After off-loading our consignment of bodies we'd often discover unbelievable amounts of cash beneath the seat cushions and on the floor; live rounds too, if the army had been involved. Though we didn't want the live rounds, neither did we want them floating around our aircraft, so they were turned in to the powers that be.

We also lent a helping hand with any faults that required rectification, for we were a team, too. Team spirit got the aircraft turned round much quicker, which left more time for the essentials, such as demolishing the remains of the liquor cabinet at the end a VIP flight.

There were stopovers in places such as Fiji, and Bangkok, where I at last got to see most of it's three hundred temples, visit the floating market on the Chao Phraya river, view the Emerald Buddha and the Royal Chapel. I had even visited Choi Cowboy, with it's wall-to-wall girlie bars, and ridden in a three-wheeler Tak-Tak, a kind of taxi that goes nowhere fast, although slightly faster than a regular taxi. Such is Bangkok traffic.

Then there was Canberra, where a week at the Rex Hotel became one continuous party. And what a party.

This was long before the Aussies and Kiwis liberalized their drinking laws, the days of the notorious "six o'clock swill" - after which hour most Australian cities exuded the kind of gaiety one would hardly expect; more akin to that of a Welsh temperance society on the Sabbath. This was to confer upon us a distinct advantage. Being resident, we were able to circumvent this archaic state of affairs by the simple expedient of propping open the hotel cocktail bar. Which, naturally, we did. The barman at the Rex, an amiable, Australian-Scot, seemed happy to have us, plus the large circle of friends we suddenly accrued. Another thing in our favour was the fact that whereas pubs were men-only institutions, women were made welcome here, especially by the likes of us.

What a week that turned out to be; so good the recollections are only fleeting. A bunch of Aussies invited us to a party, then issued a challenge to drink crew chief, Ron King, under the table. Oh no!

I recall the last of them handing Ron the key before sloping off to bed, asking him to lock the door as we left. Then there was an aircrew versus groundcrew tenpin challenge. For a cask of beer; what else? Honours to the groundcrew this time. Difficult for it to be otherwise, most of the aircrew appeared to legless even before the contest began. Can't imagine how that came about!

Other glossy-brochure type locations featured hotels in places as diverse as Wellington; Ottawa - where it was the Chateau Frontenac; Istanbul; Nairobi - the New Stanley here, on Kimathi Street, with its Thorn Tree bar; Rome; and in Nice, the Excelsior, on the seafront. Nowhere in Khartoum could ever in a million years be classed luxurious, and the Caravelle Hotel - in Saigon - missed out as it was at the time filled to capacity with "American Advisors". (Seemed a minor skirmish was brewing hereabouts.) Instead, we found ourselves to be guests of the British Embassy staff, their families having been repatriated due to the aforementioned skirmish (a hint, perhaps, that a Viet Nam-style skirmish was not to be so minor after all). And what a thirsty bunch those remaining civil servants turned out to be, not that we were exactly paid-up members of Alcoholics Anonymous ourselves, officers included. Definitely no difference between ranks in that respect. In fact it would probably be true to say the officers came out ahead; on the wrong side of the line. The stories I could tell, but won't. Needless to say had they been flying for the airlines, they probably wouldn't have been! Not on the days in question.

Myself and the radio tech, Jim - yes, the very same guy who had taken me snorkelling at Gan - found ourselves billeted with a second secretary, in rather palatial quarters. It happened to be this chap's birthday, and he was going out to celebrate with friends. So, after ensuring we were well settled, and advised on where and where not to go in town, he invited us to help ourselves to his rather prodigious stock of liquor, then left us to it. Oh, no! Not again.

Jim, I now found, was apparently a cognac fanatic - though on this occasion I'd have said more "common sewer" than connoisseur . With our host had barely out of the door, Jim immediately latched on to a bottle of Remy Martin. And so persuasive was his invitation, I found myself imbibing along with him; try anything once, me. But not right away. Seemed I needed a little gentle coaxing before adding to my assorted intake of liquid refreshment.

'Try this,' Jim suggested, pouring a decent shot into a large snifter and handing it to me. 'You'll like it.'

'Don't like whisky, why would I like that?'

'Nothing like whisky. Much better, believe me, I know about such things.'

'Like you know all about shark etiquette?' I felt the need to remind him. 'That bugger didn't seem to mind being where he wasn't supposed to be.'

'Ah yes, sorry about that, seems I was misinformed there. But no harm done, you're alive aren't you? All the necessary pieces still attached? Anyway this is first-hand knowledge.' He stuck his nose in his glass, closed his eyes, and inhaled the fumes. 'Ahhh,' he sighed, ecstatically. He looked like the Bisto Boy.

It was enough. So, despite his *faux pas* with the shark, all was soon forgiven. I followed his example. Found I rather enjoyed the ritual, the taste, the sensation, tried a second glass just to be sure. As with my first curry - at Seletar, six years before - I loved it. Either that or, after all these years, I'm still trying to make up my mind about both. Now there's a thought, or an excuse.

'Never imagined I'd like brandy,' I told him. Wrong thing to say; my *faux pas.* He was on it in a flash, like a Scotsman onto a bargain. Or a Yorkshireman, come to that.

'Cognac,' he corrected, 'not brandy. A vast difference. All cognacs may be brandies but all brandies are certainly not cognacs,' he explained. 'This,' he stated, holding up his glass like a trophy with which he'd just been presented, 'comes only from the very heart of the Cognac region, in France. Brandy can come from anywhere. Often tastes like it has.'

I did I mention he was a bit fanatical about the stuff, didn't I? Yes, thought so, and this was when the night was still young. I learned a lot more about Cognac before he was through. For instance, did you know that... ? No, maybe not.

That evening we merely finished off the half-empty bottle, before heading downtown to join the rest of our crew in what turned out to be a fairly quiet affair, for a change. No one outrageously incapable, no undue problems. Oh, we did happen across one totally legless example of expatriate humanity, but after all, it was his birthday.

It was on this same tour that we went sightseeing, to Angkor. A series of temples, each of which had served as capital of the Khmer Empire (1113-50). Phnom Bak Kheng, known as Angkor Wat, the first capital, through to Angkor Tham, the last. These vine-covered ruins lay deep inside the Cambodian jungle, all but lost to the world at large, for they were located in an area which would, in later years, become the infamous Killing Fields of the Khmer Rouge.

With entry to the area being already self-restricting, with regard to the travel safety angle, this was to be sightseeing with a difference; from the air. Which was just as well, for the site covers over forty square miles.

Our Comet C4 descended, to pass just a few hundred feet overhead. It was the closest you could safely get at that time, and I'm not too sure about that being entirely within the bounds of safety. You know, like I had a sneaking feeling we'd probably have gone even lower had the trees not prevented it. As it was I'd prayed the aircraft wouldn't suddenly decide to charge off in an entirely inappropriate direction, or that the pilot would sneeze.

Later on in this tour came the time I finally got to land at Labuan, where five years ago I'd experienced that low pass in a Sunderland. Rather marginal as far as the Comet was concerned too, it seemed, for after taxying out, the aircraft was pushed back to the very limits of the runway threshold, ensuring every inch of its length would be available for take-off. A precaution, you understand. A contrast was the runway at Easter Island, where I was to visit some years in the future. So long it doubles as an emergency landing ground for the space shuttle. Not much more to Easter Island, apart from that runway and a bunch of unexplained statues.

Naturally, there was another side to the accommodation coin. Hong Kong, for instance: a corrugated-iron Nissen hut on the RAF Base. The same old huts we'd used when based there with 205/209. Comfortable enough - considering the few hours we seemed to require their use - but noisy when it rained. They were firmly anchored, too, steel cables ensuring they stayed put during the typhoons which the colony now and again experienced. As luck would have it, not whilst we were in attendance. Which leads nicely to that NATO exercise in Greece.

*

Larissa. Thirty-five years ago! My... that long? Our home, tent city. Row upon row of what amounted to canvas billets, with few facilities. Not at all what the Air Force was used to, never mind "The Sunshine Boys". But, as luck would have it, two things were in our favour. Close-by stood what appeared to be a derelict building, along with it's adjacent scrapheap. And we just happened to have amongst our number a couple of people who were masters of resourcefulness. Well, we all were really, needed to be at times, but "Twink" Hills and "Nobby" Clarke were experts. Kind of people who could make things appear magically, as if from thin air. So it was not to be very long before, thanks to a discarded water tank, some rusting brackets and sections of pipe, we boasted the only shower in the area. Add to the recipe an open fire, beneath the tank, and voila! A *hot* shower. Luxury! Even the officers were attracted our way by this piece of kit.

Next thing was to get out of the tents, for it rained heavily. One of those freak, continuous downpours which happen but rarely. I asked one of the locals about it. "Seen nothing on this scale for at least twenty years," he insisted. "Well..., apart from the one two years ago. And the one after that."

Rather than squelch around in a sea of mud, we decided to move into the derelict building, for it looked dry and secure. It was. So secure we were obliged to force an entry, not that that required a great deal of ingenuity or resourcefulness. Nor was it derelict. We discovered it to be filled with sacks of something or other, but it was dry, the sacks soft enough to sleep on. It offered a much better option than the quagmire outside, though there was a negative factor, a profusion of bloody great, poisonous centipedes, each fully six inches long!

So, we were dry and clean, what next? Not a lot to be done about the toilet facilities, which proved to be an ideal breeding ground for microbes and flies. An open pit, a long wooden seat with the required holes in the required places. Some poles and sacking gave a modicum of privacy by creating individual stalls, though the whole thing was open to the elements. Very basic therefore, as was our preferred method of debugging the place: a light dose of Avgas, followed by a match and a hasty retreat. Effective enough, provided one took care. But, as usual, there was always the odd idiot who decided they needed a really good dousing. "Fred" was just such a person. Not one of ours, I hasten to add.

'A touch more for luck,' quoth he, upending the can he carried. As it was rather a large can I decided the time had come to relocate myself, immediately engaged every instinct in the rush to do so, as did everyone else, with the exception of Fred. Oh, and there was....

'Hey, what the....?' came a voice from one of the stalls. A futile and irrelevant question, even had it been completed; from that point on it was obvious what.

It wasn't a huge explosion, at least, not relative to nuclear standards. There was a kind of rumbling noise, which added a touch of reality to the name, *Thunderbox*. And it did clear the toilet block, literally. Shit and sackcloth everywhere. A couple of singed rear-ends, too, I assume. Bits and pieces of whatever rained down on those passing by. Unfortunate timing, that. Especially for those who had chosen that particular moment to go about their business, as it were. The shower was a popular place that day. We felt we should have been charging for the privilege.

Yes, I was happy to see the back end of that operation, if you'll excuse the pun. Not all gaiety and laughter, you see. We did struggle a little, now and again.

*

1962 was the RAF's year for ferrying the NATO Defence College around, and I had apparently bagged one of these much sought after trips - Southern Capitals, Europe. Lucky, eh? Well, in a way. But I had recently presented Flight Sergeant Holt - the very person whose job it was to allocate our schedules, amongst other things - with a bottle of his favourite whisky (any whisky in a bottle, actually), which I miraculously just happened to have left over from a previous jaunt. Miraculous indeed, given I didn't even drink the stuff! It was what I termed forward planning. Others referred to it as bribery, but I noticed that title didn't deter them from also indulging in the practice. Not Pete though (another survivor of the Dutch ambush, you'll recall). There again, Pete didn't always get the prime trips. As I mentioned, a lot depended on if you happened to be around at the right time. Must have done all right on the whisky and cigar front, Chiefy Holt. But I was happy, too. Especially so when this turned out to be the trip during which I made the most memorable flight of this whole period of memorable flights.

The chance presented itself on the penultimate stop of the tour. Paris had come and gone, as had Malta, Ankara, Istanbul, and Athens.

We'd been shown the sights, we'd been wined and dined. Now it was the turn of Napoli, Italy. See Naples and die, so the saying goes. Easy enough to imagine it happening, too, should you wander into the wrong area of this city. Our hotel happened to be in the right area: on the seafront, across the bay from the Isle of Capri; magnificent in the sunset.

We'd had a free day, another was on the schedule for tomorrow, so a trip to Pompeii had been organised. It sounded interesting enough, but I'd decided I would much prefer to join the Admirals and the Generals on their day out, if it was at all possible. Well, nothing ventured, nothing gained, so I made discrete enquiries. The Americans promised to follow it up, check on the level of our security clearance, and let us know, which they did, in the bar, later that night. Those who wished to avail themselves of the offer should be outside the hotel at some ungodly hour the following day. As it was a day whose start was bare minutes away we had a couple more drinks to see it in, a couple more to discuss the matter - although my decision was already made. We then retired for a couple of hours sleep.

Thoughts of what lay ahead ensured I was up and about in good time, even if I wasn't feeling exactly on top of the world. OK, an Alka Seltzer will fix me up, says I, popping one into a glass of water. Time was short, couldn't wait for it to dissolve. The hell with it, I thought, I'll drink the pieces. I could vaguely recall times when I had felt better.

As the astute reader will by now have gathered, drinking was more or less a prerequisite on such tours; the price to be paid, a cross to be borne. And there was everyone thinking we were having a good time. But should you perchance feel sorry for me, don't. You see, the big disadvantage to waking up bright-eyed and bushy-tailed is that you immediately know that is as good as you're going to feel all day. I, on the other hand, often had something to look forward to, and on this particular day that something happened to be much more than the simple process of recovery from another hard night.

Aircrew apart, only myself and one other made it. Just! Nothing to do with oversleeping, or the time of day; Capri had vanished overnight, swallowed up in a bank swirling cloud. And it was that weather which almost jinxed it for us, before it ended up doing us a favour. A rather large one, as it happened, much appreciated.

The trip out was scheduled to be by launch, but because the weather was inclement, with very heavy seas, travel by air became a necessity. Well, no problem as far as the Americans were concerned. If there was room we could still be included, if not, it looked likely to be the lava encrusted offerings of Pompeii.

It took half a dozen flights all told, and we had to wait until last, naturally. Don't know how many times I counted bodies, divided by the number of passengers per flight, checked my watch, crossed my fingers, promised God I'd be forever good, maybe even threatened to stop drinking, but it worked. A Grumman TF-1 Trader eventually carried me across the Bay of Naples, for a deck landing on the then mighty, *USS Forrestal*. Pretty small by modern standards, I understand, but it seemed huge to me. Let's face it, the largest ship I'd ever seen had carried me back from Singapore, and let me tell you now, twenty thousand tons was tiny by comparison to this leviathan.

Seated down the back in that windowless fuselage we were therefore blind to the approach, but despite this there was no mistaking our arrival, for the punctuation of that flight bore all the hallmarks of a car wreck; a thump, and deceleration in the one-twenty to zero knots in two seconds kind of range. You see, carrier-based aircraft aren't landed so much as thrown onto the deck. A rather violent means of arrival, but one which supposedly permits a fairly accurate prediction of the touch-down point: ideally, apparently the third of four arresting wires. I believe we hooked the second, adding yet another milestone to my catalogue of aeronautical adventures.

The NATO staff officers were escorted away by the welcoming committee: lunch, political briefing and Yankee hype, followed by a whirlwind tour, one suspects. The Britannia boys - flight-crew and ourselves - having been assigned a guide of our very own, were conducted through areas of particular interest to us: lunch, below-deck hangarage, tech workshops, launch control. No rush, no bullshit. Hype aplenty, but that was only to be expected. No booze either, not on an American flag vessel. No way.

Then came the highlight of the trip. An exclusive air show during which the carrier launched, displayed, and retrieved its complement of aircraft.

Guard helicopter apart, the piston-engined Skyraiders were first. Then came the jets: Phantom, Skyhawk, Skywarrior. These were followed by their "eye in the sky", the Grumman Tracker.

It was an awesome display. Even moreso when they each demonstrated their firepower: bombs; heat-seeking missiles fired at flares; cannon fired at the ocean. Spectacular but harmless explosions in and above an empty sea. Modern high-tech entertainment. And of course, an empty sea placed no restrictions on the speeds attained by those Phantoms, which is when high-tech became high velocity. Talk about fast and furious. It was a matter of afterburners and compression vortices. God, what I would have given for a trip in one of those beasts.

And with the NATO complement comfortably seated on deck - once it was clear of aircraft - we found ourselves sited on "Vulture's Row," halfway up the island, overlooking the whole operation. Down below, multi-coloured groups of men scuttled hither and zither about their tasks in that crowded and dangerous environment.

Ours was a spectacular viewpoint, and from it I watched with growing interest, paying particular attention to the launch procedure, excitement building as I anticipated it happening to me. But by the end of the day, the sea was deemed calm enough for us to be safely transferred ashore by boat. Pity, that. I was quite looking forward to being catapulted into the sky from the end of some British-invented steam contraption. Still, certainly not "just another day in the office," this had been the stuff of which dreams were made.

After that outing the remainder of the tour seemed rather anti-climactic. Even three days in sunny Rome failed to capture my complete attention - Trevi Fountain, Spanish Steps, Via Veneto, Coliseum; places to which all first time visitors seem to gravitate. Then there were the restaurants and bars: the pasta, pomadoro and fromagio, the Barolo and the Asti Spumante. That was Rome. From there it was back over the Alps for another short stop in Paris - one of the world's really great cities - where we deposited our guests before returning to Lyneham. Anti-climatic? Not really; a gem of a tour.

*

The next tour on my schedule was another gem, or sounded like it could have been: a Royal Tour of Nepal, with the Queen, and Prince Phillip. Hadn't a clue as to how I even came to be selected, the requirement being for DC3-experienced personnel. Well, I had seen a few, even flown in one. Watched one crash, too. I suppose that constitutes a certain amount of experience, albeit not quite the kind I would wish for. So maybe it was to do with mild personality, smartness of dress, amiability? No, not me then. In any event, after a return visit to RAF Insworth, in the heart of Gloucestershire, to be kitted-out with de-luxe, tropical uniforms, plus making various other preparations, my participation in the tour was suddenly cancelled, as was the Queen's. Coincidence, eh? Well I hardly think Her Majesty cancelled out in sympathy for my exclusion. In fact the whole thing was cancelled. For what reason, I don't recall hearing, for no one ever seemed to confide in me.

Probably as a result of all this touring, it was during this period that I turned my attention to the pleasures of gourmet cooking, and fine wines; although there was no way I was about to abandon the Indians. In fact I discovered a place in Swindon that served a real mean vindaloo. But the days when I might have walked into a restaurant and ordered an egg omelette or a red *vin rouge* were long gone.

1963. The year began with a detachment to Bahrain, where I was to spend three weeks on detachment with No.54 squadron and their Hunters. (54 squadron were also part of 38 Group, which encompassed Transport Command.) Different indeed, for a transport type, but I quite enjoyed the experience. What a pity they didn't take along a two-seat T7. Could have volunteered to go along on an airtest, I would have loved that.

Two exercises to Cyprus followed the Bahrain trip, then came a polar trainer to Thule, returning via the North Pole. Next was a quickie to Nairobi, before being rushed up to Dishforth to retrieve a grounded Comet 2. No seats fitted, so it was a "park yourselves on the floor" return trip.

The following month saw us off on a world tour, Chief of Air Staff Designate along for the ride. Or maybe I've got that the wrong way round? Trips to Cyprus and Bardufoss - Norway - allowed us to catch our collective breath before departing for Canada and the United States with Lord Louis Mountbatten. A real privilege.

We would occasionally be presented with a gift on completion of such a tour, a bottle of whisky maybe, or something equally useful. (I was usually able trade whisky for cognac. If not I could always give it to Chiefy Holt) But I do recall one Tory politician who seemed to think an autographed photo was something we might well treasure! No names, no packdrill. And it was a long time ago. I never once wondered what happened to that photograph.

The Mountbatten tour was followed by an exercise to Australia with the Royal Ulster Rifles, after which 45 Commando were ferried to Southern Rhodesia for some threatened crisis in Swaziland. Then it was back to Australia, to return with the recently dispatched RUR. Varied and interesting work, compared to the regular schedules of other service personnel. Another big plus was the fact that we were rarely around for parades and inspections.

With many departures taking place late at night, this usually meant a dawn arrival somewhere or other. Many a touchdown was therefore greeted by a warming sunrise - summer in the Arctic Circle apart, for there, at that time of year, the sun never sets.

Like seamen, whenever we MSF types got together we recalled trips, crews, countries, and, of course, girls. With more landfalls, in more cities, we probably knew more bars than did the sailors. And believe me, there are lots out there well worth remembering. Bars and girls.

But it was the VIP trips that were always the most interesting, for on those we would often spend days on the ground between sectors; plenty of time to survey the local sights. And I never once felt the least bit guilty knowing the taxpayer was funding my travel. After all, I was a taxpayer, too. Of course it couldn't last, nor did it. The 1974 Defence Review decreed that cuts had to be made somewhere, and with the Comets already gone, the Britannia was where. But by then I had gone too; long since found someone else willing to pay my way.

*

I even got to fly a Britannia, one time. Beautiful take off, even if I say so myself. The chance to experience this was courtesy of a friend (maybe ex-friend), Tony; technician in charge of Lyneham's simulator.

'Quite a time consuming job to get this lot back on line after it has been crashed on the approach,' he informed me, though possibly not quite in those words. Still, I suspect it was never intended to be flown solo. Flying controls, gear, flaps, throttles, the lot. Rather a handful for a qualified pilot, never mind your wayward instrument fitter cum frustrated fighter pilot.

That then was Lyneham. Another sackful of memories to be filed away. Three years worth. Probably the best of all. Or was that a thought generated by the fact that these happened to be the most recent. Whatever, there were many more goodbyes to be said: to friends and colleagues, Comet and Britannia, part-time lovers and romantic places. It was also goodbye to the Air Force itself, although their goodbye to me, after ten years service, was a mere ninety pounds cash. Not exactly a golden handshake. There again, could have taken a suit in lieu, but .... well, yes, exactly. Still, the Air Force had taught me a lot over the years, had afforded me more good experiences than any amount of cash could possibly buy. Valuable, those. I'd also become independent, able to stand on my own two feet, knew I wouldn't go far wrong in not relying on others to help me out of situations I was perfectly capable of getting myself into without the help of anyone. On top of which, I had seen the world. Or so I thought. Anyway it was a shrinking world, a shrinking Air Force, a shrinking Empire. El Adem, Bahrain, Aden, all gone. Given a few more years and Gan would also disappear, as would Changi itself. I decided it was also time for me to go, to move on.

So it was that my service life came to an end. I felt a wistful sadness in a way. Ten years out of my life, then. Good years, too, despite the occasional hardship, real or imagined. Anyway hardships are part and parcel of life, and overall, I think luck ran with me more than the reverse. Or maybe the volunteering had worked in my favour. Was it possible I'd manoeuvred myself into positions where luck played right into my hands? Wasn't it Louis Pasteur (or, probably, Dr Johnson, maybe even someone else) who suggested, *Chance favours only the prepared mind.*

Whatever, I had no regrets about those years, none at all. So, even though I was a little misty-eyed, I was now ready for a new challenge. But what kind? Of that I wasn't sure. All I knew for certain was that it had to be this way, despite thoughts that life in the outside world would surely be anti-climatic when compared to life in the Air Force.

For a time I felt like I was walking away from a life that had given so much, following a trail that led who knew where. But when doubt caused me to stop and look back over my shoulder, the path back there seemed to have disappeared completely. Which left me with no alternative but to forge ahead, get on with the rest of my life. I didn't even contemplate how long the road ahead might, where it may take me, or how far I would travel before I reached the end - of the road, or my life. Out there were new experiences to be encountered, new places to be discovered, old favourites to be revisited. Australia and New Zealand had wet my appetite for more of the same, as had America, despite my first visit replaying like a scene from a bad movie.

It happened during a visit to Shepard Air Force Base, Wichita Falls, Texas. Yet another exercise. This one involving elements of the British and American armies, at nearby Fort Bragg. Some new type of cannon, I seem to recall. Something that was supposedly much more efficient in the art of wiping out human beings.

Upon completion of servicing, securing our aircraft for the night, we were invited out by the American crew who'd helped refuel our Britannia. An invitation we gladly accepted. Only natural, that, bad manners not to. They took us by car to Oklahoma city - over the Red River and across the state line - where, for a change, we visited the odd bar or two.

We'd left *The Piano Lounge,* or some such, after a bit of a scuffle, one of our hosts having been threatened by a Latin type. Apparently the girl he'd been attempting to chat up was this guy's sister, and he had taken umbrage to the fact that our host had approached her. The two of them got into it, the Latin was floored, we felt it prudent to leave.

We were now cruising round, looking for somewhere interesting, when a police car passed us at speed, red lights flashing, siren howling. Real Hollywood stuff. But there was a problem, for it suddenly chopped across our bows and screeched to a halt. So did we, little choice in the matter. We'd have come to a stop for sure if we hadn't. A very sudden, and embarrassing stop.

`Out the car!' a voice commanded. We obeyed. Let's face it, they were actually pointing guns at us, just like on TV. For what, a minor traffic violation? I was aghast.

There were two of them. Not a tall thin one and a short fat one, but they wouldn't have looked out of place if they had been.

`Keep your hands in sight, and *don't* move,' ordered one. `Up against the car and spread those legs,' demanded the other.

They looked at one another, as did we. It was like something out of Police Academy whatever. But they still had guns. And those guns were still pointed our way.

'Yeah, up against the car,' agreed the first.

Had the second also reversed his opinion I think I'd have cracked up, despite the threat to life and limb. As he didn't, I decided to try the "confused-English-gentleman-abroad" trick.

'Excuse me, officer. Could you please explain what is going on?' Alec Guinness at his talented best. And it worked!

'From outa town, huh?' He seemed rather more amiable, and I thought I detected a slight hesitancy in his manner.

'From England, actually,' I replied, proudly.

'That so? Well, up against the goddamn car, limey, before I bust yur mouth.

Ah well. It almost worked.

Never did discover the ins and outs of what it was all about, for we left early next day, after we'd checked out the inside of the precinct house, making a statement on events as we saw them in that bar. Could only assume the Latin had a relative on the local police force. Maybe the chief, who knows.

Not a very auspicious introduction to a country. But that wasn't typical America, was it? I mean, we'd just been unfortunate. Wrong place at the wrong time, kind of thing, right?

Well, we had, hadn't we?

* *

Chapter Eleven
JOURNEY INTO THE FUTURE

One would think an eleven year stint in the services would be excellent preparation for release into civilian life, and on the whole this was true. But what to do with my new found freedom?

A large part of my service life had been spent touring the world, at the taxpayers' expense. It had been an occupation in which even flying was classed as work, whereas to someone like me every flight was an experience not to be missed. Where else could one encounter such a magic sensation on a grey, dull, damp November morning than by punching a hole in the murk (or whatever it is aircraft do), to break out into bright sunshine?

Take-off, and the all-encompassing darkness and gloom would gradually clear, until the cloud itself became thin and wispy. This is actually one of the few times during scheduled flight that speed becomes apparent; those final moments of breakout, or vice versa. In next to no time the overcast would be left far below, spread out like an untidy carpet. The clouds above would look fresh and washed, brilliantly white, as opposed to used and dirty, for up there is a special world. It is a world of dazzling, mountainous peaks, dream castles, chasms, and canyons; or of nothing more than a blue emptiness. Peaceful is what it can be; a sky that at times seemed surreal, full of possibilities, and of mystery. It is a world to be shared only with God, the birds, and other aviators; the sun, moon, and stars often your sole companions. Then there are the sunsets and the dawns. They can be magnificent when viewed from such an superior location. Sunrise spectacularly so, especially when it occurs at the end of a long, night sector.

At present these were all just memories, to be extracted from my suitcase of dreams, as and when required. But that suitcase was as yet only partially full; room for lots more.

Could have gone in for anything, I suppose. A fresh start. Police, accounting, mechanic, binman, all no doubt honest enough occupations, which someone has to do. But count me out. Not for me the nine to five of an office, nor a life in which unions would dictate where and when I could work, and for how much. I was too independent for that, needed something different. I was fully aware of the alternatives, prepared to go and seek them out.

For eleven years I had been living a kind of gypsy existence. Home was wherever I ended up. So I couldn't suddenly settle down, just like that. Besides, leaving the service had done nothing to diminish my interest in aviation, the passion was still evident, though perhaps not strong enough for me to commit myself to a controlled working environment, with the airlines, say. At least, not here in England. The quest for adventure had not yet been enervated, nowhere near. There still remained far horizons beyond which I felt the need to travel, so travel was the option I felt the need to pursue. The airlines I'd already rejected, mainly because of the union factor. Same rules applied to the aircraft manufacturers. Anyway, I no longer felt the need to actually touch aircraft, to see and fly in one occasionally would probably suffice. So scratch the aviation angle. I didn't have the means to go motor racing, which probably meant I also lacked commitment, which again left me with the travel. Travel, therefore, seemed like the best path to tread. So onward then, best foot forward, into the unknown. Besides, I wasn't exactly out of ideas, already had the inkling of yet another cunning plan.

Back in the old home town, a long-time friend and I had already discussed the possibility of emigrating to the United States. Ron had left the service three months prior to me, and as he held a First Mate's ticket in the Merchant Marine he'd taken a job in the North Sea, awaiting my demob. During this period Ron heard mention of a company in America with whom it might be possible for us to get a job, which was all the encouragement we needed; decision made. With any luck, working in America had to be better than working in England, and I figured it may just see me on my way to the financial freedom I sought. Not the kind of financial freedom that gives one the power to trash hotel rooms, or to drive the Rolls into the swimming pool. Such behaviour I was quite willing to leave to the upcoming generations of pop stars. All I required were funds enough to ensure my future comfort.

*

So it was - less than three months after hanging up my Blues - that I found myself airborne once more, winging my way across the Atlantic. Ringway to Idlewild (now Kennedy), via Prestwick, courtesy of BOAC and Boeing. Yet another new type for the logbook: the 707; the degree of comfort previously unimaginable. Yes, I realized, I could easily tolerate a life of not working on aeroplanes, as long as I occasionally got to fly in something like this. The difference was, this time I paid my own fare. An occurrence which, up to then, was about as rare as the loaves and fishes episode.

Ron and I had planned on a few relaxing days first, in New York City. It was a place with which Ron was quite familiar, and an area of this vast country to which I had never been; city or State. But relaxation wasn't quite what we got, the way things turned out. As was seemingly to become the norm, our plans ended up in shreds. Rather than relaxation, there was to be another confrontation with cops, instead. Not our fault, honest. It just so happened that the room we had rented was also being claimed by the landlady's ex-husband. They were apparently still in dispute over ownership of the house. No, change all that, nothing apparent about it!

On only the second night, Ron and I, in our beds at the time, were awakened when this guy burst into the room, closely pursued by his irate better-half. Didn't seem like he was here to discuss the legal implications of our tenancy, either, for he was obviously drunk, seemingly with malice in mind. Just as well his ex-wife was present, for she took the brunt of his ire. A shouting and slanging match ensued between him and his ex, during which I learned lots of new and interesting words. This tempestuous two-way invective was eventually to follow the protagonists back downstairs, out of the house, and on up the road into the depths of Queens.

Half an hour later we had another caller. He seemed equally insistent on being allowed entry, so I got up to check on things, our door now locked and barred, from the inside.

This time, as he'd previously stated - 'Open up. Police' - it was one New York's finest, fully tooled up as usual, requesting our version of events. He wasn't at all belligerent, just stood there, idly tapping one palm with his nightstick. But I knew his mate would be out there somewhere, probably lurking in the shadows, ready to lay down a hail of lead if called upon to do so. I'd seen the movies, watched TV, knew what it was all about. Didn't make a scrap of difference, even at three in the morning you don't contest such a request. We didn't. Which severely disrupted our sleep, to say nothing of our visit to the Big Apple.

Two trips to the States, two confrontations with the cops. Neither of which should have involved me, both of which had. America was not coming out of this too well. What next? I wondered. Well, as there was a requirement for us to head south, down to New Orleans, with a chance to fly in Boeing's new 727 tri-jet, we decided to do so. In fact, later that same day seemed to be an ideal time; the first available flight. This was especially true being as the company concerned had offered to pay our expenses once we arrived in their fair city, even though they did decline on the air fare. Goodbye Times Square, hello Jackson Square.

The original intent had been for me to take up residence in the United States, but the job I duly applied for, and accepted, when it was offered, was to take me - after four months in the Pacific Northwest, California and New Orleans - back across the Atlantic. Forget the immigration bit, for although a Social Security number had been assigned to me, and I was in possession of the all-important "green card", there was a requirement for me to remain in the States for some time yet before it became fully effective. Not the Social Security number, mind; as that required me to pay tax, it became effective immediately. Anyway, I still wasn't sure about the cops. Those fictional movies and TV shows were now looking less so. At this point I wouldn't have been surprised had I come across Bugs Bunny wandering down the street!

Just as well I didn't immigrate as it turned out. My service background would have almost guaranteed my being drafted into the US Forces, and a second spell in Vietnam was unlikely to replicate that first brief visit.

So began a period of intense travel. Anywhere, everywhere, anytime; all expenses paid. I couldn't believe my luck. I could be in Singapore, say, maybe South America, Brazil, and I'd think, wow, here I am on the beach at Copacabana, and someone's paying me to be here. Who'd have thought it possible. Certainly not the teacher who long ago forecast that, unless I changed my ways, I was not destined to go far. It seemed an odd prognosis, sitting there on that beach. There again, maybe I had changed my ways.

I made sure family and friends were kept abreast of my movements. Postcard from wherever, kind of thing: "Wish you were here", and suchlike. Pictures of golden beaches and palm trees. New Zealand was one such: "... the weather has been magnificent. Leaving tomorrow for Tahiti." And from that Pacific paradise, in which I arrived during a tropical downpour: "Yesterday I thought I'd forgotten to pack the sun, but it's out now so all is well." Then, from California: "Just happened to arrive in the middle of a heatwave. I hear you're having snow."

But wait. I'm jumping the gun a bit. We haven't even left America yet. Barely arrived, in fact.

*

Offshore Navigation Inc was a survey company working mainly with the oil industry, in the offshore environment, naturally. The job involved the positioning of seismic vessels, drillships, rigs, platforms, pipelines, whatever, with a relative degree of accuracy. Nothing that would be acceptable today, but standards change. That was then. (The company did in fact have the contract for navigation trials of the US Nuclear Submarine fleet (Polaris). But that was for especially cleared personnel only, not the likes of me.)

Radiolocation, was the name of the game. The desired qualifications for which appeared to be an electronics background (an emphatic "yes"), plus some knowledge of navigational and survey procedures ("yes," though maybe not so emphatic). I presumed it was also a requirement to be fit, judging by the medical I was required to endure. Serious stuff this.

There again, being the good old US of A, no doubt the charge for it would be equally serious. All was well though, that charge was to the company's account.

It seemed that, in this line of work, it also helped if you were slightly crazy (oh, oh), though it was a few months before that became fully apparent. Not, that I *was* crazy, that it may have helped if I *had* been, is what I mean. If adventure was what I craved, it was certainly what I was about to get. Served up in man-sized chunks. Was this the stuff that dreams were made of?

The idea was that a vessel could be positioned utilizing signals transmitted from two or three accurately located shore stations: similar to what Bomber Command achieved during the war with their Oboe (or was it H2S?). In fact the equipment we used *had* once been the property of the USAF, snapped up at a giveaway price by a far-sighted ex USAF officer, then pressed into civilian use. The boats needed bodies to install, operate, and repair the equipment, as did the shore stations. Lots of people, lots of logistics, lots of problems in lots of countries.

For a start the equipment was not exactly state-of-the-art. It may well have been so in 1942, when it was used for aerial navigation and bombing, or when it was last used as intended, in the Korean conflict of 1950. But this was 1964. Still, they did pay well, and as the work was worldwide I would still manage more than the occasional flight. Just what I wanted, wasn't it?

Well, possibly. Although the first job I went on had me wondering if I had made a wise choice.

I was handed a ticket and instructed to fly up to Astoria, Oregon, wherever that might be. Upon arrival, I was to report to a certain hotel, to a certain person. No problem there; this, after all, *was* America. Taxi to the airport, Delta Airlines DC8 to Memphis, St Louis, and on to Chicago - Midway. Change flights: United DC8 to Seattle and Portland, before changing again. Bit of a comedown, this: West Coast Airlines DC3 for the final, turbulent leg through down-on-the-deck cloud and rain. Ten hours total, and there I was, in the top left-hand corner of US, on the Pacific Coast. It had been sunny in New Orleans, here it pissed down, continually. Which no doubt accounted for the lush greenery.

I took a taxi and splashed my way to the designated hotel - the John Jacob Astor - where I registered, and dumped my bags. I next checked with reception as to the precise location of the person I sought.

'You'll find him in the office,' was the reply. So I took myself off in the direction indicated, right there on the premises would you believe. The "office" was where I'd been told I'd find the area supervisor; apparently a well-known character around these here parts, as they say around these here parts.

Discovery number one: This "office" went under the name of The Fur Trader. (And why not? German born John Jacob Astor, after whom the hotel was named - as was the town, come to that - had developed a virtual monopoly on the fur trade, back in the eighteen hundreds.) Discovery number two: the person whom I suspected to be my contact appeared to be well advanced in the act of trading - dollar bills, for beer. He had a glass in his hand even as I walked in, but from the look of things he was just topping up the beers he'd already had.

And just why did I suspect him to be my contact?

Had to be, didn't he? He was the only person in the place other than the barman, who was, nevertheless, being kept fairly busy.

The interior decor matched the name: log cabin effect walls and bar, beamed ceiling, real furs hanging around; minus their original occupants, of course. Above and behind the bar were pinned US currency notes of various denomination, each bearing someone's name. Emergency funds, I assumed. What a quaint idea.

The place was air-conditioned, cool and comfortable-looking. Rather inviting, one might say, so I wandered over to where my leader-to-be propped up the bar. His features matched the name I'd been given, for he had that Latin look about him: slicked-back dark hair, matching pencil-thin moustache, devious-looking eyes, beaky nose.

'Excuse me. Are you Jose?' I hoped he was, for he looked like someone you needed on your side rather than against you.

Must have been the politeness that got him, for he spun round so fast he almost fell off his stool. But he recovered quickly enough, as a good supervisor should.

'Yeah. And you're?'

'Dave Taylor. Just hired on with ONI.'

'Hey, don't bug me with your problems, Dave. Pull up a stool and have a drink.'

Sounded familiar. So, in order that the interests of world peace and international friendship and understanding should prevail, I sacrificed myself once again. Big mistake. In this job, it seemed, to be caught without a glass close to hand was tantamount to being unqualified. I was trapped, unable to make my escape. Good excuse, eh?

By the time midnight arrived there were five of us; not including midnight, that was the time. (Had it related to a person it would have been twenty-three fifty-nine, you may recall. Chapter two. Remember?) The whole bunch of us were either employees of ONI, or about to become so, all in more or less the same shape. Well, maybe not Jose. He'd had a head start, after all. There again he was supposed to be our supervisor.

Jose didn't merely drink, he threw it back like he'd heard they were going to re-introduce prohibition real soon. Like maybe tomorrow.

It showed; he picked up the tab. (See how quickly I was picking up the language.)

When we eventually departed we left midnight way behind, but like I said, time wasn't with us. Anyway, we only made it as far as the nearest pizza parlour, to which Jose insisted on driving us. He wasn't in too bad a shape, really. He could drive, even if he couldn't stand. Couldn't change gear, either. Never got out of first, although he refused to give up trying, much to the detriment of the gearbox by the sound of things. Still, it was a company vehicle, and we didn't need to cover much over a mile.

Jose also bought dinner - or was it breakfast? - no doubt on his expense account, along with those drinks. I didn't care, I was famished, hadn't eaten for ages. I had drunk rather a lot, but that wasn't quite the same; very little protein.

Then, almost as a prelude to the new day, Jose finally managed to get us thrown out. Well, we were asked to leave, really, which, in a place such as that, more or less amounted to the same thing. Seems he had been getting rather vociferous over the, Goldwater vs Johnson for President, issue. Don't even remember who it was he supported, but it doesn't really matter does it, he was standing on the table, addressing all who cared to listen, along with those who did not. Ah well, I'd been thrown out of worse places. And at least they hadn't called the cops. Couldn't have stood that. Could barely stand as it was. Needless to say, Jose was not yet finished, he found us another bar. Or maybe that was as far as the vehicle was prepared to take us, for it ground to an ignominious halt, right outside the place. Convenient, eh?

Naturally, at that time I was still under the influence of ten years RAF upbringing. Which is to say, any expenses incurred should be absolutely justifiable, otherwise the Air Ministry were liable to get... well, not just upset, they went straight for the jugular. In this industry, I learned, fiddling the expense account was a battle of wits. Could prove quite lucrative, provided you came up with a scam which would not stretch credibility beyond very elastic bounds. Why do you think oil costs what it does!

*

The moment I awoke was when I started to have second thoughts about what I might have let myself in for with this Offshore Navigation outfit.

No, I told myself, surely the second thoughts began yesterday? When I first set eyes on Jose?

Yes, of course. But things haven't improved, have they? At which point I gave up the internal discussion with myself. In fact, enthusiasm for my new job didn't just dive, it crashed straight through zero, well into the negative factor.

A boat? I couldn't remember how I'd got there, didn't know what I was supposed to be doing there, and I wasn't at all well. This was nothing like flying, not in any way, shape, or form. I figured it had to be a big sea out there, and so it was - the Pacific Ocean, to be precise, they don't come any bigger. But when I say "big," I really meant in terms of wave height. To someone like me, a self-confessed aerophile, and landlubber, it felt like they were enormous. Gigantic, even. Easy to deduce from the way the room was moving around me. Only the room was now a cabin; another deduction - and as such, not bad for a man in my state of health, even if decidedly less than helpful in terms of practical assistance.

I got up to have a look, should have stayed put. The boat - a very small boat in these seas - pitched and rolled alarmingly as it rode mountainous waves. It rose and plunged, crashed and shuddered, from one trough to the next. It also sounded very much like it was about revert to its component parts at any moment. Anything not secured was on the move. I couldn't have cared less, even though my stomach certainly wasn't secure.

It was to be two days before I again ventured out of my bunk, not that anyone seemed unduly worried. Apparently it was too rough for us to work anyway. And so it remained, for most of the time I was on board. All

I seemed to be learning were new ways in which to throw up, and a new language: topside, below, and other nautical-type terms, some of which were familiar, from my days on the flying boats. The bow was the pointy

end, I remembered, stern the rear, and those little round windows weren't, they were ports. The head was something new, and it was where I was most frequently to be found, whenever I was upright.

It was two weeks before I saw dry land again - possibly the longest two weeks of my life - and I couldn't wait to step ashore. And guess what? Jose was there to greet me. Well, not exactly greet, his mind was filled with other thoughts.

Evidently my brief spell with the equipment constituted something of an apprenticeship (compared to the eighteen months it took to reach that status in the Air Force)! I'd seen Shoran in operation, had a go myself, was apparently fully qualified, albeit with little experience. No matter, Jose was ready to offer me another assignment, along with a drink, of course. Despite the fact recollection of those two weeks started to recede into the background the moment I set foot on *terra firma*, there wasn't the slightest chance of me accepting either, and Jose, much to his credit, was intuitive enough to spot that. Which is when he started putting on the pressure. This, I recognised and understood.

It was a pleasant day out there on the dock. A hot sun, blue sky swept clear of clouds, insects buzzing around. A beautiful part of the country to be in on such a day: mountains, trees, crystal waters. We stood and talked as the minutes passed us by, and, as if there was a statute of limitations on bad memories, I slowly began to see things in a different light. Well, I was rather thirsty, and the sun was way over the yardarm, so I yielded a degree or two. I accepted his renewed offer of a drink, agreed to discuss things further, in more familiar surroundings.

He next offered a rather substantial pay-raise, which I turned down. Reluctantly, I'll admit, memories now fading significantly. Besides, where else could I go, what could I do? I had thought of trying for a job with Boeing, just down the road, so to speak, in Seattle. But that had been when things were at their worst, out there on that boat. I now realized I had no idea how to go about it, had no contacts. Anyway, Jose had by now attracted my interest. I decided to see how far he was prepared to go.

He bought another round, offered an even more substantial hike in salary. The memories were definitely dimming, hardly any recollection at all now, plus I figured ONI must be desperate for personnel. (Little did I know Jose had just had two guys quit on him, and he'd had to fire a third. No choice there, the guy in question having phoned the company president at three in the morning. He'd then told him he though Jose useless, and that he should be promoted to replace him. Not a good idea even at three in the afternoon, there again he probably wasn't drunk at three in the afternoon.)

It was about this time that I accepted a third drink, then suffered an attack of the second thoughts. Well, let's face it, oldest excuse in the world: it seemed like a good idea at the time. Especially as I wasn't to be at sea. Nor did it require the services of a chartered accountant to discern that this was a very reasonable offer. But it was the attraction of a land job that really decided me. I was to operate a navigation site high up in the beautiful Olympia National Park.

'Just yourself and one other guy, a camper-van, and a trailer, acre upon acre of green trees, snow on the high ground, the blue sky up above,' Jose assured me, sounding more like a tour guide. Although, as I was later to discover, one minor point seemed to have slipped his mind. He'd made no mention of the fact there were bears out there, too. Well, I'd faced the dual threats of snakes and tigers during my spell in the jungles of Malaya, and as with those, the bears never bothered us either, so we tried not to bother them. The Pacific Ocean was also out there. Somewhere. Way beyond my view. As far as I was concerned it could stay that way. I was going to be all right, for I was happy again.

Had Jose known, he could have got me for a lot less. My needs were few, and I wasn't even contemplating a donation to Oxfam. A bit devious perhaps, but what the hell. (Actually, thinking about it now, well after the event, it strikes me as being a lot devious. But, as I was to find, Jose wasn't exactly being straightforward, either. This was a high turnover industry; seems people switched around as the mood took them.)

It's possible sterling was a little below par at the time, but what I was to be paid was a fortune compared to what I could expect back home. Even the miners weren't raking it in on this scale.

I only recall one small problem we encountered on that specific, pre-surveyed point on that Washington mountain. Well, not us in particular, the boat. Seems they experienced some difficulty with their navigation the day my colleague drove the truck - in which was located the active transmitter - down the hill to the local supermarket. Said they felt our signal was not too reliable, the transmitted position apparently somewhat unstable!

*

Overall, I quite got to like the job, despite the fact it was male dominated. But my world had been that way ever since leaving school and joining the Air Force. Before really, for the school I attended having been boys only.

It wasn't that I could do without women in my life, no way. I needed them, but I also needed my independence. Too-close friends had always seemed to let me down in one way or another, at one time or another. I didn't find that to be the case with friends separated by distance. Maybe that's why I was a bit of a loner. Anyway, some of the female friends I met weren't exactly the long term type. Take for instance the pretty young thing I met up with in New Orleans.

After the basic introductions, she enquired, in her own inimitable way, as to, 'Where y'all from?'

I glanced round, found myself to be alone, despite her use of the plural.

'York,' I told her. Even though I still lived in Norton, with my parents, I always told them York, especially overseas. After all, I doubt even Malton would admit to the presence of Norton. So York is what I told her. 'Know where that is?' I asked.

'Sure do,' she replied. 'Up north, ain't it?'

'In a way. Up north and across the Atlantic. The United Kingdom,' I corrected.'

That stumped her, though she wasn't about to admit defeat, even if a reply did require the application of serious thought. I could almost see her mind in action. Maybe if I'd said England, or even Great Britain, the result might have been different. But I hadn't, so it wasn't.

'Well I'll tell y'all one thing,' she eventually said. 'Fer a foreigner yuh sure speak good English.'

OK, so she'd skimped on geography. Anyway, it wasn't her mind I was interested in, and as far as biology went she hadn't missed out on a thing.

That was something else I needed to get used to: American English. For instance, the slogan "Nothing sucks like Electrolux" I once saw attached to a British vacuum cleaner, would be unlikely to endear the product to a public whose understanding of the word "sucks", is for any item so described to be of extremely poor quality. Or, as Gerald Rattner later put it - in what eventually turned out to be the closing down speech of his jewelery business - "crap."

I picked it up eventually. Soon learned it was impolite to ask a girl if she required "knocking up" in the morning. At least until we were on more intimate terms.

After a month or so in the forests of Washington State - as opposed to Washington DC, two thousand three hundred miles away on the east coast - I found myself en-route to Long Beach, California, the company's West Coast office. Here I discovered I was scheduled to pick up another camper-van, drive it the better part of two thousand miles, to New Orleans, Louisiana (aka NOLA); after first picking up a co-driver at the airport in Los Angeles. Another employee, back from another assignment in another place.

'No problem,' Al, the supervisor for this particular area, told me, immediately issuing forth with a stream of directions on how to reach the airport by road, which, to my mind, sounded extremely complicated. I, meantime, was busy dreaming up some excuse as to why I would be unable to fulfil the role of driver.

'I'd much rather fly,' I told him.

'Me too, replied Al, who, I discovered, flew gliders for fun on a weekend. 'But we have all this equipment to be transferred back to head office, and two people heading that way.'

So it was that Al won the day. Of course he did. Thankfully without the need of recourse to the nearest bar. Which is how I came to end up behind the wheel of an overloaded camper-van which steered like an overloaded camper-van. That is to say, with all the finesse of a drunken hippopotamus.

It was rush hour on a Friday evening, I'd never before driven a left-hand drive vehicle on the right-hand side of the road, yet this was precisely what I ended up doing. Not only that, I was heading for the notorious Los Angeles freeway, with little idea of where I was going, or what I was about to do. The very arguments I'd been dreaming up to present to Al as reasons as to why I should fly. But I'd discounted the fact that occasionally my mind literally soaked up information, and retained it. Mostly, it appeared, irrelevant, seemingly useless trivia. (Using up brain cells which could probably have been put to good use in later life?) But I now found a lot of the recent input was suddenly becoming very relevant indeed.

A bend in the road ahead, traffic lights. "Take a left there," I remembered. Or possibly, "hang a left". Same difference, I assumed, so I hung a left, remembering to head for the right-hand side of the road. More lights, more bends, other significant points. "Right at Macdonalds, follow the signs, take the upramp". And before I knew it, there I was, on the freeway, heading in the right direction. Not one false turn to my credit. The right stuff, or what?

This was California all right. The sun shone, Peter, Paul and Mary were "Blowin' in the Wind", life felt good. As if to confirm the fact, a message loomed large over the centre of the freeway. An electronic sign which, with an obvious lack of anything important on which to offer advice, proudly announced: THE WEATHER'S GREAT TO BIKE OR SKATE. It was, too. A sky swept clear of clouds, a cooling breeze, that pleasant sun.

All I had to do now was continue on this course and follow the signs to the airport, which I did. But, not sure which lane out of five I was supposed to be in, I picked the centre one. It seemed as good a choice as any, for here the traffic appeared to be maintaining the kind of pace I favoured - not particularly slow, for they also posted *minimum* speed limits on this side of the Atlantic.

I sat there for what seemed like a long time, getting the feel of things, taming the hippopotamus, becoming complacent maybe. Traffic flashed past on both sides in those pre-restriction, pre-OPEC days; above and below also, at the multi-layered junctions.

A juggernaut semi-trailer thundered by on my right, towering above me, cars swept past on the left. Camper-vans on the left too, much bigger and more luxurious than mine, flashing past nevertheless. It was like being trapped betwixt and between the Trucker's Grand Prix and the Los Angeles 500. Then something else flashed past on my right, a brief glimpse only: Los Angeles International; the airport turnoff. Sod it! I'd seen it far too late to attempt taking a chance on slotting myself into the gap one truck had so carelessly left between itself and the one in front. Could have made it easily had I been ready. There'd have been at least a foot to spare. Nothing to do now but take the next turnoff, so I carefully prepared myself. I indicated a right turn and waited for someone to let me in. And I waited. Just as well the next turnoff was a few miles ahead, it took that long to switch lanes. Or possibly I wasn't yet aggressive enough in my tactics. But I was learning rapidly, out of necessity, which, if you think about it, sounds like the bloodline of a racehorse.

A gap appeared. Closing fast, but still room. Preparing to tuck myself in close behind another truck, I edged cautiously over, until a demented blast on a horn forced an immediate rethink. The guy coming up alongside, ignoring my indicator, glared at me, held up his middle finger. An indication, I assumed, that it was yet a mile to the next turnoff. There again, from the look on his face, maybe not.

Definitely not, it was here already. So, throwing caution to the wind, I slipped in behind him and quickly took the downramp. I then followed the freeway signs and rejoined, literally. So much for the navigation! I'd done a three-sixty instead of a one-eighty. I was in the same race, heading in the same direction. Sod it, again. Though I didn't exactly think along the lines of "sod it", you understand.

It took awhile, but I eventually made it off, and back on again, heading in the right direction this time. Now it was simply a matter of finding that airport exit again. Probably by now ten miles back.

Not only did I find the exit, and the airport - couldn't really miss that - I also found my way in, and somewhere to park. I also met up with the person I'd come to meet, was feeling pretty pleased about all that. Until he revealed his plan of attack.

'Need to call at the house first, pick up a few things. It's downtown,' Bill Gleeson told me, handing me a piece of paper on which was scrawled an address. Just like Al, he reeled off a detailed list of directions on how to go about getting there.

'Fine,' I replied, once he'd finished. 'Lets go.' I handed him the keys.

'You drive, I'll navigate. It's what I do for a living.'

Which is how I came to be, well, not really a tourist, but a kind of working tourist. The main difference being that I saw a lot that the tourists never did. Although I did miss out on one place.

'How about a night in Las Vegas?' Bill suggested.

We'd been to "his place," sorted out his things, and were now underway, well clear of Los Angeles. Bill was driving, I had the navigation in hand, so I made a quick geographical assessment from the map I held.

'It's a hundred and sixty miles off course. Across the desert and into Nevada,' I said.

'I know where it is,' Bill replied. 'And the diversion is zilch in terms of American distances.'

'If we do, can we still make New Orleans by Monday?'

'Hell, no,' he replied. 'Even without Vegas we'll have to drive overnight to reach NOLA by Monday.'

'So it's a choice of Vegas, or that job in Florida?'

'Yeah, but don't forget, Al said Florida was only a possibility.'

'Which would you prefer, Bill, Las Vegas, or the chance of Florida?'

'Florida, I guess.'

'Me too,' I said, making the decision for us, and agreeing to drive through the night. We drove through the next day, too, until the heat of the Arizona desert got the better of us.

Signs along the roadside petitioned us to eat this, drink that, Drive Ford, or Fly Pan Am. They also counselled us to buy, save, invest, spend, or visit. So we did, calling in at the next motel we saw. We had a couple of beers and a meal, then slept through the afternoon before setting off once more, in the relative cool of the evening.

Somewhere, far away, lightning flashed on and off, giving the impression that some unseen war was being staged over the horizon.

*

America is one of the few countries that has stretches of highway so long and straight you can't actually see the end, it just runs on into an ever-receding vanishing-point. A bend becomes something of an event, for you actually have to exert yourself to turn the wheel. But if in the meantime you've fallen asleep, it doesn't really matter, it's so flat you just bounce around a little more, waking up in time steer back onto the blacktop; counts as your excitement for the day.

Zip! There it was, gone. Bar, diner, filling station, house or two, motel, and a dog. There's almost always a dog, sitting there scratching, or maybe sleeping and dreaming, though he probably doesn't feature in the bullet-holed sign I noticed as we approached: Hickville, or some such: Pop 72. I wondered if they renewed the sign every time there was a birth or death. Didn't wonder long, for it all flashed past in the blink of an eye. Now we could settle down to some serious snoozing, for in this barren landscape those signs of habitation happened only rarely.

On and on we drove, Saturday and Sunday. Sunlight, ferocious in its intensity, blazed down from an azure sky, therefore it was hot and tiring. We sweated and baked, stopped for a drink frequently. Sage bush flats stretched away seemingly to infinity, presenting us with a countryside that was to all appearances featureless, although through the haze, far away, mountains were vaguely discernable. We passed by places advertising "Genuine Indian artifacts," we drove through Phoenix, Tucson, to cross the Rio Grande at El Paso. Then along came Austin, Houston, and finally - seventeen hundred miles and two days later - New Orleans. It was late Sunday night, maybe early Monday morning. Both too late and too early to do anything but find a motel and sleep.

Checking in at the office later that day, feeling rather proud of what we had achieved, we discovered that, while we'd been achieving it, Florida had been cancelled. The job that is, not the State. Should have gone to Vegas.

'Hi Bill. How y'all doing? Good to see you back, Dave.' was how we were greeted.

'A bit knackered, Ray, but ready for Florida.'

'Florida? Is that what Al promised? Aw, hell Bill, that went down the tubes long ago. Got something else though. Probably suit you, Dave.'

One of the things I'd come to realize in the short time I'd been employed was that, although the pace of life could be described as slow, it certainly wasn't boring. Couldn't see anyone suffering a coronary; cirrhosis, maybe, but that was for the future. Though the camaraderie was visible almost all the time, we were, I suspect, generally lonely and depressed. And, since alcohol is a known and accepted antidote for these conditions, we partook regularly, frequently, copiously, and often! At least I assume those were the reasons we did so. Sometimes it went on all day, other times we got down to some serious drinking. We did though, on the whole, retain some kind of decorum, in that we rarely started before ten a.m. That's not to say we'd never be *found* with a drink in hand before such a time, but if we were it was likely to be the finale of the previous day's piss-up rather than the prelude to this day's. And for this I was being paid. So there and then I made the decision to stick with it for a couple of years. See more of the world, gather together a bit of a nest egg, then make a switch to something else. Get a *real* job. A *real* life.

It never worked out that way, of course not. Should have realized by then how true was that old maxim: Few plans survive being put into action.

* *

NEW ORLEANS & OTHER STORIES
1978

⚓ he headphones clamped to my ears crackled into life; `814 is clear to take-off,' the controller in the tower at Lakefront Airport advised. Terry - another ONI employee - looked across at me and frowned. I frowned back, looked down and behind, for that's where the tower was located. Behind, and a thousand feet below Cessna Skyhawk N75814, the aircraft in which we were seated.

`Lakefront tower. 814 is already airborne, passing one thousand,' Terry answered, nonchalantly.

A pregnant pause, then the reply. '814, Lakefront. Roger.' That was all. What more could he add, he'd cleared us for take-off not five minutes ago. Didn't exactly fill me with confidence, that, a controller not necessarily in control. So for the rest of the flight I kept an extra sharp lookout, listened intently to the radio traffic, just to be sure we knew who was where, and who else was around, even if the controller didn't.

Terry Aylor and I were becoming bored with New Orleans, the world capital of jazz, but not that bloody bored! Terry was much younger than me, been with the company less time, too, but he was bit of a whiz-kid on the new systems: Transit satellite, Loran C, Argo, all of which were beginning to replace Shoran.

This was the city in which our head office was located, and we were in town for a few days, between jobs, so to speak. Terry, who possessed the relevant private pilot's licence had suggested chartering an aircraft for a couple of hours, from the local flying club. I didn't need a second invitation. It's that easy in the States, just like hiring a car. All you need is a licence, and the money. Although, naturally, you are first taken on a check ride. Take-off, climb to altitude, stall recovery, land, upon which Terry had been handed the keys.

We flew around for an hour or so, viewing sights from the air that we'd seen many times from the ground: Canal Street - the widest street in America - setting for the annual Mardi Gras parade; the Superdome indoor stadium, its simulated football field surfaced with that great American invention, Astroturf. Only here, in typical American fashion, it was called Mardi Grass. Then came the waterfront - a bend in the mighty Mississippi - with its paddle-steamers. Up the road was the French Quarter - bars, restaurants, jazz, and fine old buildings, with their filigreed balconies. It all looked a little different from the air, was different, especially Bourbon Street; up here you were unlikely to get mugged. May get mislaid by air traffic control, but what the hell.

We broke minimum altitude regulations, zoomed down over Lake Ponchatrain, to beat up the company vessel which was out training newly hired navigators (an advancement since days when I joined and was as good as press ganged, then left to find my own way around, up there off Oregon, and Washington State).

Later that same day we decided to visit the local racetrack. No horses to attract us though, an annual event was being staged; the New Orleans Jazz and Heritage Fair. It was summer and the conditions were perfect: clear blue skies, a blazing sun, Cajun cooking, a raging thirst. Which brings to mind the local roller coaster, just down the road, in Ponchatrain Park. They called it, The Ragin' Cajun, and it was a cracker: old wooden trestle kind of thing. No Red Arrows stuff, the loops or rolls, but it gave a longer, far better ride than it's modern counterparts.

Back at the track were limitless amounts of ice-cold beer, along with sizeable crowds. Oh, and there was jazz.

As we stood there taking things in, including the beer I clutched in my hand, I spotted a likely subject for a photographic study: battered straw Stetson worn low on a head which featured a fine aquiline nose, gaunt, featured face, stubbled chin, long, straggly hair, glazed-looking eyes. Very glazed-looking, in fact. Suspiciously so. Best to check first, thought I, allocating the task to Terry whilst I prepared the settings. After all, this was America. Wouldn't do for the guy to take offence and pull a gun on me. No, much better that Terry ask. Anyway, he spoke the language.

'No problem,' he reported, upon his return, though he didn't really seem sure. 'Stoned out of his tree,' he told me. 'Thought I was bumming a toke, gave me a whole joint. Fancy smoking it?'

'Why not?' I replied. 'Try anything once, me. Incest and lion-taming apart.'

'Heard about the trainee lion-tamer then?' Terry asked.

'Go on, I'll buy it.'

'Young lad. Asked what he should do if the lion approached him.

"Look him in the eye and back up," the instructor says. "Always maintain a safe distance between yourself and the animal."

"And if he keeps coming?"

"Don't panic. Keep backing up, but never take your eyes off him."

"Say I'm up against the bars. What then?"

"Ah, just grab a handful of crap and throw it in his face, that'll stop him."

"What if there's no crap available?"

"Don't worry, lad, there will be," Terry finished. He then lit up, took a drag, and passed the joint across for me to do likewise. It was as well I'd taken my photographs first.

Maybe it was the alcohol we'd consumed, maybe the weather. Or could it be that we weren't used to it? There was also the possibility of it being "good shit", as they say. *Santa Marta Gold*, from Colombia, or *Punto Rojo*. Maybe even the legendary *Panama Red*. I'd been told by connoisseurs that these were the tops.

After a drag or two I found myself studiously trying to ignore Terry, and he me, it appeared, for we looked in separate directions as a matter of course. In the end I was unable to avoid a sideways peek out of the corner of my eyes. It was as if telepathy were at work, for my eyes met Terry's, doing the same to me, and that was it.

Humans start to laugh for all sorts of reasons at all sorts of times in all sorts of moods, and I have no idea what the reason was here, but that was the moment Terry and I cracked up. Laughter became endemic if we so much as glanced at one another. And it was genuine. We giggled, spluttered, broke into uncontrollable, almost hysterical, laughter. It must have continued for a full ten minutes, and the only possible way to control it was not to look at each other, which proved nigh on impossible. The slightest pretext and off we went. I'd regain control temporarily before sneaking another glance at Terry and, as if programmed, there he was, doing the same to me. Off we went again. It brought tears to our eyes. We were airborne once more. Back up there among the clouds, no aircraft required, no flight plan to file, no clearance needed. It hit us that quickly; talk about spaced out. Which leads to a graffiti I saw later that day: yellow spray-paint on a dark wall. "Why drink and drive when you can smoke and fly?"

We eventually found ourselves watching a frisbee throwing contest, concentrating as best we could, until the effects finally wore off enough so we were back among the sane. 'Those dogs weren't really throwing the frisbees, were they?' I asked Terry, later on. 'Please tell me they weren't.'

*

Early morning is not the best time to visit the French Quarter, all you're likely to see then are hungover tourists on the way home from the night before. In the mornings they collect the garbage and hose down the streets. Every day. They need to! The bars and jazz clubs on Bourbon are shut tight, as is Preservation Hall, round the corner at 726 St Peter. Even Jackson Square is as quiet as the statue of the horse-back mounted General after whom it is named. Well, almost that quiet. There was a rumour doing the rounds which had Jackson Square as being one place ONI recruited their personnel. Said they hauled the drunks out of the gutter and signed them on! Not true of course. We weren't quite that bad. OK, maybe some of the guys looked and acted as if they could well have been recruited there. Probably had, on occasion, lay in a gutter or two, Jackson Square included. But they'd need to have sobered up before being considered as employees. As for Terry and I, one reefer was it, and that by default. Anyway, to some of the company's recruits, being signed on in Jackson Square would be seen as child's play. Like the guy I later met in Singapore. An American who seemed rather reluctant to go home. One day I asked him about it.

'Can't,' he told me. 'Not since Uncle Sam and I had a little disagreement over the validity of the Vietnam conflict.'

'So? What happened?'

'I left the army, rather hurriedly.'

'They kicked you out?'

'Not exactly. Let's just say the impetus for departure didn't come from the army's side.'

Anyway, forget Jackson Square. The early morning place to be, if you have a valid reason for being anywhere but in bed, is the French Market, north of the river - still the Mississippi. Here they serve strong chicory coffee and fresh beignets - pronounced baan-yaa - a type of French doughnut, sprinkled with sugar. (Would be French wouldn't they, with a name like that?) Delicious all the same. A little later and you can breakfast at Brennans, 417 Royale, providing you meet the requirements.

Although breakfast is not usually considered to be a memorable occasion, there have, for me, been one or two exceptions over the years. Brennans was just such an occasion.

Located in the French Quarter, Brennans is more tradition than anything. It's a place at which plantation owners of old would take breakfast. Which is where tradition comes in, requiring one to dress for the occasion - jacket and tie essential. It is also advisable to make reservations, well in advance.

My turn came one November morning in 1976. A champagne cocktail to kick things off. Eggs Hollandaise, with a Piesporter Riesling to wash it down, strawberries to follow. You also need lots of time. Ron Hewson - a New Zealand friend - and myself, along with our respective wives, found need to take the rest of the day off. At the time Ron just happened to be deputy operations manager for ONI, so no problem there.

Providing you haven't breakfasted at Brennans - in which case you won't require any - The Court of the Two Sisters is a good place for lunch. Here you can sit beneath a canopy of banana trees, have a drink, relax to Dixieland. A little different to lunch on some foreign shore. Ghana, for instance.

Relating to his early days with the company - before he was married, at least, officially! - Ron told me of the time he and his Ghanaian "wife" were out collecting crabs. She was catching them, handing them to Ron to hold.

"She was doing well. I had both hands full when one of the little sods clamped onto a finger. Naturally, I dropped the lot, and that was it. All that hard work and there went our lunch, scampering away across the sand. She was a bit upset about that, especially as it meant she had to go and catch a monkey instead."

A snippet which probably serves well as a lead in to this next, which, I suppose, could be said to concern dinner rather than lunch.

There's not a lot to be said for Tuktoyaktuk, up in the far north of Canada, apart from the name that is. I certainly found it to be different; not a tree to be seen; June, and the bay was still frozen over, that kind of different. But as the thaw got underway the so ground became a quagmire, permafrost on the surface giving way to mud six inches deep. And with the thaw came the mosquitoes. Big? I could have played badminton with these.

We didn't travel to the rig by helicopter, we went by snowmobile; until the ice melted. I recall stepping over the side at midnight, walking out to take a photograph. Summer you see; never gets dark. Different in winter though. Then, at those latitudes, dawn doesn't arrive until midday, but as that's also the time the sun sets, there's little evidence of either.

Tuktoyaktuk was where Ron was about to go, in the days before he was promoted to Party Chief - an appropriate title, maybe, though for "party" read "crew". On arrival at Inuvik airport, after a long tiring flight, he was met by a fellow Kiwi, name of Easterbrook; another ONI legend.

As Ron tells it, he found himself with barely enough time to check in at the hotel and dump his bags.

'"Let's go get a drink, and I'll brief you on the job," says Ian, who had been known to take the odd drink. So we went for a drink. Not just beer either. We sampled most of the other precious fluids with which we'd occasionally anoint ourselves.

'"Fancy something to eat?" Ian suggested, sometime later. Which meant a change of location was indicated, a place where food as well as drink was on offer. There was such a place - restaurant, bar, band, bit of a dance floor - so that's where we ended up. Even managed to find an empty table, next to the band. Bloody noisy, so not ideal, but it would do. We ate, drank some more, listened to the music, messed around on the dance floor. We then returned to our table.

'Oh God. I feel sick,' says I, holding a hand over my mouth.

'"Shit, no!" Ian replied, quickly sizing up the situation, and their particular location. "Not here."

'Too late by far. That carelessly placed hand turned defence into attack, over a much wider front, band to the fore, defenceless. Not just one, I got all five of em.

'At which point Ian seemed to develop a sudden urge to dissociate himself from both me, and that place. He hustled me outside, bundled me into a taxi and disappeared. Bare chested, soiled clothes under my arm, I arrived back at the hotel, hairs on my chest frozen bloody solid. You should have seen the looks of astonishment when I asked for my key. I could read their thoughts: *This must be one tough dude, it's about a million degrees below, outside!*'

Ron says he soaked his clothes in the bath overnight, then packed them away in a plastic bag. Early next morning he left for his station, way up the top of some Arctic mountain. Says his clothes never thawed out for weeks.

We first met in Nigeria, Ron and I. But even before joining ONI he'd spent eighteen months at the South Pole, as a member of New Zealand's 1962 Antarctic Expedition. His areas of responsibility had been the surveying, and the Huskies. Study a detailed map of the area and you'll see a Mount Hewson somewhere down there, plus a Hewson Glacier. There might also have been a crevasse, the one in which he almost perished. Said he owed his life to the fact of being tied to the sled he was riding, and this had wedged itself across the gap, leaving Ron hanging twenty feet down, nothingness beneath him! And how cool can you get? He told me he actually asked his rescuers to pass his camera down so he could take a photograph before they pulled him out. Not lying either, I've seen the photo.

*

In New Orleans the real musicians come out at night. The aforementioned Preservation Hall is a good place to start, if you must be in the French Quarter. Not much of a hall, just a very small room. Dingy, crowded, sit-on-the-floor kind of place. Ideal atmosphere for the old, and maybe not so famous, to jam it up. Good music though. But for real jazz, leave the French Quarter to the tourists. Find someone who really knows the neighbourhood and head for the outlying areas. If not jazz, then try Pat O'Bryan's, in the Quarter, for a lively night out. That's the fun place, if you can squeeze yourself in.

New Orleans in a nutshell? Not really. For that, as the cliché-mongers would have it, barely scratches the surface.

I recall my first visit there, in 1964. The office was then in the Garden District, off St Charles, with its streetcars; one of which *was* named Desire.

There was a Hungarian working with us at the time, Paul, I believe - or whatever was the equivalent in Hungarian. He'd escaped from

225

Budapest during the '56 uprising, made it safely as far as America, then gone and joined ONI. Even after eight years he was finding it difficult to adjust. I discovered this when a group of us went out to lunch with him. As usual, talk eventually embraced politics. But, not used to the idea of people running down the government, Paul would lean close to me when he talked, conspiratorial like. And he'd forever be looking round, as if half expecting the door to burst open, and people with guns to come charging in. Well, being America, I suppose that was always a possibility, though they sure as hell wouldn't be the secret police.

* *

Chapter Twelve
I'M GOING WHERE?

Four months of North American hospitality and I was on the move again, this time to a country of which I had never previously heard. Yes, I had heard brief mention of a Dr Albert Schweitzer, and of a place called Lambaréné, but not the country. Never mind heard, I wasn't even aware of the existence of Gabon. Yes, exactly! It was the first question I posed when informed that was to be my destination.

"An ex French colony on the coast of West Africa," so Ray Landry informed me. "Turn right after Nigeria, second on the left." Ray was operations manager in New Orleans, the guy responsible for despatching us hither and thither about the globe. I'd get to know Ray quite well over the years, and a phone call from him would usually end up with myself reciting what became known as the four W's down the phonelines: 'What? Where? When? What the hell!'

So, shortly after entering America as a likely immigrant - a whirlwind tour of New York, the West Coast, and the Southern States - I found myself up to my knees in mud and slime of the *Estuaire du Gabon*, outside the capital, Libreville.

Unique, compared to my air force days, certainly, but the flying hours were still piling up, especially as a lot of these flights were in piston-engined aircraft: DC3, DC4, DC6, DC7c. Douglas, it appeared, almost had a monopoly, particularly on the African run. With such types plying the routes, flights, it could be said, were conducted at a somewhat leisurely pace, for by necessity stage lengths would be relatively short. Five hours was about average, but with four eighteen-cylinder Pratt and Whitney radials, or Wright Cyclones continually pounding the eardrums, it was enough. We also used a lot of ad hoc charters, especially around Africa, and they were something else again. Real seat of the pants stuff, this.

'What about weight and balance?' I recall asking one helicopter pilot.

"Oh, just throw it aboard. If we can get off the ground, OK, if we can't we'll have to off-load something." That kind of thing.

After United had jetted me to New York, via Atlanta, it was across the Atlantic by a 707 of British Overseas Airways Corporation. (At the time the airline used the jingle, It's Quicker by BOAC, which, these being the dark days of vindictive unions and instant strikes, almost inevitably became corrupted to BOAT).

During our west to east progress we crossed paths with a sun that soon set behind us, creating darkness out there. It was a molten blackness that, although sprinkled with stars, remained deep and mysterious. A thick night through which the aircraft bored a steady passage, heading for its rendezvous with the runways of Heathrow.

Paris came next - BEA Vanguard - and a five day layover, the first of many. But from there on it was all downhill, starting with a DC6B of Air Afrique, to me ending up wading in that Gabonese river. And just what was I doing? Just what I was being paid to do, set up a navigation beacon on an otherwise inaccessible point.

This was a different Africa entirely, so far removed from the places to which I'd previously made brief visits during my service career I could well have been on a different continent. Different planet, even, for there was an overwhelming atmosphere of things falling apart: dilapidated streets, crumbling buildings, widespread decay and corruption. All pervading was the fetid heat, high humidity, and the mouldy, damp smell of disuse. Red corrugated-iron roofs were rusted through, paint long since a forgotten memory. Seedy and ramshackle. Unspoilt, they called it in the guide books. I would have said uncared for, were I being polite.

The first hotel I stayed at slotted right in to this category, for it looked as if it should have fallen down years ago. Willie, one of my travelling companions summed it up rather well. 'Jesus, what a dump! Wouldn't be surprised to find Livingstone was the last person to check in here.'

I had to agree.

'You try the shower, Willie,' I asked, when we later regrouped in the bar. 'Mine doesn't appear to be working too well. All I got was a dribble of brown, tepid water.'

'Yeah, it's working all right. Just lucky the sun was in the right position relative to water tank, eh, otherwise it would have been cold. And that dribble ensures more than one guest will enjoy the privilege of water,' he replied. He'd know, Willie, for he was an old hand with ONI. Quite a character, too, I was to find.

"A li'l ole country boy," was how W W Williams had described himself to me, which, seeing as how he came from a small town in the Southern States, was true enough. But did that small town ever cause problems when he tried to cash a cheque anywhere outside his home town. Seems no one was prepared to believe the Bank of War was for real. Believe me, it's there; War, West Virginia. Look it up in your atlas, just to the west of Bluefield. (And while you've got the atlas handy, here's another, in Norway. East of Trondheim, close by the airport, is the one place from where it is imperative you send all your friends and relations a postcard. Everyone does, for there is nothing else to go there for. Railway yards, post office, and that's about it. There is a hotel across the tracks, but I'm not sure if it's included. I mean, hell of a place to build a hotel, Hell. But I've stayed there, sent my share of postcards from Hell.) So, quite a change from the forests of Washington State, was Africa. But, as I was about to discover, America had been a holiday. This was to be the true beginning of my life as a doodlebugger.

A what, do I hear? Well, let me explain. Doodlebug, given its American definition: Any device, scientific or otherwise, used to determine the possible presence of underground minerals. Hence doodlebugging. The loose definition of which, refers to the search for oil. It's also the common name for the larval stage of a certain species of the ant lion, a somewhat predacious bug I gather. All true, I swear. I was passing a dictionary one day, looked it up.

After Gabon, I doodlebugged all over the continent. All over the globe in fact. And should your thoughts immediately turn to travel, adventure, excitement, think again. It could be, of course, but not all the time. Nowhere near. Each and every job was different. Each a new experience: different country, new dramas, different grounds for laughter, or tears. Varied, and occasionally rather unconventional means of transport. Helicopter; light plane of one kind or another, wheels, skis, or floats; boat; four-wheel drive; mule; dug-out canoe; piggy-back, or on foot. Whatever the form, it dropped me - along with that which I deemed necessary for a stay of a month or more, plus the equipment I was to operate - somewhere way out in the back of beyond, miles from anywhere. Was going to say "civilization," but that would have been superfluous. This, after all, was Africa emerging from beneath the cloak of colonialism.

There were times (quite a few, as a matter of fact) when I wondered just what the hell I was doing in a place like this; wherever *this*, currently happened to be. But that was early on, before I learned to accept any situation for what it was, ignored the things that didn't directly affect me.

The site could be high up a mountain, or on the seashore. It could be in the Arctic, or the tropics. Mainland, or some remote island. Wherever, once there I was on my own, needed to be self-sufficient, able to take care of myself, which, of course, included cooking. I soon learned how to knock up a meal out of whatever was available: a handful of rice and beans, to a tin of corned beef - a luxury, that. Talking of which, a bottle or two of cognac never went amiss, either. Not that I was still in the process of evaluating the stuff, I'd long since given it the thumbs up.

OK, so the cooking was basic, but let's face it, the rudiments of the gourmet chef would have been slightly misplaced out in the bush. Even so, there was always a choice. You know; Spam and beans, beans and Spam! It was often a case of eating whatever came to hand, no matter what state your hands might be in, or the hands that may offer you that unknown something.

"Ugh! I couldn't do that, I wouldn't." I've heard these words many a time. Said with conviction, too. Usually by a person in a state of post-prandial euphoria. Well let me tell you here and now, with absolute certainty, you will if you have to.

"But that's unhealthy," they'd say, to which I have a stock answer.

'Well, yes, I suppose it could be. There again, so could dying of starvation.'

Four months in Gabon, then I was off to Nigeria for a short spell. Barely long enough to form an opinion, regardless of which, I made one: was favourably impressed. Which only goes to show how horrendously wrong a fleeting impression can be!

The Port Harcourt Club must surely take most of blame for that, a gastronomic oasis in the midst of a culinary desert. Jacket and tie were requirements in the airconditioned restaurant, trousers and long-sleeved shirt recommended elsewhere, after dark. In theory, membership was open to all. In practice, few Nigerians could afford the annual fees, and those that could took out membership purely for reasons of prestige, they rarely used the facilities: multiple bars, golf course, swimming pool, rugby club, movies, or for plain socializing. To all intents it was really an expatriates-only club, the bars of which proved to be extremely popular. The perfect place to unwind after the trials and tribulations of yet another day in perdition.

But that was pre-Biafra, pre-coup, the country still in a reasonably stable state. Once that first coup was successfully enacted things were to change dramatically. But that is for later.

*

On the morning of March 3rd 1965, Burutu was its usual, laid-back, unexciting self: hot and sticky, despite a cooling breeze. In fact it was so laid back it was soporific. Talk about quiet, open a bottle of wine with any amount of enthusiasm they'd think the revolution had started.

There was little on this island apart from offices, the workers' accommodation, warehouse facilities, and a dock. Oh, there was also a club. Meaning, a bar - of course there was. The whole complex was owned by the United Africa Corporation - part of mighty Unilever - as were the surrounding plantations, sizeable acreage allotted to the growing a particular type of palm, from the fruit of which is extracted an oil used in the production of soap, as well as for cooking. Down river, a few miles offshore Nigeria's River Delta State, a more valuable type of oil was being extracted from deep beneath the seabed.

Out on the grassed area cleared for it sat a Hiller 12E4, three passenger helicopter. It was awaiting its complement of three before flying out to Gulf Oil's Rig 49, located off the mouth of the Forcados river. The pilot - a practical joker of the old school - having completed his pre-flight, was already on board, though few would have guessed as much. Dressed in sixties hippy regimentals - light anorak, jeans, sweatshirt - he sat in the rear, reading a week-old *Telegraph*. Out here, week-old news from back home was about as good as it got. Or bad, depending on what was in the news.

Even as the passengers arrived he carried on reading, making a show of checking the time now and again, feigning impatience.

'Where the hell's the pilot?' he asked of no one in particular, sometime later. Then, 'Oh, well, if he's not coming I'll have a go. Get in. Can't be much to flying one of these things.'

The passengers' nervousness showed as he clambered rather inelegantly into the front seat and prepared to fire up. But, amazingly, like overwrought sheep, they did as he suggested, no thought spared as to how four passengers would have fitted into three seats. They even showed some reluctance to believe him once he revealed he really was the pilot. I believed, because I knew him. And by the time he angled the stick forward, dipping the nose, machine curtsying before moving off, the others believed him, too. They plainly didn't approve, but they believed. Or made out they did. Pity one of those other passengers happened to be a high echelon executive from Gulf Oil; lacking a sense of humour to boot!

Two months and twenty-three adventurous helicopter hours later I was on the move again. This time, after a brief stopover in Rome, to the Middle East; our area office, at Khorramshahr. At the time, Iran was hotspot of the Gulf, as far as exploration went, but it wasn't to be long before the office moved on, to Beirut. A much better option in those long-forgotten days before the architecture was severely restructured; the changes wrought by civil war. Any war, come to that.

In 1965 Lebanon was considered to be the Riviera of the Middle East. From St. George's Hotel, on the waterfront, with its Ferraris, and bikini-clad lovelies decorating the swimming pool, to the exotic bars and clubs located off fashionable Rue Hamra, and the Casino Liban - up in the hills behind the city - its show a match for anything Las Vegas had to offer, so I was informed. Having missed out on Vegas I couldn't say for sure. But this time I didn't miss out.

After a while the office moved once again, relocating this time in Geneva, where it remained for years.

Even Iran was relatively peaceful back then. I recall many a night spent thousands of feet up in the mountains on my lonely outpost, ostensibly alone, but for the stars and peaks - although my second tent housed two Iranian helpers.

Back then we rarely worked after dark, so no generator to run, no lights, apart from a hissing lantern. After my evening meal I'd kill the lantern, lay on my back in silence and stare into space. Not unseeing, just not sure of what I was seeing. And believe me there was plenty *to* see, up there where the atmosphere was so thin, pure and crystal clear. Canopus, maybe, Polaris, Pegasus, Cepheus, or whatever was in view in my particular sector of the night sky. They shone with an unusual, extravagant brightness. It was as though each had been individually washed and polished, then, like precious stones, replaced on their backcloth of black velvet; blue-white diamonds which twinkled and wheeled about in the heavens. So many stars their residual light lit the ground without aid of the moon. Starlight. And if man ever feels the need of the true measure of his size and importance, he should do as I did: lay back and concentrate on that black void. And remember, it goes on for ever and ever. Further than the mind can comprehend. I felt as if I were alone. Just myself, a billion stars, and a blackness that was total. The deep, mysterious blackness of infinite space. As I lay there, watching constellations swim slowly through the cosmos, it made me realize just how insignificant and vulnerable we humans are.

There was movement in the firmament, too: shooting stars, comets, the flashing strobes of unseen, unheard aircraft. (I didn't need to see or hear to be able to deduce what they were: Jets, because of the flight level at which they were operating; civil, because of their direction and the steady course they held; DC8's, 707's, maybe the odd Convair 880 of Swissair, because those were the only civil jets plying the routes at the time. In my minds eye I could even see their clean white contrails, the sooty blackness of their efflux.) At lower altitudes were the Viscounts of IranAir. The Viscounts, it was possible to hear. What were obvious were the man made stars, the satellites which drifted across. Easy to spot, those. They wheeled past a mere two hundred miles above where I lay. Whether travelling west to east, or Pole to Pole, they orbited the globe at regular intervals, every ninety minutes or so. You could almost set your watch by them.

Up on my mountain I was as about as far from civilization as it was possible to get in that day and age, but I didn't miss it. For limited periods, that is; after all, this *was* supposed to be the Swinging Sixties. Didn't miss things as they were out here, is what I'm saying. Didn't miss the cities, the crowds, the traffic; especially the fumes they created; Teheran in particular. No, this was perfect. Myself, two Iranians, a dozen chickens; to start with.

I'd had this wild idea of a fresh egg supply, no doubt subconsciously linked to my father's post-war effort. Well, here on my Iranian mountain-top, the results were definitely similar; few omelettes, lots of chicken curry. Seems they never learn, these chickens.

Despite the climate - hot and dry - the welcome change of environment, the excitement of seeing somewhere new - to me, that is, for the place itself is older than the bible - the Middle East didn't suit me for some reason. I quickly developed an urge to return to Africa, the continent already exerting its seemingly inexorable grip on me. So that was where I ended up. And it was to be along the West African coastline that - brief excursions to Europe and the Middle East apart - I was to roam forever. Well, the next seven years. At times, it seemed like forever.

*

Up to this point I'd felt myself lucky, found it difficult to accept the fact that someone was actually prepared to pay me to travel the world, even though it wasn't quite like working for the "Holiday" programme. I'd visit all kinds of exotic places, yes, eventually. But all foreign lands are not necessarily exotic.

From Angola, north and west to Morocco and the Canary Islands, we searched for traces of those elusive hydrocarbon deposits known as oil and gas. At least we collected the data. The geophysicists did the evaluating. And it was there all right, richness of deposit seemingly in inverse proportion to the amicability of the country involved. Yes, Africa was to prove a different style of life altogether.

Outside my single-storey, army surplus tent, hissed my Coleman lantern. Inside, and it would bring with it the heat, and its plethora of whirling bugs and moths. We also used Coleman stoves, designed specifically to use white gas, unavailable almost anywhere outside the States, so we took to using regular gasoline instead. Nowhere near as efficient for cooking purposes, but very effective at burning down your tent if you got it wrong. Not a brilliant idea, that. Could be days before a replacement arrived.

It was peaceful, and I was happy enough. The job wasn't difficult, strenuous only occasionally. But not for nothing did they pay well. I was away from home for long periods, cut off from life some of the time, occasionally in places I would rather not be. Still, when thought about, lots of people out there in the big wide world weren't having it so good either. They were fighting to catch up with one another, they were being injured, mugged, robbed, raped, and murdered. No, life wasn't too bad when viewed in perspective.

So, in the evening I'd sit outside, reading. Here I'd remain until the insects arrived in strength. Then it was to bed. I'd lay beneath my mosquito net, dialling in the world on my personal, shortwave radio. It was my first action in the morning, too. I'd reach out for my radio and tune in to the BBC World Service, just to check the world was still there. Essential if you wish to keep abreast of things. Not just the rest of the world, current location also. The Beeb always seemed to be first to know.

I was working on the island of Fernando Po (Now known as Equatorial Guinea, or Bioko.) - a place most people have probably never heard of - off the coast of West Africa, tucked into the corner between Nigeria and Cameroon. It is an extinct volcano, reaching up over nine thousand feet. But such is the air quality around that area, it is visible no more than two or three days a year from the Nigerian coast, usually just after a heavy rainstorm.

The move there from Nigeria had been enforced upon us by the Biafran situation. I'd left my car behind, all my household possessions, escaped with my briefcase, some clothes, and my life. Not so bad then. But even when based on the island, at no time during my four months there did I see the peak of that mountain.

At the time of my sojourn, Fernando Po was a Spanish colony, and we'd receive company cheques from the States; operational expenses which, naturally, we cashed locally. We're talking here of cheques to the value of dollars by the thousand, one of which I was about to cash the morning I heard on the Beeb that Spain had devalued the Peseta. As a result, on arrival at the Bank I requested to see the manager, the only person available who spoke English. I asked him how much the currency had been devalued, and you know what, he hadn't heard a thing about it. He had to check with head office, in Madrid. I found that absolutely amazing. Not a quick phone-call or fax, either. It was two days before he received a reply. As a result I received considerably more Peseta's in my account than did the company in theirs. Good to keep abreast of events, then.

One day - Nigeria, of course, for most bad experiences seemed to happen in Nigeria - I reached out and touched... Not the radio, but water! That jerked me awake in a hurry, for it suddenly seemed possible the world *was* no longer there. It was, but quite a way inland from where I now reposed, for I discovered my bed to be an island. During the night the tide had risen to unprecedented levels, flooded my camp to a depth of twelve inches. Things floated and bobbed around, including my radio. Electronics were submerged, lunch swam past even as I lay there. A problem, then? Well, if it wasn't, "problem" was a concept without meaning.

Luckily, the things remaining untouched, above water level, were the most important. At least to me they were: bed, generator, transceiver. I could at least call for help.

'Help!' I called. Well, let's face it, hardly a mayday situation.

'What do you need?' asked Bill, back at base, once I'd passed on my report.

OK. This was no time for an exercise in logic. 'Pair of waders would be good,' I suggested.

'I mean, to get the station operational?' he said. Had his priorities, Bill. I could be drowning, needed to get things up and running before I took my last breath. In the event we merely raised the camp, set it atop an oil-drum and plank base. Nowhere near as comfortable as that time the river forced us upstairs in the Griffin, twenty years before.

I was later to discover I'd also contracted malaria, had to be airlifted out, after wading to dry land. A fortuitous piece of luck, really, for the water level never did go down. My malaria soon cleared, but, thankfully, before I was well enough to return, the site was finally abandoned, camp moved inland. Or should I say, ashore?

Now, had I not known better, this would have been a time when I'd have thought Bill had it in for me, for I was sent elsewhere. Only to be held hostage, against payment to the local chief for use of a piece of land in which no one had previously shown one iota of interest. A maze of mangrove-swamped channels: more water, more mud, more mosquitoes.

Everything was supposed to have been prearranged, albeit minus the hostage-taking bit. Someone had negotiated an agreement, money had changed hands. Trouble was, there now seemed to be more than one claimant for this worthless piece of real estate. We'd apparently paid the wrong chief, or hadn't paid the right one enough. Now they had a pawn with which to bargain, and let's face it, if they were requesting my worth it must have been rather a lot, mustn't it? Or was I overvaluing myself?

Seemed maybe I was, reading the note I was handed: "Until you pay, you will not be allowed to live." The last word I took to be a spelling mistake. Hoped I was right. Sure, this was still pre Biafra, Kalashnikov not yet freely available to all and sundry, but they did possess wicked-looking machetes.

We only required the use of this site for a few hours, and luckily a full moon allowed me to set everything up at night, when all but myself were asleep. Convenient, that. Though not necessarily from my point of view. I called the vessel, explained my predicament. Big mistake, telling them I was operational. They went to work. I waited; only now realizing the powers that be were unlikely to treat the threat as serious so long as the job was going ahead. But in those days we were young and impetuous; company orientated, I suppose. Meanwhile, the natives were getting restless. I may have been miserable, yet I had much more than they did. And, providing I escaped in one piece, I also had the option of quitting. They were stuck with what they had. So, in retrospect, maybe I was a bit hard on them when they attempted - often successfully - to steal anything they could carry off. I even hired guards from within the local community, but not only did the disappearances not stop, the guards themselves either stole, or directed operations. But that appeared to be the least of my problems. I was still waiting at noon. The boat, long since finished, had already left the area, and still no word on the arrival of the seventh cavalry. (Eighth or ninth either, come to that.) Good old Bill, company man to the last: as long as the job got done it seemed I was expendable.

I waited all day, finally receiving word that a helicopter would arrive the following morning, to bring money in, take me out. That evening, I was summoned to a meeting, asked to explain the situation, for want of a better term.

Lighting was courtesy of Coleman. A lantern which looked suspiciously familiar. Not as bright as when it had been mine, the glow now orange rather than white. Inferior kerosene and mantles, I presumed. Or maybe there wasn't enough pressure. It threw eerie, flickering shadows across the walls of the small room. Not very welcoming at all. The air was still and fetid; odour colonial rather than eau de Cologne. The smell was of packed earth and woodsmoke, and of unwashed bodies; their concern for personal hygiene being rather less obsessive than mine. Also, the roaches were back. Much smaller than the Singapore version, but just as proliferate. I didn't dare stamp on the bastards, they'd probably up the cost of my release if I did.

Despite the locals being well paid, the stealing continued, even as we were loading the helicopter. I made sure the electronics went on the first lift. No problems there, they were of no use to the villagers, but were our bread and butter. Tent and camping gear was a different matter altogether. I had the tent down and folded, ready to go; and go it did. Last I saw of it was as it vanished into the bush. It looked like a leaf being borne off by a bunch of ants. In fact things were disappearing so fast I had visions of the old Hiller 12E4 being next.

Not so. I wasn't about to take that chance. Old or not it was my only means of escape from this place. On its next approach I signalled my intentions to the pilot as I guided him in, leapt aboard as soon as he touched down, and away we went, leaving everything else behind. Nothing that couldn't easily be replaced. One more site we wouldn't be using again. So who were the real losers?

Thinking about it later, I realized how fortunate I had been to have a pilot who was quick on the uptake, shall we say. I recall one occasion when the locals grabbed hold of the skids of one helicopter as it tried to take-off. They literally pulled it out of the sky. And as they had all grabbed the same side, the aircraft literally rolled over, crashed, and caught fire, with fatal results.

We had a Bell 47 touch-down on one of our stations, and as it did so, out of the bush swarmed a bunch of locals, ignoring the fences we had erected. The inevitable happened, of course; one walked into the tail rotor. A glancing blow, but it was enough to wreck the helicopter's tailboom. The guy lost one arm, one ear, one eye, and half a leg, and the ducks on site had a field day, gobbling up pieces of flesh. Naturally, the helicopter company ended up paying an arm and a leg for the rest of that guy's worthless life, it could be said.

Mobil had one of their Nigerian trainee executives try to walk though the propeller of their Twin Otter, whilst the engine was running! Instant Chum, chum.

It seemed then, there were to be nightmares as well as dreams, for we all experienced minor problems on our stations from time to time.

I was sunning myself on the beach one day, and, as became natural, had an ear half cocked to the high-speed radio, via which I would occasionally converse with my compatriots, and vice versa. It helped break the monotony. This day, our tame Geordie, Bob, a dozen or so miles up the coast, was talking to Steve, operator out on the boat. At least Steve was calling Bob. The conversation casual, to start with.

'Gamba, Geo Three. How are things in paradise, Bob?'

'I'm surviving,' Bob replied. 'But there's a cloud of dust just appeared out in the bush. Hang on while I climb the mast and have a look.'

With that, the radio went quiet for a while, I dosed briefly.

'You still there, Steve?' Bob called, a few minutes later. Not exactly orthodox radio procedure, but this was Africa.

'Gamba, Geo Three. Roger, Bob, what is it?'

'Bloody great herd of elephants. On the rampage by the looks of things.'

'Copy, Bob. Heading your way are they?'

'Tell you what, Steve. You lose my signal in the next half hour, don't bother calling. I'll be gone.'

Then there was the time in Spanish Sahara when the Foreign Legion took me in, for questioning, not as a recruit (although they had me worried for a while). My fault, really. Just outside Villa Cisneros was this Beau Geste-type fort, which I decided to film. Seems they didn't take kindly to that, especially when I stuck my lens through the open gates. They demanded my film cartridge (Super 8mm), which, naturally, I gave them. Didn't fancy ten years involuntary service with that mob! Just hoped they didn't have the means of replaying the movie before I left the country, for - with a sleight-of-hand of which Tommy Cooper would have been proud - I managed to switch cartridges, gave them an unexposed version. Small price to pay for my future freedom.

And there you have it, you see. We were well paid, but, as I said, it wasn't for nothing. At times conditions could be extreme. Hazardous? Well, yes, that, too. Difficult for it not to be in countries where the roads themselves could be regarded a major hazard. As could the military dictatorsh... Excuse me. Government. But if it ever got too much, all I needed was to gaze into the empty sky. Up there was peace. An open, blue peace which stretched from horizon to horizon. The sky was my escape route, I was free to take it. And once up there, looking down, I could be anywhere, for all cities, towns, and villages become neat from the air. Height glosses over the slums, dumps, and inadequacies, much as does a recent fall of snow. Such thoughts were calming, my worries became insignificant.

*

Then there was the flying. Take for instance the time I was en-route by helicopter over the Bight of Biafra, on my way to an oil rig, just myself and the pilot. There we were, tooling along in a small, two-seat Hiller E4, when we spotted a shark cruising along on the surface, a hammerhead. Easy to spot from fifteen hundred feet. Very easy, for it was actually a rather large hammerhead. In fact, truth be told, bloody huge!

'Will you look at that!' Tom - the pilot - said, as if I might have missed it. 'How big, do you reckon?'

'Big enough,' I answered, not really curious as to the precise physical dimensions.

'Shall we go down?' Tom asked.

Stupid question, I thought. But then I realized it wasn't really a question. He wasn't asking, he was telling.

'Let's not,' I said. But I was far too late. The power came off as the collective was lowered, and we were on the way.

Descend he did, to hover, barely above sea-level, directly over the creature, measuring his length against that of our suddenly frail-seeming, single-engined machine. His? Hey, forget the Equal Opportunities Commission, or the concept of political correctness, he or she was academic, this sod was considerably longer than the Hiller's mere fifteen or so feet. Which immediately conjured up dire thoughts, as such things tend to do.

The engine did continue to run smoothly, but it didn't *sound* at all smooth, not to my ears.

'Is that a slight misfire I detect, Tom?' I asked, only to receive a wry smile in return. 'Is the clutch slipping, causing us to sacrifice what precious little altitude we have?' A muttered reply this time, although in the negative. Are we overpitching? I almost asked. I knew about such technicalities, had a wealth of experience. But it seemed we weren't, so

I kept quiet, tuned my thoughts to other scenarios, imagination working overtime, as usual. So what about you, Tom? I wondered. Are you about to suffer a heart attack? Funny, the things that come to mind now and again. Not funny ha-ha, funnily strange. But such sounds and disasters

were only in my head. Normal things to imagine at a time like that, when the potential for trouble is high. Even so, despite the temperature being in the eighties, I found my arms to be covered in goose bumps.

'Is that overgrown fish just sunbathing, do you think, or is it hungry? I mean really hungry?'

'Come on Dave. Look, statistics prove....'

'Yes, I know what statistics prove,' I interjected, 'but as far as I'm concerned, when it comes to the matter of sharks, anything that moves is lunch. Didn't you read *Jaws?*'

That was the kind of flying to which I was to be subjected, for the laws tended to be lax - what laws there were. Scheduled airlines attempted approaches that wouldn't have been contemplated by a military pilot faced by such conditions. The difference, you see, between revenue and non-revenue flying. But to fly, you first had to board an aircraft.

In America you picked up the phone to make a reservation: 'Good day, Eastern Airlines. How can we be of service?' a cheerful voice would ask. Then, once I'd detailed my requirements, 'Fine, sir, that's New York, New Orleans, confirmed. Have a good day, and thank you for calling Eastern.'

Not so in Africa, where things were slightly different. For starters, forget the telephone. You almost needed a reservation to use that, if in fact it worked at all. Then, despite holding a "confirmed" reservation, made in person, you were still likely to find yourself resorting to the greasing of a palm or two, (known as "dash") in order to secure a seat. Still, with your confirmed reservation now confirmed, you could sit back and relax, couldn't you? Possibly. As long as the head of state didn't choose that particular day to fly off somewhere or other. In such an event, he and his entourage would just commandeer the aircraft. I even experienced this phenomenon at a hotel in Gabon, the only hotel in town, as it happened. In that instance I was already occupying one of the rooms, *was*, of course, being the operative word.

The Head of State apparently needed a room. Mine! No refund, no help in finding alternative accommodation, certainly no arguments. OK, so he needed a room or two, but so did I, therefore you'd have thought one would at least have chance to discuss the situation. But discuss it with whom? I never for a minute imagined those guys sporting camouflage drill and dark glasses to be his public relations advisors. Well, I suppose they could have been, but to my way of thinking an AK-47 seemed an unlikely item for a public relations advisor to be carrying.

So much for the politicians. Now let's consider the matter of the transport itself. The flying during these formative years of Africa's oil exploration was, to say the least, varied. And, it seems, in retrospect, not entirely as safe as it might have been. Adventurous, shall we say. The average ground-check appeared to be of the "kick the tyres, light the fires" school of thought. At least in the charter sector, where most of the aircraft looked like cast-offs from some third-rate airline.

Thinking back (which in this case is the best time to think, for that implies survival), I often wonder how safe those flights had actually been. Not that it matters at all, not now. All that matters is that I *did* survive, am still around to tell the tale.

During my early days in the area I particularly recall a flight on a Nigerian Airways DC3. We were en route from Lagos to...... Well, Lagos, actually, as things turned out. Focal point of the universe, as far as Nigerians were concerned.

I boarded to find that the seats on the starboard side were what one might call... er... well, friendly is a word that springs to mind. You know, kind of thing you and your girl made a rush for in the back row of the cinema. Only in this case my seat was extra friendly, in that it was fitted with only one seat-belt. Oh, tra la la! My seat-mate happened to be of like sex, you see. Meaning he was a male. Upon complaining, a mechanic was dispatched to rectify the situation - seat-belt (or lack of) that is - whilst I stood in the aisle twiddling my thumbs and, no doubt the other passengers fumed. *Not content with securing a prized seat, he wants a bloody seat-belt as well.* Fair enough, I'd probably have though the same had the positions been reversed. They weren't, so we waited until the job was done.

Shortly after take-off, at the top of the climb - on second thoughts, taking into account the rate of climb achieved by the DC3, maybe a little longer than "shortly after take-off" - the aircraft entered a dark canyon. Its walls were formed by sheer cliffs of the evil-looking Cumulonimbus which towered out of sight above us. It suddenly went black, as if a shadow had passed over us. At which point my earlier decision to complain about the lack of restraint became fully vindicated.

It started with a mild warning. A gentle shudder, as if the craft was limbering up, preparing for the worst. The worst came with frightening suddenness and a violent buffeting. Turbulence picked us up and tossed us around like a child's toy, wings fluttering like those of a hummingbird. The darkness outside was occasionally lit by generous flashes of lightning - like maybe a trillion volts. An unseen fist punched us viciously upwards before we fell off the edge. Then the bottom just fell out of the sky, taking us with it. We were on our way down. Fast. Then it caught, held momentarily, before again surging upwards like an elevator that was rocket-propelled. A wing dropped, was corrected for, and we were yawing wildly, pilot always seeming to be a little behind nature. Then, just as suddenly as it started, it was over. The cabin brightened, and we were in smooth air. The horizon was back where God intended it to be, and we were right way up.

In conditions I was sure most aircraft would not have survived, our Sikh pilot had somehow managed to reverse course and make good his escape. So I thought. On reflection it was more likely the storm had spat us out like some unpalatable insect. It was one of those times when I wondered at the sanity of strapping myself to the inside of a metal tube, surrounded by hundreds of gallons of highly inflammable fuel. Others probably wondered the same, although none were about to admit to it. Small, nervous smiles spread throughout the cabin like a friendly virus as white-knuckled hands relaxed their grip on the armrests. The mood was now quite macho. "We have just courted death in the clouds, but it was nothing", type of thing.

But relief was to be short-lived, for again we turned, only to re-enter this monster on a different bearing. Trying to sneak up on it from behind maybe? He was a game one, this pilot. One of the more competitive types that hates to be beaten. Either that, or he had a madman's contempt for the weather. He was going for it again. Which was about the time I wished I'd never set eyes on him. Why couldn't he have been downed by a Sikh-eating missile in some minor skirmish in the Hindu Kush, or been taken out by turban guerrillas? To me, pilots were held in similar regard to doctors; I placed my faith in them. In this case, that faith was about to be tested to the full.

This time it was worse. Much worse. Weather radar would have told him that story, but lacking such modern facilities he had to find out the hard way. Violent currents punched us aloft one second, then, with contemptuous ease and a sickening lurch, threatened to drag us out of the sky the next. In reality, I suppose the longest period of free fall couldn't have exceeded two or three seconds, though you'd have had trouble convincing those aboard of the fact, myself especially. We were all over the sky, plunging one second, shooting up the next.

One person was past caring altogether, it seemed. A Texan. Well over six feet tall, he sported a straw Stetson which he wore the whole time, apart from during one particularly violent period when he snatched it off his head and waved it in the air. 'Yeeehaah!' he yelled, when what he should have been doing was praying. Everyone else seemed to be. Not me though, I was too concerned worrying about the possibility of my fiery demise.

'Yeeehaah!' he repeated. Back home I imagine he rode Brahman Bulls during his leisure hours.

A sudden, rending crash from somewhere aft signalled the end. It's literally all downhill from here, I thought. But no, it was just the end of the coffee. The small, meagrely equipped galley was suddenly larger, though now even less well equipped, cabin floor awash as the canister containing the beverage no longer did. It had been ripped off the bulkhead.

Whether (if you'll excuse the pun) at this point the pilot conceded defeat, or the elements decided to give us another chance, was difficult to determine, for the next thing we knew was that we had been spat out again. Safe. Albeit still on the Lagos side of the weather front. At which point the pilot did give up, although only temporarily. He returned to Ikeja, trading the whole lot in for an F27.

One hour later, Five November-Alpha Alpha Zulu climbed high enough to enable us to weave a stately slalom between those massed peaks, en route to Port Harcourt. Up there the sun shone brightly, as if nature were apologizing for her earlier tantrum. So eventually we did get to see our cloud castles. And we did enjoy our coffee.

*

The trip from Lagos city out to Ikeja was another of life's less exhilarating experiences. A fact attested to, and exploited by, a particularly thoughtful piece of advertising. It concerned (at that time) one of the largest of international airlines, and it was sited beside the road leading out of the city.

I'll never forget that trip, the first time I made it. The taxi was a bone-shaking old wreck. Even to call it a car was an overstatement, although it had been, once. Most of the remaining trim was hanging off, as were some important-looking bits underneath. Odds on against even making it as far as the airport, I thought, as I sat on my wooden-box seat. And had I not paid in advance that would have been guaranteed, the driver didn't have enough petrol in the tank until I gave him the money for it.

That hurdle overcome, we were on our way. Not exactly at a spine-tingling rate of knots, nor sedately, on our way nonetheless. There seemed to be roadworks every hundred yards or so, holes in between. It was hot and humid, which ensured the many traffic jams would be ill-tempered affairs, making the journey seem that much longer. Everything appeared to be against us. Then, just as frustration and hostility reached their peak, we came across this advert. A huge billboard at the roadside, not at all discreet; to me, a welcome smile-generator. It simply read, PAN AM. LET US TAKE YOU AWAY FROM ALL THIS.

Amen to that, I thought.

Don't know how they got away with it, for Africans are not a race to take criticism lightly.

That smile lasted until I came upon the only redeeming feature the

243

country had to offer, the airport departure lounge. Ikeja was not a typical Third World airport, something to patronize the area into believing they had entered the twentieth century. No way. Ramshackle rather than modern. Not cheery or welcoming at all, just the opposite. It looked like most other government buildings in Nigeria: run-down and filthy. And although civilian, given the number of Kalashnikovs on display - plus other assorted hardware - one could be forgiven for thinking it to be a military base.

Considering the degree of reluctance with which they allow you to enter their country in the first place, I never ceased to be amazed by the number of difficulties encountered when trying to leave. Therefore - once access had been granted, the hassle of check-in endured, I, and my wallet, suffering at the hands of immigration and customs - I relished the thought that I was but minutes away from boarding a flight to..... Well, anywhere. Please. Just so long as it meant leaving the frustrations and tensions and of West Africa far behind.

Such frustrations you begin to jettison even as you climb aboard your aircraft, for, of course, once seated, you are as good as back in civilization. Cleanliness and compassion rule the day here. Then there is the familiar soothing voice of your captain, a man who understands; he's seen it all before.

From here on there was no holding me, the world my oyster.

* *

Chapter Thirteen
GABON

The billowing white clouds which had formed and developed during yesterday's humid heat - my cloud castles - had gone on to produce a spectacular show after dark. Lightning forked down, illuminating land and sea alike, but the storm had remained offshore, thus sparing me. Today, in this Gabonese outpost, all was peace and serenity, apart from the continuous thudding of the roaring, crashing breakers. That sound was my constant and only companion, though I was now beginning to accept it as normal.

Five days ago two of us had left Port Gentil in a Cessna 180, landed at some unpronounceable location. From there, travelling by Land Rover, we were deposited at a logging camp deep in the tropical rainforest where my equipment awaited our arrival. Here we'd spent the night. Luxury, that, for often there was no bed at all. A sleeping bag under the stars if I was lucky, if not, the mud floor of a bush hut, or the grimy deck of a small boat as it threaded its way up some remote African waterway. Whatever was on offer was usually more than welcome.

Wasting no time we were on the road early next morning, Africa having unfolded slowly and dramatically with the dawn. Most of that day was spent in a canoe, being paddled along a narrow river. The banks crowded in on us, trees overhanging the water, soundtrack replete with noises of the jungle, yet with only the occasional monkey to be seen, or the iridescent flash of colourful plumage as a bird was startled into flight. Whatever else there may have been remained well concealed, though they no doubt kept a watchful eye on us.

A long walk followed, trek really, out of the trees then across sun-baked savanna. There was man-tall grass, which could well conceal anything from gorillas to elephants, for this was West Africa, not East. Over here a safari was a safari without the tourists, and watch where you put your feet boyo. Which, apart from recalling my days in Malaya, brings to mind that legendary tribe, the Focawee.

Being pygmies (aka short-arsed) they were sure to be vertically disadvantaged in grass such as this. In fact, 'tis said this was where the tribal name had its origins, their unique method of navigation when faced by such an obstacle. The younger warriors were apparently to be seen bouncing up and down, as if on springs, spurred on by the cries of their less able elders; "Where the foc are we?"

No Focawee around here then, but with our accompanying bearers -

whom we paid to do the work of absent machinery - we must have looked like we'd just walked out of a Daniel Defoe novel. Everything was carried on their heads, as was the African way. This had been explained to me when I first asked a Nigerian how he was going to manage a forty kilo transmitter. 'She go for head, Boss,' he told me.

Arrival at the designated site, late in the evening, saw our cast of thousands disappear. Only three of us remained: myself, my supervisor, (or Party Chief, as they were called) and the guide who would eventually see him safely on his way back, once everything was installed and operational.

It was hot, sweaty work assembling the station through the heat of the day, and we didn't stop for anything, working through till the sun went to bed. Up until then I hadn't spared a thought for food, hadn't eaten a thing all day, though I had drunk plenty. Cases of bottled water were frequently attacked. That it soon became warm didn't matter, it was wet, and all I needed was liquid. Now it dawned on me how hungry I was, so I scratched around, grabbing whatever came to hand. A tin of beans, some rice, a bottle of Tabasco. Thirty minutes, and bingo! I could have been at the Ritz but the food wouldn't have tasted better. I then collapsed on by bed and fell into a sleep that was more like a short course in death.

It was left-over beans and rice for breakfast as well, though it didn't taste anything like as good first thing in the morning. But the water was cool.

Two days more and I was alone. Myself, the sea, sky, and the scenery. No, not just that, there were the smells as well. Rotting vegetation, the aroma of exotic blooms, my own sweat, all mingled to create an atmosphere I could feel and relate to. It was naturally peaceful. Far removed from the rush and clamour of civilization there were no deadlines, no sense of urgency. Even the passage of time had little meaning. Night and day, darkness and light, yes, but not time itself. I was self-sufficient in essentials; food, water, medical supplies, electronic spares and fuel. That's right, I wasn't out here for the good of my health, had to keep a generator running, a navigation beacon operational. It wasn't ideal, but it would do for now. Had to, no way for me to escape. But why would I want to. There were swaying palms, stretches of golden sand, and the ocean. OK, the water was brown rather than turquoise, the surf curdled as opposed to creamy-white, and beyond that surf were the sharks. There were mosquitoes inland, but a breeze spared me those.

*

In either direction the beach ran straight until it vanished in a mist of spray. My immediate world consisted of sea, sand, trees and savanna. Nature in the raw. It was almost like being paid to go on a tropical holiday.

It could be a lonely life at times, but it did have its advantages. I didn't have to suffer pollution and littering, and no mains electricity or water meant I never got cut off, nor did I have bills to pay. There were no taxes, no nagging worries, few problems or responsibilities. I enjoyed the isolation, didn't mind cooking for myself. Any local purchases were all "chargeable" for which I would be duly compensated. There were no schedules to keep, I was free to do more or less as I wished, eat and sleep whenever I felt like it, as long as I was up and running when required. That kind of luxury you couldn't buy. And as I was being paid it will come as no surprise when I say there were days when I wouldn't have wished to be anywhere else. But certain things were eventually missed. Aeroplanes, and the cocktail cabinet, perhaps? Ah yes, certainly the aeroplanes. I was suffering withdrawal symptoms there. Or was I?

I had managed to odd flight, and odd they had proved to be, too. Similar to that hammerhead experience offshore Nigeria, really, when yet another helicopter pilot was to place me in a comparable position.

It was a Bell 47 this time, as in M*A*S*H, though just as flimsy and vulnerable as had been that Hiller. The pilot of this machine, spotting a family of gorillas trailing across the Gabonese countryside, felt the need to approach within feet of them. Close enough to allow a detailed inspection of their impressive dental structure, would you believe? Fair enough. Until the male - after first ensuring his family were safely ensconced within the surrounding bush - reared up to his full height and faced us. His fists beat on his leathery chest, his mouth was open in a defiant roar we could not hear, his teeth were bared in an anger we *could* see. Justifiable, admittedly. It brought to mind the scene from a film: King Kong snatching aeroplanes out of the sky.

'Hey, come on, Pete. There are limits to the conversation one can hold with a gorilla,' said I, 'Let's get the hell out of here.' And Pete must have been in agreement, for he did take us out of there, rather swiftly.

But the scene was to be repeated yet again. Different pilot, different helicopter - an Alouette two - a herd of elephants apparently deputizing for the gorillas. On that occasion we moved off and gained height once the leader started spraying sand at us. He, too, seemed slightly upset.

It's no wonder these pilots were threatened with instant dismissal if caught in any such act. But to my mind it seemed the powers that be had the wording wrong. Bugger the animals, it should have been "disturbing the passengers".

So maybe not the flying so much, after all, but there were other things missing from my life. I'd only been on site a week, when, as occasionally happens, my mind conjured up visions of female company, soft beds, and cold beer. But - being a "Yorkie, therefore somewhat of an

epicure when it came to the dish - oh for a newspaper-wrapped parcel of fish and chips. Cooked as they should be, used to be, before the authorities started to question anything that gave enjoyment. I had the potatoes, nothing with which to catch the fish. Ah well.

It was to be a couple of weeks before I had my first human visitors. Like a converse Livingstone, *they'd* come on safari to visit *me*. To them it was a day out. To me, knowing how close the nearest village was - or wasn't, actually - it was a safari. And the problems their visit posed were soon circumvented. Their version of French - which made me, with my fragmentary knowledge of the language sound like a linguist - was basically undecipherable, so we drew pictures in the sand, traded personal aromas, and shared a cognac. Well, base supplies did run to better things than bottled water, even if they didn't include a portable shower. The cocktail cabinet was alive and well after all.

*

Another week and it was visiting day again. Only this time my new-found friends asked, via a combination of mime, and more pictures in the sand, if I'd care to go fishing. I would. But, suspecting the favoured area was not the *pas loin* indicated, suggested *demain*, perhaps *apres-demain* would be better, as tomorrow, or the next day, the vessel, to which I was transmitting signals, would not be requiring any. So it was arranged.

When I eventually did get to go, I was pleased to have done so. Pleased also we'd made alternative arrangements as to the day of my going. It was down the coast a piece - as the Americans would say. The French? *Grande distance,* I'd imagine, or similar. Certainly not *pas loin,* for, to my way of thinking, "not far" meant less than the distance we covered. Substantially less! But it had been well worth the effort. A lagoon, estranged from the sea by a steep, sandy beach, but with a narrow channel that allowed stocks to be replenished at high tide. Patient, watchful wading birds also favoured these secluded waters. Out here the air was clear and fresh. The continual sound of the surf was muted by layers of low scrub and vegetation, which also formed a barrier against a spirited onshore breeze. So everything was far from perfect, for that breeze was what kept the mosquitoes and sandflies in check. No matter, my prayers were answered. The fish were plentiful, obliging, and definitely *Grande,* so I did have my fish and chip supper, even if it didn't match that of my local chippie. My expectations had never been that high to begin with.

As I settled for the night, relaxed, at peace with myself and the world, all around was tranquillity. Well, almost. Nothing stirred in the landscape except the whispering grasses, but the surf crashed and boomed along the beach like a battery of cannons.

There were days of sheer bliss. Days when the sun shone in clear blue skies, the temperature up in the nineties. Hot white sand washed by tropical waters and edged by leafy palms, their fronds barely shifting in the light, cooling breeze. And there were days of absolute hell. Days when heavy black clouds dragged their curtains of rain across the surface of the sea. Large, fat raindrops were driven horizontal on the strength of the wind, and there was thunder, intense and fearsome. Nothing remained dry, little remained undamaged.

They came for me after a month. Not the men in white jackets, but it *was* time to go in for a break. A tiny Cessna dropped by. My personal transport bouncing down on the grass of my back garden, as it were. It then carried me to town for a couple of days. I just fastened up my tent and left. Something you could do in few African countries. Well, you could, but it wouldn't be there when you returned!

Port Gentil is a pleasant little coastal town. Trees line its streets, beaches line its shores, and there are shaded sidewalk cafes and bars. It is the oil capital of an emerging African nation. French influence and language, French food and drink, for Gabon - along with other ex-French Colonial territories - although independent, is still heavily influenced by Paris.

December 31st found us at the most popular bar and restaurant in town. The Provencale was knee-deep in Frenchmen, but that didn't sway us. Rather than the overpriced, celebratory, fixed menu, our group opted for chip butties. Not really *a point,* as they say, but to appease the owner somewhat, we also gulped champagne with considerably less restraint than the price demanded. In fact we continued to do so well into the new day, which was also the New Year. It couldn't really be termed the morning after the night before, as there had been no demarcation point, the session was still in full swing. We later transferred our allegiance to the nearby beach: a buffet lunch, along with a punch that was concocted from some imagined formula. This related basically to whatever was currently available: everything from Martini to Mou Tai - the latter a Chinese spirit that appeared to possess all the properties of liquid Semtex. It smelt bad, tasted even worse, but I can confirm it to be a drink of exceptional authority, not to say some belligerence!

*

A pleasant interlude, then it was time to return to work, thank goodness. I needed the rest, or a kidney transplant.

Same old Cessna taildragger, although a different pilot this time; American. And was he ever different. As different as the Year was eventually to prove to be.

'Hi, there. How we all doing today?'

I thought he was greeting to me, until I turned to find him patting the metal of the engine cowling. He talked all the way through his walk around, addressing himself to the aircraft the whole time. Bloody silly, really, it was just a bunch of pieces screwed, bolted and rivetted together.

A collection of parts: aluminium and steel, wood, leather, rubber and wire; an inanimate object. Yet I knew how he felt, just wished he'd speak to me. The odd word would have done. No matter, the monologue continued throughout, even when my supplies had been loaded, we were strapped in, and engine started. I may as well not have been there, even though, in effect, I was paying him.

'How's your fuel then? Yeah, fine. Oil pressure? Good girl. Mixture? Carb heat? Flaps?' The litany continued as his fingers rippled over switches, buttons and levers. Then, with a final check - to make sure I was aboard, maybe? - he finally acknowledged my presence with a smile and a raised thumb. I replied in kind.

'OK, we're ready...' I thought he really was addressing me this time. Wrong again. He hadn't yet finished. '....let's see what you can do today, old girl.'

It was a relatively long take-off run with the weight we had on board, and the heat, but the runway was built to take big jets, so no problem. Still, he coaxed her all the way. 'Come on old girl, you can do it. Yeah, there you go. What did I tell yer.'

It was the last kind word he said, for the air was turbulent and it seemed the aircraft was to take the blame for that. It was now 'Bitch. You old cow,' and, upon touchdown, 'Get your ass on the ground, goddammit.'

Even after off-loading he had no time for a coffee and a chat - not with me, at least - he was back on board immediately, apparently eager to be on his way. He fired up and, propeller disappearing in a shining arc, they quickly taxied off.

The little plane turned, and with the application of power trundled across the grass. The speed built up, agonizingly slowly it seemed to me. Even empty it appeared to struggle, engine straining at full power. I could imagine the pilot urging it on: "Come on you bastard. Son of a bitch, get up." Then, seemingly with some reluctance, it responded, barely clearing the trees on its way into the sky. I watched until it disappeared from sight.

'Goodbye, old girl,' I found myself whispering. Then I was alone once more. Alone with my thoughts in the now still emptiness of this place. The only sounds were those of nature in the raw: the call of the birds, the clicking of the insects, and the familiar, at present muted, crashing of the surf.

*

A bar could be an airconditioned, glass and chrome fitted room in a hotel, a packed-earth floored shack out in the bush, decked out with home-made furnishings, or it could be anything in between. There were even subdivisions at the lower end of the scale: a shack with a refrigerator, a shack without. The only common factor was the beer, though the cost varied considerably, price relating to degree of comfort. There again, comfort was self-determined.

Tonight, my last in Libreville, we had opted for quality, deeming Antiones to be worthy of our presence. Pâté de Foie avec Truffe, followed by Coq au vin à la Bourguignon, with a Crème Brûlée to round everything off. Delightful. Naturally, bottle after bottle of wine had accompanied us on this journey of gastronomic enlightenment. At the moment life felt good. Of course it did, we'd eaten well, drank some good wine, downed a few *digestives.* That's what alcohol did, made you feel good, no matter how things really were, one reason drinking was so popular.

As he stood, Dennis *looked* as if he'd had one or two. The way he sauntered off to the toilet reminded me of the way they walked in those old westerns, the rolling gait: John Wayne, Kirk Douglas and the like; the real westerns. Dennis must have been having similar thoughts, for as he passed a full length mirror on one of the central pillars he paused, backed up a few paces, stood and faced himself, narrowing his eyes. Then, pow! pow! His hands came up, two fingers on each pointing as he attempted to outdraw himself. Pow! pow! Again, with just as much luck. So, oblivious of the attention he'd attracted, seemingly disappointed with himself, he holstered up and headed for the loo.

'Cowboy mad, Dennis,' Bob proclaimed to no one in particular. 'Says he has videos of all the John Wayne and Clint Eastwood westerns.'

'Ah,' said someone else, 'but we....' I dismissed thoughts of Dennis and looked round. It was Don, peering down into his glass as he spoke to Ted. Not about Dennis, an entirely unrelated subject. I realized this as soon as Ted expressed profound disbelief at what was being discussed. At least I assume that's what was implied.

'Bollocks,' he said. Quite loud, too.

Jerry and Big Al shared a bottle of whisky. It stood on the table between them, contents well down, a fact that seemed to form the basis of *their* current debate: the philosophical implications of the bottle's condition. Lack of a degree in philosophy apparently didn't preclude either from forming an opinion. Big Al was first with his analysis. 'Bastard's half empty!' he exclaimed, as if wondering where the other half had gone. Jerry, having once admitted to a fleeting interest in existentialism - therefore the more qualified to address such a concept - seemed to disagree. 'Bullshit! It's still half full.'

Pow! Pow! From across the way. Dennis was back, still trying to outdraw himself in the mirror.

Luckily, I had packed the previous evening. Not luckily, purposely. I had known what it would be like. The pain behind the eyes, the throbbing head, uncoordinated movements; exactly how it was. I padded around without order, unsure of what it was I wanted to achieve. All I did know for sure, was that I needed to get to the airport by a certain time.

Never again, I thought, yet again. Must have been the wine in the Coq au Vin.

* *

TALES FROM DARKEST AFRICA

Friday night. A poker game at the house of an American oil executive, who happens to have a monkey as a pet. Fans and louvred doors keep night-time temperatures down to reasonable levels, fortunate that, for his mini anthropoid likes nothing better than to perch upon the blade of the old-fashioned ceiling fan, from where, providing the speed is set at its lowest - which it is - it's only too happy to observe the world drifting past below. Which, again, it is. Literally: flush, full house, ace high, whatever. The men down there also focused on the cards, concentration absolute.

'Bet two,' a gravelled voice announced, dropping a couple of notes onto the pile.

'Your two, raise you five.' Seven more notes joined the growing stack in the centre of the table.

'Call', said the next player, adding the appropriate amount.

'Fold, dammit. Cards ain't running for me tonight.' And so it went, one hand after another, one drink after another.

Then, players attention on the cards, another hand, this one unnoticed, reaches surreptitiously through the door, switching the fan to full chat. An appropriate phrase, that, for the monkey was soon to be doing so: chattering away excitedly, whilst hanging on for dear life. His arms and legs were wrapped around the blade, head towards centre. Such a position, of course, compelled the other end to be directed outwards. As it was. So, when the terrified beast eventually lost control of its bowels...

Needless to say, from that point on the shower suddenly proved to have far more attraction than a mere pack of cards, or a pile of money.

It was one of the things us expats would get up to in an effort to relieve the tension of working in this unpredictable environment. How unpredictable? Read on.

*

Some countries have so few beggars they're known by name. Nigeria is not such a country. It is, though, a country divided by tribal rivalries - bound to be, with around two hundred and fifty from which to choose. Another thing I soon became aware of, they always seemed to be in year eight of the latest five year plan.

When I first arrived, the government was fairly stable. (For an independent African nation, that is. Which says just about everything.)

The Prime Minister, a Hausa, went by the name of Al Haji Sir Abubaka Tafawa Belewa. Exactly! In fact, I recall one BBC newsreader admitting - once trouble was brewing and this name hit the headlines rather frequently - that it was quite some days before he felt comfortable with the pronunciation. He went on to say, "I'd just about mastered it, when they shot him!"

With a dead Prime Minister being of little use to the country, it was all-change time. Next in line - not as in accession, or deputy leader of the ruling party, but as in leader of the coup - was a Maj. General named J.T.U. Aguiyi-Ironsi. Another mouthful, to be sure, even without regard to the initials; no idea what they stood for anyway. No matter. He hardly lasted long enough to trouble anyone.

Lieutenant Colonel Yakubu Gowan, a Yoruba, was next up. Once again voted in at the point of a gun. Meanwhile, away to the east, General Odumegwu Ojukwu, an Ibo, seemed to hold the opinion that it really should have been his turn. A minor disagreement ensued, the outcome of which resulted in the Eastern Region seceding from the Federation. They declared themselves to be independent: the Republic of Biafra. But as a large percentage of Nigeria's most prodigious oil-fields just happened to be located in this region, the outcome, inevitably, was civil war. Maybe not such a minor disagreement after all, then.

Sometime after that tragedy was resolved, Gowan, paying a visit to Britain - silly man - decided that this was probably a nice country in which to retire. He was only in his mid-forties, but he had lasted eight years, so early retirement seemed like a good idea. Especially as he no longer had a job back home.

During his absence, someone else had availed themselves of the army's Kalashnikovs, voting themselves into power. And from here on it became a kind of "Who's turn is it this week" situation, dictators appearing to tumble faster than England wickets in an Ashes Test.

I believe there was one brief spell of civilian rule, but it wasn't to last. Neither, it seems, was it exactly democratic. Apparently - this having become yet another country where elections were a rarity - lots of people stood around with guns; to prevent confusion as to the mechanics of voting, you understand!

In most African countries, becoming an opposition politician is not looked upon as being a particularly wise career move. In Nigeria, the same could be said for the Head of State. Not exactly a pensionable position. There again, maybe it is, certain of them allegedly depositing indecent amounts of cash in Swiss banks over the years.

But as Nigeria doesn't exactly have a monopoly on Coups d'etat the following stories may be of more interest. The salient points of each attributed to the Nigerian press.

*

As a former British colony, Nigeria observed the drive on the left rule. That was the law, though not one to which Nigerian drivers necessarily subscribed; seems they felt more comfortable in the centre. And should another vehicle have the effrontery to approach from the opposite direction, well... 'He'll give way, won't he? 'Specially if I delays veering off until de last minute?' It's a question that must pass through the mind - I won't say often, for that surmises survival - and one for which the answer often becomes all too obvious, all too late. A couple of problems arise, of course. A: The opposing driver's intentions are not taken into account - and, being another citizen of like mind..... B: Veering a largely unserviceable, severely overloaded vehicle, suddenly, tends to result in said vehicle charging off into the scenery with all the finesse of a rhinoceros running amok.

The twelve seat Volkswagen minibus - known as a Mammy Wagon - was quite popular on the long-distance taxi run, therefore it was not unusual to see newspaper reports along the lines: THIRTY-SIX DEAD IN MINIBUS CRASH! Not the multiple pile-up one would imagine, as the sub-text often revealed: No other vehicle involved. Indeed, the road-sides were littered with twisted remains of the most horrendous wrecks. Difficult to see how they could ever have extracted the bodies. There again, it's possible they hadn't. Just as, on my return from the pub - particularly during coup season - I have to admit to seeing the odd corpse lying around. (They'd hardly stand, would they?) A passer-by may toss a banana leaf over it, maybe not. Most didn't seem to care. No wild, drink-induced dream, this, either, a figment of the imagination given substance by the enveloping darkness. This was reality. Come morning those bodies would still be dead. And, in all likelihood, they'd still be there. The only mourners were likely to be the vultures.

As I was on leave when the next story broke, it was joyfully related to me upon my return, by a colleague. Hearsay as it were, thus unsubstantiated. There again, Al being a conservative type, not prone to exaggeration, and this being Nigeria, neither can it be categorically rejected out of hand.

'A group of us sat in the hotel bar,' Al began. This I was quite prepared to believe. A not unlikely venue for such as us.

'In fact the place was crowded,' he continued. 'With good reason. For this night, as well as drinking and raising hell, we were there to watch the news on TV. And sure enough, on screen, as had been rumoured, the Minister of Transport put in an appearance. He was there to make a special announcement.'

'"The decision has been made," the Minister said, "to better tie in with the ex-French colonies, (which bracketed this most populous of West African countries) to switch to driving on the right." The Minister went on to announce that the change-over would be implemented in two phases, over a two-week period. "During the first week, taxis, buses, and commercial vehicles will make the change. Private vehicles will comply with the edict the during second week. This will, I feel, alleviate some of the confusion that would be bound to occur if everyone changed at the same time."

'Us expatriates thought this to be a splendid idea, and many glasses were raised to the minister's health and well-being.

'That we had not already been suffering from the effects of too much alcohol, or had miss-heard, was confirmed when the following morning's newspapers appeared. There it was in black and white; taxis, buses, and commercial vehicles one week, private cars the next. Amazing!

'Same bar, same hour, following evening. The news again. It was announced in Lagos that the Transport Minister, in a sudden fit of patriotism, had resigned his post, volunteering to drive a jeep on the Biafran front. A number of his staff - presumably feeling similarly patriotic - had volunteered along with him. The new Minister, by the way, felt that, after close study of the drive-on-the-right situation, the confusion would not be as great as at first anticipated, therefore everyone would change over on the same day.'

Everyone I talked to confirmed this story as being correct, and judging it alongside other stories I read in the local press, I could well believe it. One in particular comes to mind. Well, it would, wouldn't it, a story of true romance. There again, maybe not, for it concerned a man who was up in court for... well, not exactly indecent exposure, more like... er... Oh, what the hell, screwing in public is what it amounted to. Rape, in fact.

A woman was apparently bending over a well to fill her bucket, when along comes the accused and fills her, so to speak. Sounds like rape. There again, apparently no objections were raised until... well, later, when the woman faced the perpetrator of the dirty deed - or penetrator. Anyway, when the defence questioned as to why she didn't protest sooner, the woman replied to the effect that, until she faced him she'd thought it was someone she knew!

Can you imagine? "Oh! Hello there. Is that you, Sunday? Or is it Joshua?"

Then there was one about a girl who collapsed and died on a dance-floor. Not immediately, mind. She apparently convulsed a little first. Everyone else, it seemed, carried on dancing around her until the number

257

finished. At which time it was discovered, so was she. When questioned as to the reason they hadn't offered help, other dancers replied that they were of the opinion she was demonstrating a new style!

One thing for sure, it would never catch on.

Frustrations were part of the daily routine, if you didn't laugh you'd cry. Take the time Ian Easterbrook (yes, he who had been known to take the odd drink) managed to get hold of a leg of New Zealand lamb. A real coup, that. Especially so, being as Ian was a Kiwi. Looking forward in anticipation, he instructed his house-boy to prepare it for that evening, when he would be bringing some friends home for surprise dinner.

Just as well Ian had only revealed his fare as being "something special" rather than roast lamb, planning to surprise his guests. And surprised they were, for what they sat down to was lamb stew.

The replacement house-boy proved to be no better.

'What you want for dinna, massa?' he asked one morning as Ian left for work .

'Oh, I don't know what time I'll be in, Sunday, just get a chicken from the market and put it in the fridge.'

That evening, on arriving home, Ian went to get a beer. But as he opened the fridge door he found himself facing a live chicken. He said it stood there, centre stage, like an artist in the spotlight, head hunched, shivering on its feet.

So, as can be seen, in Nigeria, as in Africa itself, life was rarely boring. Roadblocks became rife. Driving to work one day I was confronted by armed troops. Then one of them was inviting me to step out of the vehicle, to open the boot. This I saw as being a reasonable request, he was carrying a Kalashnikov after all, pointing it at my head. So out I got. They wouldn't be looking for anything in particular, I knew, just going through the motions, enjoying doing so. Power at the point of a gun. I knew the feeling, recalled that exercise in Seletar, the officer I'd challenged. Difference was, that had been a game, my gun not loaded. These would be, that was for sure.

Even safe in the knowledge that he didn't intend shooting me was no great comfort. Gun safety being as sloppy as it was this was no guarantee I wouldn't end up getting shot. I could imagine the scenario:

'What dat noise? Why you lay down, you tired? Hey, dis man leaking.'

It happens, but at the time the mind is occupied by other thoughts - the likelihood of my liberty being seriously curtailed, for instance - so it was only later, when I thought about the situation, that my heart fluttered for a second or two.

Another such situation occurred in South Africa, during the apartheid period. Getting lost when driving into Johannesburg from the south, my wife and I inadvertently ended up in the township of Sowetto. Without the necessary permit, needless to say. Easy enough to find our way in, getting out was another matter altogether. It was dusk and we certainly didn't wish to stop and ask directions. But maybe the dim light was to our advantage, for we were neither stopped nor, apparently, noticed for what we were. From all I'd read before, and heard since, that also had been a time of grave danger. Or had it?

*

It was another fine day over the Gulf of Guinea. The sun hung high in a sky dotted with fleecy white clouds. Nothing serious or threatening, yet. But they would build throughout the day to form billowing cumulus, possibly the towering cu-nim. A thousand feet below was the placid sea, its calmness disturbed only by a long, rolling swell.

There were six of us in the S55's cabin, on our way to Mobil's Ocean Master Two. This was a Mk.10, the turbine version, more reliable and powerful than the Mk.4 we'd used in air force. We were fifteen minutes out from the island of Fernando Po, twenty from the rig, and I was well into the latest edition of *Playboy* when my attention was diverted.

Something serious, then! Had to be if it were to unglue my eyes from the centrefold.

It was.

There was a whoosh, a sheet of flame out of the exhaust, then the silence of a shut down engine. So smooth was the transition from forward flight to autorotation I immediately assumed it to be a practice, as in Malaya, all those years ago. My inner self told me otherwise, an opinion confirmed when we actually set down on the ocean, the pilot calling for us to launch, and board, the liferaft. As we complied, he sat, half in, half out of the cockpit, transmitting a mayday. This was picked up by the captain of a overflying airliner, the call relayed to Santa Isabel tower. They, in turn, informed Mobil, which is when things really got moving. Just as well.

Within sight was a large freighter, steaming towards Cameroon, so, to attract attention we set off distress signals.

Given the conditions, there was no way for him not to see those billowing clouds of orange smoke, but despite maritime laws that specify ships must offer assistance to anyone in distress, he steamed willy-nilly on his way. Maybe he also assumed it to be an exercise? It had been so perfectly executed it could almost have been so. No injuries, no panic. Little time for it really. It was over almost before we realized it had begun.

The chief pilot also seemed to regard it as an exercise, for when later circling overhead - awaiting the arrival of the first of many vessels steaming towards us - he was to instruct our pilot not to let us touch the supplies.

'They're for emergencies,' he advised.

This from a man who was later to remark upon the size and number of sharks with which we were unbeknowingly encircled. They were probably gnashing their teeth just waiting for us to be served up.

All ended well though. After four hours bobbing around, sunbathing - not to be recommended, even on a day as calm as that - the rescue vessels arrived to pick us up. The helicopter remained afloat on its buoyancy cushions and was towed back to the island. A quick engine change, a check, and it was back in service.

*

Customs officers were a continual bugbear, so, over the years I developed a few ideas for dealing with them upon arrival. As most were only capable of concentrating on one thing at a time, I felt it a good idea to divert their attention from the thing they were supposed to be doing, which they didn't want to do anyway. I'd pick the most senior officer, talk to him as if he were a long-lost friend, for they love their staff to see they have the respect of a European. I'd pull out a cheap calculator, pass it to him, show him what it could do, tell him to keep it.

Then there was the toy dog ruse I once resorted to, purely as an experiment. I had back-up calculators in my briefcase, didn't need them. The dog was wound up and made to perform. It yelped, ran around, did somersaults, wagged its tail. The officer was delighted, grinning and clapping his hands like a child. 'Keep it,' I told him. He did, wished to see nothing more. Out came the magic chalk, on went the indecipherable squiggle. Alongside, those not so wise were having their souls bared to the world.

Departure was even more difficult. First came the queue for your tax exemption certificate to be stamped, which allowed you to queue up at the ticket desk only to learn that your ticket, which clearly indicates your reservation to be, OK - in airline parlance, confirmed - is not. Confirmation in most third world countries can only be taken for granted once you actually clear their airspace. Not merely when seated and airborne, mind, that's no guarantee you'll not be returning, aircraft required by the President, say. One reason not to use the local airline. No, best not to relax until you clear their airspace.

I recall the time Ron Hewson and his crew had just completed a job in Ghana, were about to depart for another. Different job, different country. Life was like that. We'd roam around for months on end without going home. Sometimes it was years. We got our breaks transferring from one place to the next, as in this instance.

As usual, it seemed pre-dinner drinking had got out of hand, and by the time dinner was over some of the crew decided to visit the Accra casino. Come midnight, Ron, and Lynne, his legal wife, decided it was time to round them up, remind them they had a plane to catch very early the next morning. Two of the party refused to leave, so, nothing else to be done, Ron left them to it.

When the rebels finally departed they discovered there was no longer any transport running. So what did they do? Used their initiative, naturally. Talk about pushing your luck, these guys actually flagged down an army patrol, managed to commandeer a personnel carrier to take them to the airport, for a fee, of course. Too late, though. The flight had already left.

They eventually turned up in Gabon some days later, after an adventurous trip. But so it had been for the rest of the crew, it seems. Ron and Co. had boarded the Cameroon Airlines scheduled flight, as planned. The aircraft, a brand new 737, was routed from Accra direct to Libreville, Gabon. Only, this being Africa, that wasn't the way things went. It made an unscheduled stop en-route, in Douala, Cameroons.

The newly created airline had a fleet of just three 737's, and, it appears, that day was to be the official inauguration. Airline officials decided they wanted all their aircraft lined up for the ceremony, hence the diversion, or was it a skyjacking?. Upon landing, the passengers were disembarked, bundled aboard an old, chartered DC4, and sent on their way. Albeit quite a few hours late. And if you'd had a connection scheduled in Libreville? Tough luck. That's Africa for you.

In March 1972 came my turn to depart this continent, and I made it relatively unscathed. The *quid pro quo* for this was... well, several quid, actually. An amount that just so happened to coincide with the total contents of my wallet. Plus my watch! But at least I'd broken free of Nigeria, at last.

So there you have it. As can be seen, after living there for so long, anywhere else was bound to offer more than a passing attraction.

And so they did.

* *

Chapter Fourteen
DOODLEBUG DOODLES

'What do you actually do?' It is a question that has been put repeatedly over the years, my answer is usually evasive. This I feel is due to one of the following: To the layman, it is difficult to explain; There are times when I'm not entirely sure myself; I automatically assume the person behind the question is merely socializing, therefore not particularly interested.

I could always bluff my way, I suppose, say I'm a racing driver, for I have driven racing cars at Brands Hatch. But no, driving a racing car didn't make me a racing driver, just as flying an aircraft never made me a pilot. (By the same rules I was no gigolo.)

A result of this evasiveness is that people tend to get the wrong idea. Either that, or they have just finished the latest Le Carré novel. Which in turn can lead to an even more oblique line of questioning, as happened at a recent party.

After making a show of looking round, just to be sure no one else was taking an interest - or maybe to ensure I knew he knew what he was about - words were whispered, voice as hushed as that of an atheist in a cathedral. The words were along the lines of, 'You're not involved with the Foreign Office, are you?' A reference, I assumed, to Queen Anne's Gate, or Vauxhall Cross, as it now is. You see, I read the novels too.

'What? You mean the security services?' I replied. 'Not me. Pass on that.'

Despite such denials I'm sure people still occasionally presume I am. After all, it's not a thing someone of that ilk would be likely to admit to, is it? And my departures can, at times, be rather rapid, and unexpected. Take for instance the evening I was urgently required in Norway, and no scheduled flight could guarantee my arrival in time, the vessel I was to join, due to sail at dawn.

I was instructed to take a taxi to the military base of RAF Leeming - a bare twenty miles from home - from where, I'd been advised, onward transportation had been arranged. Upon arrival at the guardroom I received a salute - it was rather grand for a taxi, I'll admit - along with an escort out to the airfield, where a light, twin-engined aircraft was scheduled to arrive. When it did, the door opened, a hand beckoned, and I stepped aboard. Without shutting down, or a word being exchanged, Bandeirante and myself, its lone passenger, disappeared into the darkness of the night. So what had been going through the minds of those airmen, do you think? Probably suspected me to be one of those "funny people"; the serviceman's euphemism for agents. In actual fact I was whisked up to Glasgow, where I spent the night in a plush hotel. Next day it was off to Haugesund in another chartered twin - one of Piper's American Indian tribe this time (Apache, as it happened) - just myself and the pilot. It was a perfectly uneventful trip in the still, early morning air, and we landed at our destination long before the first scheduled flight was due. A flight I could well have been on, for the ship's departure had been delayed due to reasons previously unforseen.

'You'd be embarrassed if I revealed how much it cost to get you here,' I was later told. Try me, I thought.

So, not one of those funny people at all. In reality, nothing more than a plain old doodlebugger, which, you'll recall, is a term pertaining to anyone engaged in the search for oil. Not the development and production side of the business, but exploration. A vast difference.

*

A prime requirement for any seismic exploration is an acoustic source. Offshore this can range from the twenty to forty pounds of basic dynamite mix as used back in the pioneering - non-environmental days - to the two thousand plus pounds per square inch compressed air of a contemporary, tuned array.

Oh, oh. Here we go again. Mention of dynamite brings to mind a Norwegian guy I once found myself seated next to, on a flight to... well, Norway, would you believe. He introduced himself, then - usually a good move, to my way of thinking bought me a drink. (The Scandanavian Airlines must have been almost the last to offer complimentary drinks.) Anyway, we got to discussing something or other when, after a couple more drinks, the conversation drifted on to a totally unrelated subject, as makeshift conversations generally tend to do. This time it was the merits or otherwise of building houses with the lower floor located below ground level. Interesting, eh?

'Difficult in Norway,' I prompted, knowing it was exactly what they did do over there. This despite the whole country appearing to be formed of solid granite.

'Ya, not so,' Olaf replied. A contradiction of terms for a start. 'I do it myself. A few sticks of dynamit' - that was how he pronounced it, dynamit - 'and whump.' His hands flew up. 'Ground or Germans,' he said. 'Same for both. Finish.' He then went on to explain how he'd gained his experience. 'During the war years, serving with the resistance.' Underground, I thought, would have been a more appropriate term, given the subject under discussion.

An acoustic source, then. The next requirement is a means of recording energy pulses reflected from beneath the seabed, ie, hydrophones. These are towed behind the vessel, wired together in groups, the complete assembly - up to two miles in length - known as a streamer.

This acoustic source generates sound waves which penetrate ocean floor, and as depth of penetration is dependant upon strata and frequency, then a multi-frequency signal will give a variable return. These seismic data are recorded, and it is from these records a geophysicist, working his sorcery and bullshit, will come up with an answer. This can range from, "No likelihood of oil here, old son," to the infrequently muttered, "Looks promising." In which case the area in question is subjected to further exploration magic, and or, the drilling of a very expensive hole; in the end, the only true test. And that, basically, is it. Except... It's not a lot of use someone finding something like that if they don't know where it was to begin with, which is where we come in.

Every shot, hole, platform, pipeline, or whatever, requires an accurate position, for which we supply the coordinates. Simple, eh? Well, today, with the advent of GPS satellites (for Global Positioning System) it is. Though not as simple as it could be. The reason? GPS - primarily a US military system - is strictly controlled by the Department of Defence, ie, the Pentagon, who trust hardly anyone. So, to deny access to unauthorized users - in DoD speak, the Point Element (the enemy, or bad guys, to you and I) - the data is coded. Data available to the general public is transmitted on a separate code to that intended for military use, the quality of our data degraded by deliberately induced clock errors - termed, Selective Availability. Maybe thirty metre accuracy, as opposed to plus or minus one metre. OK for yachtsmen and the like, nowhere near good enough for the oil industry, or the airlines. We need the kind of accuracy the military use for tossing their missiles around.

But a solution was soon devised.

With a receiver placed at a known location it is a simple matter to calculate any data errors. You know where *you* are, you know where the GPS *says* you are. *Voilà!* as the French say. If these data - differential corrections - are then applied to any other receiver operating in the general area, almost all errors can be eliminated. In theory, error-free position data. And guess what? It works in reality too. Bingo! American prestige remains intact, we achieve the required accuracy. I still have a job.

A point of interest: During the Gulf War - you remember, the world's first televised, as-it-happens, real-time war - SA was dispensed with, ie, switched off. This became necessary, as at the time there were not enough military-code receivers to go round. The military therefore found a need to pop down to the local Tandy store, there to purchase commercially available equipment. The SAS, for instance, were said to have used hand-held, yachting type receivers which, predictably, suddenly became extremely accurate. What chance now, those Scud missiles?

Another GPS story concerns itself with the early days, when I was still unfamiliar with the system and all its nuances. An "expert" was dispatched to help with the installation, and to give me a few pointers as to its use. He was very helpful. Set everything up and checked it out before getting ready to leave.

'Great,' he says. 'Perfect.' He then handed me his card. 'If you experience any problems, give me a call. Any time. Home number's on the back.' With which he disappeared rather swiftly, as if he was late for something. The bar, for instance? Still, I was impressed. Until I did experience a problem. After hours, naturally; a weekend at that. So I called him at home, got his mother. Nice person by the sound of her. She talked about our Michael, how he wasn't in right now. She talked about the weather, the flowers she'd just planted, and wasn't it terrible how the government.... On and on it went. Trouble was, during all this she didn't once mention anything about what to do if the system hung up because your GPS receiver refused to accept the downloaded ephemeris data. Ah, well.

But that's GPS, and now. Way back when, in the Stone Age, so to speak, before the advent of such sophistication, things were very different. Radio beacons located at a number sites on shore, transmitted a signal to a receiver on the vessel. This signal needed to be lined up on a marker pulse, the range read off a scale. Nothing automatic or fancy, navigation solely in the hands of the operator or, more often than not, fate.

What you had were two pre-computed ranges, fixing a point at which you needed to position the vessel - although, before the advent of the portable computer (yes, there was such a time) even these needed to be computed by use of the human brain. You also had two indicated ranges, from which could be derived your present position. It was then down to the operator to instantly calculate range and bearing - you remember, Pythagoras, square roots etc - then position the vessel on the preplotted point. Not too difficult, for a single point. But for a preplotted line of any number of evenly spaced points, down which a seismic vessel was required to run, not so easy. Difficult in fact, bearing in mind the streamer needed to be straight at the start of the line; ie, you were navigating two miles of ship, needed a long run in, needed to be accurate. When I say accurate, I mean relatively so. Back then? Plus or minus fifty metres, maybe. But even that required a well tuned installation; weather conditions which permitted the reliable propagation of radio waves; accurately located stations ashore, at least two of which were operational. It rarely happened. Therefore it has been known for an operator to run on time and bearing, an acceptable method for a very limited period, should you find yourself with but one, not altogether perfect, signal - again not entirely unheard of! Providing you started with two, ran long enough to establish the timing between shots, and course made good, it should, in theory, be possible to track the one station, maintain present heading, and call the shots off a stopwatch. Hopefully, once both signals returned, the line could be completed with but slight corrections to timing and heading. No one any the wiser, none of that dreaded "down-time" for either party. Alas, things don't always work out as planned.

'You can stop calling the shots now, Dave,' one not so gullible Party Chief called up to the bridge. 'We've been aground five minutes.'

Oh, oh! *In flagrante delicto,* like.

Onshore meanwhile, many other problems, which is where ingenuity and adventure came to the fore. Stations needed to be set, on pre-surveyed sites. Then the equipment had to be imported, by fair means or foul. Yes, many's the time a large dugout canoe has rendezvoused with a seismic vessel offshore Africa, equipment hastily off-loaded, secreted ashore and assembled. Those smugglers of old had nothing on us.

Thus unhindered by stifling government regulations, the survey could well be completed before the mountains of bumph, bureaucratic dallying, size and number of kickbacks etc, had been negotiated and resolved. Sometimes they were never resolved, for communications out in the bush were often non-existent. And as for your hypothetical bush telegraph, well..., even drums could be silenced for a few notes; provided such notes bore a true likeness to the presidential incumbent!

Of course, the powers that be were often only to blissfully aware of our presence, happy to overlook such burdensome bureaucratic details, just so long as the relevant papers changed hands. Naturally, such paper featured a number, preferably followed by enough zeros to mount an attack on Pearl Harbour - as Clive James would have it. Free enterprise? Maybe. Though more than somewhat outside what is the conventional framework as regards such a system.

Apart from Africa, where corruption is anyway blatant, the financial handshake is also the natural way of doing business in South America, and elsewhere. Thus it was - following in the wake of the Lockheed scandal (where large amounts of cash were handed out in order to secure military aircraft sales) - that word came down from the parent company of a seismic operator, to whom we were at the time contracted, that forthwith, everything was to be done by the book. Which is how we came to be standing by for two weeks in a Caribbean hotel. Whereas previously a day or two would suffice, this was the time it now took the relevant application to be officially approved. Not that we were complaining. There *are* worse places to be stuck, on expenses!

As is the way with memories, it always seems to be the exotic which spring to mind. How easy it is to remember ten days in a luxury hotel in Rio, awaiting clearance of equipment that some aggrieved customs officer had deemed not to be accompanied by the correct documents. As before, such documents - usually coloured - bore a portrait of the current dict... er President, followed by a large denomination number. Or perhaps it was someone higher up the scale who decided the correct procedures had not been adhered to: ie, the above-mentioned documents fell somewhat short of expectations. It happened, and forgive me if I admit to not feeling entirely sympathetic towards my employers at these times.

Columbia was another country in which I was to spend an enforced layover. The capital, Bogota, was a place that left me breathless. Not because of the sights - breathtaking enough, admitted - but the altitude, over eight thousand feet above sea level. Takes some getting used to, that. One beer and you know you've had a drink. Bogota is also the kidnap capital of the world, so after a couple of days I left for Cartegena, on the Caribbean coast, a far more satisfactory option.

Or how about a week in Paris, awaiting a work permit for Gabon? This, we discovered, could be readily obtained in two days, were one prepared to bow and scrape to some third world clerk, or to speak French. Both reasonable requests, considering the location. But we can't be perfect can we? Not all the time. Got to know Paris quite well over the years.

*

The limited range of our equipment required stations to be moved many times during the course of a survey, presenting us with many headaches and logistical problems, plus the means of generating a little extra revenue for that account in the Bahamas! A bank that was later to crash, taking with it a considerable chunk of my savings. Actually, it was a guy called Robert Vesco who took with him my savings. Such is life. Easy come, easy go.

There has been the odd bad investment, I'll admit. That bank apart, there was an Investment Fund - again, obviously investing in someone else's future. There'd been the odd gold mine, not to say gold itself (which dived in value the moment I became involved), and like that. Thing is, I never invested more than I could afford to loose - always a wise move - and, thankfully, the good investments more than covered the bad.

Back to the job. This equipment, Shoran, (for SHort RAnge Navigation) I used as late as 1984. Although by then in the last vestiges of retirement, enough was rescued from the rubbish skip to conduct a survey in the Indian Ocean, off the Andaman Islands. It seemed the Indians were unwilling to pay for the greater accuracy of modern technology.

Now, it is mainly computerized, digitized, automatic tracking GPS. All singing and dancing Pentium, and Network for Windows. The only physical input required, is for someone to install, and troubleshoot the system, and to control the quality. Oh, and this paper-less office is also required to generate prodigious amounts of paperwork! Most of which will rarely be looked at by anyone ever again. Such is progress.

But all this gadding about meant I still got to fly. Quite a lot, in fact, in a variety of aircraft. I was to log many an hour on the scheduled airlines; piston engined aircraft in the early days, the DC's by Douglas. They flew relatively slowly, through or around the weather rather than over. And letdowns could be quite scary in adverse conditions, wingtips lost in the fog. Bad enough in a Trident on the approach to Heathrow, and they were fully automated: auto approach, auto-throttle, Autoland. In the third world there were no such facilities, it was a matter of trusting tired pilots. Then there were the semi-private, semi-personal flights; the charters. Nothing routine or scheduled about those, each one an adventure in itself.

Undeterred by what they saw as petty rules and regulations, pilots often flew low, almost down on the deck at times. I appreciated these flights almost as much as the pilots obviously enjoyed them, although they were of course illegal. But with no radar control, little air traffic, few reporting points, what the hell. We could have been back in the barnstorming days.

Even the aircraft were different; whatever was available at the right price. Although we regularly used such as the DC3, Britten Norman Islander and Trislander, there were also many oddities: Beech 18, Westland Widgeon, Shorts Skyvan, Partenavia P68B, Max Holste Broussard; one I well remember, that. Gabon again, very low level. A bit lax on air traffic, so get it down on the beach, kind of thing.

Flying along the shoreline like that was exhilarating. Big, noisy radial engine throbbing away out front, leading the way as it were, high wing affording us a clear view. The creamy surf blurring past on the right, high ground to the left, yellow sand directly below. Real flying. Possibly, even a little risky at times. But what the hell, life is full of risk, isn't it? No risk, no adventure, which in itself equates with boredom. The thing to remember, as ever, are the margins. On no account must you allow those to be cut too fine.

* *

Chapter Fifteen
ROMANTIC INTERLUDE
1968

T he aircraft was a VC10; BOAC rather than Nigerian Airways (who also flew one of the type, until it crashed on the approach to Lagos. There were murmurings of extra bodies being discovered in the cockpit, and of guns being found in the wreckage).

Here I was, home again. To England. To all the feelings that are generated by the sight of that familiar landscape sliding past beneath the wings. Rolling, green countryside, a patchwork of fields and woodland, the occasional golf course. Is there anywhere so green as England?

The romantically rural eventually gave way to suburbia, then along came London and its environs: the Isle of Dogs and the silver thread of the Thames; Westminster; Twickenham - stadium apart, row upon row of identical houses situated on narrow streets along which were parked a rainbow necklace of toy-like cars - Windsor, if approaching from the west. A football ground passed by, still way below; twenty-two colourfully striped insects moving purposefully about in pursuit of an invisible ball.

Up here the smooth, aeronautical lines were now broken, slats and flaps emerging from the leading and trailing edges of the wings, spoilers above; the geometry of low-speed flight. Beneath us, felt but unseen, the undercarriage would be sliding into place, four-wheel bogies ready to support that which the wings would soon be incapable of supporting. Lower and lower we edged, feeling our way down, a perfectly controlled descent, vortices spiralling away behind in our turbulent wake.

Buildings: houses and shops; a school; commerce in its many guises; traffic filled roads. All flashed past, for even low speed flight in a large jet is well on the way to two hundred knots.

Very low now, slower too, almost at touchdown. Cars parked, people watching. White faces turned up towards the sky, towards us. Enthusiasts, like myself, unable to pass up on yet another wondrous and graceful approach. Over the boundary fence, shadow rushing up to meet us, to be reunited on the rubber-streaked runway. Away in the distance other aircraft depart their stands, fully refreshed, setting off to seek new adventures of their own.

To someone like me, that's what flying is all about. It's not just a matter of getting from A to B. The travel is incidental, every flight is an adventure. The smaller the aircraft, the more personal the adventure. The mere act of settling myself into my seat fills me with excitement rather than apprehension, anticipation rather than trepidation..

So much for the arrival. I now felt slightly deflated as I joined the throngs rushing to clear immigration, to collect and manipulate a maverick baggage trolley, to clear customs, then transfer myself to Terminal One. I found the Domestic terminal to be slightly less chaotic, now was the time to relax.

There would be other such arrivals over the months to come, just as many departures, for I had time on my hands, plans to fulfil.

In Nigeria, or wherever it was I happened to be, I listened to the news from home, read the week-old papers, and the magazines, so I was well aware of what was going on. I felt the Swinging sixties were passing me by, longed to be part of it. So here I was, ready and waiting.

*

It was my brother, George who first afforded me a glimpse of Sixties lifestyle. A brief glimpse it was, too. Nor was it happening in Yorkshire, I'll tell thee that for nowt. So, after a quick trip up to the family home, or pub, I was soon to be retracing my steps. This time by rail, for looking out of train windows is a good way to conjure up memories. In days past I recall seeing advertising hoardings located in the fields alongside the track, now there were none. I wondered if this was evidence that trains now travelled too fast for anyone to be able to read adverts, or had attention spans contracted. No matter, they'd been eyesores more than anything. Industrial adverts. Not the kind of thing that invited one to do anything interesting, or seductive. Now, I noticed, any industry sited close to the tracks advertised themselves, gratis; large letters painted on walls or roofs. I also had this vision of a landscape dotted with the scars and eruptions of the mines. Now I could barely distinguish pithead gear from factory. But the telephone lines were as remembered, up to their old tricks: the seeming wish to droop towards the ground, only to be jerked back into place every few seconds.

*

London is big. Over nine million souls huddling together for shelter. To me, caught up in the mass of humanity funnelling into the underground, en-route to the centre, it seemed they had all come out together. It would be the same all over the city at this hour: commuters flowing in at one point, being whisked through a dark tube to various destinations around the metropolis, where they would again spew out onto the streets. Be the same above ground, too, on the buses. Only the buses travelled at a more leisurely pace, caught up in the traffic snarl that was London. Too many cars, too much noise, too many people, too humid, too much hustle and bustle; I loved it all the same, it was another of my favourite cities. Not only that, it also contrasted sharply with the life I'd been living.

On the underground I saw a man with a bicycle. Imagine that if you will, in the rush hour at Piccadilly Circus. "No smoking" signs were everywhere. No signs against graffiti though, which also was everywhere. Baker Street station seemed out of line with the rest, dim and aged, as if still awaiting the arrival of Sherlock Holmes.

George had taken a job in London, set up home here, a small flat which he shared with an old school friend - one of mine, not his. We'd never been close, George and I. Rarely went out together, never played together, never even walked to school together; my choice, the latter, for more often than not he'd be late. I'd had no wish to be, knowing the consequences such rashness could bring in those days of corporal punishment. Got my share as it was. But that was all in the past. Anyway, this was different; George now had something which could be of use to me. His flat became a base to any friends or relatives visiting the capital. I recall times when, incumbents apart, there would be two or three of us staying there together, one on the sofa, two on the floor. A bit of a crush in the morning, for bathroom and toilet - two floors down - were shared with the occupants of other flats.

I recall my visits mainly as a series of cameos. Not all that distinct, either, though not because of the usual Sixties reasons. I do remember Lyons Corner house, located somewhere near Hyde Park. Breakfast or lunch there, if not at the Ace Cafe, out on the North Circular. The Ace was a classic example of The Great British Transport "Caff," as they were known to the majority (cafe, far too pretentious a word. Foreign too). Almost a lost institution in these days of health food mania. Health foods? To me health foods were things my father suggested I should eat; or else!

In the evenings it was often Mac's, 100 Oxford Street. We'd go there for the jazz: Colyer, Lightfoot, Barber, Bilk, *et al.* A crowded atmosphere, where waves of sound washed over us. Smoky, too; though by then I no longer smoked. Then there were the parties to which we were invited. The absolute fringes of sixties parties, these. Must have been, for the recollections are clear. (That shared joint back in New Orleans had been a one and only.) It was all there: The music; rock 'n roll, Trini Lopez, and of course, the Beatles; the long hair and short skirts. The clothes: colourful, outrageous, smart. The beautiful people, the good times; none of the drugs. Or if there were, people were very discreet.

I'd stroll down Carnaby Street and the King's Road, "in" places those days, heyday of the sixties revolution. The hippies had been there, and the weirdos. Those on their way to the top, too. Brief glimpses, if you were lucky, kept your eyes open: Beatles, Stones, Hockney, Twiggy, Terrance Stamp, and from York, John Barry; the carnival that has long since left town. I also recall Sunday lunches at the aforementioned Ace Cafe. Ah yes, do I ever. One in particular. There were four of us, and we'd arrived late. Not unusual, that. Our day had been late in starting, due mainly to the late finish of the previous one, each overlapping the other. Life wasn't lived to some mystical twenty-four hour period, you see, so our days didn't necessarily end at midnight. They ended when you crashed, started when you got up. Anyway, by the time we arrived at the "caff", all that remained on offer was minced beef, or Yorkshire Pudding - so the menu would have us believe.

'Bloody cook would get lynched if he served these up in Yorkshire,' Martin suggested, ordering both.

'Minced beef and Yorkshire pud! You'd likely get lynched, too.' I said. 'Still, there's nowt else, is there? I'll have the same, lass,' I told the waitress.

We all had both, on the same plate - something we'd have been lynched for in Yorkshire. "Up There" - as opposed to "down south" (upper case for the former, you'll notice. Same rules that applied to "The Countryside"). Be that as it may, but "Up There" puddings are traditionally served first, with lashings of beef and onion gravy.

We favoured the Ace because it also was an "in" place, for the likes of us. Plus it was cheap, which probably amounted to the same thing. Just how cheap I was to discover that night, or the following morning, take your pick. Zero three hundred hours to be precise.

We must have retired early, for that was the time I awoke from a deep sleep, and I didn't feel at all well. In the inky blackness I groped my way two floors down to the toilet, confident in the knowledge that, at this ungodly hour, I'd at least be assured of a seat.

Wrong! In fact, there was a queue on the stairway. Only to be expected, I suppose. Could have been the original "greasy spoon", the "caff".

That was to be my last visit to the Ace.

*

It was the change in environment that gave the game away; I was back in Yorkshire, with its isolated farms and smallholdings, or as isolated as one can get on this crowded island. There was a lone cow in a field. A skinny cow. A silly cow, in fact. A scarecrow cow, I realized. A tractor trailed a flock of seagulls along behind it, and away in the distance was the power station at Ferrybridge, its cooling towers creating an environment all of their own.

Not far now and I would be home again. Back from yet another Continental Grand Prix; Monaco this time. I was in my element, but not yet in paradise. Although from Norton my idea of paradise was but a short drive away. And it now had added impetus. I was to visit there quite often during this break, along with this girl I'd met on my way to the Belgian

Grand Prix, at Spa. Not across a crowded room kind of thing, more an airport departure lounge. Nevertheless it had been one of those rare occasions in which that penetrating first assessment - ranging far beyond the physical sight - was to colour the relationship for the future. A look. A question. A coffee. And before I knew what was happening it seemed I was in love. Not certain, but I suspected so, for it had never happened like this before. The moment she raised those sunglasses, wedged them in her hair, I was smitten. As was she, I suspect, for it was her that had initiated the approach. Nor was the physical sight of her at all lacking: Smiling, hazel eyes, pearl-white teeth, eyebrows which could well have been purpose-built for seduction, gave her the look of a mischievous pixie. She wore tights rather than stockings, out of necessity, I would have thought, and they were wrapped around legs that were... well, enough to say those legs were something else again. The mini had been designed with legs like that in mind. And the kind of minis she wore really showed them off to advantage. More than her legs at times.

If anyone ever accused me of being a chauvinist I'd probably agree with them, but I found the type of girl I took out usually preferred me to be that way. They liked men to do the things they expected men to do. Janette - an Essex girl who certainly did - was just such a girl. Not only that, here was a girl who laughed with me, not at me. In fact, this auburn-haired beauty was to have such an effect on me I suddenly, inexplicably, became afraid of flying. Me, the person who thrived on flight now required the aid of a drink, or a Valium, to get me in the air. Strange, that, as to someone like me romance was the sun rising over a remote airfield: the orange glow of the dawn, an ethereal mist, stark, immobile silhouettes, angular and noiseless. That to me was tranquillity personified. Peaceful, still, silent, yet also alive; or at least ready to burst into life.

No longer, it seemed.

I'd rented a car, and we'd drive all over the countryside. Familiar places from times past. I found I didn't need to check maps or look at signposts, my brain having memorized the way with such precision. I also managed to divert us to Silverstone, for the British Grand Prix, and we visited a certain little airfield in Bedfordshire. Not so much memories and vivid flashbacks, here they were in the flesh, some of them original, some replicas: machines I'd thought to be forever in the past. Aircraft of the Shuttleworth Collection.

Our time in Yorkshire was spent walking in the country, with only the odd day in town, buying whatever it was we needed, showing Janette whatever it was she wanted to see: Minster, Shambles, Clifford's Tower, a walk along the Bar Walls - everything that was worth a visit, which took some time. But the moment our shopping and sightseeing was complete we'd return to the country. It really was paradise, this. A peaceful place. A place for lovers. Cloud shadows chased each other across the rolling countryside. Not a hurried chase. Slow and gentle, in keeping with the environment, and our actions. We breathed the scent of heather, caught the bleating cry of sheep as we strolled along hand in hand, crossing babbling brooks via stepping stones or ancient bridges. The only intrusion as far as Janette was concerned, the occasional RAF fighter. Music to my ears, anathema to hers. Up there at least, but she did attend the air shows with me. So maybe she saw it as an intrusion because of what we occasionally did up there amongst the heather. We were, you see, well past the teddy-bears and dolls stage by then.

'Listen,' I said one day, just after we'd made ourselves decent again. 'What do you hear?'

She tilted her head. 'Nothing.'

'Right. That's the countryside. Country silence if you like. But if you concentrate the sounds gradually start to filter through.'

So she listened, found they did. Common sounds that were all around, going unnoticed until you tuned yourself in to them. Birdsong, crickets, the bees, sheep and cows. There were smells too; the perfumed fragrance of the heather, the sweetness of the new mown grass, even the distant sea. The sights, sounds and aromas of a summers day. Peaceful, relaxing. Nature in the raw.

She spun round suddenly, startled, eyes wide, ears filled with... not sound, noise; loud and shattering. The curtain of silence was ripped apart by the sudden blast of a jet aircraft. It passed low, directly overhead, banking sharply to disappear into the next valley, following the contours of the land, dragging its sound along behind.

'And *that* was the Royal Air Force. The Moors are a designated low flying area,' I explained. 'That was a Canberra PR9, by the way. Photo reconnaissance. Just as well it didn't appear sooner or they'd probably be displaying pictures of us in the mess this evening. Your posterior could have been recorded for posterity by a post-graduate pilot.'

'Your posterior, lover.'

'Ah, yes.'

Oh for the passion of youth. That which so often made us disregard the risk of discovery.

Perspectives changed continually. The turn of a path and one scene would vanish, to be replaced by something entirely different: moorland for a wooded copse; a sea of heather for fields of grass; and there, forming a glittering horizon, the waters of the North Sea off Whitby. Another turn reveals a pretty little village previously hidden in the fold of a familiar view, country cottages huddled together, as if for warmth and protection. Dry-stone walls criss-crossed the countryside, walls which were totally innocent of cements and adhesives, yet which had remained intact for generations. We turned our backs on the golf balls of Fylingdales.

Down in the valley we leaned over a hump-backed stone bridge, watching children and dogs play in sun-depleted crystal waters. Sheep browsed on the verges as birds swooped and circled overhead, whilst in the distance echoed a metallic ringing: the ancient game of quoits being played on the village green. This was Beck Hole. Little more than a pub and a row of stone cottages which nestled in the folds of this great, green and purple, rumpled quilt. Here we stopped for a bite and a pint.

'It's lovely up here,' Janette said.

'Yes,' I agreed. 'But this is only the nursery slopes of the Moors. Up there, away over the hills, they can be remote and forbidding, especially in winter. Then, people have been known to get lost up there.'

And when evening came - stealing in like a thief, with its gathering cloak of mist - we could be found in yet another a pub; oak beams and cosy surroundings. We'd settle comfortably by a flickering fire, supping and chatting, happy in each others company. We'd then drive home in reflective silence as another perfect day faded into history. Well, almost!

They really were days of wine and roses, or close enough to appear so in retrospect. Halcyon days, and nights, when I found myself to be at peace with my very being. Satisfied, for a time. I now had something I'd wanted, yet other things were missing. To me, important things. Selfish, I realized. Far too late in the day, of course. There again, the one thing love never did have was logic.

It is not always necessary to see or hear it to know that a door has been closed to you. This particular door closed when it came time for me to return to work. Marriage? I wasn't yet ready for anything quite so drastic. At present, thoughts of solitude took precedence over presumed domestic chaos. The Valium were no longer needed, the wanderlust was still in my blood, raring to go, and it would have been impossible for anyone to travel with me to my work. So it was that I lost Janette, although I thought of her often, my longing as acute as it was pointless. Her place in my heart was now filled with emptiness. Right person, wrong time? Possibly.

I though of her a lot, especially in my dreams; those moments when you have no choice as to your thoughts. She was there in my head, free to roam around at will.

Yes, we did meet up now and again over the next couple of years, but it was never to be the same. Although the flame had not been fully extinguished it had diminished significantly. Then, as eventually had to happen, my place in her heart was filled by a new love.

"Oh how bleak the moors look now." It was a line I remembered from somewhere, either read or heard, didn't matter which, it fit the scenario well enough. It also matched my mood to perfection.

Good times then, while they lasted, and memories of those youthful days of naivety were to remain with me for some time. And even though relegated to the far recesses, they were memories coated with sugar and spice. But, given time, that coating dissolved, and the memories along with it, which, of course, is what always happens.

Ah well. The next one would not escape me, I promised myself. Wrong again, for things started to go wrong between Catherine and I shortly after we lost our daughter to what was termed a cot death. I had left home for Paris that morning, en-route for the Congo, when I received a message to call home, only to receive the dreadful news. I took the first available flight back. Helen had been just short of two years old. Catherine and I remained together for another two years, seven eventful years in total.

Okay, then, the one after the next. Right this time, for this was where Elizabeth walked in to my life. And although we occasionally have our differences, she remains my wife to this day, though I'm still not clear as to whether or not she ever did come to understand my interest in aviation. Soon got to grips with the wine, though.

William, our son, was born in 1985, just six months after we were married. Oops!

* *

PHOTOGRAPHS-4

Page 278: Top: Hong Kong as it was, 1958. The new runway (as yet uncommissioned) can be seen stretching out into Kowloon Bay at the top of the picture.
Bottom: The airfield at Gan. Situated on one of the Maldive group of islands in the Indian Ocean it became a major staging post on the Far East run before becoming a holiday Isle. A colour shot would reveal golden, palm-fringed beaches. Wonder if they still hold cycle races on the jetty?

Page 279: Top: Not quite Biggles. In the left-hand seat, complete with moustache & shades - KL, 1959.
Bottom: Mozambique, 1985, back in the left-hand seat . Close-up, in Jetranger ZS-HJY.

Page 280: 216 sqdn. Comet C2 (XK697 - Cygnus), on Lyneham dispersal at night. Both Comets and Britannias were named after heavenly bodies of the cosmological kind. Upon retirement this particular aircraft became a clubroom for the ATC at Wyton.

Page 281: Night servicing of a Britannia (XM498) at RAF Lyneham. Both 99 and 511 squadrons flew the Britannia, the aircraft being pooled and allocated according to serviceability and requirement.

Page 282: Top: Naples, Italy. A Grumman TF1Trader, the type of aircraft which flew the author out to the USS Forrestal in 1962.
Bottom: F4U Vought Crusader gets airborne from the Forrestal's steam catapult.

Page 283: Top: Douglas B66 Skywarrior on finals.
Bottom: Skyraider hooks the No.1 wire. USS Forrestal, Bay of Naples, Nov.1962.

Page 284: Top: Almost like and exercise: engine failure offshore Nigeria. Help is nigh for G-AOCZ of Bristow Helicopters. (Wonder if this qualifies me for membership of the Goldfish Club?)
Bottom: "My" Jetranger; ZS-HJY in Mozambique. Can't imagine what it could have been doing on this deserted stretch of beach, honest. (Wonder if Bill Maher (left) is trying to tell me something!)

Page 285: Top: Antonia Gordhino maintains station whilst I latch an antenna onto the hook in preparation for my balancing act, one hundred & fifty feet up.
Bottom: Helicopter landing, offshore style An S58, Brazil, 1980.

Chapter Sixteen
WATERS OF THE CARIBBEAN

Slightly north and east of the point at which the Isthmus that is Panama tags itself onto the emerald jungle of Colombia, is located the city of Cartagena, one-time glittering citadel of the Spanish Main. A jewel it still is, albeit slightly tarnished by the drug trade now. The very fortress that had at one time or another defied the likes of Edward Teach - of Blackbeard fame - Henry Morgan, and Drake (Sir Francis, that is), still stands, as do the massive cannon that once protected it, along with the old walled town gathered below. The narrow streets and 17th century Spanish architecture look to be clinging to the fort for protection - much as would a child to her mothers skirts - and so it was; or had been. All this, and more, I discovered when dispatched to the area, post haste, back in 1977. A far better option than Africa or the Middle East.

I'd arrived in that modern galleon of the skies, the DC10.

Just imagine, an all expenses paid trip to the Caribbean, wi' handsome salary to boot, forsooth! Aye, but 'twas not to be all rum and pina-colada. There was o'course ye small matter o' work, blast me bollocks an' by yer leave - Oops! sorry. 'Tis the environment, d'ye see; tends to remind one of what had once been afoot hereabouts, belike, an' a curse on that. Romance and skulduggery. Captain Kidd, Sir Henry Morgan, and such. Galleons, gold, and moonlit nights beneath which the water gleamed like silver, an'all. Could go on about the fearsome boom of cannon, the glint and clash of Toledo steel, but I think you get the picture. One thing's for sure, you will if you go there. History is reflected everywhere around the islands of the Caribbean; in the buildings, along the waterfronts, in the forts high on the hillsides, and in the names scattered about like grape shot. In Antigua we find Nelson's Dockyard, at English Harbour; St Thomas, in the US Virgins, has its Drake's Seat, Blackbeard's Tower and Bluebeard's Castle. The British Virgins also honour Drake, naming a channel after him, and there is the oddly named island of Dead Chest. (Arr, Jim lad. Could that be where ye treasure lies buried?) Or what of Great Dog, Little Dog, George Dog, West Dog, Cockroach, and Fallen Jerusalem. Not a lot of thought given to the naming of those islets.

*

This trip was to signal the start of my Caribbean, Central, and South American phase of operations, and fond memories there are of the area, too. So let me recall some, share them with you.

Magens Bay, on St Thomas, is probably the prettiest, most perfect, cliche ridden of all Caribbean beaches. An elongated, sheltered bay of crystal clear, but turquoise-coloured, water. A crescent of golden sand at one end, the whole surrounded by lush tropical growth. Only one problem: in the afternoon, when the little hand hits three and the big hand twelve, watch out. Without fail, millions of pesky no-see-ems would rise from beneath the sand; a particularly aggressive form of sandfly. Like something from a Stephen King novel they set out to devour whatever tasty morsel they could latch on to, human blood apparently top of their shopping the list. Talk about flying teeth!

Charlotte Amalie, capital of St Thomas. An evening drink at one of the waterfront bars here is served up with the kind of sunset that even Hollywood at its most imaginative couldn't dream up. This, I imagined, sitting there with wife number one, on completion of one job, was as good as things got to be. We sat outside, watching life pass by along the centuries-old waterfront. Just down the road was an old fort, now the police station, up a hill somewhere behind me was Bluebeard's Castle. Reputedly, once a pirate stronghold, now a hotel. Probably never had anything to do with buccaneers, there again it could well have, for.... Buccaneers. The word conjures up all kinds of imagery, especially in this setting: water gently lapping the shoreline, a susurrus of breeze to stir the palm fronds, the moon high overhead. Was that a plunge of oars I heard, the faint creak of timber, a whisper of command, or was that, too, imagined? In my mind's eye I saw silent figures flitting through the shadows, a brief glint of steel.... Bluebeard's Castle eh? We'd dine there later on that night.

There is a local grog which goes by the name of Miss Blyden, said to have been a great favourite of the buccaneers. Rum based, as are most drinks in this part of the world where rum is even cheaper than bottled water. The rest of the ingredients were, as far as I could gather - the exact constituents being a closely guarded secret - the spices of the islands: cloves, cinnamon, aniseed, nutmeg. These are ground to a fine powder and boiled in syrup before the rum is poured over. The mixture is then strained and bottled, after another secret process. Most of the islands have a variation of their own, and although not habitually a rum drinker, I felt it my duty to sample a few.

*

A light pinged above my head, the fasten seatbelts warning. Across the aisle a woman did so, she then gripped the armrests tightly, as though that were an integral part of the instruction. Not a secure flyer, then. I relaxed and looked outside as Trinidad hove into view once more.

I was in an appropriately named aircraft, an Islander, returning from

279

a short stay in Grenada. I'd taken the opportunity during our enforced stay in Port of Spain, where we were awaiting a replacement streamer. Ah yes, nearly forgot to tell you. Rather embarrassing for the client party chief, that, having to call corporate headquarters, in order to order a new streamer. (You remember the streamer - hydrophones, etc., one and a half to two miles a of it?)

'An extremely long silence was what greeted me,' the party chief later revealed, as he related the passing on of his report. That wasn't hard to believe, for I could well imagine management, back in Dallas, experiencing some difficulty in absorbing the news. Twenty four hundred metres of seismic streamer - worth the better part of a million dollars - required replacing? Well, it did happen that now and again the streamer would get torn up on an uncharted reef, or be severed by a passing tanker and suchlike. Even so, the majority was usually recovered. But it wasn't the loss that so astounded, it was the answer received to the inquiry: "What happened to the old one? Didn't you recover anything?"

'Oh, we recovered it all. In fact it wasn't actually lost. It was run over by a train.'

'Another silence. Rather prolonged, and at overseas rates, quite expensive in itself.

'"Yes, well excuse me if I sound a little confused, but could you explain in a little more detail. After all, it's just possible the insurance company may ask."'

And so Dave related events as they had unfolded. How they'd needed to work on the streamer when the vessel was alongside the dock, had unreeled it, laid it out on the quay.

'I did query the railway tracks, across which it would be necessary to lay it,' he'd told them. 'Was informed they were rarely used. Suppose this must have been one of those rare moments.'

I could well sympathize with the guy, for a similar incident once befell me when the crew were off loading our equipment on the dockside, inadvertently placing it in the path of a crane, the operator of which seemed to have a grudge against us!

Thus it was I got to tour Barbados and Grenada, on expenses, the trip from which I was now returning. The airline was LIAT - officially, Leeward Islands Air Transport. Colloquially, this became, Leaves Island Any Time, which tells you something about their schedules. About as reliable as British Rail during a strike. But that was the way of life out here in the West Indies, laid back. Their airports are not counted amongst the worlds greatest, either, little better than a grass strip and a thatched shack in places. But who's complaining, this is the Caribbean.

No matter, before long I was at Doc Bishop's house in the

Trinidadian capital, Port of Spain. Doc was our Party Chief on this job - only natural, being as he was local - and we now sat out in his back garden. He had no need of the greengrocer, this guy, they were all here; bananas, avocados, papaya and oranges. All within reach of where I was seated beneath the magnolia tree, sucking on a rum and something. The sun streamed down and humming birds fluttered about their business.

I'd been conveyed here by Doc's son, in a car of indeterminate age, top down, Eagles - Hotel California - playing as we circumnavigated the race track cum cricket ground, the upside-down Hilton on the rise to our right. Strange place, that. After checking in, you took a lift *down* to the rooms. I was familiar with it, for we'd often visit. This was where the airline crews stayed, so we'd sit around the pool, drinking, eyeing up the British Airways hosties. Ah, yes. Life could be hard at times, on these islands where cannon were to be found everywhere. Remnants from the glory days: Nelson, Raleigh, Picton, Abercromby. Of buccaneers and the Spanish Main; Yo, ho, ho and a bottle of rum, kind of thing.

Most are now painted black, those cannon, mounted vertically in concrete, often with chains strung between them. But this leaves an adequate number in situ, their barrels, though no longer threatening, still directed towards a point from which a threat could once have been expected. Some are embossed with the date of their casting; 1742, was one. Others carried the arms of their patrons: dukes, earls, kings, and emperors.

*

'Hibiscus,' I said, when the plant was pointed out to me. Back at Doc Bishop's, we were comparing names by which the various plants were known. Not unexpectedly, we seemed to use more or less the same names. Until now.

'Choublac,' Doc said. 'You don't use that word?' He seemed surprised I called it something different.

'No. Why should I? Never heard of it.'

'I always assumed it to be the English name,' he said.

'What gave you that impression?'

'Choublac is actually the Haitian name,' he told me. 'But it comes from a word the English buccaneers used when cleaning their shoes it.'

To give the story credence he plucked a flower and gave it to me, indicating I should rub it on my shoes, being as he wasn't wearing any! When I did, lo and behold, a purplish juice ran out of the crushed petals and dried on the leather as a shiny black varnish. Then I understood: Choublac was a corruption of shoe black. Not many people know that. Funny, the things you learn. Different things, different situations, different places.

Then there were the steel bands. And believe me, steel bands here were different. Or maybe it was the ambience that made them sound so. These were steel bands in steel band country, and they, along with the rum, could really get you going. Even to the extent of a mass streak down a public beach! Not me, I captured it on my 8mm.

Another thing I came to understand around these parts, South America, mainly, but it could well usefully apply in the Caribbean: "Manana" doesn't actually mean "tomorrow." To be precise, it means, "not today."

Prithee. 'Twas ever thus.

DOWN THE GRINGO TRAIL

Rio de Janeiro is one of the most glamorous cities in South America, about which it could be said the guide books understate the case. It has to be one of natures most glorious settings, the geography adding greatly to its charm. Beautiful beaches, and even more beautiful, the girls. You could go mad just looking at the girls, most of which appear to have misplaced their bathing suits. But it's not only your inhibitions that can disappear. If you're not careful, wallets and jewellery will perform a similar feat!

Away from the busy harbour area in the central business district, the city spreads itself along the coastline, stretching out over a series of beaches whose names are known the world over: Copacabana, Ipenema, Leblon.

There is of course another side to Rio, not too far removed from all this luxury, either. Geographically speaking. In fact, well within sight of the hotels which line Copacabana, but high in the hills behind. Up here perch the Favelas, and despite advice to the contrary, I'd wander up for a look-see. But I'd dress the part. No jewellery or watch, no flashy, ostentatious clothes, mini Pentax in my pocket, out of sight. I'd keep my eyes open, remain friendly. A wave here, a smile there. It all helped, and as I rarely encountered problems, it either works or I've been extraordinarily lucky. But the people always seemed happy to see me. Maybe that was in part because they never expected me to be there, were pleased that I was.

Up there the air was tainted with the stench of poverty. It was a sad-looking kind of place. You couldn't say run-down, as in certain areas of certain English towns: boarded-up windows, overgrown gardens, incomprehensible graffiti - this whole place was run-down, had never been up. Shanties and lean-to's were constructed of cast away wood, corrugated iron, cardboard, beaten-flat tin. Anything useful or handy, a lot that was not. Still they crumbled with decay. Between them ran festering, open drains. Rubbish served only to block already inadequate gutters, giving birth to fetid pools in which children played, floating things around. Indescribable things.

That was me, needed to see everything for myself, good and bad. Same thing went for Bogota, no one bothered me there either, though from recent reports I don't think I'd attempt it today. Got to see rather a lot of the rest of Colombia, too, away from the cities, for some of our stations were located in the high mountains. I'm talking eight to ten thousand feet now, real mountains, the station often lost in the clouds. But it was the journey up there that could be spectacular. Dusty, one-street villages of neat little houses with pantiled roofs. Those that stretched themselves to more than one street usually also boasted a square, in which would be sited a wedding-cake church. All around were hills and valleys, green, though fading to purple with distance. But let's face it, this was the Andes, where 2-3000 feet is barely above sea level. Those hills are mountains, some of which seem to reach up forever. There were occasional splashes of colour, too; red, and yellow, and pink, as though some careless artist had dripped paint on his canvas. I recall looking across vistas of subtropical forest, with coffee and bananas growing in the areas cleared for them. And, who knows, maybe even coca - basis of cocaine - a major product of the area. Certainly the height was right, between two and six thousand feet.

To arrive at one of these villages at the wrong time - siesta - was to find a place that looked deserted; windows and doors shuttered and closed. Like one of those Mexican towns in the Westerns, where the occupants are expecting a visit from El Baddo. Abandoned by all, with the possible exception of a flea-bitten mongrel stretched out in the sun, even that too lethargic to scratch.

As things turned out, with the usual impeccable sense of timing, our arrival always seemed to coincide with an hour when it was possible to partake of the odd tepid beer or two. It would be the same Western though: groups of men sitting around drinking beer from the bottle, their horses hitched up in a line, waiting. The difference was in the headgear. Here they wore battered trilbies rather than Stetsons. Further on down the Gringo Trail, say in Peru, or Ecuador, they favoured the bowler.

*

I was never caught up in drugs at all, dead set against them, but in Colombia they were never far away. Many of the gringos we spoke to were probably involved. Almost certainly, in fact, for the hotel at which we usually stayed when in Bogota, the Tequendama, was supposedly the place favoured by the dealers, the buyers, and the couriers - the mules. So the intrigue, the scheming, and the machinations of the drug trade were no doubt being enacted all around us. I'd probably even shaken hands with the odd cocaine baron or two. (Just as in Sicily I had almost certain shaken the Mafia's hand. One had even invited me to take a ride with him, though not the kind of ride from which one never returns; this was in a Ferrari.)

The drug syndicates were certainly operational up along the Caribbean coast, where most of our work took place: Cartagena, Barranquilla, Santa Marta, and Riohacha - on the Guajira Peninsula, with its hidden coves and airstrips. Not only was the area naturally inhospitable, those who had business there made sure it remained so. Their kind of business brooked no uninvited guests, no unwanted interference. In fact, not only were strangers decidedly unwelcome, they were likely to face extreme danger, for this was an area where it would not be too difficult to put on weight. That is to say, 44 magnum, 250 grain type weight! We were even refused permission to install a station on the rising ground to the south of Santa Marta. Was this because the area was a known site for illegal marijuana growing, and some official was protecting his interests? After all, we did carry radios and other electronic devices - no matter how ancient and seemingly innocent-looking - so who was to say it was only a navigation station? Or maybe the authorities had no involvement whatsoever, just felt unable to offer sufficient protection in that particular area. We certainly made the odd contact offshore. One time playing our part in terminating a smuggling operation, albeit inadvertently.

We were conducting a survey off the Columbian coast, a round-the-clock operation, as is most oil related business, where time is money. Naturally, when towing a streamer, up to two miles in length, in the dark, one needs to keep a sharp eye on the radar.

'Strange, eh?' the skipper remarked. 'Lots of green blobs on the radar, nothing to be seen outside! They're close enough, too. If they were running with lights, we couldn't fail to spot them.'

'Have you tried calling on the radio? the client representative enquired.

'Sure have. But no one answers.'

'Just have too keep an eye open then, if they look like getting too close, fire off a red.'

All we were interested in was protecting a multi million dollar legitimate business. But on this particular occasion someone's luck was "out to lunch," as was ours.

'We've got noise on the tail end,' came the call from the recording room. 'Streamer tension increasing.'

This told us all was not well.

'OK, abort the line, we'll have to pick up and check it out.'

Nothing else to be done, and as it takes hours to recover everything, it's not exactly top of the list of popular activities among those involved. This time the operation was proving even more labourious; lots of backing down, which suggested the tail end was still supported. Probably something related to the two large green blobs on the radar screen.

'No! Not two,' the skipper said. 'Three, four, ten. They're breeding. Anyone see anything out there?'

But in the dark nothing was visible.

With dawn came the mist, and after a time, out of the mist loomed our tailbuoy, in the shape of a pleasure cruiser. Another stood off, close by. The one we'd caught was large - ten plus metres, twin screws - and he wasn't going anywhere. He must have crossed the end of the streamer, caught the tailbuoy rope in a propeller. Panic, full power, which only served to wrap the streamer around his propshaft. And the foundations of a streamer are three, very strong, stainless steel cables. No way he was escaping without assistance. Our assistance, as it turned out. Not because we empathized with him in his plight, we needed to get back to work. Luckily, we had scuba gear on board, plenty of volunteers. We went over in pairs, one with a hacksaw, one on shark watch; didn't fancy old Jaws sneaking up on us.

It took a long time, but we were eventually successful, even going so far as to make him a new propeller key. Had to, really, being as the person to whom I was handing the original dropped the thing. Quite deep in places, the Caribbean. Lucky not to drop the prop, too! Much heavier than imagined. Just as well we had a line attached when we removed it.

So, eventually both vessels roared off into the haze, our captain logging names and registrations; a report would need to be filed.

It was then we came across the cause of our spurious radar returns: bales of hay, bobbing around in the water. Only it wasn't hay, that was marijuana. They must have dumped it in panic, probably suspecting they'd been caught by the authorities.

No, we did not recover it. I kid you not.

*

What is said of criminals and thieves seemed also to apply to dedicated aviators: Takes one to know one. Many's the time I've been invited to take the vacant right-hand seat, alongside the pilot. This, in the main, applied to charters. But in the realms of the Spanish Main it happened on a small airline named Antilles Airboats. They operated scheduled inter-island flights, utilizing such aircraft as the Grumman Goose, and Mallard. Aptly named, these, for like their amphibian namesakes, they too appeared to waddle as they left the water to taxi up the slipway.

Take-off whisked me back in time, to Seletar: The spray, the lurching run to get up on the step, the dripping climb. Then it changed dramatically, the scene below, magnificent. Typical Caribbean, yet it was a view of which I would never tire. Emerald, yellow fringed islands were set in a sea that seemed constantly to change colour. Blue, green, turquoise, azure; from the blue-black of the depths to the creamy-white where it foamed over the reef.

The flight was but a short half hour. I could happily have stayed up there all day. Which brings to mind an operator named Mike Bergstrom, a Swede: his comments on a GPS reference station at which he was based, in Norway.

'I could happily spend the rest of my life there,' he told me.

And so it came to pass.

I replaced him on the site a week later, after he died of a heart attack. I thought it a good station, too. Though I took care not to give voice to the thought.

* *

Chapter Seventeen
MOZAMBIQUE

'Stow those for me, please, Dave. In the boot,' he added, his English almost perfect. 'Plenty of room in there.' He handed me the various covers and tie-downs which he had just removed, carried on with his inspection.

1985 and I was back in Africa. It was well in to October, a couple of minutes into sunrise. Dawn is an hour in the past.

I've always found early mornings to be such a wonderful time of day, more's the pity that to enjoy them one needs to rise at such an ungodly hour. But here the setting was far from perfect. A yellow ball struggled to free itself from the pall of haze and pollution which mantled this remote corner of the continent, with not a breath of wind to clear it. Immobile, angular, fuzzy silhouettes were visible over on the far side of the airport. They looked to be abandoned, probably were. Antonovs, Mils, Migs, and Ilyushins; remnants of yet another failed Soviet incursion. Before me on the dispersal sat an American made helicopter, and in front of the terminal, a member of Boeing's 737 family of twin-jets; signs of now-favoured Western influence.

A peaceful stillness ensued, even though nature's gentle awakening had already broken the silence. Man was about to add his contribution to this start of yet another day's aerial activity.

*

A week had passed since my arrival in Mozambique. Air Zimbabwe from London to Harare, where a six hour layover had afforded me chance to reacquaint myself with the capital. The only change appeared to be the name; it had been Salisbury on my last visit, twenty-three years ago. In a similar vein the country had more or less disassociated itself from the memory of Cecil Rhodes, dropping Rhodesia and reverting to the ancient name of Zimbabwe. Sad, really, but what's in a name? Quite a lot, it seemed. I learned that Rhodesia used to export the very goods Zimbabwe now found a need to import.

I'd already been reacquainted with the bush during our approach to the airport. Well, almost. It had been the captain's last flight before retirement and, receiving permission to buzz the airfield, he had done so (first advising us passengers of his intentions). Made a good job of it too. Lowest I'd been in a 707 with the undercarriage retracted.

From Harare I was booked on Linhas Aereas De Mocambique, to Maputo, another capital which had suffered a change of name; previously,

Lourenco Marques. In the hands of whoever had been running it these past years it also had suffered a change of fortune. Once the playground of wealthy Portuguese, and South Africans, it was now extremely run down, almost derelict. Its wide, tree-lined avenues were unkempt and overgrown. The once-upon-a-time abundantly-stocked stores were now empty, and closed. Grandeur had given way to decay. With all this in mind I'd expected to fly in some Russian cast-off - such as the Antonov AN24 of Lina Congo, which had once conveyed me between Brazzaville and Pointe Noire, or the Ilyushin IL14 of China's CAAC, neither of which had been exactly relaxing experiences - so I was pleasantly surprised to find C9-BAD, when it arrived, to be one of Boeing's finest. A 737 of one series or other. But that registration did happen to be appropriate. We sat on the ground in Beira for an hour and a half, awaiting the arrival of some politician, or general. Same thing, really, out here. This being the case, it should have come as no surprise to find that the country was a war zone. A group named Frelimo vs a group named Renamo this time. Frelimo - the Marxist Government - apparently controlled the cites and towns. Renamo - what would, in a democratic society, be the opposition - controlled a good deal of the countryside, the very place I needed to be to do my job. We'd already felt the effects of this still-lingering war, the threat of attack making it impossible to transport our equipment from Johannesburg by road, and as LAM didn't have the capacity to carry it, we had to charter a South African aircraft to do the job. Despite this, LAM insisted we pay a fee of US$1.00 per kilo for them not flying it in. Typical Africa, charging for something they were not able to do themselves.

Now the gear had finally arrived, we were ready to go to work, about to depart on our first sortie. All covers and locks had been removed and the pilot had completed his pre-flight walk-around, particular attention being paid to the rotor head and blades, the most important parts of a helicopter. Now he climbed aboard and strapped himself in alongside me. It felt comfortable to be back in familiar surroundings, seated up front.

The first streaks of sunlight cleared the surrounding hills, filling the cockpit with promised warmth. And as I watched from the left-hand seat, my pilot ran through the start-up checks, reading off each item from a checklist located somewhere in memory, answering himself as the appropriate action was taken.

'Master switch? On.

'Fuel? Checked. Levels, OK.

'Mixture? Set.

'Rotor brake? On.'

His hands appeared to run through their tasks automatically, as I'm sure they did - immediately assuring me of his competence - and whilst awaiting the correct response to a particular action, after first initiating it, his mouth hummed a Beatles number, thus divulging his age group. It was a triple act in which he performed all three parts.

'Battery master?' the mouth asked. At which a hand reached out to flick a switch. 'On,' came the reply, followed by a couple of bars from *Yellow Submarine*. There was a clunk as a heavy duty relay thumped home, a click had the instrument panel flickering into life, needles jumping attentively, recording whatever it was they were supposed to record. Lights glowed brightly, other things clicked and whirred.

'We have power,' he exclaimed, almost sounding surprised. The eyes and fingers were just as busy as the mouth, which itself had now switched to an atonal version of *Hey Jude, Yellow Submarine* apparently having sunk without trace somewhere between "Battery? On", and "Rotor brake? Check".

A break in the musical improvisation allowed him to pose the question, 'Clear to start?' apparently at the door, for that was to where his eyes were looking. His head swivelled, allowing him to check the immediate locality, presumably for the odd stray camelopard. Obviously there were none, his answer being in the affirmative: 'Clear to start.' More switches were snapped on. His left hand now dropped to the twistgrip throttle on the collective pitch control, wound it fully open, closed it again. He then opened it fractionally as, simultaneously, his forefinger stabbed a button recessed into the end of the lever. The engine turned over with a low, dry, whine, turbine steadily building up speed. Another switch had the igniters clicking away merrily like love-sick crickets, until, with a wumph, fuel ignited and the whine became the gentle roaring of hot gasses. His right forefinger now redirected his eyes to a gauge by pointing at it. Its needle rose quickly through the green segment, touching briefly into the red before dropping back into the top end of the green. This was apparently OK, as the finger was removed, a thumb raised in acceptance.

EGT 760c. Exhaust gas temperature, I decoded.

Antonio had introduced himself to me during the drive out to the airport. Short, dark-haired, with a cheerful smile and a wicked sense of humour, he was to be my pilot. His machine, a Bell 206 Jetranger, was at my beck and call, to use as and when required.

My first task was to install navigation beacons on pre-surveyed sites along the coast. These would be used to position a seismic vessel working offshore. The beacons were battery-powered, the batteries charged by solar panels. At least that was the plan. It had sounded good the previous evening, when I and the rest of the crew had sat down and discussed it. We were in a bar at the time, lubricating our throats in traditional manner. We needed to, for this was to be subjected to some serious thought, which in turn required a drink. There again, none of us being single-drink people......

At some time during the proceedings it became obvious I was slightly drunk. No, let me correct that; completely pissed. Had to be. Slightly drunk is on a par with being slightly pregnant, or slightly dead: you either are, or you ain't. Anyway, as I have previously related, it's a well known fact that no battle plan survives being put into action, so it was hardly surprising to find this one didn't come anywhere near.

The problem was with the solar panels. They just weren't up to the job, which meant I needed to change batteries every two or three days, on each of five stations. Antonio was delighted about this, for between times we stayed on board the vessel, and I was left with the distinct impression he wasn't at all happy with that arrangement. In fact it took very little time for this to become apparent. After only twelve hours I noticed him mooching around his aircraft, tied down on the helideck. Next morning he swept in to my cabin like a pocket rocket; a one man tornado.

'Any batteries to change, Dave?' he asked hopefully. His eyes reminded me of spaniel; pleading. We'd gone a full twenty-four hours without lifting off. He was bored. Well, so was I. And as I could easily justify flying off, away we went, Antonio's grin a sight to behold. We were going to get along just fine. But I'd already ascertained that we would.

The sites were located on such as a convenient lighthouse or, if there wasn't one, the highest point around. Trouble was, the highest ground was usually a sand dune, very difficult to climb when carrying a twenty-four volt battery, especially in what were to be extremely high-digit temperatures; sun, plus the reflection factor off the sand. This was when I really came to appreciate Antonio. He offered an alternative, which we discussed en-route, deciding to give it a try. On arrival he eased the machine sideways, feeling his way, touching a skid gently on the sand at the top of the dune. This provided him with a reference, me with a chance to leap out, my helicopter background serving to remind me to watch my head. There was no wind, which helped, but I was relying totally on Antonio's skill. I looked up briefly from my task to observe him. He was very good. The machine remained in the hover, barely moving. It reminded me of a bumble-bee pollinating a flower. Perfect. So from then on it became standard practice. No hauling awkward bits and pieces up the insides of lighthouses, either. I assembled everything at ground level then attached it to the sling as Antonio hovered above me. I then rushed up - as fast as one does rush up hundreds of narrow, winding steps, in darkness, temperatures of ninety plus - and secured it to the light, balancing myself on top of the safety rail, Antonio releasing the sling when I gave the word. I shudder to think of it even now. One false move and it was one hundred and fifty feet to oblivion. But we were both careful, so all went well. Almost perfect, actually. It saved me hours of toil and frustration. Just as well, for the only lighthouse available also happened to house a detachment of the local militia; sort of Mozambican Observer Corps, though these were heavily armed. The walls of their room were plastered with recognition photos of SAAF aircraft, for South Africa was looked upon as a likely enemy of the State. Or at least a friend of the State's enemies. And in the room where my equipment was located lay a suspicious-looking tarpaulin-covered bundle. I peeked, of course. Well, you never know, it might have been something that would affect the operation of my gear. What I found were even more suspicious-looking wooden boxes, complete with Cryllic lettering. Well, I just had to open one of those, didn't I, couldn't read a word of Russian. All sounded quiet so I eased to top one open a crack. Bugger me, hand-held ground-to-air missiles! And why not? This was the Third World. These guys might be starving, have ragged uniforms, not get paid, but they were well equipped when it came to the tools of war. Could come in handy, those, thought I. I later warned Antonio not to get stroppy with me, or else!

I also made sure the militia had a good look at our aircraft. It may not have looked much like a Mirage or a Hercules, but it did carry South African registration. Those guys we kept happy by bringing them cartons of Marlboro ciggies and tins of food, both of which were freely available to us, but not to the general population. There was a government-controlled store in Maputo, name of Interfranca. A kind of duty free Tesco, access to which was by passport only - unless you happened to be a member of the government, of course. Payment was in South African Rand or US Dollars, for even the locals weren't interested in the local currency. No wonder, either. I'd been forced to change twenty dollars at the airport upon entry to the country, the resulting barrowload of Meticais good only for the purchase of postcards and stamps; which is the reason everyone and his dog received a postcard from me that trip. But even though cigarettes and electronic goods were plentiful at Interfranca, fresh food was not. I recall a few boxes of apples putting in an appearance one day, and brief wasn't the word to describe it! Fleeting, maybe. Or how about "bloody swift?" Which is what you needed to be if you fancied one - apple, that is, not a boxful. Expatriates were almost coming to blows over them. It was like watching a news clip of relief supplies arriving during yet another African famine. Suppose in a way it was.

As with my butter and sugar during WW2, to the militia pure gold was of less value than those ciggies and cans. The inference was that we would be their friends, forever. Hey! Now hang on a minute... These guys neither washed or changed their clothes, or if they did they needed a serious rethink on their choice of washing powder. I carried a can of air freshener, sprayed it ahead of me as I ascended the stairs. Antonio stayed with the aircraft. Didn't blame him.

It was a perfect partnership I had with Antonio, and we had some great times together. I helped him with refuelling and servicing in the field, he helped me, even taught me to fly the thing - a far cry from the old Mk.4 Whirlwind.

He'd originally been out here with the Portuguese Air Force, still had friends scattered around the area. Handy, that, too. Many of them, out in the sticks, lacked basics such as rice and potatoes, we had access to both, if not in Maputo, then off the boat - which resupplied in South Africa. Whenever we flew up their way we took them supplies. They, in return, provided hospitality and beer whenever it was necessary for us to spend a night away from base. They also kept us supplied with things of which they happened to have a surplus: crayfish and prawns, freshly caught. Both were almost unobtainable back in the capital.

Come the weekend it was a simple matter for me to suddenly discover there to be a problem on one of the stations. Something which required my presence in the area. Naturally, it would be a station that just happened to be located on a particularly agreeable site. Near enough a nice safe stretch of beach, and whatever other facilities the area could muster. Some of those problems could take quite a time to sort out, believe me, so we always carried a picnic lunch with us. No point flying with empty seats, either, so we invited others of the crew along. You know, I had this weird idea that maybe the sea was affecting propagation of the radio waves, had to go in and find out. Well, you can't be too sure can you? Lucky I thought to carry my swimming gear with me, eh?

Even on genuine sorties Antonio would often tire of the distance-induced illusion of slow motion flight at five thousand feet, take us down for a boredom-relieving spell of the low-level stuff.

'Look, Antonio, flamingoes,' I said, pointing ahead.

'Ah, yes, the flamingoes' he replied, as though it was a sight with which we were familiar. Which, I soon discovered, to him it was, and on this job was to become so to me.

When viewed from above, against the backdrop of a lake and surrounding savanna, huge flocks of flamingoes are an incredible sight, especially when they suddenly have an urge to become airborne *en mass,* as they tend to do when a chopper screams in over the trees. And although a hundred and twenty knots may not be much to a racing driver, to us mere mortals, travelling five feet above the sand, or skimming the waves, it was exhilarating. Dogs and other four-legged creatures - inspired to remarkable sprints of terror - took off like they were turbo-charged. They'd disappear into the undergrowth, leaving their somewhat braver, if foolish, owners to stand tall and shake a defiant fist in the air. More or less as had that gorilla in Gabon, but presenting much less of a threat. Then the message would filter through: *Steel bird at five feet, lower than dis head at six feet* (or whatever was the local equivalent). Next thing they'd be hurling themselves ingloriously flat on the beach, face down to the sand, or into the sea. Sometimes the thought processes would prove rather more lethargic than usual, it was then up to Antonio to remedy the situation; a quick jink left, right, or up.

We flew low over the Limpopo - its supposedly crocodile-infested waters the colour of milky coffee - until it abruptly turned left to begin a series of wide, looping turns, meandering this way and that, as if in an attempt to delay its arrival offshore. We followed it. A real African river this, no banks to be seen. The jungle began right at the water's edge, a dense, verdant landscape through which the river had sliced a path. And although I never did see any crocs I did once see a swirl of vacant, muddy water, where a second or two previous I had spied a bird of some kind, so I could well imagine it hosting them, along with other exotic beasties: snakes, hippos and such.

There were many canoes being paddled around too, their progress seeming tranquil, yet at the same time intent. In this country of poor to nonexistent roads that river was a motorway.

At the last moment Antonio hauled us up, clear of the trees, climbing high enough to inform Maputo control of our imminent landing at Xai Xai (pronounced, Shy Shy). We had the rice, were ready for some crayfish and beer.

*

I particularly recall one flight, early on in the project, when we were still in the process of evaluating procedures. We'd removed the rear doors from the cabin, so as to allow the ten-foot mast sections to be carried athwartships, across the cabin floor. On other projects I'd just lash them to the skids, fore and aft, but the skids on this aircraft were fitted with floatation devices. Could have gone ahead anyway, but there are limits as to how far you push the safety angle. There were extensive overwater sectors on our route - especially if we were returning to the vessel, up to forty miles offshore - and we only had one engine. So we went for the cabin-floor option. It worked fine, with a full load, at fairly low speed. Not so good on the return trip, with an empty cabin, when we found the airflow threatening to rip out the rear seat cushions. Well, no problem, this was a helicopter, wasn't it. We put down in a convenient spot. A clear, open area, for we weren't about to take a chance on being captured and held hostage, either. Here I removed the offending items, stowed them in the boot. And so we went merrily on our way. For a while, that is, until the seat-backs attempted the same trick. OK, down we went again, off they came, into storage. A little later and a flapping noise brought to our attention the fact that now it was the turn of the sound-proofing. It was being torn loose; airstream getting beneath and popping the press-studs. Another unscheduled stop, yet more of the aircraft disappearing into the spacious boot, which was by now becoming crowded. Not only that, the rear cabin was looking pretty stark. Once again underway I looked behind me, just checking, I then looked across at Antonio, the smile on his face breaking into uncontrollable laughter. With tears streaming he explained the reason for this outbreak of mirth. He fantasized arriving back at base flying the bare skeleton of an airframe, explaining to his engineer the whereabouts of the remainder: "It's in the boot." That got me going, too. It was probably one of those incidents no one else would have found

funny, but it had us in stitches. Spur of the moment humour.

Referring back to the safety angle, and those floatation devices. Almost had a need to use them one time, when we pushed the margins to the maximum. We were heading back to the vessel, almost at the limit of our range when considering the need to retain enough fuel to get back ashore, should that prove necessary. This time, it almost was.

The boat could be more than twenty miles from where we left it, depending on how long we were away. No problem. We figured we only needed to navigate ourselves to within a ten mile radius, and we should be able to spot them. Only this day it was hazy, got steadily worse as we proceeded, making things very difficult, for we had no radio contact, either. We were almost at the point of no return when for some reason Antonio happened to glance back; he later said it was one of those subconscious things. There was the boat, behind us and well off to the side, barely discernable on the very edge of our vision. We drastically revised our procedures after that, remained ashore more often. Better to get wet inside rather than out!

Then it all came to an end. The job, I mean. This area of Africa had been new to me, though I had once been fortunate enough to visit Luanda, capital of Angola, over on the west coast. It had still been a Portuguese colony at the time, and in my opinion, a city unmatched for beauty in few places on this continent, outside South Africa, that is. Maputo - when it had been Lourenco Marques - had been similar, that was plain to see. I recall they used to hold an international sportscar race through the streets of this town. Not any more. Just as Luanda was no more.

We flew out to Nelspruit, in South Africa, by charter - a Cherokee 6 - and I recall the border as being a distinct line: unkempt nature to well tended fields in the blink of an eye. There was no mistaking it from the air, reminded me of a pudding-bowl haircut.

Believe me, after six weeks in Maputo, Johannesburg was the best place on earth. Absolute luxury. That night I dined on surf and turf: succulent steak and lobster tails, washed down by wines of the Stellenbosch area. I also discovered a sound local brandy, a ten year old KWV. As good as any reasonable cognac.

Next day South African Airways were good enough to upgrade me to Diamond Class for the long haul back to the UK, which put me upstairs on their 747. And travelling north meant no jet-lag to contend with.

* *

NOTEBOOK SIX
THE PLEASURES OF FLIGHT

Waiting around in airports is purported to be one of the most trying features of modern life. So many people, so many flights, you imagine it all grinding to a halt once you leave. Surely it can't be the same every minute of every day? Where could all the people be going to? Where would they all come from? But it does go on all the time, day in day out, even when you are not around. When you are, there's a need to accept it. You must be prepared to queue, or to time your arrival for the last minute. But I'm a person who hates unnecessary rush, so when travelling, especially alone, I always allow plenty of time. I much prefer to sit and wait for an hour or two rather than face the hustle and bustle of a late check-in. Anyway, I find airports to be fascinating places, full of interesting events, happenings, people. You just never know who you're going to bump into.

Terminal Two was particularly crowded. I'd done my shopping, was having difficulty finding an acceptable seat, so, even though my flight hadn't yet been called, I decided to make my way to the gate - airside, as it's officially known; past immigration and the security checks. Experience had taught me it was a place where I could sit and read in relative peace or, alternatively, stare out of the window, soak up the atmosphere. Even the endless corridors - of which Heathrow appears to have a surfeit - are always infinitely less crowded than the departure hall. Today, in fact, I was all alone. Until *was* became the operative word, that is, for I suddenly found myself to be surrounded. People rushed past, turned, then I was facing a battery of cameras, a barrage of flashguns. At last. My fifteen minutes of fame. But for what reason? Had I contravened some hitherto unknown Heathrow ordinance, such as proceeding to gate before flight was declared ready for boarding? Highly unlikely. I had spent rather a long time in the newsagents, flicking through various lower-shelf magazines without actually making a purchase. But unless they'd passed a bill in the last hour...? No, not that either. Maybe I was the millionth person to check in today, had won the holiday of a lifetime? A possibility, it seemed. So I smiled and awaited the outcome. But *my* fifteen minutes were to be but a ten second dream.

A straw boater drifted past on my right. There was someone beneath it. Someone wearing a familiar smile, a striped blazer and funny glasses. Someone who looked suspiciously like Elton John. It was. Ah well, so much for the holiday of a lifetime. Didn't need it anyway, my life appeared

to be one long holiday. On occasion.

A similar situation occurred the time I chanced upon Richard Burton, again at Heathrow. Crowds of photographers walking backwards. Not for Christmas, as Peter Sellers would have it, but from the arrival gate, towards immigration. What I remember most clearly about that was the lady who complained she shouldn't have to put up with this kind of thing; the flashguns in her face and what all. Fact was, had she joined the rest of us - walking ahead of the rich and famous, the glitterati - she wouldn't have been. I suspect she chose to place herself in the line of fire, no doubt hoping for a cameo appearance on the front pages of the tabloids.

We'd travelled back from Geneva together, Mr Burton and I (along with Mrs Suzie Hunt, soon to become the next Mrs Burton). We hadn't travelled in the same class, admitted. Whilst they were up at the sharp end - of life, as well as seating - I elected to sit back in Business; at least, my company elected on my behalf. But I did have Mr Burton's full-length fur coat on the rack above my head. The rack up front had been declared too dusty, so the steward informed me. I asked him to relay an offer for me: five quid for the coat. Never did get a reply. Strange, that.

Then there was Gregory Peck. An extremely tall person, Mr Peck. And for some reason I'd always thought him to be short. He was also, I suspect, a heavy tipper. He had his hands behind his back, fiddling with a tenner as someone did his checking in for him. I'd have done it for a fiver, had he asked!

Paul Hogan I snared in the baggage hall. He was clutching a carton of Marlboro. This was in the days before Crocodile Dundee, and I felt the need to remind him that he advertised a different brand back home in Oz.

'Can't get 'em here,' he replied, smiling knowingly. We'd both just arrived on the same flight, from Australia. Which leads nicely into that Winfield advert. It featured said Mr Hogan - never one noted for his sartorial elegance, at least on his shows - suavely dressed; black tie, ankles crossed in James Bond fashion, cigarette in hand. HAVE A WINFIELD, the billboards, or Mr Hogan, invited. Eye catching all right, but nothing sensational. No, the clever ad was to follow a couple of months later. The Australian government had meantime passed a piece of anti-smoking legislation which forbade personalities from promoting tobacco products, a situation that was immediately exploited by WINFIELD, or whoever runs their advertising campaign. Mr Hogan duly disappeared from the billboards, as was now law. In his place? Nothing; a blank space. Below which was the message: HAVE A WINFIELD ANYWAY.

I recalled some of these anecdotes some weeks later when out for a drink, thinking to impress the locals. Even had autographs to substantiate them. They listened politely, then, after the briefest of pauses, someone said, 'Did tha' 'ear about Mrs Daniels? Has ti go back to t'hospital next week ti have 'er foot fixed.'

So much for assumed fame by limited association.

*

Few people who travel by air know what it is to fly. They miss the essentials, the magic. From an airconditioned terminal, viewed through soundproofed glass, passengers see only something which will transport them through time and space whilst they are fed and watered, their needs pampered to. Sort of! Most, upon entering an aircraft, being seated and strapped in, meekly surrender their option to take individual action. Until touchdown all decision making becomes the responsibility of the crew, which is as it should be. Some passengers may know that aircraft outside to be a Jumbo, but that's about all, the important things go unseen. The beauty of the machine. From the finely rounded contours of the cockpit surrounds and drag resisting nose, to the harsh, stark, heat-discoloured metal of the jet efflux things take on a sudden reality, and hugeness. But they're more than huge. Compared to the majority of aircraft the 747 is massive. Brutal almost, yet at the same time functional and purposeful. Next time the opportunity occurs, take look at that wing: the size, the profile, the surface area; the very things that enable us to fly. These are the things that usually go unnoticed, they impress few. I imagine Sir George Cayley would have been suitably impressed, as would his coachman pilot, along with Wilbur and Orville. (Maybe they are, who knows?) There are other aspects, too. Some visible, some not. Down on the tarmac the engineer walks around beneath those wings, completing his visuals. The captain will be checking the on-route weather, calculating all-up weight and unstick speed, logging radio frequencies, checking Notams (notices to airmen). Or he may already be in the cockpit, programming the computers to fly him where he wants to go; hopefully the same place all the passengers wish to go! The first officer - having completed his external checks - will also be aboard, applying his magic, whilst the cabin crew check the galleys, prepare for the boarding. Until then, the passengers interest will be focused on Duty-free, the newsagent, or the bar. Especially the bar.

In the departure lounge a certain amount nervousness is sure to be apparent. People stand and make their way towards the gate well before the boarding announcement. Like lemmings that have received the call, they surge forward, pushing and elbowing, this despite the fact that seats are already allocated. I, of course, am forced join them. But my only worry is for space in the overhead lockers. No fun with your briefcase beneath your feet for ten hours, and some of that "hand baggage" should really be in the hold.

So, we are finally seated. Baggage stowed, seatbelts fastened, safety briefing complete, engines running, tension high. I relax, others check the seat pockets for freebies, glance around, fiddle with things, unimportant things. Then there is the hesitant conversation, the forced smile; both, nervous reactions. Of the technicalities they neither care, nor do they wish to, which is what breeds the fear they feel, creates the tension and nervousness. Fear is brought about by ignorance. Up front are the people who understand, up there in the cockpit. The crew, with their little codes and a language all their own: VFR, and ILS, for Visual Flight Rules and Instrument Landing System. Quebec Foxtrot Echo - QFE - the barometric pressure at the airfield (or, alternatively, Quebec November Hotel - QNH - the pressure at sea level). Then there is the all-important, V-one, or velocity one, the decision point on the take off run. Beyond this speed the aircraft is committed to take-off, no matter what. Given their all-up weight and the prevailing climatic conditions, there will not be enough runway remaining to enable a safe stop to be made. Which is exactly what the crew would have been calculating, earlier. V-R comes next, velocity rotate, lift-off speed achieved. At which the pilot in control will gently ease back on the column - or sidestick controller. This brings the nosewheel off the ground, a brief pause and we are flying. The real danger period, this. A few seconds only, then V-two, flying safety speed; the airspeed is such we are now able to continue the climb should we have the misfortune to suffer an engine failure. We don't, so now everyone can settle back and relax. Until it comes to the landing. But that is yet hours in the future.

For now, the aircraft hauls itself into the sky, slowly gathering in those bits and pieces - gear, flaps, slats - which, after getting us airborne, would now slow us down if not neatly tucked away. From this point on it would take an unlikely combination of circumstances, or failures, to endanger either the aircraft or us, which makes flying the safest way to travel. You see, it usually takes more than one failure to bring an aircraft down, it takes what is known as an event cascade: a problem on top of a problem on top of a problem.

Generally, though, flying is as safe as the pilot makes it. His safety is in his own hands. By the same token, so is mine. Even though the best of pilots - commercial or private - are unlikely to be too concerned with the safety of his (or her) passengers, they do worry for their own safety. Which more or less amounts to the same as thing them worrying about mine. The main danger down there at the "back of the bus," it seems, often comes from your fellow passengers.

*

I was happy, felt like talking, especially as I had a sympathetic ear available. Someone I'd never see again once we landed; an American, who shared my row of seats. I greeted him briefly.

Big mistake, for not only was he large, amicable and jovial-looking, he also turned out to be a gregarious type, obviously felt the need to talk himself. It was as if he had been waiting to pounce. From the moment I opened my mouth it took no time at all for him to reveal that, although he'd been christened James Jonathan, and that the family name was Haverslicker, or some such, I should refer to him as JJ, as did all his friends. I refrained from pointing out that we were yet to become friends. Was possibly prevented from such by lack of a suitable pause in which to do so.

'You're British?' he enquired. Or maybe he was telling me, for he certainly didn't allow me the time to answer. 'I just love that limey accent. Say, can I get y'all a drink?' he asked, his eyes locking onto an approaching stewardess like a heat-seeking missile onto a jetpipe. And for that I thanked him; the drink, I mean. Another mistake. Out came the wallet, and the photos. Mrs Haverslicker and a whole tribe of infant Haverslickers. I'd say this for JJ, he was a prolific talker. He went on and on, even throughout the meal. Well, I'm not a good listener in such circumstances, even if the speaker is plying me with drinks. In fact, to be more forthcoming with the truth, I'm a very *poor* listener, if not rotten. But, as luck would have it, JJ was .....well, I suppose it could be said, he drank efficiently. Very efficiently; at least two to my one. And so eventually he slept. I was saved.

Across the aisle a little grey-haired old lady, whom, I assumed - from the amount and quality of her jewellery - was not exactly short of a coin or two, was busily stuffing her handbag with left-over freebies from her lunch tray. In the row ahead, a small, bespectacled gentleman from the land of the rising economic miracle - probably having just redesigned a 64 bit processor on the back of his napkin - was attempting to separate cheese from plastic wrapping, with little success. The stewardess showed him how.

'Ah so,' said he, rather predictably.

Another flight, another American. One who seemed to possess intimate knowledge of every calamity or misfortune that could possibly befall a human being. He also seemed determined that I should hear about them, in all their gory details.

'Once saw a biker run headfirst into a Mack truck. I mean dead-centre of the radiator, man! Splat!' His palms slapped together. 'Jeez, what a mess. Take some cleaning up, that lot.'

Certainly will, thought I. One hand had been about to open his carton of coffee creamer, now it was; open and empty, the contents luckily missing me. He didn't seem to notice, carried on. 'Forget about crash-hats, I mean his head was somewhere down by his ass. Shit, man.. talk about strawberries. Which reminds me, once saw a guy leap from an airplane. Sport they called it. Only his chute candled on the way down. Jeez, yuh should'a seen....'

'Serves him right for jumping out of a totally serviceable aircraft,' I cut in. Couldn't stand any more, so, assuming nervousness to be the cause of this verbal diarrhoea I decided to exploit the fact. Maybe wind him up a touch.

'Different to down there, eh?' I inclined my head towards the window that overlooked the rest of the world.

'How so?' Just that. I knew then I was right.

'Let's face it, down there's a madhouse. Up here we're free of all that lunacy. It's kind of an escape, isn't it?'

'How so?' Again, just that. Figured I had him now, hook line and sinker.

'From the pressures of life,' I answered. 'No problems, no bills, no worries, especially no inquisitive women. Look out there. Sun, blue sky, white clouds. Perfect. We could be on our way to heaven.'

'Yeah! That's what worries me.'

Ah yes. In for the kill. I'd give him the Spike Milligan treatment. 'Why should you be worried?'

'Why? Flying's why. Ain't natural. Goddamn dangerous if you ask me.'

'Nah, come on, flying's not dangerous. Safer than crossing the road.' I allowed a couple of beats. 'Crashing. Now that's something else. Crashing's dangerous.'

Ended up ordering him a drink, double brandy. I eventually coaxed a laugh out of him, though. After that he was fine.

Then, on another sector, there'd been the woman. American again, of course. They almost always seem to be excessively friendly. She'd also wasted little time getting round to the photographs, as if she felt the need to explain why she was travelling without her Elmer.

'That's Elmer,' she said, 'in the middle. Taken shortly before he went, that was.'

I felt like asking "Went where?", but it was plain to see he'd obviously gone to where he couldn't take it with him. Gold, silver, and diamonds hung from everywhere jewellery could hang. At least everywhere that was visible. If I had that kind of money I certainly wouldn't have been sitting back where I was. It was foggy when we landed and I could barely see her ahead of me, walking across the tarmac to the coach which would transport us to the terminal. I could hear her though, jangling along like an alpine cow.

These days, fog rarely shuts an airport down, especially an airport with the stature of Heathrow. They, in conjunction with the aircraft that use them, possess magical electronic systems which allow landings to be made in conditions of zero visibility, and it is landings that are all important. The main reason for fog to close an airport was because it prevents a landing. Take-off wasn't the problem, it was the possibility of a problem occurring *during* take-off which closed the field. A problem which would dictate a speedy return to the runway.

Heathrow has possessed the capability of allowing hands-off landings since back in the sixties. That BEA Trident on which Mr Burton and I returned from Geneva did so. Fog so thick you couldn't see the wingtips, auto-throttle sounding very erratic indeed, crew relying totally on technology. Which I imagine could be very frustrating, from a pilot's point of view. Like a back seat driver who also has control. Those were early days though, and Heathrow was surrounded by wide open spaces. Not all airfields are so lucky. Take Tegucigalpa, capital of Honduras, for instance: I recall the take-off from there as being quite er... well, what shall we say? Exhilarating? Yes, that'll do nicely. Vague memories of a runway which terminated on the very lip of a steep valley. More of a canyon, really, for once this point was reached the aircraft became airborne no matter what. The job of engines and crew from here on in was to ensure it *remained* airborne. But it was a canyon within a canyon, if you see what I mean, the airfield itself surrounded by towering mountains, thus compelling the pilot to circle within their walls until he had the altitude to clear them. Probably not quite that bad, but those are the images I recall.

Or how about Kai Tak, in Hong Kong. Here wingtips scythe through the air perilously close to buildings either side of the flight-path. Close enough to allow a brief peek into people's living rooms, therefore their lives. Can you believe that?

If not, try this. Apparently true.

An aircraft, cruising at thirty thousand feet, was requested by an American sector controller to climb immediately to thirty-two thousand. "For noise abatement purposes", he said.

The captain complied, then, puzzled as to the reason given - after all, noise abatement procedures normally relate to operations close to populated areas, ie: during take-off - he requested clarification.

`Did you say noise-abatement? At this height?'

"Roger," came the laconic-sounding voice. "Y'all ever heard the noise of two 747's meeting head-on?'

Such are the pleasures of flight.

* *

Chapter Eighteen
TALES FROM THE NEW WORLD

I've always welcomed the opportunity to depart for warmer climes, at least for part of the long European winter; don't really need a valid excuse. At the back end of 1962 therefore, it was pure coincidence that found me revisiting an old haunt: RAAF Butterworth, in northern Malaya (that Far East Tour with the S of S for Air - Comet C4). Good place to be I'd thought at the time, what with the world seemingly poised on the very brink of nuclear annihilation, the Cuban Missile Crisis in full flow. It had seemed like a comfortable, away-from-it-all kind of place in which to hide away if the worst came to the worst. (Maybe that Secretary of State knew something we didn't?) Now, here I was again, 1991, another coincidence, similar feelings for a similar situation, only this time my destination was New Zealand: Aoreatoa to the Maoris - Land of the Long White Cloud. Good place to be anytime, but especially now, just when it appeared the United Nations, led by America, were - to use an American term - about to kick ass in Iraq. Or maybe....?

No matter, all would become clear once the action began. What mattered to me was that I should be well separated from it. Could even sit and watch it happen this time around. Did so, in fact; cold Steinlager to hand. Well, I saw as much as Stormin' Norman, or the Department of Defence, thought I should see. But gosh and golly weren't those laser-guided bombs something else; testimony to mankind's inventiveness and absurdity apart. Talk about impressive. I swear I must have seen fifty, every one a direct hit.

What?

Ah, yes, the targets did look rather similar, I must admit. But doesn't one bunker or bridge look very much like another? I mean, they wouldn't cheat, would they? After all, this is the Pentagon we're talking about. Upright, to-the-point type people. There again, how far could you trust the kind of people who would lumber a simple nut (you know, that fits on a bolt) with the term "hexaform rotatable surface compression unit". Which I didn't just make up, believe me. Try that down at your local ironmonger and see where it gets you. 'A 25mm HRSCU, if you please, squire.' Think he'd be the one to pose the questions then.

Okay, so New Zealand may not have been as far away as I could possibly get, but I certainly couldn't have wished for better.

*

York. Eight am: The omens looked good. Taxi arrived ten minutes early;

a frosty winter morning, clear yet sunny; a leisurely journey; arrive LBA (Leeds/Bradford Airport) with plenty of time in hand. Too much, as it happened, a one hour delay on the incoming flight. Fog at LHR (London Heathrow), we are told (an occasion when it did affect operations). Ah, well, my onward flight isn't scheduled to depart until thirteen hundred.

Nine thirty: The delay had become an hour and a half. No problem, airborne now. Forty minutes to Heathrow, another forty transferring to LGW (London Gatwick). Two hours to spare, I calculated.

Light smattering of snow on the Dales, down below, remnants of the blizzard conditions which had recently swept this part of the country. Skies clear and untroubled now. 'Absolutely perfect flying conditions,' the captain informed us. 'It's possible we'll make up time.'

Make up time we did, but to no avail. We joined the stack, over Epsom. Delayed flights piled above and below like tiers on a wedding cake. One thousand feet below, mirroring our movements, a British Airways 757, resplendent in the sunlight; grey, blue, and red paintwork gleaming. Below that, green fields, fingers of fog still stretching out in the tucks and folds.

Ten thirty: LHR. Met by courier: passport, work permit, ticket, as planned. 'You'll miss the ten forty-five bus, but there's another at eleven,' she advised. 'Should make that.'

Didn't. Delays with the baggage due to delays with.... etc, etc.

Eleven zero-five: Close. Nowhere near close enough. 'Next bus, eleven fifteen,' the ticket girl answered sharply. Sullen type, couldn't care less. Clearly, on this day, a person who hated her job, her country, the world, and everyone in it.

Twelve fifteen: Traffic delays meant late arrival at Gatwick. I wanted the North terminal, naturally we called at the South first. My reserves of patience and time now becoming sadly eroded. Only one person off, but we had to wait for pick-ups! Time becoming a valuable commodity.

Twelve thirty: North terminal, at last - not an area with which I'm familiar. Ten precious minutes to locate and struggle to the correct desk. Late check-in means no choice of seat selection; allocated a seat well to the rear of the Air New Zealand 747, area of maximum discomfort due to torsional stresses, among other things. I prefer to be above the wing. Would actually prefer First or Business, my client apparently wouldn't. Ah well, at least I'm on board, on my way, out of the cold and the chaos. Well clear of that sullen ticket girl.

Aircraft were lined up ahead, each awaiting its take-off slot. There is a calculated interval between departures, spacing dependant on aircraft type and size. For instance, a Jumbo jet could take off close behind a

Shorts 360, say, but not vice versa. The wake turbulence generated by a 747 is such it could easily flip anything smaller onto its back and into the ground. No such problems here, I was in the biggie. Airborne at last, aerodynamically clean; gear, flaps, slats, retracted. Back in my element.

Poor service. Lousy meal. Especially to someone to whom it is the first meal of the day. Wine didn't show until almost too late, but at least that was reasonable. Postprandial brandy - as opposed to the Cognac I'd requested - more akin to something from Spain. What the hell, settle back to a good film. Oh, no! Teenage Mutant Ninja Turtles, which, very much under duress, I had taken my son to see the previous week.

Spent an hour or so chatting to a New Zealand film producer, outside the lavi. We weren't queuing to use it, it just happened to be close to the galley, ie, the drinks. Fancied another Muller Thurgau, ordered same. What I received was what was currently on offer: Cooper's Creek chardonnay. Well, it had legs, was spicy, with excellent clarity and a lingering aftertaste.

'Not bad at all. Give us another,' the film producer later requested.

Middle of the night: Los Angeles. A four hour layover - secure in a mini transit lounge. Not the fresh air I'd hoped for. Still, being LA the air inside was probably purer.

For some unexplained reason there was a change of aircraft here. Same flight number, but 747-200 traded in for the latest model, a dash 400. More comfort, no discernable improvement in service. Still, couldn't complain, at least we hadn't crashed on take-off.

With clouds, sea, and sky our only companions, the aircraft droned on through the night. I was secure at Flight Level 360 (thirty-six thousand feet) enclosed in an aluminium shell, with its associated plumbing; electronic, hydraulic, pneumatic.

Then, almost before I realized, we were there; top of descent. Depressurization so fierce, background noise was reduced to zero. New aircraft, maybe the pilots hadn't yet got the hang of it. Did good on the approach and touchdown, though, really greased it on. Welcome to Auckland International, probably the least crowded of the world's major airports, no hustle and bustle here, one reason I like this laid back, friendly country. A twelve hour time difference, six month seasonal variation. The sun shone, and it was as warm as the welcome of the New Zealanders.

*

The little plane was dwarfed by the majestic, snow covered peaks of the Southern Alps. Precipitous walls dropped away to the fields and pastures, and the rivers which meandered through them, five thousand feet below our flight level. Directly ahead was a crystalline peak. It towered a further two thousand feet above us, ice and snow clinging to the summit like icing on a cake; brilliant, smooth, dazzlingly white. This was Mount Tasman, its peak only one thousand feet lower than Mount Cook itself, which was but a stone's throw away; highest point in the Southern Hemisphere, so the guidebook told me. But it was Tasman which now filled our windscreen, its jagged slopes seemingly close enough to reach out and touch. I say our, in relation to the windscreen, for the old magic had worked its spell once more; my being offered the copilot's seat.

Almost at the last minute it seemed, the pilot banked the aircraft steeply, as if flying a terrain-hugging fighter. Then, around the corner, our destination floated into view; top end of the eighteen mile Tasman glacier - eight thousand feet above sea level. The virgin surface sparkled in the sunlight as we made an up-hill approach. With a soft bump we touched down, skis hissing over crisp, recently fallen snow as we ran on, pilot turning the machine, bringing it to a halt, side on to the slope, before switching off. With a final hiccup the engine cut, propeller shuddering to a stop.

I scrambled out eagerly and stood transfixed, awed by the incredible stillness. The brittle metallic tick of the exhaust as it cooled and contracted bearing sole responsibility for the disruption of nature's silence. As if on request, I and the other two passengers automatically lowered our voices, so as not to disturb the magic of this enchanted place. At this altitude the sky was a brilliant blue, the air sharp and clear. So clear that when I looked into space I felt quite vulnerable, exposed; as when one's cover is stripped away.

'Absolutely fantastic.' It was all I could manage.

'Isn't it just,' agreed the pilot, materializing at my side. 'We don't get too many days like this, so make the best of it. A pleasure to fly in these conditions.'

I was happy to fly any time, though I had to admit, this took some beating. I breathed in lungsfull of the pure, invigorating, mountain air as I wandered off to stretch my legs, footprints disrupting the pristine surface.

A few yards on I turned and looked back at the tiny, blue and white Cessna, Charlie Charlie X-ray, of Mount Cook Airlines, its orange dayglow stripes standing out brilliantly against the snow. Towering imperiously above, and forming a spectacular backdrop, was the peak of Mount Cook itself. It made the aircraft look like a child's toy, discarded and forgotten on a sheepskin rug. I recalled the description: Highest peak in New Zealand, Mount Cook is known as Aorangi by the Maoris, the literal translation of which is "The Cloud Piercer". Now of course it is named after Captain Cook, who never actually set eyes on it; so it told me - that same guidebook.

The surface around me glistened, giving the impression of handsful of diamonds, cut and polished, having been scattered in the sunshine. That same sun struck blue-black shadows in the gullies and undulations, the edges of which were smoothly contoured, that having been attended to by a recent fall of windblown snow.

All too soon the pilot indicated it was time to leave, so we clambered back on board, the fragile little machine rocking on its spindly undercarriage as we settled ourselves, and strapped in.

The propeller kicked jerkily, once, twice, then the engine coughed, caught, and roared into life, shattering the peace. Airframe vibrating as the throttle was pushed open, the pilot turned us to face down the gradient, slipstream raising a cloud of fine white powder behind. Then we moved off. Slowly at first, speed building as we bumped over the surface, pilot making fractional corrections with the rudder to hold us straight between encroaching walls. We were schussing down the piste. Vibration lessened with the onset of speed, ceasing abruptly as the tail rose and we became airborne once more, free, floating gracefully in the still conditions, propeller describing a glistening arc as it pulled us through the sky.

Retracting skis and flaps, the pilot throttled back and trimmed the aircraft for the short flight back to Mount Cook airport. It was downhill all the way. Five thousand feet.

But I wasn't here to fly or play, I was here to work. It just so happened that for the first month or so, working was really a bit of a misnomer, under the circumstances. Therefore, as the project experienced delays not associated with my part in it, I seemed to spend more time playing golf (to the detriment of the local course, I might add), trying my hand at fly fishing (anything under three pounds went back. OK, would have, had anything come out to begin with), and ....er... drinking a little. Still, the pay was the same.

*

Remember Brian, my old school mate? Course you do, way back there in chapter two. Met up with him again this trip. He took me fishing over by Taupo. Forty years and he hadn't changed a bit. No, I lie. He didn't have the beard at school, grey or otherwise.

'How come you ended up in New Zealand?' I asked.

'Emigrated after leaving the army,' says he. 'Opportunity was there so I took it. Figured I may as well be poor and warm, as poor and cold.'

That was Brian, you see, no real ambition. No pretensions, either. But whether he realized it or not, he was no longer poor. He'd done all right. His own house, family, garden, fishing most weekends - probably the best waters in the world for it - and a good group of friends. Not really my friends though, they caught all the fish! Experience, I suppose. My only experience had been gained forty years ago, on the banks of the Derwent.

I hadn't been too successful then, either.

Seemed obvious my technique with rod and line had not improved over time, but Brian's had. Still a Norton lad at heart though, Brian; down at the bookies most days. What a life! All that, and New Zealand.

But here in New Zealand it was the scenery I loved. The ever-changing countryside. Trees, lush undergrowth, open pastures, and the ubiquitous Toi-toi; an indigenous form of pampas grass. There were lush forests, pine clad hillsides, the folds of which accommodated river valleys and smallholdings. And beyond the sheep-speckled fields were snow-capped mountains and turquoise lakes. On the banks of one, a little old lady, secure beneath a straw hat, perched on a stool. She was faced by an easel, brushes and paints to hand, as were her sandwiches and flask. Green was in an abundance. Tree trunks, rocks, virgin ground; all upholstered in a rich, velvety moss, whilst a myriad of ferns complimented the scene. The reason? The copious amount of rain to which the area was subjected. One minute dry, next, you're looking for a boat, kind of thing.

*

The twin engined Islander sat poised on the grass, waiting, the pilot completing his visual inspection with a well aimed kick at one of the tyres.

With some forethought I chatted him up whilst we awaited the rest of the passengers, and, as hoped, was yet again invited to occupy the right-hand seat. He was quite young, the pilot, but his familiarity with, and competence in operating the machine were immediately obvious as hands and eyes completed their checks, started the engines. His fingers flicked switches, and operated levers and buttons, whilst his eyes checked the gauges. That nonchalant tyre check had obviously been just for show.

As the brakes were released the nose bobbed up, as if in relief, then the little plane surged forward, airspeed rising quickly as the ground fell away. A starboard turn had us heading back towards Te Anau and up the centre of the lake, climbing steadily. We needed to, there were mountains all around. The highest of the peaks were substantially lower than those of the Mount Cook range, a result of which was that only the tallest - to be seen ahead - still retained a dusting of snow.

On a narrow plateau I noticed a group of walkers, knapsacks on their backs, striding out along a trail which traversed the ridge.

'Milford Track,' the pilot announced over the intercom. 'Said to be the finest walk in the world. Thirty three miles. Takes about three days to complete,'

The almost sheer walls fell away a couple of thousand feet, to end on the banks of a river far below. One false move, they'd be falling forever. We circled, the hikers looked up, waved. We followed the track, circled again over Lake Quill, watched awestruck as it spilled over the lip, creating the one thousand nine hundred foot triple drop of the Sutherland Falls. Light, scattered clouds floated by as we climbed once more, before the ground suddenly dropped away beneath us to form Milford sound. Those mountainous walls continued their downward progress, a further thousand feet beneath the surface of the fjord; plenty deep enough for the QE2 to visit, which it had.

Down we zoomed, to within a few hundred feet of the water, following the course of the fjord out to the open sea. Bank left, around the point, and we were following the coastline. Breakers crashed against the cliffs, throwing spray and spume high into the air, the white foam contrasting starkly with the yellow sandstone and the emerald clad land behind. At Doubtful Sound we turned inland, climbing to clear high ground before again descending over Lake Manapouri, back to the flat grazing land which doubled as the airfield. Look out, sheep, here we come.

*

In New Zealand as with anywhere else, in my view, the idea is to leave the cities behind. Rather than Auckland, one needs to be on the North Shore, over the bridge known as the coathanger, with it's Japanese-designed outer-lane extensions, referred to locally as the Nippon Clip-on. North of Albany and the chaos begins to subside. In the South Island things are altogether different. Down there, even in the cities life is lived at a much reduced pace.

Our pace wasn't exactly hurried either. The job, scheduled to last six weeks, sort of overran a little. Four months and it was still ongoing. Not what you could call a success, from someone's point of view, but I loved it.

By now, the Pohutukawa - otherwise known as the New Zealand Christmas tree - had ceased to display their bright red flowers. They put in an appearance only during the Christmas period, hence the name, although out here Christmas was the height of summer. It was now autumn, time for me to move on.

As I was driven over the harbour bridge for the last time, on my way to the airport out at Manukau, I looked once more at the Auckland skyline, the Westhaven Boat Harbour and St Mary's Bay, jam packed with yachts. Come weekend, most of them would be out on the Waitemata, colourful spinnakers billowing. Ashore there would be parties, and barbecues. I felt sad to be leaving my friends, Ron and Lynne. Sad to be leaving these warm and friendly islands. I recalled a Maori telling me they had a saying, a form of welcome when meeting someone for the first time: "Not a stranger. An old friend I haven't yet met."

Then I was on my way, winging across the Tasman Sea to another island, an island that was also a continent; a place known colloquially as

Oz, the language, "Strine."

*

`Yuh have a prison record?'
    No problem with the language there. It was the immigration officer at Perth airport, and he was asking, not stating a fact.
    Oh! I didn't realize it was still a requirement. Didn't really say that, but I'd have liked to. Don't imagine it would have scored too many plus points though, so I kept my silence and went on my way.
    'Emma necks?'
    Yeah, well I was always going to have trouble with that, despite the fact that this was not my first visit to the Lucky Country.
    I looked up, puzzled. Not only did I not know the answer, didn't even understand the question.
    'Emma necks? he asked again. 'For brekkie?'
    Ah ha. If it was my preference for breakfast he was enquiring about, it could well translate into ham and eggs. I found out it did, so I ordered, breakfasted, paid the bill, and prepared to leave.
    'Scona rine,' the girl said, handing me my change. Easy, this one, for she also gave me a clue, taking time out to appraise the sky. I guessed right away it was a meteorological term, for it did indeed look like rain.
    That had been my re-introduction to English, as she is spoke in "Oz".

*

Over the years many people have gone to Australia for many different reasons. The early settlers had little choice, they were said to have been transported, though not quite in the fashion of Star Trek! Next came the prospectors and adventurers, to be followed by the immigrants - voluntary, but their journey heavily subsidised. Then came the tourists. I fitted none of these categories, for I was here to work - a non-resident. It wasn't my first trip, I'd previously been here with the Air Force. I'd also worked the Bass Straight, out of Melbourne and Tasmania - lovely place, Tassie. Melbourne was OK, but Victoria's weather was too variable for my liking, and the unions were unbelievable. Seems the people who couldn't make it back home had come out here to stir things up.
    In our business time is money, so when we found the Aussie Dockers Union members to be slow organising themselves, insisting on a "smoko" before they would begin to even think of off-loading our equipment, taking themselves off somewhere instead, we decided to do it ourselves. We were in the usual hurry, and figured it was all part of what we were paid for.
    Not out here. A definite no no. But we already knew that, were therefore prepared when the expected confrontation occurred.
    When they eventually turned up, they asked what was going on.

'Going on? We're loading *this* equipment onto *that* boat,' we told them. Which is when they became extremely belligerent.

'Run that by me again. You're doing what?'

'Putting our equipment on the boat.'

'And what makes you think you have the right to do that?'

'Part of our job. Always has been.'

'Not on this bloody dock, mate, bloody oath. Yuh trying to put someone out of a job, or what?'

'No. But there was no one here, and we're in a bit of a hurry.'

'Jeez! Bit of a hurry is it you pommy bastard? Well, now it's just going to take a little longer, isn't it,' they informed us. So we stood around and watched as they went aboard, carried everything off, loaded it onto the waiting trucks. Exactly what we'd been doing. Just about shut the port down when we drove off!

So much for the south coast, now it was to be the North-west again, the part of Oz I enjoyed most. Exmouth, Dampier, Port Hedland, Broome, Derby. Virtually the whole of the West coast, from Perth up; the Pilbara, as it is known. It is a vast, scarred and ancient land. An area of contrast and colour. Natural colours, red predominant. The soil is red and its dust covers everything around. It comes from the iron ore which is mined and shipped from here. Ore of such high grade, I'd heard tell it was possible to weld fragments of the rock together.

If not the outback, these towns are at least on the very edge of it. There may be a government in Canberra, but up here the land is ruled by nature, not people. The riverbeds are dry most of the year, a dusty dryness. So dry in fact, they look like they have little recollection of the feel of water. The gum trees on the banks stand silvery white against the deep blue sky, and there is the yellow flower of the Wattle. The rains would come eventually ("The Wet"). Gentle at first, making a drunkard of the parched earth. Then faster and heavier, until the ground was overcome and the channels began to fill.

Some of this I knew, some I was told about whilst standing around sucking on a tinnie, outside the Roebuck Inn, in Broome. Fancy name for a not so fancy place. Safer to drink outside on the western-style boardwalk than in the inn itself. Could get dangerous in there, we were told. At least I assume that was the inference.

'Doesn't take much to start a bit of a ding. Bloody oath,' said our guide.

I could well imagine it. I noticed the juke box was chained to the wall, as had been the case in the bars of KL, all those years ago. Only difference here, no glass in the window frames, just chicken wire. I'd been to similar bars in Africa, only those contained no juke box, no chicken wire. Lucky if there was electricity.

As we stood there, soaking up the sun, the stories, and the amber nectar, I allowed my thoughts to drift, back to another time, a previous visit to the Pilbara.

*

It was a job we were about to start in the King Sound.

First there was a requirement for us to set up a navigation chain in the area, around the town of Derby. And as there wasn't much around this particular town, apart from lots of bush, scrub, and saltwater, we were experiencing difficulty locating the preferred sites; known survey points.

We had, at some cost, obtained maps of the area from the Lands And Surveys Department, before departing Perth. Only trouble was, those maps were quite old. They therefore related more to what had been, rather than what now was!

Onto the scene stepped the lanky, very personable, John Hughes, here to represent the oil company's interests. Arriving from Sydney, to oversee the calibration, he was a little early, as it happened. Difficult to calibrate something you don't yet have. Still, it gave us chance to get to know one another, and a more pleasant, amiable company rep I had yet to meet, as it turned out.

For a variety of reasons we'd up to now only been able to locate one of the sites, and that with some difficulty. Still, we'd definitely face few problems when returning: all it required was for us to follow the trail of destruction created by our illustrious leader's "point and stop" method, as used on that first run: What I referred to in an article for the company magazine as "Clarke 1880 - Heavalo 1980". The first being the survey datum, and the year in which it had been established, the second, a reference to our Party Chief's more recent effort.

Don had seen the high ground away in the distance, couldn't miss it really, peak protruding above the surrounding dense scrub. Had to be the place, but with no obvious trail in sight, how to reach it? No problem. Don just pointed the Land Rover in the right direction, put his foot to the floor, more or less stopped when he arrived at the base of the hill. That run took an hour and a quarter, a time that was to be reduced somewhat once the trail had been blazed. On one memorable occasion I donned my Mario Andretti gloves, lowered the Jackie Stewart sunglasses and, accompanied by Mike "White Knuckles" Jarvis, managed to lower the record to fifteen minutes. Figured I could have shaved the odd minute or two off that had the wheels remained in contact with *terra firma* a greater percentage of the time. And Mike hardly spilled a drop of his gin and tonic. There again, Mike being Mike, it didn't get much of a chance to spill!

As a result of these difficulties a conference was called, in the bar of the Baobab Inn, naturally, this being our home away from home, up here. Anyway, this being the Outback, we were feeling a little parched. The outcome was that John decided the expense of an aerial search was warranted, so the appropriate flying machine was duly chartered: a twin-boom, push-pull Cessna 337. We were then introduced to our pilot "The Crazy Kiwi". But only after taking to the air did the reason for this sobriquet become apparent.

We were en-route to Oobagooma station - Australianese for cattle ranch - where one of the sites was apparently located. I, in my customary seat, up front, explained what we were looking for, supplied him with an approximate location. He'd need that, the pilot, for stations up here covered thousands of square miles.

'That look like the place?' Crazy Kiwi asked, some time later, stabbing a wingtip towards a pile of rocks on top of a hill, whilst pulling a rate four turn around it for a minute or so, the resultant G, forcing me down in my seat. I clawed at a window - which, due to our attitude, was now the floor - attempting to elevate myself enough to be able peer out. John, seated behind, supposedly checking the charts, was instead wrestling with a plastic bucket. For some reason, he appeared to be shouting at it. Difficult to understand the words, but it sounded like "Hughie", "Ruth", or some such thing. Very strange.

The pilot took us down low, so as to get a closer look. Very low! Then he was fiddling with something down the side of his seat, seemingly unconcerned about what lay ahead. As if to compensate, I kept my eyes glued to the windscreen. Yeah, that looked like the place all right. No need to get any closer.

Sometime later, back at five thousand feet over the King Sound, peace and tranquillity having been restored, a sudden shout of "BANZAI" had nose hard down, sea rushing up to meet us.

Jesus! It didn't look at all tranquil from this attitude. I said my goodbyes and silently chanted my hellos. No recovering from of this, I thought, whatever *this* was. Yet the pilot didn't appear to be fighting for control, seemed rather relaxed, in fact. The bugger was.

'It alleviates boredom,' he told us, once he'd recovered, somehow without tearing the wings off the thing. John and I could only agree. It did tend to have that effect. A minor coronary usually does.

His later offer of, 'Another "banzai" before we land?' was firmly declined. John, who was after all effectively paying the bill, managed, with a notable lack of subtlety, to convey the fact that he was not entirely thrilled by the offer.

After landing we again retired to the bar at the Baobab. Not exactly because we were parched, more medicinal, this. But we didn't stay long, transferring our allegiance after a couple of beers to the disco at the

Spinifex Hotel. A much livelier option, this. Typical outback pub; rough as guts. A notice advised us of the minimum dress requirements: singlet, shorts, sandals (called thongs). Some of the clientele even exceeded this, going so far as to wear a hat. Sweat-stained and battered, but then so was the rest of their gear. There was a second notice pinned up, I noticed. For sale, it offered: *Encyclopaedia Britannica*. Complete set. Now married, no longer needed. F***ing wife knows everything about everything.

It was interesting country all right. During "The Wet" the roads double as quagmires, become all but impassable to anything but four-wheel drive and a lot of luck. In the dry season they are rutted and rough but can be negotiated by car, so long as you don't mind the odd piece falling off. We opted for the latter. It was a hire car anyway.

Not a good place to be during the cyclone season, either, as one party chief had discovered years before. He'd been in Darwin at the time, capital of the Northern Territories. The date, December 25th 1974; the day Tracy came to town. He'd apparently been asleep through the whole thing - unconscious would probably be more accurate, he'd have to have been. His first words upon waking were classic, eternally recorded in the doodlebuggers bible.

`Serious trouble up here last night,' he told the telephone.

`Didn't wreck the pub again, surely?' the boat manager, in Perth, queried upon hearing this.

'No, the pub's OK. More or less intact, fortunately. About the only place that is though. I wake up in the hotel, in bed, looking at the bloody sky. Jesus! Must have been some party, thought I. Until I looked outside, that is.'

`And...?'

`Gone! The whole bloody town's gone. Wiped out by a cyclone.'

`Like you said, must have been some party if you slept through that.'

There are many things I like about Australia, for it is a likeable and diverse country, as is New Zealand. In Australia, weather apart, it was birds, booze, and barbies, in NZ....? Ah, Yes. Same thing, come to think of it. Different scenery though.

* *

Postscript: Three months after the King Sound job I was to work with John Hughes again, by which time we had become close friends. He'd always fancied attending a European Grand Prix, so I made reservations for us to visit Monaco. Before it came about, John was gone; killed in the crash of a light twin during one of our scheduled crew changes. The aircraft on which he was a passenger lost an engine on take-off from Portland, west of Melbourne. With the machine way over the weight limit - it was subsequently found - the pilot attempted to make it back to the runway but failed. The aircraft broke apart on impact, catching fire a couple of minutes later. Everyone escaped except John. He was unconscious, trapped by his legs when the main spar broke. It had proved impossible to free him before the wreckage was engulfed.

A harmless person, come to harm.

It's always traumatic to learn of the death of a friend, much worse if you happen to be close by when it occurs.

* *

Chapter Nineteen
MIDDLE EAST MEANDERINGS.

It can be quite a daunting experience to travel on certain middle eastern airlines, especially on the rare occasions when they make an announcement over the public address. You know the kind of thing; 'The flight time today will be one hour forty minutes.'

The difference here is the message extension; just one word - 'Inshallah!' It is that final intonation which brings one up short: "If God wills." It's as if the pilot were declining to accept responsibility for anything that may go wrong.

Then there is the safety briefing. That seems not to change no matter where you are bound. 'In the unlikely event of the aircraft settling down on water.....'

Yeah, right. Would be unlikely wouldn't it, as would flying into a mountain in Holland. With an intended flight-path that routed us over the desert, finding water of a quantity large enough on which to settle an aircraft would require a navigational error of unprecedented magnitude. I settled for a quick glance at the safety instruction card. Nothing new there, either, apart from a hiccup in translation informing me of the presence of a "live" vest beneath my seat. Ah, well, I'd longed for international travel, and here I was, in Egypt.

*

Wandering around the Western Desert, along the shores of the Red Sea, is a gaunt reminder as to the futility of war. Acre upon acre of sand and scrub, seemingly of little use to anyone, but which had been fought over almost continually since time began. The odd wreck bore testimony to some of the later clashes, steel skeletons of tanks and other vehicles of combat, the people who had been inside, long gone, in one sense or another.

Occasionally I chanced upon barbed wire fences, but they didn't stop me, merely slowed my progress as I clambered through to some choice stretch of beach away in the distance. It was only later, after hearing the following tale, that I decided to curtail the walking, resume the drinking.

Another station, another country, but not that far removed; next door, in fact. Gadhafi-land, but before it became so. The remnants of another, earlier war. The station operator, just like myself, would wander around freely. Until the night his bearer - parting for home after bringing the daily water supply - parted from this life altogether when his camel stepped on a mine. It had apparently been uncovered by the shifting sands of a passing storm.

So Abdul was gone, we had survived. Inshallah, as they say. Yet another of those instances where death, or serious injury, could have been but a whisker away. Those little skull and crossbones signs weren't an indication that pirates once roamed hereabouts then! Thank God for Allah, or vice versa. Certainly someone up there was on my side. If not, then I'd been spared by factors unknown: Geographic location, fate, luck, or simply the old nine-lives syndrome? Who knows? What I did know was that I didn't care, I was still alive.

One day I stumbled across a sulphur lode, yellow crystals glinting in the sun from some way off. My heart raced, along with my feet, only for my hopes to be dashed. Always, at the back of my mind, I had visions of one day blundering into something precious, often willed it to happen. It was my favourite get-rich-quick dream. Picking up diamonds off a beach in South West Africa, for instance (not much chance of getting away with it if I had, the way they searched our equipment), or a nugget of gold in Australia. (When there I read in the Australian press of a case where a guy had stubbed his toe on a piece of half-buried junk, kicking at it in disgust, only to discover a lump of gold that was to make him rich. The Hand of Fate, as it became known; 20 kilos of the stuff.) Then there were rubies in Burma, emeralds in Columbia, other gemstones in other countries. Alas, it never happened. There again, I never stepped on one of those Egyptian mines either. Exciting times, eh? Maybe that doesn't sound like excitement, but what you have to realize is that Egypt can be a pretty dull place. At least along the Red Sea coast. Travel inland, to Luxor, and it can be just as different again.

Like the sea, the desert is timeless. Look at it today and it could be any period in history you wish to make it. Something similar could apply to the tombs in the Valley Of The Kings. Those interior paintings look as if they could have been completed only recently, rather than five thousand years ago, so bright are the colours. Worth seeing, those ruins. Trouble is, they seem endless. Tombs and temples on either side of the Nile, each that little bit different, all worthy of a look. Just one problem: given time it can become boringly repetitive. After inspecting acre after acre of ruins you find yourself approaching the next with a certain lack of enthusiasm. In fact, the only thing that keeps you going is the sure knowledge that, should you discuss this place with anyone else, they, for sure, will have been there. Not only that, they will end up enthusing about the one you missed out.

For our trip to the Valley of the Kings, we decided to eschew the comfort and cost of the touristy taxis and coaches for the novelty of a four legged beast of burden. Certainly different. The one I drew completely redefined the meaning of the word recalcitrant. If it was actually alive it had to be a very good actor. But alive it was, for when I dug my heels into its ribs it did move, if only to accelerate with all the enthusiasm of a three-toed sloth. I named it Muffin, although there was nothing puppet-like about it; definitely had a mind of its own, this one. So set in its ways, I suspected it of being female, but I never thought to check. In fact it must have been, for it turned out to have more sense than I did. When I attempted to turn right it went straight on, or to the left. It apparently knew the trail intimately, would brook no input from me whatsoever. I could shout, quietly coax, kick, it made no difference. Naturally, when seated on the back of an animal you can't see a lot of its face, so all I got in return for my commands was a mysterious twitching of the ears. That was the only indication I had that it had even heard me. It knew where we were heading, where the best views were to be had, the most economical pace at which to travel. It even knew when the track was too lose for me to ride in safety, for it just stopped, refusing to move until I dismounted. But it was definitely worth the pain and frustration, for we were afforded views the tourists would miss; quite spectacular from high in the hills. Away in the distance was the ribbon of the Nile, a darker brown against the surrounding sand, graceful feluccas gliding along its surface. But replicating the course of the river, probably quarter of a mile either side, was the green fertile area in which a large percentage of the county's fresh produce was grown.

We had previously done the Giza bit, in Cairo. The Sphinx, etc, Arabs and camels. Nowhere near the impact of Luxor. And the *son et luminère* at the Temples of Karnak was far superior. Besides, Giza is too touristy. One guy even offered to sell me a pyramid; Cheops. Can you believe that? Well, we had a bit of a discussion about it. Not all that easy an accomplishment when my knowledge of his language was mainly confined to ordering a beer. He fared rather better in mine, even if it did appear to be limited to numbers, seemingly in multiples of ten. Anyway it was a pretty ridiculous exercise. He must have thought I was gullible or something, but I wasn't going to fall for that. I mean, how I would get it home?

*

Travelling across the desert can present all kind of problems. Due to a lack of roads and tracks there was a need to complete our journey before darkness fell. For this I employed guides, which in itself created further problems.

By my reckoning we still had a way to go, and evening was nigh, yet we suddenly ground to a halt, everyone apart from myself piling out. They were about to brew up. Something that occurred rather too frequently.

'Fahad, I need to get to the boat, urgently.'

`Okay,' he replied, settling himself onto a mat, patting the space beside him, an indication that I should join him. He then turned and called over his shoulder. `Abdullah, etnayn chai.'

But I understood, if not their ways, a little of their language. 'We don't have time, I need to get there quickly. They're waiting to sail.'

'No no no.' He shook a finger at me, but at the same time he smiled. 'Patience. First tea, then business.'

This is the way of the Middle East, and I knew whatever I said wouldn't effect a change. And maybe they're right. Relaxation should come first.

And so darkness enveloped us well before we reached our destination. More tea and prayer stops the cause, but also, possibly our saving. Who knows what might have happened if they'd signed off with Mohammed early, as I frequently suggested. My thinking was that we should put in as much travel as possible during hours of daylight, not keep stopping, so as to check in with some superior being. He'd know where we were. We, on the other hand, appeared at times not to. But all turned out well. A full moon replaced the sun. The payoff, maybe?

I really did need to reach the boat before they sailed. Not for the usual reason, either, a decent meal. Not on this particular boat. No way, for the cook was Finnish. Not exactly a gourmet experience, let me tell you. Not wholly unexpected, of course, for the Finns are not specifically renown for their cuisine. So maybe I'm being a teeny bit harsh on the guy. I mean, who's to say he wasn't an expert on reindeer steaks and mooseburgers? Probably was. There again, as you can imagine, moose and reindeer are pretty thin on the ground in the Middle East.

* *

RETURN FROM A FOREIGN LAND.

Insipid sun; an overcast sky,
Coastline below, unseen to the eye.
Then round and round, we're in the stack,
High over Epsom; welcome back.
Thank God for that, about time too,
Fourteen hours with little to do
But sit and think, and maybe dream,
Until 14A starts to yell and scream.

We're informed of emergencies, yes indeed;
Of masks which materialize, in case of need.
Life-vest located beneath your seat;
And we'll show you a movie.' What a treat!
Not much chance of anything blue,
But.. Oh, my God, no! Mutant Turtles 2.
We're offered headsets, magazines and hot towels.
We're served "plastic" meals, which play hell with our bowels.
`And, Sir. Something to drink for you?'
`Yes, please. I'll have a gin and schw..... you know who.'

Blindly following a radio beam,
We start the descent, earth still unseen.
Down, down, down, through cotton-wool clouds,
Grey and clinging, just like shrouds.
Suddenly, it's there below,
The sparkle of a river's flow.
Green, green pastures, Elysian fields,
Pleasant memories, emotions revealed.

Buildings, modern and ancient are viewed
Through eyes which now are moisture dewed.
Anonymous houses, blocks of flats.
Vortices stream back off the slats.
Buckingham Palace, the gardens at Kew,
And, is that...? Yes! Twickenham, too.
'Gear down, please. Flaps, one third.'
Only up front are these words heard.
For us it's, seat belts, no smoking, and,
'Remain in your seat until safe at the stand.
'Welcome to Heathrow. Have a good day.
Thank you again for flying BA.'

Chapter Twenty
FINALE? Well...almost

Given a clear day, from thirty thousand feet you can almost see forever. Well, hundreds of miles. At present Bucharest would be sliding past below, almost imperceptibly. Ahead would be Hungary. Out to port, Bulgaria, with the USSR off to starboard. Difficult to be sure for there are no marked boundaries, and from up here everything looks the same. But they would be there all right. No point looking though, for this wasn't day, clear or otherwise. Out there the blackness was almost total but for the stars, suspended like globules of molten silver, the flash of a wingtip strobe, and a rare sign of habitation far below. Very rare, for the ground over which we now passed, be it Hungarian, Bulgarian, or Romanian didn't matter, it was dark and mysterious. So dark it could well be hidden beneath a coverlet of cloud, though I knew it not to be. This was pre-democratic Eastern Europe (assuming it to be now post-democratic), and I could well imagine assorted nefarious characters flitting in and out amongst the buildings down there, darker shadows among shadows, going about whatever business it is that requires such nefarious characters to flit. Seemed it was only to be expected in the communist world. A world I had only visited one time, although by then the Iron Curtain had crumbled. Still, I expect my details had long since been on file with the KGB, for I had visited many an African country that fell under Moscow's one time sphere of influence. Places where my passport had disappeared into some back office for long periods, and where any expatriate's seen flitting about in the background - whether Boris or Ivan - were certainly nothing to do with the Ministry of Tourism.

Then, just about the time you expect the lights to flicker out completely, they burst into life again, Eastern Europe having slipped astern. In next to no time we were approaching France, breakfast was being served. The flight was serene in the still air, but that was about to change, for far ahead, and below, nature began a pyrotechnic display of some considerable brilliance. Lightning flashed on and off, clouds lit up and went out like flashbulbs at the Academy Awards ceremony. These were obviously the wrong kind of clouds for us: Cumuli Nimbus. They revealed themselves as such, lit from within; dark, threatening silhouettes. There was danger in such clouds: thousands of gallons of water and ice, enough electrical power to light this continent for a year. Worst of all were the winds, updraughts and downdraughts. The turbulence they created was capable of tearing an aircraft apart, in exceptional circumstances, admitted. And they straddled our course as we began the descent. A line of battlements towering over the approaching landscape. There didn't seem to be any way to avoid them. Nature's barrier would need to be challenged once more. Or would we concede defeat, divert to an alternate haven? It didn't seem likely, at least not without giving it a try.

Wings flexed and flapped, the gyroscopic effect of spinning turbines causing the engines to move around alarmingly. Lightning flashed, thunder crashed, and we dropped as the bottom fell out of the sky. Chaos reigned, for of course when an aircraft goes down the food trays go up, as do you if you're not strapped in. But all was well, aircraft kitted out with the latest in electronic aids the crew soon had us safely down at Heathrow. (In some cases, shaken but not stirred.) Another return from another job in another place. It still goes on today, you see, though less frequently now. And I still travel on the old blue and gold passport would you believe; sixth issue. See me through the millennium, that, no change there. No change either in the way I dress to fly; comfortable, but smart, just the way it used to be for everyone that flew. It often pays off, too; dress well and you could be rated SFU at the check-in desk (suitable for upgrade). If not an upgrade it can see you allocated a seat by the over-wing exit, with its extra leg-room. Or maybe that's the "takes one to know one" syndrome coming into play?

*

1994. In the ever-changing pattern of service life paths cross and recross before finally parting, often forever; hello and goodbye. Then here we were, thirty four years on, meeting for an evening of reminiscence: The Far East Helicopter Association (Malaya Operations). There was George Puddy, bubbling and effervescent as ever, Taff Walker and Tom Browning. Tony and Spider hadn't changed much either. In fact none of them looked a day older to me, probably because we'd all aged. Tom Bennett was there, too, he of the stinkwheel bike, with its attached box, "for putting things in". Ended up an Air Commodore, Tom, and here I was, a lowly ex-corporal, on first name terms. It didn't feel quite right at first, but I soon realized it was. Although I still respected him, I learned to accept the fact that rank didn't count for much now, we were all civilians. The main thing was, we were friends.

Then the hangar doors were opened once more. It happens all the time when old service pals meet up. The greetings over a pint or two, the usual qualifier, "Do you remember when....?" I attempted to dredge up the images. Rather old images. But I found them all right, as did everyone. We talked of times past. Brief mention was made of pull-off checks and blade tracking, then it was people and places, helicopters and Hondas. Long-forgotten incidents were soon to be recounted with the help of photographs in albums. We swapped yarns and talked the night away, and the early hours of the new day. We were still capable of that.

It was good to meet them all again, to find out where they had gone, what they had done, what they did now. I also learned what they would be doing next year around this time; they would be back for another reunion.

Wrong.

It was the last time I was to see George.

*

I now know many things about many places, for I'm lucky enough to have been there, to have seen them. Most remain as picture postcards in my mind, and the luck seems intact. It is something we all need a little of now and again, good luck. That some people appear to have more than their fair share is not necessarily unjust, for some luck is engineered. Was it coincidence that Winston Churchill just happened to be in the right place at the right time when Chamberlain resigned, for instance, or did he place himself there on the off chance? The same could be said for Senator Johnson accepting the vice-presidential nomination under JFK. It could be said that such luck is deserved, earned rather than chanced upon. In a similar vein I didn't appear to have fared too badly, even though there'd been times when I'd seriously dispute that. But on balance I'd say I came out rather well, for I'd taken opportunities as they were presented, a lot didn't. No point waiting for fortune to smile upon you, it rarely does, that was my reasoning. What you must do is go out and grab it, or at least make the effort. I had been determined to fly, to see the earth from a bird's viewpoint. I had achieved that, spending over four thousand hours of my life in the air, and I don't have any regrets. Apart from that DC3 in Nigeria all those years ago, I can honestly declare I have never refused to board an aircraft. Mind you, there were numerous occasions when, once airborne, I wished I had taken the train instead. This of course includes those assorted, rivet-popping, oil-spewing Illyushin, and Antonov cast-offs of what could well have been called "The Honourable Gravity-Defying Chinese Flying Machine Company," but in those instances I don't suppose even the train would have presented an acceptable alternative. And although I see pilots as a special breed, I must admit to flying with the odd one or two with whom I wouldn't wish to fly again, given the choice.

So why didn't I ever become a pilot myself, or racing driver for that matter? Well, it's the physical side of things that excite me; the design and shape of the cars and aircraft, the sounds they make, the way they move through the air, along the ground. The way they behave, react to differing situations, the way they are controlled. Skill and ability, courage and dedication were things I could observe and appreciate, even if I didn't necessarily possess them myself. And that, I suppose, was basically the true reason: lack of confidence. I never felt I would be capable of being up there amongst the best, and average would never have been good enough for me. As pilot of a fast-jet I'd probably have found myself as misplaced as a stunt man on Songs of Praise. Or maybe I'm just one of life's observers, as opposed to a doer?

*

Bearing in mind the fact that I claim not to be superstitious, I must admit to there being more than a few good-luck charms over the years. First was the shark's tooth on a gold chain - not too lucky for the shark, admitted, he was dead. But my possession of one of his teeth was a by-product of his death, not the cause. We happened to catch him when fishing off an oil-rig in Nigerian waters. OK, so we used a crane and a trash basket as our tackle, a pound or two of beef as bait, it was still a fair catch. Skill and timing were required in the operation of that crane. There was a need for luck to be with us, too, against the shark.

Next came the New Zealand greenstone Tiki I wear to this day. Superstitious rubbish I tell myself, God is my good-luck charm. But I wear them anyway. Insurance, I suppose, should God be away on holiday or something. Or maybe I wear them in an attempt to ward off the dreams I occasionally experience; nightmares, really. Maybe a couple of dozen over the years, though long after leaving the Air Force. A worrying, recurring sequence: an aircraft seemingly about to crash. Sometimes I'm aboard, sometimes not, it doesn't matter, I always wake up before the crash occurs, if it ever does.

One such had me staying at a London hotel, my brother visiting. We heard the characteristic whine of a large jet passing overhead.

'DC10,' I guessed aloud. 'Sounds low.' I frowned.

'Much too...' But George's words were drowned out by a fearful noise; the heart-rending "whump" of a fuel-heavy explosion. I raced to the window, looked out. Nothing to see, nothing to hear. That was normal, too, I never actually saw the crash, or its after-affects.

I awoke in an instant, with a jolt. There was a kind of swishing and whooshing going on inside my head, the death throes of a disturbed dream. Then I was wide awake, yet calm and clear-headed. The images in my mind had been vivid, unnaturally lucid, as if they'd been real. Images from a dream life, or of one yet to be? As usual, I briefly wondered about this, then dismissed the thought, cast it the way of the others. Possibly the images were brought about by subconscious visions of crashes I had witnessed: that DC3 at Dishforth, and the Valetta. Or the extremely public loss of that French Air Force Breguet Atlantic; Farnborough, 1968. A terrible piece of asymmetric flying; turning on the dead engine. I'm no pilot and even I'm aware that is something you should never do. Stands to reason when you think about it.

*

So what else has changed over the years? The aircraft themselves for one. A visit to the cockpit of a modern airliner served to remind me that the contemporary cockpit was far removed from those I remembered: Sunderland, Hastings, even Comet and Britannia. Digital readouts now (as opposed to analogue - a direct reading rather than an easily misinterpreted pointer), all singing and dancing, lots of colours on lots of screens: blues, yellows, greens. Red was reserved for attention-getters: the not to be exceeded limits, and the "what-the-hell-do-you-think-you're-doing" warnings. Although the basic blind flying panel was still evident it was no longer in a form I recognised. It was now much more accurate and responsive. And where in hell was the control column, that pole to which pilots habitually clipped their notes? Replaced by something known as a sidestick controller. OK, but what about the notes, where were they? How could a pilot fly without those scribbled reminders? Ah yes, the red and amber lights, the audio and visual reminders. Then there is George mark whatever. Not only does he fly the aeroplane he also makes the decisions, based on what the pilot programmed into him to begin with - more of those missing notes, they, too have gone digital. Which leaves the crew to get on with their real function, to keep an eye on things, to be able to react instantly, if and when things go wrong. To prevent that event cascade. It also allows them time to enjoy their meal - though never the same menu for everyone! Just in case.

Then we come to shape and size. To watch an aircraft perform - a present-day fighter, say, free in its natural element - is to observe smooth beauty. Compare the same machine in the static mode and size seems strangely exaggerated. There is a sense of balance, symmetry, power, yes, yet it now appears chunky and angular rather than sleek and smooth. A brooding presence, crouching, patiently awaiting its time. It is dead and silent until the moment the pilot climbs aboard and straps it to his back. Confident hands now set the controls, push buttons, and flick the switches that are to bring it back to life. Pressures build, electrons flow and pulse, gyros spin, turbines whine, until the silence disappears in a storm of sound. From the moment that throttle is advanced as the machine lines up at the end of the runway, shuddering and straining like a hungry predator, nose oleo compressed, it is invested with an air of sinister intent.

A little jiggle, nose bobbing up as the brakes are released and, given a second or two, things happen very quickly indeed. The sudden build-up of speed, throttle pushed into afterburner, an explosion of flame and sound - excruciating, or music to the ears, depending on one's viewpoint - aircraft roaring past before rotating smoothly into flight. Gear up quickly, then it's away, into the wild blue yonder, climbing at an unbelievable rate. Somewhere between twenty and fifty thousand feet per minute for the latest and greatest. And you thought it was dead and silent.

Now it is the massed crowds who become silent as they stand and watch, eyeballs fused to camcorder viewfinders. The clothing they wear is that of the enthusiast: Flight jackets of leather or nylon are pleated, buttoned, zippered and pocketed. They are also badged and patched, the battle honours of previous engagements: IAT '85, Duxford '87, Farnborough, Mildenhall, etc. Clothes far removed from sartorial elegance, but not out of place in the macho world of aviation. And in this context, it would appear that the word "macho" could also apply to the female of the species. (Watch the video Reaching For The Sky, part 12, The Adventure of Flight: hear Lynn Rippelemeyer's story, watch her at work, flying the 747, then tell me I'm wrong.)

I could have been at any of the above air shows, at any time during the eighties and nineties, but I wasn't. This was Elvington, 1995. These days, you see, I have no need to fly to satiate my love of aviation, a visit to an aeronautical museum will do, even the quiet of an empty hangar can be enough to stir the memories: the different aircraft that have served to transport me on my peregrinations of the globe. The Oxford that carried me on that first flight, the nostalgia inducing biplanes: Tiger Moth, Stearman, Waco, Pitts Special. (Wow! Was it ever. Turned me inside out that one.) There were the tri-engines, the first flight in an aircraft whose airspeed indicator was calibrated in mach numbers rather than knots: Comet 2 (all gone now, apart from the one used as a restaurant, a couple as clubrooms. The Comet 4 is still around though, reincarnated today as the Nimrod). Then there are the helicopters, the seaplanes, amphibians, and floatplanes, and the ski-planes - refreshingly different, those. Silent flight is a sailplane, and there are the toy-like micro-lights; as serious as anything that ever left the ground, make no mistake about that.

Then there are the flights I missed out on: Concorde to Bahrain, cancelled at the last minute; Concorde from New York, likewise; being catapulted into the air from the deck of the USS Forrestal; that HD31, in Gabon. There were others too, missed because the chance had never been there to begin with. Aircraft I'd loved to have flown in, but hadn't: Meteor T7, Vampire T11, Hunter, the T4 Lightning, any of the V-Bombers, and most of all, the Canberra. Still, as I said, I hadn't fared too badly: one hundred and sixty assorted types, disregarding various marks of the same type. There were the countries to which those aircraft had carried me, too; eighty seven at last count. The most well remembered? Okay, remembered but not liked was Nigeria. Had to be for I'd spent quite a few years there. Of the places remembered with pleasure there were many.

I'd been and seen, as the saying went: African dawns and Caribbean sunsets. The day-lit nights of the Arctic summer, the night-time days of its long, hard winter. Periods of calm, moments of storm. I'd relished the good, suffered the bad. There'd been plenty of both, naturally. That, after all, was life. There are many countries to which a return visit is always something to look forward to with pleasure, few I would wish to live in if it meant rejecting England. But my out and out favourites have to be Australia and New Zealand, countries where life is lived at a much relaxed pace.

*

It's a long way back to those binocular-toting days of the fifties, but I still live in Yorkshire. Those same binoculars - now battered, aged, and long since retired from horse racing - continue to give valuable service, spotting aircraft. Only now the sleek-lined, propeller-driven aircraft of the fifties and sixties have been replaced by those angular, aggressive high-tech types of the eighties and nineties. They'd stand no chance in an avian beauty challenge, there again, that was never their intended role. And as for those old airfields, some still remain, Elvington more complete than most, now a museum. But don't despair that others fared not so well, for a trip to a deserted airfield is something else again, even if its runways are no longer active. No aircraft approach them now - no more Lancasters, no Halifaxes, no B17's - but what stories those runways could tell: tales of young men at war. The men and women are gone, too. All that remains, apart from those runways - grass thrusting up through cracked concrete - are a few derelict buildings - glassless window-frames and broken doors - and the clouds in the sky above. The clouds may look the same, but clouds are silent, they tell you nothing. At times though - if you listen, concentrate, imagine - familiar sounds still seem to echo in the early morning sky: air crackling with the short sharp messages of man, the popping and banging of throttled back engines, the seemingly relieved screech of rubber on tarmac, relaxed-sounding voices raised in song; bar-room ballads to the accompaniment of a piano improvisation: the lads down at the mess. Then there is the real music: a once familiar theme, this. An orchestration seemingly composed especially for the Rolls-Royce Merlin. The returning ghosts of long lost heros. All in the past, all gone.

But I do still have my suitcase. It is much bigger now, well packed, its complement of dreams now fulfilled. Well... almost. I shall continue to fly and to travel as long as I remain fit and capable. For the good times are surely by no means over. In fact, I rather hope the best is yet to come.

* *

AIRFIELDS VISITED
(Dates refer to year of first visit)

UNITED KINGDOM (RAF):

Driffield	1950	Edinburgh		1991
Leuchars		Birmingham		1996
Waddington				
Finningley	1951	**LYBIA**		
Dishforth		Castel Benito (Idris)		1955
Rufforth		El Adem		1961
Cosford	1953			
Millom		**EGYPT**		
Lyneham	1955	Fayid		1955
Valley		Cairo		1975
Aldergrove		Luxor		1976
Abingdon	1962	Hurgadha		
Benson				
Colerne		**FRANCE**		
Scampton		Istres		1955
Waterbeach	1963	Paris (Orly)		1962
Wyton		Toulouse		
Wattisham		Paris (Le Bourget)		1964
Leeming	1983	Paris (C de Gaulle)		
		Nice (Cote d'zur)		1968
UNITED KINGDOM (Civil)		Marseilles		1973
Doncaster	1952	Bordeaux		
Stanstead	1957			
Heathrow	1962	**MALTA**		
Manchester (Ringway)	1964	Luqa		1955
Glasgow (Prestwick)				
Luton	1968	**ITALY**		
Southend		Brindisi		1957
Gatwick	1970	Rome (Ciampino)		1962
Leeds/Bradford	1972	Naples (Capodichino)		
East Midlands	1982	Sardinia		1963
Sutton Bank		Rome (Fiumicino)		1965
Inverness	1987	Genoa		1968
Aberdeen	1990	Isola de Lampedusa		1972
Sumburgh		Crotone		
Humberside		Forli		1976

Bologna		**VIET NAM**	
Milan (Linate)	1977	Saigon	1960
Trapani (Sicily)			
Palermo "		**TAIWAN**	
Catania "	1979	Taipei	1960
IRAQ		**KENYA**	
Baghdad	1957	Nairobi (Eastleigh)	1961
PAKISTAN		**ADEN**	
Karachi (Drigh Road)	1957	Khormaksar	1961
INDIA		**CYPRUS**	
Delhi (Saftar Jung)	1957	Nicosia	1962
Calcutta (Dum Dum)		Akrotiri	
Bombay (Santa Cruz)	1975		
Port Blair (Andaman Is)	1982	**MALDIVE ISLANDS**	
		Gan	1962
THAILAND			
Bangkok (Don Muang)	1957	**CHANNEL ISLANDS**	
Haadyai	1974	Jersey	1961
SINGAPORE		**NEW ZEALAND**	
Payar Lebar	1957	Wellington (Rangotai)	1962
RAF Seletar		Auckland (Whenuapai)	
RAF Changi	1958	Christchurch	1981
		Te Anau	
HONG KONG		Manapouri	
Kai Tak	1958	Mount Cook	
Chek Lap Kok	1998	Auckland (Manakau)	
		Rotarua	
MALAYA		Palmerston North	
Kuala Lumpur	1958	Queenstown	1989
Butterworth		Dunedin	
Malacca	1959	New Plymouth	
Ipoh		Taupo	
Kuantan	1960	RNZAF Wigram	
Penang		Tekapo	
Labuan	1962	Glentanner	
Kota Kinabalu	1979		
Kerith	1997		

GREECE
Larissa	1962
Athens (Hellinikon)	
Kavala	1974
Thessaloniki	
Kos	1992

TURKEY
Ankara (Esonboga)	1962
Istanbul (Yesilkoy)	
Samsun	1972

SUDAN
Khartoum (Wadi Seidna)	1963

LEBONAN
Beirut	1965

GHANA
Accra (Kotoka)	1965

CANADA
Gander	1962
RCAF Rivers	
Goose Bay	
Toronto	1963
Ottowa (Uplands)	
Quebec City	
Calgary	1978
Edmonton	
Yellowknife	
Inuvik	
Tuktoyaktuk	
Halifax	1979
Saglek	
Fort Chimo	
Scheferville	
Montreal (Dorval)	
Vancouver	

FIJI
Nadi	1980

JAPAN
Osaka	1960
Tokyo (Haneda)	

NIGERIA
Lagos (Ikeja)	1964
Port Harcourt	1965
Kano	1966
Warri	1967
Kalabar	1970
Enugu	

IRAN
Abadan	1965
Boushehr	
Karg Island	
Tehran (Mehrabad)	1972
Isfhan	
Shiraz	

CAMEROON
Douala	1964
Victoria	1967
Yaounde	1972

GABON
Libreville	1964
Port Gentil	
Gamba	1973
Mayumba	
N'Dindi	

CONGO
Brazzaville(Maya Maya)	1973
Pointe Noire	

DAHOMEY(BENIN)
Cotonu	1972

TOGO		**GREENLAND**	
Lome	1973	Thule	1963
FRENCH POLYNESIA		**RHODESIA (ZIMBABWE)**	
Tahiti (Faaa)	1981	Salisbury	1963
Moorea			
		GIBRALTAR	
UNITED STATES		Gibraltar	1968
Sheppard AFB	1962		
Elmondorf AFB	1963	**NORWAY**	
Hickam AFB		Bardufoss	1963
Andrews AFB		Andoya	
Norfolk		Bergen	1983
Jacksonville		Haugesund	1984
New York (Idlewild)	1964	Stavanger	
Baltimore		Oslo (Fornebu)	
Atlanta	1964	Kristiansund	1985
New Orleans Int		Trondheim	
New Opleans Lakefront	1978	Sondnessjoen	
Memphis		Alesund	
St Louis		Bronnoysund	
Chicago (Midaway, O'Hare)		Molde	
Seattle		Bodo	1988
Portland		Rost	
Astoria			
San Francisco		**SPAIN**	
Los Angeles		Valencia	1966
Orlando	1976	Seville	
Tampa		Madrid (Barajas)	
Dallas/Fort Worth		Barcelona	1968
Miami		Alicante	1987
Washington (Dulles)	1978	Ibiza (Balerics)	1990
Denver			
Cleveland	1979	**SPANISH SAHARA**	
Anchorage	1989	**(WESTERN SAHARA)**	
		El Aaiun	1971
SWITZERLAND		Villa Cisneros	1973
Geneva (Cointrin)	1972		
Zurich		**CANARY ISLANDS**	
		Las Palmas	1968
		Teneriffe	

MOROCCO
Casablanca 1968
Tangier

FERNANDO PO (BIOKO)
Santa Isabel 1967

LINE ISLANDS
Kiritimati(Christmas Island)1963

SWEDEN
Stockholm (Arlanda) 1974
Stockholm (Bromma)
Ronnerby
Malmo
Kalmar
Visby 1976

DENMARK
Copenhagen (Kastrup) 1974
Billund 1998

GERMANY
RAF Wildenwrath 1962
Stuttgart 1968
Cologne
Frankfurt-am-Main 1972

BELGIUM
Ostend 1968
Brussels (Melsbroek) 1974

HOLLAND
Amsterdam (Schipol) 1974
Den Helder 1997

AUSTRIA
Vienna (Schwechat) 1993

ROMANIA
Constanta 1993

PORTUGAL
Lisbon (Portela) 1978

INDONESIA
Medan 1974
Seunagan
Jakarta (Kemayoran) 1991
Surabya (Juanda)
Bali (Denpasar)

CHINA
Canton (Baiyun) 1979
Zhanjiang
Hai Koi
Ningbo

CEYLON (SRI LANKA)
Colombo (Ratmalana) 1982

KOREA
Seoul 1989
Pusan
Cheju

SOUTH AFRICA
Durban(Louis Botha) 1983
Jo'burg (Jan Smuts)
Port Elizabeth
Nelspruit 1985

MAURITANIA
Nouakchott 1973

SENEGAL
Dakar (Yoff) 1973

IVORY COAST
Abijan 1972

ZIARE
Kinshasa 1983

MOZAMBIQUE		**US VIRGIN ISLANDS**	
Beira	1985	St Thomas (HSTruman)	1977
Maputo		St Croix (Alexander Hamilton)	
Xai Xai			
		BRITISH VIRGIN ISLANDS	
ISRAEL		Tortola (East End)	1977
Tel Aviv (Lod)	1972		
Tel Aviv (Ben Gurion)	1983	**ST MAARTEN**	
		Princess Juliana	1977
SAUDI ARABIA			
Dahran	1976	**ANTIGUA**	
		Coolidge	1977
QATAR			
Doha	1976	**GUADELOUPE**	
		Le Raizet	1977
DUBAI			
Dubai	1977	**MARTINIQUE**	
		Lamentin	1977
ABU DHABI			
Abu Dhabi	1983	**BARBADOS**	
		Grantley Adams	1977
MUSCAT & OMAN			
Masirah Island	1963	**GRENADA**	
		Pearls	1977
BAHRAIN ISLAND			
Bahrain	1963	**TRINIDAD**	
		Piarco	1977
KUWAIT			
Kuwait	1965	**BELIZE**	
		Belize City	1978
ADEN PROTECTORATE			
Khormaksahr	1961	**HONDURAS**	
		San Pedro Sula	1978
BERMUDA		Tegucigalpa (Toncontin)	
Kindley Field	1973	La Ceiba	
BAHAMAS		**PANAMA**	
Nassau	1973	Panama(Tocumen)	1978
PUERTO RICO			
San Jaun	1977		

AUSTRALIA
RAAF Richmond (Sydney)1962
Canberra
Melbourne
Edinburgh Field
Woomera
RAAF Pearce (Perth)
Darwin   1963
Sydney (Kingsford Smith)
1980
Launceston
Perth
Devonport
Flinders Island
Bairnsdale
Port Hedland
Broome
Adelaide
Derby
Kununurra   1981
Garden Point
Elcho Island
Geralton
Carnavon
Learmonth
Karratha
Warrnambool   1982
Narrogin
Brisbane   1989
Alice Springs   1997
Mackay
Hamilton Island
Cairns

ANGOLA
Luanda (Belas)   1972

EQUADOR
Quito   1978

COLOMBIA
Bogata (Eldorado)   1977
Cartegena
Isla de San Andres   1978
Barranquilla
Buenaventura
Cali   1979

BRAZIL
Rio de Janeiro(Galeao)   1979
Brasilla
Sao Paulo (Congonhas)
Rio (Santos Dumont)   1981
Macae

CHILE
Santiago (Pudahuel)   1982
Easter Island

PERU
Lima (Jorge Chavez)   1979

VENEZUELA
Caracas (Simon Bolivar) 1978